The Wilson Chronology of Ideas

Other Titles in the Wilson Chronology Series

The Wilson Chronology of the Arts

The Wilson Chronology of Science and Technology

The Wilson Chronology of Women's Achievements

The Wilson Calendar of World History

The Wilson Chronology of Asia and the Pacific

The Wilson Chronology of World Religions

The American Book of Days, Fourth Edition

The Wilson Chronology of Ideas

George Ochoa and Melinda Corey

The H. W. Wilson Company

New York • Dublin

1998

120208

Library of Congress Cataloging-in-Publication Data

Ochoa, George.
   The Wilson chronology of ideas / by George Ochoa and Melinda
Corey.
      p.   cm.
   Includes bibliographical references and index.
   ISBN 0-8242-0935-4
   1. Civilization—History—Chronology. 2. Thought and
   thinking—History—Chronology. 3. Idea (Philosophy)—
   History—Chronology. I. Corey, Melinda. II. H. W. Wilson
   Company. III. Title.
CB151.O37 1997
909—dc21   97-17591
                                                            CIP

Printed in the United States of America

07 06 05 04 03 02 01 00 99 98   10 9 8 7 6 5 4 3 2 1

The H. W. Wilson Company
950 University Avenue
Bronx, NY 10452

http://www.hwwilson.com

To Paul Fargis,

who is always coming up with great ideas

Contents

Acknowledgments

We are indebted to the following contributors: Tom Brown, for entries on political science and political thought, 1880–present; John Cameli, for the history timeline, 1500–present; Abbott Katz, for the sociology timeline, 1825–present; and Timothy Wright, for the timeline of criticism on visual and performing arts, antiquity–present.

We also thank Paul Fargis and Sheree Bykofsky of The Stonesong Press, Doug Grad of Ballantine, and Michael Schulze, Hilary Claggett, Lynn Amos, Joseph Sora, Frank McGuckin, and John O'Sullivan of H. W. Wilson. Finally, we thank Mary F. Tomaselli for indexing the book.

Introduction

The word "idea" can mean many things. There are technological ideas, such as the concepts behind the wheel and the light bulb. There are scientific ideas, such as the germ theory of disease. But there is another class of ideas that aim less at practical effects or explanation of nature and more at illuminating the meaning and purpose of human existence. Epic social changes may result from such ideas, but only after many people have been convinced of their claim to truth. This category of thought is the subject of *The Wilson Chronology of Ideas*.

The thinkers whose achievements are recorded in this book include philosophers, prophets, scholars, critics, educators, revolutionaries, and reformers. Their ideas include the Trinity, nirvana, the categorical imperative, the sublime, the bourgeoisie, the public school, and the equality of women. Saints and humanitarians are represented, from Francis of Assisi to Mahatma Gandhi; so are doers of evil, such as Adolf Hitler, and victims of delusion, such as Stephen of Cloyes, leader of the Children's Crusade. Some ideas, such as feudalism and Zeus, have no single authors; others, such as Nietzsche's *Übermensch*, only make sense in connection with an author's thought. What all these ideas share in common is persuasive power—the power to convince people of their truth or of the need to refute and suppress them. For the purposes of this book, the test of an idea's significance is its influence.

The Wilson Chronology of Ideas charts, from prehistory to the present, milestones in philosophy, religion, mythology, political and social thought, history, criticism, linguistics, education, and journalism. Also included are developments in psychology and the modern social sciences—particularly anthropology, economics, political science, and sociology. The history of ideas about women and about the rights of women receives special attention. So do the historical turning points that resulted from the application of ideas. No timeline of democratic liberalism or Marxism can be complete without the American and Russian revolutions, any more than the history of Christianity can omit the conversion of Constantine.

As far as possible, the chronology attempts to pinpoint the moments when an idea was first expressed and first grew in new directions. It does not attempt to record every new artistic expression of an idea. The birth of chivalry is noted, but not every painting or novel that includes chivalric heroes. Similarly, although it includes scientific ideas (such as Darwinian evolution) that had a strong impact on other forms of thought, it does not offer a history of science. For comprehensive treatment of those areas, see *The Wilson Chronology of the Arts* and *The Wilson Chronology of Science and Technology*.

The Wilson Chronology of Ideas is global in scope. All great religions are included, as are political and philosophical systems from the Americas to China. In addition to noting the dates of events, the timeline attempts to provide concise summaries of their significance. Sidebars spotlight interesting and little-known aspects of the history of ideas, from the inventor of "A.D." to the founder of est. An appendix offers easy access to the birth and death dates of many of the persons named in the book.

Nothing is so controversial as a claim to truth. One person's crackpot is another's sage. Many of the ideas expressed in this book will be anathema to some, gospel to others, and perplexing to many more. The aim of this book is not to pass judgment but to show as thoroughly as possible what great thinkers and ordinary followers have believed, argued, and put into action. This chronology is a record not only of the life of the mind, but of its impact on human life.

GEORGE OCHOA and MELINDA COREY
Dobbs Ferry, New York
December 1997

A Note to the Reader

The Wilson Chronology of Ideas is arranged by year and within each year by category. The categories are as follows:

ANTH	Anthropology
CRIT	Criticism of literature and the arts
ECON	Economics
EDUC	Education
HIST	History and biography
JOURN	Journalism
LING	Linguistics and language
MISC	Miscellaneous
PHIL	Philosophy
POL	Political thought, including political philosophy, political science, and political ideas as embodied in action
PSYCH	Psychology and parapsychology
REL	Religion, theology, mythology, and spirituality
SOC	Sociology, social criticism, and social reform ideas as embodied in action

In the timeline, B.C. dates are indicated by negative numbers, A.D. dates by positive numbers.

Throughout prehistory, antiquity, and the early Middle Ages, it is often difficult to place exact dates. Therefore, most of the dates in this book up to the year A.D. 1000 can be considered approximate. After A.D. 1000, dates can generally be considered exact unless marked with a *c.* for *circa*.

Birth and death dates have mostly been left out of the main text. However, the birth and death dates of many of the thinkers named in the chronology are included in the appendix.

B.C.

−48,000	In Mesopotamia (Iraq), the Neanderthals, a hominid people related to modern humans, place flowers in graves, possibly indicating respect for the dead. Neanderthals may also believe in an afterlife, as indicated by the placement in graves of such useful items as tools and food. REL
−30,000– −20,000	In Germany and elsewhere in Europe, modern humans make sculptures that may represent religious images. Made from stone, bone, and antler, they include animals, hybrid animal-people, and "Venuses," sculptures of exaggerated female shapes; the Venuses may function as fertility figures. REL
−20,000– −10,000	In France and Spain, paintings are made on cave walls. The images of animals, abstract designs, and stenciled hands may be associated with religious belief and ritual. REL
−10,000	In the Middle East, the dead are buried in cemeteries and under the floors of huts, often with personal articles such as necklaces and bracelets. REL
−10,000	The oldest known solar calendar, possibly associated with seasonal rituals, is engraved on bone in France. REL
−8000	In Mesopotamia (Iraq), agriculture is developed, along with the first large farming settlements, later to grow into cities. Civilization, with its high levels of organization, stratification, and division of labor, will follow. POL
−7500	The earliest known cemetery in North America is dug in what will become Arkansas. Tools buried with the deceased indicate belief in an afterlife. In Africa about this time, red ocher is sprinkled on the dead in their graves. REL
−7500	Skulls of deceased ancestors, with flesh modeled in plaster and shells in eye sockets, may be used in ancestor worship in the Levant. REL
−7000– −6000	Shrines, decorated with paintings and figures of animals and women, are built in southern Anatolia (Turkey). REL
−6000– −5000	At Mehrgarh, west of the Indus Valley, funerary offerings, including gems, are buried with the dead. REL

–5900–   The Ubaid culture of Mesopotamia (Iraq) builds temples containing altars.   REL
–3100

–5500   By now, agriculture, with its shift to a more settled way of life than hunting and
           gathering, has developed independently or been introduced from outside in
           parts of Europe, China, South Asia, and the Americas.   REL

–5000–   In the predynastic period in Egypt, sculptors carve monolithic figures and clay
–3100   figurines of gods. Funerary offerings often include sculptures, pottery, and
           weapons.   REL

–4500   Communal burial places known as megalithic chamber tombs are built in
           northern and western Europe.   REL

–4300–   During the Uruk period in Mesopotamia (Iraq) , Sumerian city-states such as
–3100   Uruk (or Erech) take shape. Relying on extensive canal systems for irrigation
           and on trade networks for supply of raw materials, the city-states have complex
           political and economic dimensions, reflected in the development of systems
           of accounting, law, and writing. The latter, known as cuneiform, consists of
           wedge-shaped signs on clay tablets.   POL

–4300–   In Mesopotamia (Iraq), the authority of the political ruler of the city-state of
–3100   Uruk is reinforced by his association with the goddess of love and war, Inanna.
                                                                                       POL

–4000   Temples, ritual monuments, and burial grounds are constructed in the Andes
           region of South America.   REL

–4000   Aborigines in Australia create rock paintings of rainbow serpents, snakelike
           beings believed to have created the landscape along a "dreaming track" as they
           traveled inland from the sea.   REL

–3100   The Egyptians invent an early form of hieroglyphics, enabling the textual
           recording of ideas.   MISC

–3100   Upper Egypt and Lower Egypt are unified under a single ruler as the Old
           Kingdom begins. The king (pharaoh) is considered divine or quasi-divine. POL

–3000   In Egypt and Sumeria, education in reading and writing is offered to young
           males.   EDUC

–3000–   Sumerian civilization flourishes in Mesopotamia (Iraq). Sumerians live in sep-
–2340   arate city-states ruled by kings; periodically, the king of one city-state estab-
           lishes dominion over others. Conquering kings are believed to rule by divine
           right, with the gods periodically transferring the right to rule from one city-
           state to another.   POL

−3000– −2600	In China, perforated disks made of jade and hardstone are used in ritual human sacrifices as symbols of heaven. REL
−3000– −2600	The dead are mummified in northern Chile, in an expression of concern for the afterlife. REL
−3000– −2340	Sumerian religion, a blend of Sumerian and Semitic traditions, contains numerous deities. At the top of the hierarchy is a triad: the sky-god Anu, the storm-god Enlil, and the water-god Ea or Enki. REL
−2550– −2470	As monuments to their glory and the importance of the afterlife, the kings of the Fourth Dynasty in Egypt (Khufu or Cheops, Khafre, and Menkaure) build for themselves the pyramid tombs of Giza, including the Great Pyramid. Khafre also builds the Great Sphinx at Giza, a colossal representation of a mythical man-lion associated with the pharaoh as an incarnation of the sun-god Ra. REL
−2500	The Egyptians mummify the corpses of the wealthy and powerful. REL
−2500	The oldest written story, the Sumerian *Epic of Gilgamesh*, meditates on the themes of human mortality, civilization, and relations with the gods. REL
−2500– −1700	Stonehenge in southwestern England, near Salisbury, is constructed. With its concentric circles of stones, ditches, and holes, the monument serves religious and astronomical purposes. REL
−2465– −2323	Rulers of the Fifth Dynasty in Egypt build monumental temples to the sun-god Ra. REL
−2400	In Mesopotamia (Iraq), the body organs of sacrificed animals are used to divine the future. REL
−2300– −1800	The Indus Valley civilization flourishes in India and Pakistan, at such sites as Mohenjo-Daro and Harappa. Though the Indus culture is later superseded by Aryan culture, it is possible that modern Hinduism owes some of its beliefs and images to the Indus people, including those related to the Great Goddess (Shakti) and the god Shiva. REL
−2100	The Sumerians of Mesopotamia (Iraq) build the ziggurat at Ur. A pyramidal brick platform capped by a temple and ascended by means of zigzag ramps, a ziggurat is envisioned as a mountain reaching toward the heavens, where the gods reside. Mesopotamian reverence for the sky and high places will be a characteristic of all Middle Eastern religions, including Judaism, Christianity, and Islam. REL

−2000   Abraham leaves Ur in Mesopotamia (Iraq) and settles in Canaan. The first
             Hebrew patriarch, he worships one God; their covenant is symbolized by the
             circumcision of his male descendants. Through his son Isaac, he is considered
             the father of the Jewish people; through his son Ishmael, of the Arab people.
                                                                                        REL

−1800−   Sun worship is practiced in Scandinavia.   REL
−1600

−1800−   The myth of Osiris, god of the underworld and symbol of death and rebirth,
−1700   pervades Egyptian belief in the afterlife. Osiris is slain by his brother Set, res-
             urrected by the goddesses Isis and Nephthys, and made ruler of the nether-
             world, where the deceased reside for all eternity.   REL

−1760   Mesopotamian ruler Hammurabi establishes the empire of Babylonia, with its
             capital at Babylon. His code of laws, one of the greatest of ancient legal codes,
             concerns business, property, family, labor, and personal injuries. Though rely-
             ing on retributive punishments ("an eye for an eye"), it will be considered
             humanitarian for its time.   POL

−1760   As Babylon becomes an imperial city, its patron god Marduk (Bel) becomes
             the leading deity in the Mesopotamian pantheon. Mesopotamian religion
             includes over 2,000 deities, associated with particular places, forces of nature,
             abstract qualities, and deceased rulers.   REL

−1600   The Phoenicians, or Canaanites, develop the world's first purely phonetic
             alphabet, based on symbols for sounds rather than objects or syllables. The
             alphabet will be the basis for all future Western alphabets.   MISC

−1580−   During the 18th Dynasty, Egyptian religious beliefs are recorded in the first
−1350   collection of the *Book of the Dead*, a literature of spells, charms, and other
             writings to aid the deceased in the afterlife.   REL

−1500   During the Shang dynasty (1533–1027 B.C.), the Chinese develop a system of
             writing.   MISC

−1500   The Aryans, a nomadic people originating in southern Russia and Turkistan,
             invade and conquer the Punjab region of northwest India. In subsequent cen-
             turies, Aryan and indigenous cultures will mingle, producing the distinctive
             religious-philosophical tradition known as Hinduism.   REL

−1500   The Aryans in India compose the *Rig Veda*, which, as a sacred text of Hinduism,
             will remain the world's oldest living religious literature. It consists of 1,028
             hymns to be used in ritual sacrifice performed by Brahmins or priests. This
             early phase of Hinduism is known as Brahmanism.   REL

−1200	In the event known as the Exodus, Hebrew lawgiver Moses leads the Israelite people out of slavery in Egypt. They learn the name of God ("Yahweh"), receive the Hebrew law, including the Ten Commandments, and enter into a covenant with God. After 40 years of wandering in the Sinai wilderness, they enter and occupy the promised land of Canaan. REL
−1100s	The earliest parts of the Old Testament, or Hebrew Bible, based on still older oral traditions, are written down. The oldest parts are found together with more recent material in the Torah or Pentateuch, the first five books of the Bible. These comprise Genesis, Exodus, Leviticus, Numbers, and Deuteronomy. *See also* 850–650 B.C., REL. REL
−1027– −256	The Chou dynasty reigns in China. Dating from this period are China's oldest work of divination, *I Ching* (*Book of Changes*) (*see* 600s B.C., REL); oldest historical work, *Shu Ching* (*Book of Documents*); and oldest poetry collection, *Shih Ching* (*Book of Odes*). *See also* 600 –256 B.C., PHIL. MISC
−1010– −970	David is king of Israel. The story of his life, recorded in 1 and 2 Samuel, 1 Kings, and 1 Chronicles, becomes part of the Old Testament. Many Psalms are attributed to him, and later messianic tradition will claim that the Messiah (or savior) will be descended from David. The New Testament will claim that Jesus is the promised "son of David," the Messiah (or Christ). REL
−1000– −400	In Greece, a number of independent city-states (Greek *polis*) develop, comprising a variety of forms of government, including monarchy, oligarchy, tyranny, and democracy. POL
−1000– −800	Aryan invaders occupy (Persia) Iran, bringing with them Aryan religion similar to that found in India. REL
−800s	Greek poet Homer composes the epics *The Iliad* and *The Odyssey*, based on legendary material concerning the Trojan War (believed to have taken place about 1200 B.C.). Homer's depiction of the religious and moral beliefs of heroic Mycenaean society will long reverberate in Western thinking. REL
−884– −860	The conquests of Ashurnasirpal II of Assyria inaugurate the period of Assyrian domination of the Middle East, lasting until 612 B.C. The king ensures centralized control by installing Assyrian governors in conquered lands. POL
−884– −612	During the period of Assyrian domination of the Middle East, the Assyrian god Ashur is the chief deity of the pantheon, although the Assyrians borrow many gods from the religion of the conquered Babylonians. REL
−850	In India, religious leader Jina Purshva flourishes. Like Vardhamana Mahavira (*see* 599–527 B.C., REL), who followed in his tradition, he is revered by Jains. REL

5

–850–
–650
The Yahwistic (J) and Elohistic (E) strands of the Pentateuch (*see* 1100s B.C., REL) are composed about 850 B.C. and 750 B.C., respectively, and edited together by 650 B.C.   REL

–850–
–650
A rationale for the subjugation of women is offered with the recounting of the story of Adam and Eve, in the book of Genesis. According to the Bible, her disobedience of God's command after being beguiled by the Serpent necessitates a painful existence for all women and submission to a husband, who "shall rule over you."   REL

–850–
–650
In the Old Testament, the monthly act of menstruation is considered to render women and their surroundings unclean for seven days.   REL

–800
By this date in India, three collections of Vedic literature have been compiled in addition to the *Rig Veda* (*see* 1500 B.C., REL). They include the *Sama Veda* and the *Yajur Veda*, both of which are based heavily on the *Rig Veda*, and the *Atharva Veda*, which contains spells and incantations. Known as the *Samhitas* (collections), the four works become part of the canon of Hindu scripture. REL

–800–
–600
In India, the Brahmanas, prose interpretations of the Vedic hymns, are composed. As part of Vedic literature, they are considered sacred by Hindus.   REL

–700s
Greek poet Hesiod writes the *Theogony*, the oldest surviving account of the origin of the Greek gods, and *Works and Days*, advice on farming and moral life. REL

–776
The Olympic games begin in Olympia, Greece, as a festival incorporating religious and athletic elements. Held every four years, they will be discontinued in the late fourth century A.D. The modern, secular, worldwide version of the games will be established in Athens in A.D. 1896.   REL

–740–
–701
The Hebrew prophet Isaiah preaches. His prophecies include attacks on social injustice and predictions of the fall of Judah and Assyria, along with visions of a Messianic redeemer and renewed state of Israel. Isaiah's own prophecies, as well as later ones attributed to him, will be collected in the Old Testament Book of Isaiah (*see* 538 B.C., REL).   REL

–722
The northern kingdom of Israel is captured by Assyria. The ten tribes of Israel are exiled to Assyria, leaving only the two tribes of Judah and Benjamin (the southern kingdom of Judah). In folklore and religious belief, the ten lost tribes will be variously identified with Arabians, Indians, Ethiopians, and Native Americans.   REL

–600s
The *I Ching* (*Book of Changes*), the classic work of divination, begins to take form in China. Based on ancient Chinese philosophy, mythology, and history,

it is meant to be used in tandem with the casting of coins or sticks to foretell the future. It will gain adherents in China, Japan, and the West.   REL

−600s   Etruscan culture develops in Italy. Etruscan religion includes a heavy emphasis on the afterlife and divination.   REL

−639–   Athenian legislator Solon lives. He revises the aristocratic constitution of
−559   Athens to make it more democratic, liberalizes the legal code, and ends serfdom.   POL

−628–   Persian religious leader Zoroaster (Zarathushtra) lives. The founder of
−551   Zoroastrianism, he is the author of the hymns called the *Gathas*. He teaches that there are two gods—a good one, Ahura Mazda, and an evil one, Ahriman—and that people must choose to follow the good one. He also foresees an apocalyptic triumph of good over evil and judgment of individuals after death.   REL

−621   Athenian legislator Draco flourishes. His code of law, which prescribes death for many crimes, will be associated with harsh punishment for minor offenses. POL

−610–   Greek philosopher and astronomer Anaximander of Miletus lives. His cos-
−547   mology is rooted in the concept of an infinite, eternal surrounding called the apeiron.   PHIL

−600   In Mesoamerica, the Zapotec invent a system of hieroglyphics that is the earliest known writing system in the western hemisphere.   MISC

−600–   In Greece, the pre-Socratic philosophers develop cosmologies and seek to
−400   understand the nature of reality. They include the Milesian school, the Eleatics, the Pythagoreans, Democritus, Empedocles, and Heracleitus.   PHIL

−600–   This period of the Chou dynasty (founded 1027 B.C.) in China is known as the
−256   Age of Philosophy, the period of the "hundred schools of thought." Philosophers Confucius, Meng-tzu (Mencius), Hsün-tzu, Mo-tzu, Yang Chu, Lao-tzu, and Chuang-tzu flourish.   PHIL

−600–   In India, the Aranyakas, treatises on meditation, and the Upanishads, mystical
−300   and speculative treatises, are composed. Part of the sacred Vedic literary canon, these Hindu works elucidate the spiritual significance of the Vedas. The Upanishads introduce the doctrines of samsara (death and rebirth), karma (bearing the effects of deeds done in a previous life), and nirvana (escape from the cycle of death and rebirth). They also speak of the identity between Brahman, the absolute reality, and Atman, the inmost soul of each individual, and advocate the practice of yoga, or spiritual and physical discipline, to attain consciousness of that identity.   REL

−500s   Greek elegiac poet Theognis advises duty, moderation, and faithfulness in ele-
               gies to his friend Cyrnus.   PHIL

−500s   Legendary Chinese philosopher Lao-tzu is said to found the system of philos-
               ophy and religion known as Taoism. As a philosophical system, Taoism advo-
               cates humility, simplicity, freedom from strong passions, and passivity or inac-
               tion. The term *tao* (way) refers both to the way the universe functions and the
               techniques used to achieve peace. Taoism will later develop into a complex
               religious system, with alchemical elements and a pantheon of gods. *See also*
               200s B.C. and A.D. 400s, REL.   PHIL

−500s   Greek teller of fables Aesop lives. His satirical and moral tales will be the sub-
               ject of commentaries by later philosophers.   PHIL

−500s   The Milesian school, also known as the Ionian school, is the first school of what
               will become known as pre-Socratic philosophers (*see* 600–400 B.C., PHIL).
               Centered on Miletus in Asia Minor, it develops a speculative cosmology and
               argues that the primary substance of the universe is water. Its adherents include
               Thales of Miletus (flourished 585 B.C.), Anaximander, and Anaximenes.   PHIL

The Birth of the Buddha

To Christians, the story of the signs and wonders attending the birth of Jesus are well
known, and commemorated every Christmas. To Buddhists, the story of the Buddha's
miraculous entry into the world is equally familiar.

According to scripture, Siddhartha Gautama (c. 563–483 B.C.), who would grow up
to become the Buddha, the Enlightened One, was born of an unusual conception. His
mother, Queen Maha-Maya, dreamed that a white elephant circled her three times,
then entered her. This elephant was the Future Buddha.

Ten lunar months later, in a grove called Lumbini, the queen gave birth while standing up and clutching a tree. Angels brought a golden net to catch Siddhartha, who
descended like "a preacher descending from his preaching-seat" and spoke these
words: "The chief am I in all the world." At his birth, as at his conception, 32 "prog-
nostics," or signs, were apparent, including these: a brilliant light flashed throughout
the 10,000 worlds; the blind saw; the deaf heard; the dumb talked; the lame walked;
prisoners were freed; diseases ceased; musical instruments spontaneously played; the
weather became fair; and all flowers bloomed.

Unlike Jesus's mother, Siddhartha's did not live to see her son grow up. Scripture
says she died seven days after his birth, because a womb that has been occupied by a
Future Buddha "can never be occupied or used again."

−500s   The great temple to Apollo at Delphi, Greece, is built. It houses the oracle sacred
               to the gods Apollo and Dionysus. The authoritative advice of the oracular mes-
               sages, spoken by a priestess in trance, is sought by people all over Greece.   REL

−500s   Greek lyric poet Sappho, born in Lesbos, leads a group of women devoted to
               music and poetry. She will be a model for later feminists.   soc

−599−   Indian religious leader Vardhamana Mahavira lives (alternatively, his dates
−527   may be 540–468 B.C.). Revered by Jains, he is considered the last of 24 leg-
               endary and historical saints who attained liberation and whose teachings help
               others do the same. Jainism rejects the Brahmanic institutions of Hinduism
               and advocates asceticism and nonviolence as a path to liberation.   REL

−586   The Babylonians destroy the Temple of Jerusalem and exile the Jewish people
               to Babylon. *See also* 538 B.C., REL.   REL

−582−   Greek philosopher and mathematician Pythagoras lives. He is the founder of
−507   a religious society whose doctrines include transmigration of souls. The
               Pythagoreans also teach that the basis of music and the universe is numbers,
               and that the heavenly bodies produce music (known as the harmony of the
               spheres).   PHIL

−570−   Greek pre-Socratic philosopher Xenophanes of Colophon lives. He argues for
−475   the existence of a single, eternal God rather than anthropomorphic deities.   PHIL

−563−   Indian religious leader Siddhartha Gautama, founder of Buddhism, lives.
−483   Known as the Buddha (Sanskrit, "Enlightened One"), he preaches the "eight-
               fold path" to escaping suffering and attaining *nirvana* (transcendence).
               Emphasizing meditation, monasticism, and right action, Buddhism will even-
               tually spread throughout Asia and the world, developing into many forms
               within two principal traditions, Theravada and Mahayana Buddhism.   REL

−551−   Chinese philosopher Confucius lives. His political and ethical teachings
−479   emphasize humanity, reverence for ancient sages and ritual, and personal
               virtue in government. Aimed at establishing a just and peaceful society, his
               views are embodied in the *Analects* (*Lun-yu*), a collection of sayings and anec-
               dotes compiled by his disciples. Confucianism will be a dominant strand in
               China's intellectual and spiritual history.   PHIL

−550−   By the Achaemenid period in Persia (Iran), the Zurvanite sect has grown out
−333   of the Zoroastrian faith. Zurvanites believe that both God and the devil
               emanate from an undifferentiated One, a divine being named Zurvan who
               exists beyond duality. Meanwhile, Zoroastrianism exerts a powerful influence
               on both official and popular religion in Persia (Iran).   REL

–550–   Mithras, god of light and truth, is widely worshiped in Persia (Iran) during the
–333   Achaemenid dynasty. Mithras represents the power of truth and order against
        evil. *See also* 60 B.C., REL.   REL

–546   Greek philosopher Anaximenes of Miletus flourishes. He argues that one pri-
        mary substance, *aer*, is the source of all others.   PHIL

–538   Cyrus the Great of Persia (Iran) conquers Babylon and permits the Jews to
        return from exile to Jerusalem (*see* 586 B.C., REL). At about this time, new
        prophecies attributed to the Hebrew prophet Isaiah (*see* 740–701 B.C., REL) are
        composed and will be included in the Book of Isaiah.   REL

–522–   Greek lyric poet Pindar lives. Known as the Dircaean Swan, he writes numer-
–438   ous odes and hymns for religious occasions, including *Epinicia* (victory odes),
        Encomia (odes of praise), *Scolia* (festive songs), *Hymns*, and *Choral Dithyrambs
        to Dionysus*.   REL

–516   The rebuilding of the Temple in Jerusalem (the Second Temple) is completed.
        See also 586 B.C., REL.   REL

–515   Greek philosopher Parmenides of Elea is born. Founder of the Eleatic school, which
        will also include the Greek philosophers Zeno of Elea and Melissus, Parmenides
        argues in *On Nature* that reality is single, perfect, indivisible, and unchanging. The
        contrast between reality and the world of appearances will influence Plato.   PHIL

–509   The Roman Republic comes into being when the people of Rome overthrow
        their Etruscan kings. *See also* 200s B.C., POL.   POL

–506   Athenian statesman Cleisthenes establishes a true democracy in Athens for all
        of its free adult males, though not for women or slaves. Athenian democracy
        will provide a model and mythic point of origin for democracies of the mod-
        ern age. The fifth-century-B.C. achievements of Athens in literature, philosophy,
        and the arts will remain lasting parts of Western heritage. The great age of
        Athenian democracy will end in 404 B.C. with the city's defeat by Sparta in the
        Peloponnesian War (431–404 B.C.).   POL

–500–   Greek philosopher Anaxagoras of Clazomenae lives. His views include the
–428   concept of mind as prime mover and the principle of homoeomereity (all
        qualities are present in all things). Exiled from Athens for impiety, he dies in
        Lampsacus.   PHIL

–500–   During the postexilic period (*see* 538 B.C., REL), the biblical books of Psalms
–100   and Proverbs are completed and put in their final shape.   REL

-500– -200	In India, the sutras—Hindu treatises concerning sacrificial ritual and customary law—are written. They include the *Dharmasutras*, the oldest source of Indian law, and the *Kamasutra*, on the practice of love. REL
-400s	In Greece, traveling teachers known as Sophists are active. Though they include such respected philosophers as Protagoras (*see* 490–420 B.C., PHIL), they will come as a group to be associated with specious reasoning for financial profit. The Greek philosopher Plato is among their harshest critics. PHIL
-400s	Greek philosopher Cratylus lives. He argues that the flux of reality is impossible to capture in words or categories. PHIL
-400s	The Megarian school of philosophy, known for its subtle logical analysis, flourishes at Megara, near Athens. Its members include Eucleides, the founder, and Philo of Megara. PHIL
-400s	In ancient Rome, the term *patrician* refers to the wealthy hereditary class. Until the third century B.C., when plebeians (people of common birth) will become able to hold office, only patricians are able to rule. Over the centuries, the term patrician will gain the more general meaning of "aristocratic." POL
-400s	The Avesta, the Zoroastrian sacred book, is set into writing in Persia (Iran). It includes the *Gathas*, or hymns, of Zoroaster (*see* 628–551 B.C., REL), as well as liturgical texts and prayers. REL
-493– -433	Greek philosopher Empedocles of Acragas lives. In *On Nature*, he argues that the universe is made up of four elements—earth, air, water, and fire—and that it moves through cycles during which one or another of these predominates. He also believes in the preexistence and transmigration of souls and the omnipresence of Love, or the principle of organization. PHIL
-490	Greek philosopher Zeno of Elea is born. Contesting the reality of a pluralistic world, Zeno develops arguments against motion known as Zeno's paradoxes. He will be considered by the Greek philosopher Aristotle the inventor of dialectic. PHIL
-490– -420	Greek philosopher Protagoras of Abdera, a Sophist, lives. He will be best known for his doctrine that "man is the measure of all things," often considered the first classical statement of relativism. PHIL
-485	In China, a land distribution program known as the equal-field system is adopted. It allows peasants an allotment of land for personal use throughout their lives. The system will be used until the eighth century A.D. POL

-483–   Greek rhetorician and philosopher Gorgias of Leontini lives. His philosophi-
-376   cal works include *On That Which Is Not, or Nature*.   PHIL

-480–   Greek historian Herodotus lives. Known as the father of history, he mixes
-425   anecdotal and legendary material with more factual information in what will
         come to be known as his *History of the Persian Wars to 479 B.C.*   HIST

-480–   Athenian orator and sophist Antiphon, an opponent of Greek philosopher
-411   Socrates, lives.   PHIL

-480   Greek philosopher Heracleitus of Ephesus flourishes. He will be remembered
         for his idea of flux in the world of appearances and for his concept of the
         divine *logos*, or law, governing the universe.   PHIL

-479–   Chinese philosopher Mo-tzu lives. Taking a utilitarian approach, he argues in
-381   favor of protecting the common weal (the greatest good for the greatest number)
         and emphasizes the moral value of individual sacrifice for the sake of one's
         community. The *Canons of Logic* summarizes the teachings of his school. PHIL

The Learning Tree

Famous teachers often produce famous students, but few lines of intellectual descent
have been more illustrious than the one that leads from Socrates to Plato to Aristotle.
All three men were great thinkers, jointly credited with founding the Western philosophical tradition; each was also a great teacher.

The Greek philosopher Socrates (470–399 B.C.) was renowned for his "Socratic
method" of teaching, in which the teacher uses a series of incisive questions to prompt
the learner to achieve knowledge. The most famous of his many pupils was Plato
(427–347 B.C.), who was so impressed with the personality and methods of Socrates
that he made them the basis for his extant works, the "Socratic dialogues," in which the
character of Socrates leads his listeners to wisdom.

Plato in turn attracted many students to his school, the Academy, the most important of whom was a Macedonian named Aristotle (384–322 B.C.). Aristotle went on to
found his own school, the Lyceum, where he was famous for his lectures on virtually
every subject under the sun. His extant works are actually written versions of his lectures, interspersed with notes made by his students.

None of Aristotle's pupils achieved his intellectual stature or that of his two predecessors, but one became world-famous for entirely different reasons. In about 343
B.C., the 41-year-old Aristotle began tutoring the 13-year-old son of King Philip of
Macedon. That boy grew up to be Alexander the Great, conqueror of the known world
from northern Africa to northern India.

−470– −399	Greek philosopher Socrates lives. Renowned for his devotion to inquiry in pursuit of wisdom, he develops the method of Socratic dialogue, or dialectic. Condemned on charges of corrupting the youth and introducing strange gods, he refuses to escape from prison and willingly accepts execution by drinking hemlock. He will be the central figure in the dialogues of his pupil Plato. PHIL
−460– −400	Greek historian Thucydides lives. His *History of the Peloponnesian Wars*, covering the period 431–411 B.C., shows more concern with objectivity and accuracy than the histories of Herodotus (*see* 480–425 B.C., HIST). HIST
−460– −370	Greek philosopher Democritus of Abdera lives. His theory that the universe is composed of atoms will be rejected by Greek philosophers Plato and Aristotle but resurrected by modern science. PHIL
−460	Greek physician Hippocrates (*d.* 377 B.C.) is born. He will classify human temperaments according to the supposed preponderance of one of the four humors or bodily fluids: sanguine (optimistic), melancholic (sad), choleric (aggressive), and phlegmatic (placid). The system will influence medicine, psychology, and literature until Renaissance times. PSYCH
−450– −420	Greek philosopher Leucippus of Miletus lives. Like the Greek philosopher Democritus, he espouses an atomistic view of nature in the works *On the Mind* and *The Great World System*. PHIL
−445– −360	Greek philosopher Antisthenes, a follower of Greek philosopher Socrates, lives. PHIL
−443– −359	Greek historian Xenophon writes such historical works as the *Anabasis* and the *Hellenica*. His *Cyropedia* is a didactic biography of King Cyrus of Persia (Iran). HIST
−436– −336	Greek orator Isocrates lives. A student of Greek philosopher Socrates, he becomes the most influential pedagogue of the era. Positioning himself against the Sophists and some Platonic tenets, he believes in the combination of a noble existence and powerful oratory to form the finest minds. Among his works is *Against the Sophists*. EDUC
−427– −347	Greek philosopher Plato lives. A pupil of Greek philosopher Socrates (*see* 470–399 B.C., PHIL) and teacher of Greek philosopher Aristotle (*see* 384–322 B.C., PHIL), he is among the world's most influential thinkers. His works, written as dialogues, are divided into three phases: early, such as *Apology, Crito, Euthyphro, Gorgias,* and *Meno*; middle, such as *Phaedo, Republic,* and *Symposium*; and late, such as *Laws* and *Parmenides*. The views most often considered "Platonic" come largely from the middle dialogues. Plato believes in the independent, objective existence of "Forms," which are the ideal,

unchanging originals of temporal phenomena. The highest form is the Good; virtue consists in increasing knowledge of and harmony with the Good. Political justice would be best served under the rule of a philosopher, who understands the Good. Aesthetic appreciation is understood in the context of the love of ideal beauty. *See also* 387 B.C., EDUC, and A.D. 205–270, PHIL.   PHIL

–400   In Athens, the type of school of advanced learning known as the gymnasium becomes popular.   EDUC

–400   From ancient Roman times until well into the Renaissance, a "liberal" education will refer directly to *liberalis*, meaning "of or relating to free men." Such education is aimed at refining the qualities of the gentleman, who has wealth and time to study.   EDUC

–400   Astrology develops in Chaldea as a system for divining the future based on the presumed influence of celestial bodies. Horoscopes become available, describing the influence of the sun, the moon, and the planets given their position in the zodiac at the time of one's birth. (The zodiac is the band of constellations that includes the apparent paths of the sun, the moon, and the planets.)   PHIL

–400–
–325   Greek philosopher Diogenes of Sinope lives. He is the founder of the Cynics, a school that emphasizes self-mastery, renunciation of desire, and contempt for social convention.   PHIL

–300s   Greek philosopher Aristoxenus, a student of Greek philosopher Aristotle, rejects the musical theory of Greek philosopher and mathematician Pythagoras in *Harmonics*, a revolutionary handbook on the philosophy of music.   CRIT

–300s   Chinese philosopher Yang Chu lives. Adopting views similar to the Greek Epicureans, he argues that people should strive for self-preservation and personal integrity.   PHIL

–300s   Greek philosopher Anaxarchus lives. A traveling companion of Macedonian emperor Alexander the Great, he is a follower of Greek philosopher Democritus and the teacher of Greek philosopher Pyrrho.   PHIL

–300s   Belief in physiognomy, the art of systematically interpreting character on the basis of facial features, arises in Greece. The idea will be resurrected in the Renaissance.   PSYCH

–396–
–314   Greek philosopher Xenocrates of Sicyon records a history of fine arts consisting of brief statements about silverchasers, workers in bronze, painters, sculptors, and stylistic comparisons.   CRIT

−387	Greek philosopher Plato founds the Academy of Athens, the most famous school of antiquity. <div align="right">EDUC</div>
−384– −322	Greek philosopher Aristotle lives. With Greek philosopher Plato, he is one of the two most influential thinkers of classical antiquity. Aristotle's works provide the starting point for much of Western philosophy and scholarship since the Middle Ages. His works include the *Organon* (treatises on logic), *Physics, Metaphysics, De Anima* (*On the Soul*), *Nicomachean Ethics, Eudemian Ethics, Poetics, Rhetoric,* and *Politics*. In logic, he defines the theory of the syllogism; in ethics, he defines virtue as moderation and regards the goal of life as happiness. In his *Poetics*, he founds the Western critical tradition with his analysis of tragedy; in *Politics*, he considers what types of government best contribute to the public good. In general, he is more concerned with categories and observed phenomena than is his teacher Plato, and he does not share Plato's emphasis on ideal, transcendent forms. <div align="right">PHIL</div>
−375	The legend of Atlantis is first given literary form by Greek philosopher Plato in the dialogues *Timaeus* and *Critias*. The lost continent, with its advanced civilization and ideal society, is supposed to have existed in the Atlantic Ocean before being inundated. <div align="right">PHIL</div>
−372– −289	Chinese philosopher Meng-tzu (Mencius) lives. His collection of teachings, *The Book of Mencius* (*Meng-tzu*), is a classic of Confucian philosophy, propounding the importance of a virtuous ruler in maintaining order and peace. <div align="right">PHIL</div>
−372– −287	Greek philosopher Theophrastus lives. His treatise *The Characters* is a vivid collection of personality types and contains a discussion of the importance of character portrayal. <div align="right">PSYCH</div>
−369– −286	Chinese philosopher Chuang-tzu lives. The work attributed to him, *Chuang-tzu*, is a seminal Taoist text that stresses the relativity of concepts and conventions and the primacy of nature. The *Lieh-tzu*, another important Taoist work named for its putative author, is also written about this time. <div align="right">PHIL</div>
−367– −347	Beginning at age 17, Greek philosopher Aristotle (born at Stagira, Macedonia, in 384 B.C.) studies under Plato at the Academy in Athens. Fragments from Aristotle's dialogues from this period will survive. <div align="right">PHIL</div>
−367	In Rome, the Sibylline oracles are systematized. <div align="right">REL</div>
−366	Greek political leader Dion of Syracuse is exiled from Sicily to Athens after trying to establish a model government based on ideas inspired by Greek philosopher Plato. Dion later returns and takes power. <div align="right">POL</div>

-365- -275	Greek philosopher Pyrrho of Elis lives. He is the founder of Skepticism, a philosophical school emphasizing the limits of knowledge and the inaccessibility of ultimate truth. PHIL
-365- -285	Greek philosopher Crates of Thebes, an itinerant Cynic dedicated to poverty, lives. PHIL
-347- -339	Greek philosopher Plato's nephew Speusippus succeeds him as head of the Academy in Athens. He emphasizes mathematical studies over other forms of philosophy. PHIL
-342- -339	Greek philosopher Aristotle tutors the Macedonian prince Alexander. PHIL
-341- -270	Greek philosopher Epicurus lives. Adopting the atomistic metaphysics of Greek philosopher Democritus, he advocates a life dedicated to such tranquil pleasures as friendship, aesthetic contemplation, and peace. He also argues that ethical action will help bring about *ataraxia*, a state of serenity or freedom from pain. His detractors will associate his name with hedonism, or indulgence in sensual pleasures, despite his own opposition to that way of life. PHIL
-335	Greek philosopher Aristotle opens the Lyceum, a school in Athens. His followers, the Peripatetics, get their name from the *peripatos*, or covered walk, where he often lectures. Aristotle will teach here until 323 B.C., a year before his death. EDUC
-332	Macedonian emperor Alexander the Great founds Alexandria, Egypt, which will remain a great center of learning through Hellenistic, Roman, and Islamic times. EDUC
-331- -232	Greek Stoic philosopher Cleanthes lives. His *Hymn to Zeus* presents a Stoic theory of physics. PHIL
-321- -298	During the reign of Indian emperor Chandragupta, his chief minister Kautilya, also known as Visnugupta or Chanakya, is the principal author of the *Arthasastra*, or *Science of Material Gain*. This political treatise on governing a kingdom will prove highly influential in India. POL
-321- -298	Indian emperor Chandragupta flourishes. On converting to Jainism, he is believed to have abdicated to become a monk. During his reign, a council of monks called by Sthulabhadra at Pataliputra compiles the canon of Jainist scriptures. At this council, a schism arises between the Digambaras, who practice nudity as part of their ascetic renunciation, and the Shvetambaras, who wear white robes. REL

−316− −242	Greek philosopher Arcesilaus lives. He founds the New or Middle Academy of Athens, which takes a skeptical position and engages in controversy with the Stoics. PHIL
−312− −238	Chinese philosopher Hsün-tzu lives. Taking a materialistic, rationalistic, human-centered approach, he argues in favor of education and scholarship and defends Confucian thought against rival philosophies. PHIL
−300	Egyptian historian Manetho, writing in Greek, composes a history of Egypt from legendary times to 323 B.C. His division of Egyptian history into 30 dynasties will endure. HIST
−300	Greek mathematician Euclid, living in Alexandria, Egypt, writes the *Elements*, a textbook summarizing Greek mathematics, including geometry. As an example of the axiomatic method, his geometry will influence subsequent philosophers. PHIL
−300	Greek philosopher Zeno of Citium founds Stoicism, a system of metaphysics, epistemology, and ethics named for the *stoa*, or portico, where the philosophy was taught. Stoicism, whose early proponents included Cleanthes of Assos and Chrysippus of Soli, will become highly influential in the Roman world. Proposing a material universe ordered deterministically by the pervasive force of God, it advocates dedication to duty and justice and renunciation of passion and indulgence. PHIL
−200s	Chinese philosopher Tsou Yen, a leader of the Cosmologist movement, develops a cyclical theory of the universe and of history. It incorporates the theory of the five elements (earth, wood, metal, fire, and water) and the opposing principles of yin (dark, female, weak) and yang (light, male, strong). PHIL
−200s	The Roman republic reaches its mature form. It balances democratic participation for adult male citizens with oligarchic institutions and controls, designed to protect the interests of the privileged classes. Republics of the modern age will learn from its organization, particularly its system of checks and balances. The U.S. Senate will take its name from the Roman Senate, one of the Roman republic's ruling bodies. Other components include the Centuriate and Tribal Assemblies. POL
−200s	During Aśoka's reign (*see* 273–232 B.C., REL), Buddhism is introduced to Sri Lanka, where the Theravada form of the religion will flourish. REL
−200s	The biblical books of 1 and 2 Chronicles, the Song of Songs, Ezra, and Nehemiah are composed. REL

-200s   The *Tao te ching*, the principal text of philosophical Taoism, is probably writ-
            ten about this time, although it is ascribed to Chinese philosopher Lao-tzu,
            legendary sixth-century B.C. founder of Taoism (*see* 500s B.C., PHIL).   REL

-200s   By now, Chinese religious practices include the cult of heaven and the worship
            of divine ancestors, both related to Confucianism, and augury and shamanis-
            tic magic, both related to mystical Taoism.   REL

-200s   In India, the Sanskrit epic the *Ramayana* is composed. It concerns the adven-
            tures of Rama and his three half-brothers, who collectively comprise an avatar
            (incarnation) of the god Vishnu.   REL

-200s   The Druid religion is practiced in Celtic Britain, Ireland, and Gaul (France and
            the Benelux countries). The Druids are priests who lead highly ritualistic wor-
            ship of nature deities, principally in sacred oak groves and at lakes and river
            sources. Wielding both political and religious power, the Druids will be elim-
            inated by Roman conquerors (*see* A.D. 58, REL).   REL

-280-   Greek Stoic philosopher Chrysippus lives. Though reputedly the author of 705
-207   books, none of these will survive.   PHIL

-273-   Indian emperor Aśoka reigns. After converting to Buddhism in 257 B.C., he
-232   helps to make it a world religion by sending Buddhist missionaries to many
            parts of Asia and as far west as Greece and Egypt.   REL

-250   A council of Buddhist monks at Patna, India, settles a philosophical schism by
            deciding in favor of the Sthaviras, who affirm that only present events are real,
            and reject the Sarvastivadins, who claim that past, present, and future events
            are all real.   REL

-250   Hellenistic Jews, possibly living in Alexandria, Egypt, compose the Greek
            translation of the Hebrew Bible (Old Testament) known as the Septuagint. REL

-234-   Roman statesman Cato the Elder lives. In his life and writings, he defends such
-149   traditional Roman virtues as simplicity, honesty, and courage. Only his treatise
            on farming, *De re rustica* (or *De agri cultura*), will survive.   PHIL

-221-   The Ch'in dynasty reigns in China. Following the teachings of the philosoph-
-207   ical movement known as the School of Law, the dynasty's founder, Ch'in Shih
            Huang Ti, abolishes feudalism in favor of a bureaucratic, harshly legalistic
            form of government. He orders the burning of most of the intellectual works
            produced during the Age of Philosophy (600–256 B.C.). The event is an early
            example of book-burning, which will become a recurrent practice of political
            and religious ideologues.   POL

−202– A.D. 220	During the Han dynasty in China, Confucianism becomes the state religion, with Taoism persisting as a popular religion. The Han period is marked by the compilation of dictionaries and encyclopedic histories, among other intellectual and cultural achievements. REL
−200	Greek Peripatetic philosopher Alexander of Aphrodisias, a commentator on the works of Greek philosopher Aristotle, flourishes. PHIL
−200– A.D. 200	In India, the Laws of Manu are compiled. Traditionally ascribed to legendary Hindu lawgiver Manu, they offer rules about ritual and everyday life. REL
−200– A.D. 200	In India, the encyclopedic Sanskrit epic the *Mahabharata* is composed. The longest poem in world literature, it is ascribed to the ancient sage Vyāsa but is actually compiled by many hands. It incorporates legendary history, theology, and moral and political philosophy. It includes the spiritual classic *Bhagavad-Gita* (*The Song of God*), which takes the form of a dialogue between Lord Krishna, incarnation of the god Vishnu, and Prince Arjuna. The *Bhagavad-Gita* advocates detachment from the fruits of action, self-knowledge, and personal devotion to Krishna. REL
−100s	In India, the *Yogasutras* of Patanjali are composed. The basic text of the Yoga philosophical school, it systematizes the practice of spiritual and physical discipline with the goal of attaining higher consciousness. REL
−100s	In India, the Hindu cult of the god Shiva arises. Devotees are known as Shaiva. Lakula, the founder of the earliest known Shaiva sect, is considered an incarnation of the god. REL
−100s	The earliest known devotees to Vishnu, known as Bhagavatas, practice their worship in India. REL
−100s– A.D. 100s	The Essenes, a Jewish religious sect active from the second century B.C. to the second century A.D., are celibate males who practice communal ownership, ritual purification, and asceticism. Messianic beliefs associated with the sect will influence the rise of Christianity. REL
−185– −109	Greek philosopher Panaetius of Rhodes lives. His Stoicism is combined with Aristotelian ethical views. PHIL
−179– −104	Chinese scholar Tung Chung-shu lives. In his works, the Confucian thinker outlines the five cardinal virtues of decorum, love, righteousness, trustworthiness, and wisdom. PHIL
−170– −90	Greek grammarian Dionysius Thrax lives in Alexandria, Egypt. His *Art of Grammar* will be a model for subsequent grammars. LING

-167– -142	The armed Jewish rebels known as the Maccabees revolt against Syrian rule of Judaea and repression of the Jewish faith. Under leader Judas Maccabaeus, the movement succeeds in restoring the Temple in 165 B.C. REL
-155	Greek Skeptic philosopher Carneades delivers a critique of justice in two speeches in Rome. PHIL
-150	The Alexandrian School is founded in Alexandria, Egypt, the first Christian institution of higher education. In its programs, it aims to integrate Christian orthodoxy and Greek culture. EDUC
-150	By about this time, the Pharisees, a Jewish religious and political sect, have originated in Palestine. They believe in strict adherence to Mosaic Law, practice debate on fine points of law, and develop the synagogue as an alternative place of worship to the Temple. Though some members will be excoriated by Jesus Christ as hypocrites, the sect introduces ideas that are essential to the rabbinic Judaism that will survive the fall of the Temple (*see* A.D. 66–73, REL). REL
-150	By about this time, the Jewish sect known as the Sadducees have originated in Palestine. They deny the authority of the oral law, upholding only that of the written law. They will be noted in the Gospels for their denial of the resurrection of the body. REL
-145– -90	Chinese historian Ssu-ma Ch'ien lives. His *Shih-chi* (*Records of the Historian*) includes dynastic annals, biographical and geographical accounts, and chronological tables. The work will serve as a model for later Chinese dynastic histories. HIST
-135– -51	Greek philosopher Posidonius of Apamea lives. He combines Stoic teachings with an imperialistic, universalistic view of history; his ideas will influence the Roman philosophers Cicero and Seneca, among others. PHIL
-130– -68	Greek philosopher Antiochus of Ascalon lives. Taking an eclectic position, he argues that the prevailing philosophical schools of his day are in basic agreement. He will be known as the founder of Middle Platonism, a movement that breaks with the Skepticism of Philo of Larissa to reintroduce the possibility of a positive science of philosophy. PHIL
-110– -40	Greek philosopher Philodemus of Gadara lives. He is known for his Epicurean philosophy, including aesthetic views that prefigure the doctrine of art for art's sake (*see* A.D. 1818, CRIT). PHIL
-106– -43	Roman orator and philosopher Marcus Tullius Cicero lives. In *De inventione*, he makes the first written reference to the term "artes liberales." EDUC

| −100 | The Roman republic institutes educational programs for boys and girls.   EDUC |

−100–
A.D. 100
During this period in India, Mahayana Buddhism becomes distinct from Theravada Buddhism. The Mahayana form emphasizes the potential for enlightenment of all beings, takes a liberal approach to rules and practices, and introduces the concept of the bodhisattva, the person capable of entering nirvana who postpones entry for the sake of enlightening others. Theravada Buddhism, the older form, emphasizes salvation through a strict monastic life. REL

−100–
A.D. 200
During this period, Jewish rabbinical scholars known as tannaim compile the Mishna, the Hebrew Oral Law, an authoritative interpretation of the written law, the Torah or Pentateuch. REL

−98–
−55
Roman poet Lucretius lives. His philosophical poem *De rerum natura* (*On the Nature of Things*) is based on the atomistic teachings of the Greek philosophers Democritus and Epicurus. PHIL

−88
The Academy of Athens, founded by Greek philosopher Plato in 387 B.C., closes when its last head, Philo of Larissa, moves to Rome. PHIL

−65–
−8
Roman poet Horace lives. The theoretical and practical aesthetics of his *Ars Poetica* (*The Art of Poetry*), together with the example of his satires and epistles, will prove highly influential to poets and critics as late as the 18th century. CRIT

−63
The Romans conquer Palestine, homeland of the Jews and future birthplace of Jesus of Nazareth. REL

−60
The cult of the Persian god Mithras (*see* 550–333 B.C., REL) enters Rome. One of several mystery cults popular in the Roman empire near the time of Christ, it includes a baptism ritual, a regular communion meal of bread and wine, and a promise of resurrection in return for living a moral life. Mithraism is also popular in India, Mesopotamia (Iraq), and Asia Minor (Turkey). REL

−59–
−17
Roman historian Livy lives. He is the author of the multivolume history of Rome, *Ab urbe condita libri* (*The Annals of the Roman People*). HIST

−59
The widespread dissemination of public information is instituted with the posting of the bulletin *Acta diurna*, in Rome. Its publication is decreed by Roman general Julius Caesar. JOURN

−58
Roman general Julius Caesar writes the historical work *Commentaries on the Gallic War*. He will write *Commentaries on the Civil War* in 45 B.C. HIST

−54
Roman orator and philosopher Marcus Tullius Cicero writes *De publica*, a work of political philosophy. POL

−51   Emperor Hsüan ratifies the conclusions of a council of Confucian thinkers, establishing an orthodox interpretation of Confucian thought, particularly as related to government. By now, Confucian classics have come to dominate the educational system and Confucian ideas of worship comprise the official imperial religion.   PHIL

−50   Greek Skeptic philosopher Aenesidemus of Cnossos flourishes. A defender of Pyrrho's philosophy, he articulates ten tropes that will be important to late Hellenic Skepticism.   PHIL

−47–
−44   Roman orator and philosopher Marcus Tullius Cicero writes several philosophical works, including *Tusculanae disputationes, De natura deorum, De divinatione, De senectute, De amicitia,* and his guide to Stoic morality, *De officiis.*   PHIL

−40   Roman architect Vitruvius writes *De architectura,* ten volumes devoted to the establishment of formal categories for architecture and city planning. His discussion of the Greek orders of temple building will be extremely influential among Renaissance architects.   CRIT

−40   In China, *The Book of Rites (Li chi)* is composed, incorporating preexisting material on correct behavior and ritual.   REL

−37–
−4   During the reign of Herod the Great over Judaea, the religious sect the Essenes establishes monastic communities in the Dead Sea region. *See also* 100s B.C.–A.D. 100s and A.D. 1947, REL.   REL

−37–
−4   During the reign of Herod the Great, the Jewish rebel group known as the Zealots forms to oppose his idolatrous practices and collusion with Rome. They will carry out sporadic revolts before being crushed in the last great Jewish rebellion against Rome (*see* A.D. 66–73, REL).   REL

−31   Roman statesman Gaius Octavius, who will later be known as first Roman emperor Augustus Caesar, defeats Marc Antony at the Battle of Actium. Augustus founds the autocratic system of government that will survive, with modifications, until the collapse of the Roman empire in the fifth century A.D. (*see* A.D. 476, REL). Though actual power is held by the emperor, the forms of republican rule are maintained, including the existence of a Senate. *See also* 200s B.C., POL.   POL

−28   Roman emperor Augustus begins a program of temple renovation, marking a renewed interest in traditional Roman religion as a support for state power.   REL

−25   Greek scholar Dionysius of Halicarnassus flourishes. Teaching in Rome, he writes important critical works, including *On the Arrangement of Words, On Imitation,* and *On the Eloquence of Demosthenes.*   CRIT

−20	Greek philosopher Arius Didymus, teacher of the Roman emperor Augustus, flourishes. PHIL
−20– A.D. 50	Hellenistic Jewish philosopher Philo Judaeus lives and teaches in Alexandria, Egypt. Drawing on Greek philosophy, he interprets Old Testament scriptures as allegories of divine truth. PHIL
−6– A.D. 30	Jewish prophet Jesus of Nazareth, known as the Christ (Greek translation of the Hebrew *Messiah*), lives in Judaea. Working miracles and preaching the Good News of the Kingdom of God, he attracts followers, including 12 apostles, who believe him to be the promised savior. After his crucifixion as a rebel by the Roman authorities, his followers will claim that he has risen from the dead and appeared to them. Declaring that Jesus Christ is the incarnate son of God who died to redeem humanity from their sins, his followers, led by the Galilean apostle who will be known as St. Peter, establish the religion of Christianity. *See also* A.D. 30, REL. REL
−6– A.D. 30	In his teachings, Jesus of Nazareth ascribes goodness and power equally to men and women, largely discounting prevalent cultural beliefs and practices. REL

Year One

Like many seemingly value-free pieces of information, a date is actually fraught with meaning. To say that the United States was founded in 1776, for example, is to add silently "A.D.," which is to say, "anno Domini," or "in the year of the Lord," which can be taken as a tacit acknowledgment that Jesus Christ is Lord and that his birth marks the central point of history.

The inventor of A.D. was a Roman monk named Dionysius Exiguus, who, by his own system of reckoning, died about 545. Calculating dates is a tricky business, and Dionysius is believed to have been a few years off in determining when Jesus was born. Christ is now thought to have been born roughly six years "before Christ," or B.C.

Before Dionysius, the Romans calculated dates from the legendary founding of Rome, equivalent to 753 B.C. Most Jews in the Roman world had gone along with this system, but when the Christians brought theology into the matter, Jews felt the need to express their dissent. It became common for followers of Judaism to reckon dates from the biblically determined year of the creation of the world, equivalent to 3761 B.C.

Muslims introduced yet another "year one"—the year of the Hegira, Muhammad's flight from Mecca to Medina, where he first established a theocracy. That year is equivalent to A.D. 622.

In our multicultural age, Westerners who desire the convenience of the dominant chronology without religious trappings convert A.D. to C.E. ("of the common era") and B.C. to B.C.E. ("before the common era").

–4–   Roman statesman and philosopher Seneca the Younger lives. His works of
A.D. 65 Stoic ethics include *Moral Letters*.   PHIL

A.D.

23–79   Roman naturalist Pliny the Elder lives. He provides an account of the devel-
         opment of the technique of painting in his monumental *Historia naturalis*.CRIT

30   Jesus of Nazareth (*see* 6 B.C.–A.D. 30, REL) is crucified on Golgotha (or Calvary)
         outside Jerusalem. His followers declare that he was resurrected soon after-
         ward. The day of his death will be traditionally known as Good Friday; the day
         of his resurrection Easter Sunday. He is believed to have ascended into heaven
         40 days later. His followers begin preaching the new religion of Christianity on
         Pentecost, the day on which they receive the Holy Spirit.   REL

33   Stephen, an early convert to Christianity, is stoned to death in Jerusalem by
         Jews who consider his preaching blasphemous.   REL

33   Saul of Tarsus, a defender of traditional Judaism against Christianity, converts to
         Christianity upon hearing Christ in a vision on the road to Damascus. As Paul, he
         will become a great apostle and missionary. As the author of many important
         epistles (letters) in the New Testament, he will play an important role in defining
         orthodox Christian theology.   REL

35–97   Roman rhetorician Quintilian (Marcus Fabius Quintilianus) lives. He will be
         known for tutoring some of the great minds of the period, including Pliny the
         Younger, but will gain his most lasting importance through his oratory and
         writings on oratory, including *Institutio oratoria*. Lost for years, the text will be
         rediscovered in 1416; it will have a great influence on the development of
         Renaissance humanism.   EDUC

47–49   Christian apostle Paul travels on his first missionary journey to Asia Minor and
         Cyprus, where he establishes churches.   REL

49   A Christian church council at Jerusalem determines that Gentiles can become
         Christians without being circumcised and that full adherence to Jewish law is
         not required of Christians.   REL

50   An unknown author traditionally called Longinus writes the Greek treatise *On
         the Sublime*, which discusses the qualities comprising an elevated style. It will

influence much future criticism, particularly in the 17th and 18th centuries. *See also* 1554, CRIT.   CRIT

50–117   Greek rhetorician Dio Chrysostom lives. He contends that a divine ideal does not exist until an artist has finished the process of making a statue or poem containing his version of the god who is waiting to be delivered from chaos.   CRIT

50–53   On his second missionary journey (to Philippi, Salonica, Athens, and Corinth), Christian apostle Paul writes First and Second Thessalonians, among the earliest of the epistles that will be included in the New Testament.   REL

50–135   Palestinian rabbi Akiba ben Joseph lives. He compiles the collection of Hebrew Oral Law known as the *Mishna of Rabbi Akiba*.   REL

53–57   During his third missionary journey, Christian apostle Paul writes the epistle to the Romans and the two epistles to the Corinthians.   REL

55–117   Roman orator and historian Tacitus lives. He is the author of *Germania*, a social history of Germany; *Annales*, a study of the Julian dynasty; and *Historiae*, a history of the years 69–96.   HIST

55–135   Roman Stoic philosopher Epictetus lives. The moral teachings in his *Discourses* and his simple way of life draw many followers.   PHIL

55   Peter, born as Simon in the Galilee region of Judaea, travels on a missionary journey to Rome, the capital of the Roman empire. In the eyes of Roman Catholics, his status as the Christ-appointed leader of the apostles and first bishop of Rome (or pope) gives him and his successors primacy over the entire Christian church. Eastern Orthodox and Protestant Christians will not accept the pope's primacy.   REL

57–59   In Jerusalem for the last time, Christian apostle Paul is arrested for provoking a riot and held prisoner. He is sent to Rome under guard to make an appeal, and will arrive there in 60, where he will die a martyr (*see* 67, REL).   REL

58   Roman general Suetonius Paulinus destroys the last stronghold of the Druid priesthood on the island of Anglesey in the British Isles.   REL

64   Roman emperor Nero orders the first of several imperial persecutions of Christians, whom he charges with starting the fire that burned down much of Rome.   REL

65   By now, Buddhism has been introduced to China, with at least one Buddhist community described at a princely court.   REL

66–73   The Jews of Palestine carry out a major rebellion against Rome. Its suppression results in the destruction of the Temple in 70 and the worldwide dispersion (diaspora) of the Jews. The last resisters, members of the Zealot party (*see* 37–4 B.C., REL), withstand a two-year siege by the Romans at the mountaintop fortress of Masada. Although Masada finally falls in 73, the Romans find that virtually all the besieged Jews have committed suicide rather than be captured.   REL

66–73   For Judaism, one result of the destruction of the Second Temple is a movement away from a religion based on sacrifice at a central location under the hereditary authority of a priestly class to one focused on the local synagogue, private deeds and ceremonies, and local leaders, particularly rabbis or teachers.   REL

67   The Christian apostles Peter and Paul are executed by the Roman emperor Nero. Linus succeeds Peter as the second bishop of Rome, or pope, a post he holds until his death in 76.   REL

69–140   Roman historian Suetonius lives. He writes *De vita Caesarum* (*Lives of the Caesars*), a series of biographies of the Roman leaders from Caesar to Domitian.   HIST

70   The Gospel of Mark, the earliest of the four gospels in the New Testament, is written.   REL

81–96   The reign of the emperor Domitian is marked by persecution of Christians, inspiring the writing during this period of the New Testament Book of Revelation or Apocalypse. The Gospel of Luke and the Acts of the Apostles are also written at this time.   REL

95   Clement, an early pope, argues in a letter that the leaders of the church have inherited their authority from Christ and the apostles.   REL

95–105   Certain New Testament epistles attributed to the late Christian apostle Paul are written, including Hebrews, Titus, 1 Peter, and 1 and 2 Timothy.   REL

100s   Chinese philosophers Ma Jung and Cheng Hsüan write commentaries on the Confucian classics.   PHIL

100s   Theravada Buddhism is introduced to Thailand.   REL

100s   The Jewish mystical tradition known as Merkavah, a forerunner of the cabalistic tradition, flourishes. *See also* 1000s, REL.   REL

100s   The Jewish religious sect the Essenes fades from existence. *See also* 100s B.C., REL. REL

100s	Gnosticism flourishes in the Mediterranean world. Combining Christian and Hellenistic beliefs with influences from Zoroastrianism and Babylonian and Egyptian mythology, the religion offers salvation through gnosis (knowledge or revelation) about the nature of reality. Jesus is believed to have come to restore knowledge about how to bring to fulfillment the divine spark residing in humanity. Gnosticism is condemned as a heresy by orthodox Christianity. REL
100	Greek biographer Plutarch writes *Parallel Lives*, a series of paired biographies of famous Greeks and Romans. HIST
100	The Gospel of Matthew is written. The Gospel of John will follow within the next quarter century. REL
100–165	Justin Martyr, one of the first Christian apologists, lives. Extant works defending Christianity include *Apology* and *Dialogue with Trypho*. REL
120–200	Greek prelate Irenaeus lives. Known as Apostle of the Gauls, he writes against Gnosticism in such works as *Against Heresies* (c. 180). REL
120–145	Gnostic teacher Basilides flourishes in Alexandria, Egypt. His brand of Gnostic Christianity, epitomized in his *Exegetica*, a gospel with commentaries, has a strong following. REL
121–180	Roman emperor Marcus Aurelius lives. Esteemed for his moral character and humane rule, he writes the *Meditations*, a classic work of Stoic philosophy. PHIL
129–199	Greek physician Galen of Pergamum lives. He elaborates on the theory of the four humors, which he believes must be kept in balance to preserve well-being. *See also* 460 B.C., PSYCH. PHIL
132–135	Jewish leader Bar Kokhba leads a major but ultimately unsuccessful revolt against Rome. REL
136–160	Gnostic teacher Valentinus flourishes in Alexandria. Founder of the Valentinians, the best-known school of Gnosticism, he teaches about the restoration of humanity to the divine order. Works associated with his school include *Pistis-Sophia* and *The Gospel of Truth*. REL
140	The ecclesiastical system of the early Christian church, including bishops, priests, and deacons, is detailed in the *Shepherd of Hermas*. REL
144	Christian Gnostic leader Marcion is excommunicated for heresy. Founder of several Marcionite churches in North Africa, Egypt, Asia Minor (Turkey), and Gaul (France and the Benelux countries), he rejects the Old Testament, arguing that the God of the Old Testament is a different and inferior God from that

of the New Testament. His dualistic views will be absorbed by Manichaeism (*see* 216–277, REL).   REL

148   In Lo-yang, China, a Parthian Buddhist missionary named An Shih-kao leads the translation of Buddhist scriptures into Chinese.   REL

150   The four canonical gospels—Mark, Luke, Matthew, and John, composed from about 70 to 125—are collected.   REL

150   The School of Alexandria, a center for early Christian theology, is established in Egypt.   REL

166   Han Chinese emperor Liu Chuang sponsors Buddhist and Taoist ceremonies in the royal palace.   REL

175–242   Alexandrian philosopher Ammonius Saccas, a self-taught laborer, lives in Alexandria, Egypt. Though no writings of his will survive, his ideas will influence those of his pupil Roman philosopher Plotinus, the founder of Neoplatonism (*see* 205–270, PHIL).   PHIL

178   Roman or Alexandrian Platonist philosopher Celsus writes the first important attack on Christianity, the *True Discourse*. Greek Christian father Origen will respond to it c. 248 in *Contra Celsum* (*see* 185–254, REL).   REL

180   The first known alchemy manuscripts appear in Egypt. Forerunner of chemistry, the tradition of alchemy is thought to have originated in Egypt or China several centuries earlier. Its principal goal is a way of turning base metals into silver and gold (transmutation). Its secretive teachings are often connected to Hellenistic Greek philosophy, mysticism, and magic. Medieval Arabs and Europeans will carry on the tradition.   PHIL

184   A peasants' rebellion spreads across China. Known as the Revolt of the Yellow Turbans, it is inspired by a Taoist apocalyptic belief that the "yellow heaven" is about to replace the "blue heaven" as the dominant force in the universe, ushering in an age of peace. The rebels wear yellow kerchiefs on their heads. Though suppressed, the revolt draws attention to the strength and organization of the popular Taoist church, which has a hierarchical priesthood and offers rites and services related to personal atonement and salvation. Its leaders claim descent from Chang Ling, a Taoist teacher of about the first century B.C.   REL

185–254   Greek Christian father Origen lives, writing such works as *On Prayer* and *Exhortation to Martyrdom* (both in the mid-230s); textual studies of the Old Testament such as the *Hexapla*; and *Contra Celsum* (c. 248), a defense of Christianity against the philosopher Celsus (*see* 178, REL).   REL

197	Roman theologian Tertullian converts to Christianity. Although his writings will strongly defend the church against paganism, he will develop heterodox opinions and leave the Roman church to join the Montanist sect (213) and later his own sect, the Tertullianists. REL

200s   Buddhist philosophers Nāgārjuna and Aryadeva are central figures in the school of thought known as Mādhyamika or Shunyavada. They believe that all attributed properties are relative and that absolute reality can only be thought of as a void.   PHIL

200s   Greek writer Diogenes Laertius writes *Lives of Eminent Philosophers*, which provides indispensable information about philosophers of antiquity, many of whose works will be lost.   PHIL

200s   *Sefer Yezirah* (*The Book of Creation*), a mystical work of Jewish theology ascribed to Jewish patriarch Abraham, is written. Its use of numerology and concepts from Neoplatonism will provide one of the sources of the cabala (*see* 1000s, REL).   REL

200s   Christian and Jewish interpretations of the Old Testament depict women as examples of evil and a danger to society.   REL

200   Greek physician and philosopher Sextus Empiricus flourishes. His works, collected into the *Outlines of Pyrrhonism* and *Adversos Mathematicos*, codify and extend classical Skeptical thought.   PHIL

200   The canon of New Testament books is by now substantially fixed.   REL

200   Palestinian Jewish scholar Judah ha-Nasi completes the compilation of the Mishna, the Hebrew Oral Law, begun under the early tannaim, or scholars (*see* 100 B.C.–A.D. 200, REL).   REL

200–500 The amoraim, Jewish scholars, comment elaborately on the Mishna, the Hebrew Oral Law. Their commentary, in Aramaic, will become the Gemara, which, with the Mishna, will become part of the Talmud, the Jewish Oral Law.   REL

205–270 Roman philosopher Plotinus lives. Influenced by the Alexandrian philosopher Ammonius Saccas (*see* 175–242, PHIL), he will be regarded as the founder of Neoplatonism, an idealistic philosophy derived from Greek philosopher Plato (*see* 427–347 B.C., PHIL). Plotinus describes the universe in terms of levels of reality and argues that contemplation can lead to mystical union with the divine. His teachings are collected in the *Enneads*, published after his death by his pupil Porphyry (*see* 233–301, PHIL), the Palestinian-born Greek philosopher. Plotinus's ideas will influence subsequent pagan, Christian, Jewish, and Islamic thought. Educated in Alexandria, Plotinus founds a school in Rome.   PHIL

215   Theologian Clement of Alexandria dies. The teacher of Origen (*see* 185–254, REL.),
               he attempted in his writings to synthesize Platonic and Christian thought.   REL

215   The earliest surviving text of the Christian liturgy of the Eucharist is set forth
               in the *Apostolic Tradition* of Hippolytus.   REL

216–277   Persian religious leader Manes (Mani), the founder of Manichaeism, lives.
               Declaring himself the last prophet of God, he preaches a dualistic combina-
               tion of Zoroastrianism and Christianity, in which the body is considered evil
               and the soul good.   REL

220–265   During the period of the Three Kingdoms (Wei, Shu, and Wu), the Han empire
               of China is replaced by political disunion. Taoism and Buddhism grow more
               dominant (and more determined as rivals) as Confucianism falls into decline.
               This "Age of Faith" will last until the beginning of the Sung dynasty
               (960–1279), when neo-Confucianism will gain ground.   REL

233–301   Palestinian-born Greek philosopher Porphyry lives. A student of Roman
               philosopher Plotinus (*see* 205–270, PHIL.), he publishes the treatises of his mas-
               ter as the *Enneads*, the founding work of Neoplatonism. He develops Plotinus's
               mystical doctrines and defends Hellenic paganism against Christianity. He
               also writes biographies of Plotinus and Pythagoras.   PHIL

247–635   During the Sassanian period in Persia (Iran), Zoroastrianism is the state religion. REL

249–251   The reign of the Roman emperor Decius is marked by persecution of Christians.
                                                                                                REL

250   In China among the aristocracy, a new form of speculative philosophy known
               as the "dark learning" develops, a blend of ideas from Confucianism, Taoism,
               and the *I Ching* (*Book of Changes*).   REL

250–900   During the Mayan Classic period in Mesoamerica (Mexico and Central
               America), the Mayans construct pyramidal temple complexes. The Moche of
               Peru (first to eighth centuries) also construct ceremonial pyramids.   REL

274   Roman emperor Marcus Aurelius declares the sun-god to be the supreme deity
               of the empire.   REL

284–305   Christians are persecuted during the reign of the Roman emperor Diocletian. REL

285   Christian hermit Anthony of Egypt lives. Known for resisting the devil's temp-
               tations while dwelling in seclusion in the desert, he becomes the focus for a
               colony of hermits, or anchorites. Anthony is considered the father of Christian
               monasticism.   REL

300s	The Yogacara (or Vijnanavada) school of Mahayana Buddhism reacts against excessive intellectualism by emphasizing moral and meditative aspects. Philosophically, the school affirms the reality of pure consciousness. Its principal exponents are Asanga and Vasubandhu. REL
300s	After a period of rivalry in Sri Lanka between the Mahayana and Theravada forms of Buddhism, the king decides in favor of the latter, which becomes the dominant form in that country. REL
300s	A Hindu-Buddhist culture flourishes in the Katmandu valley of Nepal. REL
300s	The Romans establish Christianity in Britain, but the religion will be nearly wiped out by pagan Anglo-Saxon invasions beginning in the fifth century. REL
300s	Nicholas, Bishop of Myra in Asia Minor, lives. The patron saint of children and sailors, he will become identified with the legendary figure Santa Claus, deliverer of gifts at Christmastime. REL
300s	Taoism has a strong influence on the courtly, literary, and artistic life of China. REL
312	Before the battle of the Milvian (or Mulvian) Bridge near Rome, Roman emperor Constantine the Great (reigned 306–337) sees a vision of a flaming cross with the words *in hoc signo vinces* ("by this sign thou shalt conquer"). According to legend, the vision persuades him to convert to Christianity, and he ascribes his ensuing victory to Christ. Constantine's reign marks the beginning of state acceptance of Christianity. *See also* 313 and 380, REL. REL
313	Roman emperor Constantine the Great promulgates the Edict of Milan, which grants legal rights to Christians, ending state persecution. REL
320	At Tabennisi, Egypt, Christian cenobite (monk) Pachomius founds the first monastery, to be governed under a regular rule. REL
323	Alexandrian ecclesiastic Arius writes his major work, *Thalia*. The founder of Arianism, he teaches that God is utterly unknowable and separate from the created world; that Jesus was a created being, not the supreme God but a secondary deity; and that when incarnate Jesus was not fully human but a divine being with a fleshly exterior. Arianism will be condemned as a heresy at the Council of Nicaea (*see* 325, REL), though it will remain a powerful movement throughout the fourth century. REL
325	*The Art of War*, by Sun-tzu, is the first book of war strategy. POL
325	Convened in Nicaea in Bithynia, Asia Minor (Turkey), at the order of the Roman emperor Constantine the Great, the Council of Nicaea is the first ecumenical

council of the Christian church. It condemns Arianism as a heresy (*see* 323, REL) and promulgates the Nicene Creed, which precisely defines the doctrine of the Trinity. The Nicene Creed will be used in Roman Catholic, Eastern Orthodox, and Anglican liturgies and will be accepted by most Protestants.   REL

328–373   Greek theologian and prelate Athanasius serves as bishop of Alexandria, Egypt. A vocal opponent of the Arian heresy (*see* 323 and 325, REL), he is exiled five times for his views but is eventually vindicated by the church. His works include *Apology Against the Arians* and *Four Orations Against the Arians*.   REL

330   Roman emperor Constantine the Great establishes Constantinople (formerly Byzantium) as the capital of the Eastern Roman empire, later known as the Byzantine empire. It will become the center of Eastern Orthodox Christianity until 1453, when it will fall to the Ottoman Turkish empire. In 1930 the Turkish city will be renamed Istanbul.   REL

334–416   Chinese Buddhist Hui-yüan lives. He founds the Pure Land school of Buddhism, which advocates prayer to the buddha Amitābha (Chinese O-mi-t'o) in the hope of attaining rebirth in the paradise known as the Pure Land. Pure Land will become the most popular form of Buddhism among Chinese laypeople.   REL

Julian's Religion

After Roman emperor Constantine (reigned 306–337) embraced Christianity, those in the empire who still cherished Greco-Roman paganism were at a disadvantage. However, in one of history's most famous rearguard actions, the young Roman emperor Julian (reigned 361–363) attempted to restore the faith of his fathers. Although he nominally decreed toleration of all religions, he took steps to favor paganism and discourage Christianity. Believers in the pagan gods were given preference for appointment to official posts, and Julian himself set an example by worshiping the sun and performing animal sacrifices. Christians, on the other hand, were forbidden to teach, bishops were banished, and churches were closed and sometimes burned. Such repression was augmented by Julian's own contemptuous writings against the Christian religion, which he dismissed as "the trickery of the Galileans."

Julian's attempt to restore the old religion was short-lived. In 363, only two years into his reign, he died in battle against the Persians. His successor, Jovian, promptly restored Christianity to its place of honor. Some considered the untimely death of "Julian the Apostate" a sign of divine retribution, although his Persian enemies were not Christians at all but Zoroastrians—members of a religion unrelated either to Christianity or Greco-Roman paganism.

358–364	Greek prelate Basil the Great frames the monastic rule that will be the basis for subsequent Eastern Orthodox Christian monasticism. REL
361	The Roman emperor Julian the Apostate renounces Christianity upon taking the throne. While tolerating Christianity, he attempts to restore pagan polytheism as the prevailing religion. His efforts will end in 363 when he is killed in battle in Persia (Iran). REL
367	The Festal Epistle of Greek prelate Athanasius gives the earliest extant listing of the enduring form of the New Testament, substantially fixed since about 200. REL
370–415	Greek philosopher Hypatia lives, teaching a version of Neoplatonism. PHIL
371	French monk Martin, who will later be named the patron saint of France, becomes bishop of Tours. REL
374–397	Roman prelate Ambrose serves as bishop of Milan. Through his strong influence over the imperial court and his many written works, including homilies, orations, hymns, and exegetical treatises, he helps establish the medieval ideal of the relations between church and state. He is responsible for the conversion of Augustine (see 387, REL). REL
379	Cappadocian church father Gregory of Nazianzus is named bishop of Constantinople (Istanbul). As a theologian, he will combat the Arian heresy. REL
380	The views of Priscillian, a Spanish Christian religious reformer and bishop of Avila, are declared heretical. He will be executed in 385. REL
380	Roman emperor Theodosius I makes Christianity the official religion of the empire. REL
381	The First Council of Constantinople, convened by Eastern Roman emperor Theodosius I, establishes the orthodox teaching on the Trinity, declaring that the Holy Spirit has the same divinity as the Father and Son. It also condemns Apollinarianism, the doctrine taught by Eastern bishop Apollinaris that Christ possessed the Logos (or Word) in place of a human mind, and was therefore not fully human. REL
387	North African church father Augustine of Hippo is converted to Christianity by Roman prelate Ambrose and baptized. He renounces his earlier Manichaeism (see 216–277, REL) and will soon be made a priest (391) and bishop of Hippo (396). His writings will provide an important foundation for Roman Catholic and Protestant theology and help to combat such heresies as Manichaeism, Donatism, and Pelagianism. REL

395	On the death of Theodosius I, the Roman empire is permanently divided into east and west, contributing to the growing separation between the Roman and Eastern Orthodox churches. REL
397–401	North African church father Augustine of Hippo writes his *Confessions*, the first great work of spiritual autobiography. REL
397–434	Chinese Buddhist teacher Chu Tao-sheng flourishes. As an opponent of the idea of merit, he influences the development of the Ch'an (Zen) school of Buddhism. REL
398	Syrian prelate John Chrysostom is made patriarch of Constantinople (Istanbul). He will later be exiled for his criticism of the imperial court. His writings will have a strong influence on Christian thinking. REL
399–414	Chinese Buddhist priest Fa-hsien travels in India in search of greater knowledge of the Buddhist tradition and discoveries of sacred relics and texts. REL
400s	The *Books of Chilam Balam*, a collection of Mayan historical records, begin to be composed. Combining myth, prophecy, and history, they will be transcribed in the 17th and 18th centuries, after the Spanish conquest. HIST
400s	Indian Buddhist scholar Buddhaghosa writes commentaries on Buddhist scripture and expounds Buddhist doctrine in such works as *Visuddhimagga* (*The Way of Perfection*). He is responsible for restoring the reputation of scholarship and texts written in the Pali language. REL
400s	By now, both Theravada and Mahayana Buddhism have been introduced to Burma. REL
400s	By now, Buddhism has been introduced to Java in Indonesia. REL
400s	By this century, Taoism in China has developed into a complex, popular religious system, incorporating elements drawn from Mahayana Buddhism, Confucianism, alchemy, and local beliefs. With a large pantheon of gods, religious Taoism is concerned with achieving longevity and immortality, yogic practices, and yin and yang theory. REL
400s	In India, worship of a mother-goddess begins to flourish. In Hinduism, such deities are identified as aspects of the Great Goddess or Shakti, spouse of the god Shiva. REL
400s	A council at Valabhi in India revises and finalizes the canon of Jainist scriptures (*see* 321–298 B.C., REL). REL

400s	The Talmud Yerushalmi (Jerusalem Talmud) is compiled. *See also* 500, REL. REL
400s	In China, Indian Buddhist monk Kumārajīva organizes a translation bureau that produces numerous translations of Buddhist scriptures. Through the seventh century, this and other translation bureaus in China will continue to gather and translate Indian works of devotion, doctrine, science, and philosophy. REL
400–416	North African church father Augustine of Hippo writes *On the Trinity*. REL
405	The Chinese system of writing is introduced to Japan, bringing with it many Chinese ideas and cultural motifs. LING
405	Christian scholar Jerome finishes the Vulgate, the first complete Latin translation of the Old and New Testaments. It will remain the official Latin Bible of the Roman Catholic Church for centuries. REL
410–485	Greek philosopher Proclus lives. The last major philosopher of classical antiquity, he publishes his Neoplatonist views in *Elements of Theology* and other works. PHIL
413–426	North African church father Augustine of Hippo writes *The City of God*, a 22-volume treatise defending Christianity against the pagan charge that it was to blame for the deterioration of the Roman empire. REL
418	English monk Pelagius, who denies original sin and the need for baptism and argues that justification can be gained through good works, is excommunicated as a heretic. REL
431	The ecumenical Council of Ephesus condemns Nestorianism, the view advanced by Nestorius, patriarch of Constantinople (Istanbul), that Jesus had two separate natures, one human, one divine, and that Mary was the mother only of the human part, not the mother of God. REL
432	Scottish-born Patrick arrives in Ireland to preach Christianity. He will succeed in converting the indigenous pagans and in founding many churches. REL
448	Church leader Eutyches is condemned for heresy and deposed from his position as archimandrite in Constantinople (Istanbul). He has preached an extreme form of Monophysitism, the view that Christ was purely divine in nature, with no human nature. Eutyches will be reinstated by the illegitimate "Robber Synod" in 449, but condemned again by the Council of Chalcedon (*see* 451, REL). Monophysitism is a reaction to Nestorianism (*see* 431, REL), which declared that Christ had two separate natures, one human, one divine. REL

451   The ecumenical Council of Chalcedon meets and declares that Christ's divine
           and human natures are distinct but inseparable, a doctrine that refutes the
           views of church leader Eutyches and the Monophysites (*see* 448, REL). The
           Eastern churches invalidate the council, leading the pope to excommunicate
           the east until 519. Monophysitism will persist in Syria (as the Jacobite
           Church), in Egypt (as the Coptic Church), and in Armenia (as the Armenian
           Church) from the sixth century onward.   REL

476   The Western Roman empire falls, as Roman emperor Romulus Augustulus is
           deposed by barbarian king Odoacer. The Roman Catholic Church will survive
           as the most prominent authority in western Europe.   REL

484–585   Roman statesman and writer Cassiodorus lives. He founds two monasteries;
           one of these, Vivarium, will be a leading center for Christian learning and will
           provide a link between the the pagan liberal arts and the Christian church.   EDUC

496   Frankish king Clovis is baptized a Christian on December 25, along with
           3,000 followers.   REL

500s   By now, Buddhism has spread from China to Korea and Japan. In Japan, the
           cult of the bodhisattva Amida (or Amitābha), who promises to bring his fol-
           lowers to paradise, or Pure Land, is especially strong.   REL

500s   Indian Buddhist monk Bodhidharma, who will be esteemed by later Ch'an
           (Zen) Buddhists, lives.   REL

500s   The word *Shinto* is coined to distinguish the ancient religious tradition of
           Japan from newly arrived Buddhism. Shinto is the worship of *kami*, or super-
           natural powers.   REL

500   A group of philosophical papers are written that are ascribed to first-century
           martyr Saint Dionysius the Areopagite; the author will customarily be referred
           to as Pseudo-Dionysius. Including letters and such treatises as *The Celestial
           Hierarchy* and *Mystical Theology*, they help transmit Neoplatonism and angelol-
           ogy to medieval Europe and will influence Italian philosopher Thomas
           Aquinas and other scholastic philosophers.   REL

500   The Talmud Babli (Babylonian Talmud) is compiled. Distinct from the
           Talmud Yerushalmi (*see* 400s, REL), it will become the authoritative compila-
           tion of Jewish Oral Law, consisting of the Mishna (which comments in
           Hebrew on the Torah or first five books of the Hebrew Bible) and the Gemara
           (which comments in Aramaic on the Mishna).   REL

524   Roman philosopher Boethius writes *The Consolation of Philosophy* while in
           prison awaiting execution on charges of treason against Theodoric, the

Ostrogoth ruler of Rome. Concerning the vicissitudes of fortune and the ultimate goodness and happiness found in God, the work draws on Neoplatonism and Stoicism. It will be highly influential throughout the Middle Ages. In his lifetime, Boethius also writes on logic, theology, arithmetic, and music.   PHIL

529   Italian monk Benedict founds the first Benedictine monastery at Monte Cassino. His rule, known as the Benedictine rule, will be the basis for future Western Christian monasticism.   REL

538–597   Chinese Buddhist monk Chih-yi lives. He founds the T'ien-t'ai school of Buddhism, which promotes scholarship and advocates a moderate balance of scripture study, meditation, moral discipline, and ceremony.   REL

545   Roman scholar and monk Dionysius Exiguus dies. He has collected early church documents and was the first to use Christ's birth as the starting point for the calendar.   MISC

550–615   Irish abbot and missionary Columban lives. He converts many pagans and establishes monasteries in Gaul (France and the Benelux countries).   REL

553   The Second Council of Constantinople, convened by Byzantine emperor Justinian, condemns Nestorian writings while attempting to reconcile moderate Monophysites to the Christian church.   REL

574–621   Japanese Prince Regent Shōtoku lives and gives state preference to Buddhism. The Horyuji temple at Nara is built during his reign.   REL

581–618   The Sui dynasty reunifies China after a period of disunity and favors the growth of the Taoist church. Taoists will continue in imperial favor through the early T'ang dynasty (618–906).   REL

590–604   Gregory the Great reigns as pope. He reforms the church and expands papal supremacy over spiritual and temporal affairs. He encourages monasticism, fights against the Donatist heresy, and refuses to recognize the title "ecumenical" for the patriarch of Constantinople (Istanbul), thereby contributing to the division between eastern and western Christianity.   REL

596   Pope Gregory the Great sends Italian Benedictine missionary Augustine to England, where he converts King Aethelbert. Augustine will become the first archbishop of Canterbury in 601.   REL

600s   Chinese philosopher K'ung Ying-ta writes commentaries on the Confucian classics that serve to unify Confucian doctrine.   PHIL

600s   Buddhism is introduced to Tibet. Tibetan Buddhism will evolve into a distinct variety, one that will also prevail in Bhutan, Mongolia, and parts of Siberia and southwest China. It incorporates elements of tantra (an esoteric tradition of ritual and meditation, including mystical words called mantras and sacred diagrams called mandalas) and the indigenous Tibetan religion of Bon shamanism. REL

600s   Christianity, in its Nestorian form (*see* 431, REL), reaches China. REL

600s   The Paulician sect, a Manichaean group (*see* 216–277, REL), forms in Armenia. REL

600–1200   In Tamil Nadu in India, the Vaishnava movement (the cult of the god Vishnu, recognized as the supreme deity by his devotees), flourishes. Its saints, known as the 12 Alvars, write vernacular devotional poetry. REL

610   At about the age of 40, Arab prophet Muhammad, founder of the religion of Islam (meaning surrender or acceptance), receives his call to serve as the prophet of Allah (God). The revelations he receives will become the Koran, the Holy Book of Islam (*see* 651, REL). He will slowly gather followers who accept his call to become Muslims (those who surrender to the will of God). REL

622   Arab prophet Muhammad flees from Mecca to Yathrib (ever after called Medina, the City of the Prophet), where he establishes a theocracy and begins to build an

Whose Deadly Sins?

For centuries, people have spent their lives trying to avoid or atone for the Seven Deadly Sins—anger, covetousness, envy, gluttony, lust, sloth, and the worst of the lot, pride. Christian teaching holds that they are deadly because they can lead to further wrongdoing. With whom did this list originate? It doesn't appear in the Bible or other early religious documents. The source, according to Italian philosopher Thomas Aquinas, is a sixth-century pope named Gregory the Great.

Gregory I (c. 540–604) served as pope from 590 to 604, on the cusp of the Middle Ages. During his reign he established programs of care for the poor and infirm, and wrote copiously on pastoral duties. After witnessing human abuse in England, he sent Augustine of Canterbury and a band of monks to England to serve as missionaries. His leadership strengthened the church in a time of change; his life and ideals have served as inspiration for centuries of religious stewards. His definition of himself as a "servant to the servants of God" has been adopted by popes to this day.

Islamic empire. The Hegira, or flight from Mecca, becomes the starting point of the Islamic calendar. REL

624 The Battle of Badr, in which the Muslims of Medina achieve their first military victory against the pagan Meccans, unites and encourages the Muslim community. REL

629–645 Chinese Buddhist pilgrim Hsüan-tsang travels in India, documenting the decline of the religion in its native land. REL

630 Arab prophet Muhammad becomes the ruler of Mecca, the city that had forced him to leave eight years earlier. By the time of his death in 632, most of Arabia will be under Muslim control. REL

Muhammad's Successor

The Shiite Muslim sect—a form of Islam often in the headlines in recent years—is actually as old as the death of the prophet Muhammad, founder of Islam. Upon Muhammad's death in 632, the party of Ali (in Arabic, Shiah Ali) argued that Islam's leaders should come from Muhammad's family. They therefore supported the accession of Ali ibn Abi Talib, who, as Muhammad's cousin and son-in-law, was the Prophet's closest male relative. The Shiites were overruled when Abū Bakr, Muhammad's father-in-law and an early convert to Islam, was chosen as caliph or ruler. To this day, the Shiites regard Abū Bakr and the two caliphs who followed him as illegitimate.

To the satisfaction of Shiites, Ali became the fourth caliph in 656, but his rule was short-lived, and neither of his sons succeeded him upon his assassination in 661. The older son, Hasan, declined to rule, and the younger, Husayn, was killed by political opponents in 680. The martyrdom of Husayn remains an important religious event to Shiite Muslims and is commemorated annually. Ali and his line of descendants became known as imams or leaders, who were believed to possess special access to divine truth.

The largest sect of Shiites, the "Twelvers," believe that there have been 12 imams, and that the last is still alive but in hiding. He will return again on the Last Day as the messianic figure known as the Mahdi, or rightly guided one. Twelver Shiism is the official religion of Iran.

Only 10 to 15 percent of Muslims are Shiites; most of the rest are Sunni Muslims (from sunna, or established practice). The title ayatollah, familiar to all those who followed news accounts of Ayatollah Khomeini and the Iranian revolution of 1979, is a modern honorific meaning "sign of God."

632   Upon Muhammad's death, his close follower Abū Bakr is named caliph, begin-
            ning a line of succession that will be accepted by Sunni Muslims but contested
            by Shiites. Shiites argue that leaders should be members of Muhammad's fam-
            ily, and that therefore the caliphate should pass to Muhammad's closest male
            relative, his cousin and son-in-law Ali ibn Abi Talib. Shiites consider Ali and the
            line of his descendants imams, or divinely guided leaders.   REL

635   The establishment of Islam in Persia (Iran) will eventually force many
            Zoroastrians to flee. Communities that settle in India will be known as Parsis,
            or Persians.   REL

636   In the Battle of Yarmuk, Arab Muslims defeat the Christian Byzantine empire,
            thereby winning control of most of Syria and Palestine. See also 638, REL.   REL

637–713   Chinese Buddhist teacher Hui-neng lives. His pupil, Shen Hui, will be a
            founder of Ch'an (Zen) Buddhism (see 700s, REL).   REL

637   Muslim Arabs capture the Sassanid Persian capital of Ctesiphon, thereby
            bringing Mesopotamia (Iraq) under Muslim control. Islam will replace
            Zoroastrianism as the state religion.   REL

638   Muslim Arabs capture Jerusalem, ending Byzantine Christian rule over its holy
            places.   REL

641   Muslim Arabs conquer Egypt, except Alexandria, which soon falls also (see
            642, MISC). With Egypt's Byzantine rulers defeated, Islam replaces Christianity
            as the official religion. Persia (Iran), formerly held by the Sassanid Persians,
            also falls this year.   REL

642   Alexandria, Egypt, long a center of Hellenistic and Roman learning, falls to the
            Arabs.   MISC

651   The teachings of Islam's founder, Muhammad, believed by Muslims to be
            divinely revealed, are collected into the Koran (Qur'an), a sacred volume of
            114 chapters.   REL

656   Ali ibn Abi Talib is chosen fourth caliph, temporarily satisfying his Shiite fol-
            lowers, who believe he should have been caliph since the time of Muhammad's
            death in 632. However, Ali's reign will be short-lived (see 661, REL).   REL

657   The Khariji Muslim movement is founded. Claiming that only virtuous
            Muslims have a claim to leadership, members of the movement will oppose
            the caliphs of the Umayyad dynasty, whom they consider apostates.   REL

661   The fourth Arab caliph `Alī ibn Abī Tālib is murdered, bringing an end to the
            line of the Rashidun (the "Rightly Guided" caliphs). Ruling power passes to
            Mu´āwiyah ibn Abī Sufyān, founder of the Umayyad dynasty, which rules from
            Damascus, Syria, and will survive until 749. The Umayyads will be criticized
            for abandoning traditional, religion-centered Islamic ways in favor of Near
            Eastern models of government and organization.   REL

661–750   During the Umayyad dynasty, Islamic theologians debate the doctrines of pre-
            destination (favored by the Qadariyah) versus free will (favored by the
            Jabariyah). The former is associated with supporters of the ruling caliphate, the
            latter with its opponents. Debates about the relationship between faith and
            works also arise.   REL

670–749   Japanese holy man Gyogi lives. One of several religious leaders who combine
            ascetic Buddhism and traditional shamanism, he sponsors the construction of
            the Buddhist temple Tadaiji in Nara.   REL

671   By now, the Srivijaya kingdom of Sumatra is an important Buddhist pilgrim-
            age site and center of Buddhist learning.   REL

673   English prelate Theodore, archbishop of Canterbury, organizes the Christian
            church in England into dioceses and parishes.   REL

675–754   English missionary Boniface lives. Known as the Apostle of Germany, he con-
            verts many pagan Germans and establishes many bishoprics and abbeys,
            including the abbey of Fulda (743). He becomes archbishop of Mainz in 747. REL

680   The Third Council of Constantinople condemns Monotheletism (the view
            that Christ operated with only one will, though he had two natures) and an
            earlier pope, Honorius I.   REL

680   On October 10, Husayn, a son of Muhammad's cousin Ali ibn Abi Talib, is
            martyred by troops of the Umayyad government at Karbala, Mesopotamia
            (Iraq). The date will be sacred to Shiite Muslims, who consider Husayn an
            imam and rightful heir to the caliphate.   REL

691   The Dome of the Rock, the oldest surviving Islamic mosque, is built over the
            ruins of the Jewish Second Temple in Jerusalem. Believed by Muslims to be
            built on the rock where Muhammad ascended to heaven, the location of the
            structure embodies the Islamic claim to supersede the other religions—
            Judaism and Christianity—that hold Jerusalem holy.   REL

692   The Trullan Synod, considered by the Eastern Orthodox Church to be ecu-
            menical, meets in Constantinople (Istanbul). It upholds the canons of the

Apostolic Constitutions, a late fourth-century compilation of administrative rules and guidelines for worship. REL

700s Borobudur, one of the greatest Buddhist stupas, or relic-mounds, is built in Java. REL

700s The Hindu cult of the god Shiva, known as Shaivism, is widely accepted and practiced in Indian society. REL

700s Southern Thailand comes under the influence of the Sumatran kingdom of Shri-Vijaya and its religion, which blends Mahayana Buddhist and Hindu elements. REL

700s Early this century, the Ch'an school of Buddhism develops in China. Taking its name from the Sanskrit *dhyana* (meditation), and known as Zen in Japanese, Ch'an Buddhism emphasizes meditative practice and inner enlightenment achieved through the instantaneous realization that all is Buddha-nature. Ch'an will flourish in this and the next century, and will have a strong impact on China's intellectual and artistic life. REL

700s The Chen-yen (True Word) school of Buddhism develops in China. Drawing on tantric beliefs, it emphasizes magical practices and esoteric knowledge. REL

700s The Karaite Jewish sect is founded in Persia (Iran). It accepts only scripture, not the Talmud (tradition of oral interpretation), as valid. It will gradually spread to medieval Europe. REL

700s The earliest extant Mandean writings are set down. This religious sect, combining Persian, Semitic, and Gnostic elements, will persist indefinitely in Mesopotamia (Iraq) and Persia (Iran). Their central belief is in the Absolute Being, known as the King of Light. REL

700–900 History is referred to as *Akhbar* ("stories") in the Arab world, and it consists of series of descriptions of events that do not necessarily relate meaningfully to one another. HIST

700–900 The Mu´tazilah school develops the first systematic Islamic theology. Drawing on Greek philosophy to produce a rational interpretation of their religion, the Mu´tazilah emphasize the unity of God, the createdness of the Koran, and the existence of free will. REL

711 Following several years of military expansion across North Africa, Muslim conquerors invade Catholic Spain. By 715, most of Spain will be under Muslim rule. REL

712   The Japanese work *Kojiki* (*The Record of Ancient Things*) is composed. Like *Nihongi* (*Japanese Chronicles*), which will be written in 720, it will provide valuable information on early Japanese history and mythology.   HIST

712–756   Emperor Hsüan-tsang reigns in China. He founds the Han-lin Academy, the highest center for learning in the nation. It will remain active for more than a millenium, closing in 1911 when the last Manchu emperor is overthrown. MISC

712   A Muslim state is established in Sind, India.   REL

721–815   Arab alchemist Jābir ibn Hāyyan (or Geber) lives. His own works and those later attributed to him build on the ancient mystical, quasi-scientific tradition of alchemy (*see* 180, PHIL) and help transmit it to medieval Europe.   PHIL

726   Byzantine emperor Leo III condemns the religious use of images (icons). His iconoclasm will lead to a violent controversy marked by riots, rebellions, and the waning of Byzantine suzerainty in Italy. *See also* 787 and 843, REL.   REL

731   English scholar and historian the Venerable Bede publishes *Ecclesiastical History of the English People*.   HIST

732   In battle at Tours, France, Frankish ruler Charles Martel stops Muslim conquerors from advancing further into Christian Europe.   REL

749–1258   The Abbasid dynasty, descendants of Muhammad's uncle Abbas, rules over the Islamic empire, after replacing the Umayyads (*see* 661, REL). Their principal capital is Baghdad, Mesopotamia (Iraq). The Abbasids strengthen the religious basis for their rule by employing religious specialists and judges to ensure that governance takes place in accord with the Koran and the *sunnah*, or sayings and practice of Muhammad.   REL

754   In what is known as the Donation of Pépin, Pépin the Short, first Carolingian king of the Franks, grants the pope the territory that will grow into the Papal States.   REL

767–822   Japanese Buddhist monk Saicho (Dengyō Daishi) lives. He introduces the Tendai school of Buddhism to Japan. Named for the Chinese T'ien-t'ai school, the sect is an eclectic one that combines Zen, Pure Land, esoteric, and other strands. Saicho founds the temple Enryakuji on Mount Hiei near Kyoto.   REL

774–835   Japanese Buddhist monk Kūkai (Kōbō Daishi) lives and founds Shingon (Pure Word) Buddhism, which emphasizes mystery, ritual, and symbol. Kūkai is largely responsible for developing Ryobu-Shinto, the characteristically Japanese blending of Buddhism and Shinto.   REL

781   English scholar Alcuin (Albinus) arrives at Frankish king Charlemagne's court
           at Aachen, Germany. Influential in promoting the Carolingian Renaissance in
           culture and art, he urges the preservation of ancient texts and begins the
           medieval tradition of a curriculum spanning the seven liberal arts. Informed
           by the *artes liberales*, or liberal education of free men in Athens during the
           fourth and fifth centuries B.C., the liberal arts include the trivium of grammar,
           logic, and rhetoric, and the quadrivium of arithmetic, geometry, astrono-
           my, and music.   EDUC

787   The Second Council of Nicaea condemns iconoclasm, the movement in Asia
           Minor (Turkey) opposing religious use of images (*see* 726, REL). The Council
           declares that religious images should be venerated but not worshiped. It is the
           last council to be accepted as ecumenical by both the Roman Catholic and
           Eastern Orthodox communions.   REL

788–820   Indian philosopher Sankara lives. Working in the Vedanta tradition of
           Hinduism, he develops the philosophy of the Upanishads into a monistic sys-
           tem in which the soul is regarded as an aspect of the Absolute (Brahman) and
           the world is regarded as illusion (maya).   REL

800s   Several Islamic schools of law develop. Four of these, including that based on
           the teachings of ash-Shāfiʿī (*see* 820, REL), will persist indefinitely.   REL

800s   Books are written to defend the traditional Zoroastrian religion of Persia (Iran)
           against Christian and Muslim opponents.   REL

800–1400   The system of land ownership known as feudalism is practiced in Europe.
           Through it, feudal lords pass the rights to fiefdoms (parcels of land) to their
           vassals, or lesser noblemen, who pledge loyalty and protection. Vassals, in
           turn, pass rights to smaller fiefdoms, ending with serfs, who perform manual
           labor and are attached to the land. The system provides for crop production
           and maintenance of a military.   ECON

800   On Christmas Day, Pope Leo III crowns Frankish king Charlemagne emperor of
           the West at Rome, thus laying the foundation for the Holy Roman Empire. Its
           rulers will claim legitimacy as God's temporal vicars from their appointment by
           the pope, believed to be God's spiritual vicar.   REL

802–850   Cambodian monarch Jayavarman II lives, founding the Khmer empire.
           Reigning from Angkor, he ushers in the Angkor era (9th to 15th centuries),
           marked by urbanization, public works, and elaborate Hindu religious temples.
                                                                                        REL

810–877   Irish philosopher John Scotus Erigena lives. Teaching at the court of Holy
           Roman emperor Charles the Bald, he helps transmit Greek thought to

medieval Europe and develops a philosophy influenced by Neoplatonism. His works include *On the Division of Nature*.   PHIL

810–870   Muslim scholar al-Bukhari lives. His collections of hadiths (oral traditions about Muhammad's words and actions) will be one of the most respected of such works. It and other systematic compendiums of hadiths produced this century are known as the *Six Sahih (Sound) Books*.   REL

813–833   Abbasid caliph al-Ma'mūm reigns. He attempts to reconcile Shiite Muslims by appointing as successor 'Alī ar-Ridā, who is held acceptable by many Shiites.   REL

820   Muslim jurist ash-Shāfi'ī dies. His theory of jurisprudence, based on the idea of the four roots (*usul*) of the law (the Koran, the *sunnah*, the traditional consensus of the community, and analogical reasoning) becomes widely accepted by Muslims. He argued for the binding authority of the *sunnah* (sayings and practice) of Muhammad, while rejecting the authority of the *sunnah* of other early Muslims. Ash-Shafi'i also argued that the *sunnah* is known through hadith (oral tradition). His school of thought will be known as the Usuli school.   REL

827–849   Mu'tazilah rationalist theology (*see* 700–900, REL) is made the official doctrine of the Abbasid Islamic state. The eventual repudiation of the policy is largely due to opposition from such traditionalist theologians as Ahmad ibn Hanbal, who believe in literal adherence to the Koran and the *sunnah*.   REL

843   Byzantine emperor Michael III restores the worship of icons in the East, ending the controversy over iconoclasm.   REL

866   Arab philosopher Yaqūb ibn Ishāq al-Kindī lives. Living in Baghdad, Mesopotamia (Iraq), he translates works of Greek philosopher Aristotle and Roman philosopher Plotinus and begins assimilating Greek philosophy into Islamic thought.   PHIL

869–870   The Fourth Council of Constantinople confirms the condemnation of Photius, patriarch of Constantinople, who has clashed with the pope over papal authority, treatment of repentant iconoclasts, and certain practices of the Western church. The Roman Catholic but not the Eastern Orthodox Church regards this council as ecumenical. *See also* 879–880, REL.   REL

870–950   Muslim philosopher Abū Nasr al-Fārābi lives. Author of the utopian work *The Virtuous City*, he expounds and expands on Greek philosopher Aristotle's thought.   PHIL

873–936   Muslim theologian Abū al-Hasan al-Ash'arī lives. Reconciling Mu'tazilah rationalist theology with conservative Islamic views, he argues that revelation has priority over reason, but reason can aid in defending revelation against its opponents.   REL

879–880   A synod, regarded by the Eastern Orthodox Church as an ecumenical council, affirms the restoration of Photius as patriarch of Constantinople (*see* 869–870, REL). The controversy over Photius marks the growing division between eastern and western Christianity.   REL

881   In Cambodia, Khmer king Inravarman I builds the Bakong, a step-pyramid temple and royal tomb. Like other such Cambodian temples, it is modeled after Mount Meru, the mythical peak at the center of the universe.   REL

882–942   Babylonian Jewish scholar Sa'adia ben Joseph lives. He writes new commentaries on the Bible, compiles a Hebrew lexicon, and translates the Bible into Arabic. He also writes the philosophical treatise *Sefer Emunot ve-Deot* (*Book of Beliefs and Opinions*).   REL

900s   Arab historian at-Tabari completes his *Annals*, a year-by-year history of the world from Creation to A.D. 915, which is notable for its great detail and which will become perhaps the most famous Arabic history.   HIST

900s–1400s In the Balkans, particularly Bulgaria, the Bogomil sect flourishes. Believing in a dualistic universe, Bogomils reject as evil all aspects of the material world.   REL

909–1171   The Fatimid dynasty rules Egypt and North Africa. They are supported by members of the "Sevener" or Ismaili sect of Shiite Islam, who venerate Muhammad ibn Isma'il, the seventh imam. The Fatimids claim to be successors to Isma'il.   REL

910   The Cluniac Order, a Christian reformed monastic order, is founded at Cluny, Burgundy.   REL

922   Sufi mystic al-Hallaj is executed for heresy (*b.* 858). He represents a mystical, ascetic form of Islam that will grow in popularity.   REL

958   Pope John XV proposes the truce of God, a rule limiting days of warfare between feudal lords. It will first be applied in 1027, and will outlaw fighting during most of the week and on religious days. The truce of God will fall out of favor by the 13th century.   REL

960–1279   During the Sung dynasty in China, Confucianism revives in a new form. Such neo-Confucian philosophers as Shao Yung, Chou Tun-i, the Cheng brothers, and Chu Hsi develop an orderly sytem of ideas about the nature of knowledge, humanity, and the universe. By the 13th century, neo-Confucianism has displaced Buddhism and Taoism as the official system of belief and the basis for state education. Buddhism and Taoism will slowly decline in China in the centuries that follow. PHIL

969   In Egypt, Cairo's first congregational mosque, al-Azhar, is founded. An important center of Shiite (and later Sunni) learning, it will endure for at least a millenium, by which time it will be among the world's oldest surviving universities. *See also* 1171, REL. REL

973–1048   Arab scholar Abu ar-Rayhan al-Biruni lives. He writes treatises on many disciplines, including astronomy, mathematics, medicine, and history. His best-known histories are *Chronology of Ancient Nations* and *A History of India*. HIST

980–1037   Muslim Persian scientist and philosopher Ibn Sina (Avicenna) lives. Translated into Latin and drawing heavily on the Greek philosopher Aristotle, his works will have a profound effect on medieval European medicine, science, and philosophy. Ibn Sina's works include the philosophical-scientific tome *Kitab ash-shifa* and the mystical religious treatise *Kitab al-isharat wa at-tanbihat*. PHIL

988   Grand Prince of Kiev Vladimir I declares Eastern Orthodox Christianity the state religion of Russia. REL

1000s   Chinese historian Ssu-ma Kuang writes *Comprehensive Mirror for Aid in Governing*, a narrative history of China over 14 centuries, which will be considered perhaps the greatest historical work ever written in Chinese. HIST

1000s   Indian monk Atīśa reforms Tibetan Buddhism by founding the Kadampa sect. A number of sects flourish throughout this period, each concentrating on a different aspect of the religion, such as yogic practices, monastic discipline, or philosophical ideas. REL

1000s   In India, certain Hindu monasteries such as Vikramasila and Nalanda, and in Tibet, Buddhist monasteries, develop into great centers of learning. REL

1000s   In South India, Hindu theologian Ramanuja expounds the theology of the Vaishnava movement and its practice of devotion to the god Vishnu. REL

1000s   In France, the Jewish esoteric tradition known as cabala (or kabbalah) develops. Influenced by Neoplatonism and drawing on ancient material, it offers a Neoplatonic interpretation of scripture based on numerology and allegory. REL

1000s   The use of koan, a riddle or paradox meant to lead a Ch'an (Zen) student toward enlightenment, is introduced in China and will spread to Japan. REL

1000s   Sultan Mahmud of Ghazni conquers a portion of India's Punjab, bringing it under Muslim control. REL

1000s   The Must'li sect, a Shiite Muslim group, spreads throughout South Asia after taking root in Yemen. From this sect will grow the Bohra, the community of Hindu converts to Islam.   REL

1000   In Mexico, the Aztecs begin making codices, books with leaves stitched together. Written in pictographs and ideograms, the codices record royal history and administrative information.   HIST

1000–1049   Javanese monarch Airlangga lives. Reunifying central and eastern Java, he recognizes both Hinduism and Buddhism and promotes indigenous Javanese culture.   REL

1000–1400   Eastern Thailand comes under the influence of the Khmers of Cambodia, who introduce elements of Hinduism.   REL

1000   Ch'an (Zen) and Pure Land Buddhism are the most popular forms of Buddhism among monks in China. Pure Land is stronger among Chinese laypeople.   REL

1010   Buddhist monarch Ly Thai-to becomes Vietnam's ruler, establishing a lineage that will continue up to 1225. The Ly dynasty will be marked by a strong adherence to Ch'an (Zen) Buddhism.   REL

1022–1057   Spanish Jewish philosopher Solomon ibn Gabirol lives and writes the Neoplatonist work *Fountain of Life*.   PHIL

1040–1105   French Jewish scholar Rashi (Rabbi Solomon bar Isaac) lives. His commentaries on the Bible and Talmud, which interpret the older texts for Jews living in medieval Christian Europe, will become a lasting part of Jewish exegetical tradition.   REL

1040–1123   Tibetan poet and mystic Milarepa lives. The second patriarch of the Kargyupa sect of Tibetan Buddhism, he popularizes Buddhist teachings through poems and folk songs known as the "hundred thousand songs."   REL

1044   Northern Burmese king Anawrahta begins his reign. Converting to Theravada Buddhism, he eliminates the tantric Mahayana Buddhism formerly practiced in his kingdom. Theravada Buddhism already predominates in southern Burma.
                                                                                  REL

1049–1054   Leo IX reigns as pope, marking the beginning of the 11th-century papal reform movement, which opposes simony (the buying and selling of spiritual benefits or offices) and clerical marriage and concubinage. *See also* 1073–1085, REL.   REL

1053   In Uji, Japan, the Buddhist temple Byōdōin, sacred to the Amitābha Buddha, is consecrated. REL

1054   Centuries of division between the Roman Catholic and Eastern Orthodox churches culminate in the Schism of 1054, when Pope Leo IX and patriarch of Constantinople (Istanbul) Michael Cerularius exchange anathemas of excommunication. REL

1058–1111   Islamic theologian Abu Hāmid al-Ghazālī lives. He develops a mystical theology in *A Short Treatise on the Creed*. He also attacks Aristotelian philosophy in *Self-Destruction of the Philosophers* and writes *The Revival of the Religious Sciences*. REL

1059   The College of Cardinals is established as the body that elects popes. REL

1073–1085   Gregory VII reigns as pope. His continuation of Leo IX's (*see* 1049–1054, REL) marks a turning point in Roman Church history. In 1075, he condemns lay investiture, the practice by which temporal rulers, such as emperors, appoint spiritual ones, such as bishops. Holy Roman emperor Henry IV, who opposes Gregory's action, will be excommunicated in 1076 but be reconciled upon humbling himself before the pope at Canossa, Italy, in 1077. *See also* 1083, REL. REL

1075–1141   Jewish poet and philosopher Judah ha-Levi emphasizes the concept of the Return to Zion, an idea that will be taken up by the Zionist movement in the 19th and 20th centuries. REL

1076   A well-attended Tibetan Buddhist council is held at Tho-ling, Tibet. REL

c. 1077–1166   Iraqi Sufi leader ´Abd al-Qādir al-Jīlānī lives. His followers will form the Qadiriyah order, which will flourish in the 14th century. His shrine in Baghdad will draw worshipers from distant places. REL

1078–1130   Moroccan religious reformer Ibn Tūmart lives. He is believed by many to be the mahdi, a divinely guided leader who would purify Islam. He and his followers found the Almohad empire, which holds sway over North Africa and parts of Spain. REL

1083   Holy Roman emperor Henry IV invades Italy, capturing Rome and forcing Pope Gregory VII to withdraw south to Salerno. Henry installs the antipope Clement III (Guibert of Ravenna). At issue is the lay investiture controversy (*see* 1073–1085, REL). REL

1084   The Carthusian Order, a Christian monastic order known for its strictness, is founded at the Grande Chartreuse, France. REL

1089–1164   Spanish Jewish scholar Abraham ben Meir ibn Ezra lives and writes linguistic
             and philosophical commentaries on the Bible.   REL

c. 1090   Persian religious leader Hasan-e Sabbāh founds the Assassins, or Nizaris, a
             secret Muslim Shiite sect whose devotees practice murder (assassination) in
             strict obedience to superiors. The order will dominate Persia (Iran) and Syria
             for two centuries (*see* 1256, REL).   REL

1093–1109   Italian-born scholastic philosopher Anselm serves as archbishop of
             Canterbury. He is the author of the treatises *Monologion*, on the attributes of
             God, and *Proslogion*, which puts forth the ontological proof for the existence
             of God. Anselm is a founder of scholasticism, the medieval Christian philo-
             sophical approach that uses reason to deepen and systematize human under-
             standing of the contents of faith. *See also* 1200s, PHIL.   PHIL

1095   At the Council of Clermont, Pope Urban II calls for the launching of a war to
             liberate the Holy Land from the Muslims. The result is the First Crusade
             (1095–1099), which will culminate in the conquest of Jerusalem in 1099.
             Eight other crusades, aimed primarily at assisting Crusaders already in the
             Holy Land, will follow, the last one in 1271–1272. The Latin Kingdom estab-
             lished in the First Crusade will not fall completely until 1291.   REL

1098   The Cistercian (Trappist) Order, a Christian monastic order that will be famed
             for its strictness and rule of silence, is founded at Cîteaux, Burgundy.   REL

c. 1099   The Knights Hospitalers, a military religious order known formally as the
             Order of the Hospital of Saint John of Jerusalem, is founded. Dedicated to the
             protection of pilgrims in the Holy Land, it will become rich and powerful.
             Other military religious orders follow, including the Knights Templar (Knights
             of the Temple of Solomon, or Poor Knights of Christ), which will be founded
             c. 1118.   REL

1100s   In India, the Virashaiva, or Lingayat, sect begins to form even as an older sect,
             the Kalamukha, fades. Both Hindu sects are devoted to the god Shiva; both
             practice Sanskrit study and worship of the *lingam*, or stone phallus.   REL

1100s   Indian poet Jayadeva publishes the *Gitagovinda*, a devotional work dedicated
             to the cult of Krishna and his lover Radha.   REL

1100s   Sri Lankan king Parakrāmabāhu leads a reform of Theravada Buddhism. The
             influence of the reform extends to Thailand, where Theravada Buddhism sub-
             sequently becomes dominant.   REL

1100s   The Rifa´iyya order of Sufi mystics is founded in Mesopotamia (Iraq).   REL

1100–1300   The Christian sect of the Albigenses flourishes in southern France. Taking posi-
             tions similar to Manichaeism (*see* 216–277, REL), they argue that good and evil
             are both ultimate principles, that matter is evil, and that Jesus's body was an
             illusion. Condemned as heretics by the pope, the ascetic movement long per-
             sists despite church opposition. *See also* 1233, REL.   REL

1100–1300   The ethical code of chivalry develops in western Europe, providing ideal stan-
             dards for the behavior of Christian knights. Aspects of chivalry include piety,
             loyalty, honor, valor, courtesy, and devoted love for a chosen lady. *See also*
             1185–1333, SOC.   SOC

1110–1180   Jewish physician and historian Abraham ibn Daud lives and writes *The Exalted
             Faith*, in which he takes an unorthodox approach to reconciling Aristotelian
             philosophy with Jewish faith.   REL

1115   French clergyman Bernard of Clairvaux founds a Cistercian monastery where
             he will remain abbot until his death in 1153. Famed for his intellect and holy
             ways, he will influence the Roman Catholic spiritual tradition known as *devo-
             tio moderna*, help bring about the condemnation of French philosopher Peter
             Abelard, and advocate the Second Crusade.   REL

1118   French philosopher and theologian Peter (Pierre) Abelard begins his romance
             with his pupil Héloïse. They will soon marry secretly, angering her uncle,
             Canon Fulbert of Notre Dame cathedral, who will have Abelard emasculated.

The Last Knight

In the 12th and 13th centuries, the ideals of chivalry took shape in France and Spain
and spread throughout Europe. An amalgam of military virtue, aristocratic bearing,
and Christian ethics, the chivalric ideal encompassed such characteristics as courage,
courtesy, piety, chastity, and loyalty. The true knight served God, his liege lord, and the
lady who commanded his heart. If the lady was a married woman or an unattainable
virgin, all the better, since the love affair should be conducted from a distance, perhaps
never to be consummated.

The chivalric ideal was never fully realized; more often, it served as a cloak for military aggression and adultery. "True knights" were generally those who, like King
Arthur and the men of his Round Table, existed in the legendary past. But every so
often some knight gained a reputation for true chivalry even in his own day. One of the
last such knights was the French warrior Pierre Bayard (c. 1474–1524), who was
renowned for his courage during the Italian Wars, the conflict in which he lost his life.
He was known to his admirers as *le chevalier sans peur et sans reproche*, the knight without fear or reproach.

Abelard will become a monk and Héloïse a nun. Abelard's rationalistic philosophy will lead to his condemnation for heresy (*see* 1140, PHIL).   PHIL

1122   The Concordat of Worms, Germany, puts an end to the controversy over lay investiture (*see* 1073–1085, REL), as Holy Roman emperor Henry V and Pope Calixtus II reach a compromise about their respective roles in the appointment of bishops and abbots.   REL

1123   The First Lateran Council, summoned by Pope Calixtus II, is held in the Lateran Palace, Rome, to confirm the Concordat of Worms (*see* 1122, REL). It is the first Christian council to be held in western Europe.   REL

1126–1198   Spanish Islamic philosopher Ibn Rushd (Averroës) lives. Through his commentaries on Aristotle and other philosophical works, he becomes an important interpreter of Aristotle, showing that faith and reason are not in fundamental conflict. He will have a lasting influence on Western thought.   PHIL

1130–1200   Chinese philosopher Chu Hsi lives. He extends and systematizes the neo-Confucian ideas developed throughout the Sung dynasty (*see* 960–1279, PHIL).   PHIL

The Confucian Aquinas

Italian philosopher Thomas Aquinas (1225–1274) is remembered for developing a clear, orderly intellectual system that became orthodox for Roman Catholics. Less well known in the West is his near-contemporary Chu Hsi, or Zhu Xi (1130–1200), the Chinese philosopher who set into final form the philosophical synthesis known as neo-Confucianism.

Chu Hsi lived during the Sung dynasty (960–1279), a time when neo-Confucian philosophers were attempting to revive the ideas of Confucius (551–479 B.C.) and from them develop an orderly system that would deal with such matters as metaphysics, cosmology, and ethics. After a long period in which Buddhism and Taoism had gained many adherents at the expense of Confucianism, these philosophers succeeded in revitalizing the ancient doctrines. The greatest of the neo-Confucian thinkers was Chu Hsi, who wrote extensive commentaries on the Confucian classics. Emphasizing the distinction between *li* (inner essence) and *chi* (external appearance), he argued that "investigation of things," coupled with ethical action, would lead to realization of one's own essence and knowledge of the Great Li, or Supreme Essence.

After his death, Chu Hsi's interpretation of Confucian thought became official orthodoxy. Until the coming of Maoist Communism, neo-Confucianism reigned supreme in China as the basic belief system of educated Chinese and as an influential force in Chinese popular religion.

1133–1212	Japanese Buddhist monk Hōnen lives and popularizes Pure Land Buddhism, the sect devoted to the Buddha Amida (Amitābha). REL
1135	English writer Geoffrey of Monmouth publishes the Latin chronicle *History of the Kings of Britain*, one of the main sources of the legend of King Arthur and his knights drawn upon by later writers. HIST
1135–1204	Spanish-born Jewish philosopher Moses Maimonides (Moses ben Maimon) lives. Working principally in Egypt, he codifies Jewish law in the *Mishne Torah* (Repetition of the Law) and writes *Guide for the Perplexed*, in which he tries to reconcile Aristotle's philosophy and Jewish theology. The latter work will become accepted as authoritative by medieval Jews and influences Christian scholastic philosophers, including Italian philosopher Thomas Aquinas. REL
1139	The Second Lateran Council, summoned by Pope Innocent II, condemns clerical marriage and concubinage, simony, usury, and the use of bows and crossbows in fighting Christians. REL
1140	The teachings of French philosopher and theologian Peter Abelard are condemned as heretical by the council of Sens, at the urging of French clergyman Bernard of Clairvaux (*see* 1115, REL). A popular lecturer, Abelard has employed the dialectic method of Aristotle, applying logic to the content of faith. His approach to the question of the reality of universal concepts is known as conceptualism. His works include *Sic et non*, a compilation of contradictory theological arguments. PHIL
c. 1140	In his best-known work, the *Decretum Gratiani*, Italian legal scholar Gratian presents a codification of all parts of canon law, including reasons why only men could "validly" receive ordination. REL
1147–1149	The Second Crusade, urged by French clergyman Bernard of Clairvaux, takes place, ending in failure. REL
1148–1151	Italian theologian Peter Lombard writes his *Sentences* (*Sententiarum libri IV*), a four-book compilation of quotations from church fathers and medieval authorities. It will become an official theological textbook in medieval universities and the subject of many commentaries. Its discussion of the sacraments is especially important. Lombard studied under French philosopher and theologian Peter Abelard (*see* 1140, PHIL). REL
c. 1160–1260	In Europe, the first universities are developed from a number of urban or cathedral schools. The word *universitas* refers to a common name for a guild and has no previous link to an educational institution. EDUC

1170   On December 29, English prelate Thomas à Becket, archbishop of Canterbury, is assassinated by four knights of King Henry II. Becket had defended the independence of the church against interference by the king.   REL

1171   Syrian leader Saladin defeats the Shiite Fatimid caliphate, destroying much of its royal city of Cairo. Prayers and lessons at the mosque of al-Azhar (*see* 969, REL) are abolished. In 1287, prayer and teaching will resume, but under the Sunni, not the Shiite, system.   REL

1173–1262   Japanese Buddhist monk Shinran lives and develops Jodo Shinshu, the "true" Pure Land sect. Unlike his teacher Japanese Buddhist monk Hōnen (*see* 1133–1212, REL), who believed in the power of good works, Shinran advocates pure passivity before the grace of Amida.   REL

1176–1180   English prelate and philosopher John of Salisbury is bishop of Chartres, France. He is best known for his treatises *Policraticus*, on government, and *Metalogicon*, on the scholastic controversies of his day. He proposes moderate realism as an alternative to nominalism. He is important in the history of education for his defense (in the *Metalogicon*) of the teaching of the liberal arts together with philosophy.   REL

1179   The Third Lateran Council is convened by Pope Alexander III. It deals with papal elections and condemns the Albigenses and Waldenses.   REL

1185–1333   During the Kamakura period in Japan, the bushido code of samurai warrior conduct is formulated, emphasizing loyalty, honor, and courage. It is analagous to chivalry in Europe (*see* 1100–1300, SOC).   SOC

1187   Saladin, Syrian leader and Muslim sultan of Egypt, captures Jerusalem from the crusaders. The Third Crusade (1189–1192) will be an unsuccessful attempt by Europeans to recapture the city. Christians will remain in power on the coast of Palestine and in Antioch and Tripoli.   REL

1191   Japanese Buddhist monk Eisai founds the Rinzai school of Zen (based on the Chinese Ch'an school), which emphasizes the use of koan, a riddle or paradox meant to lead a student toward enlightenment.   REL

1194–1270   Jewish rabbi Moses ben Nahman (Nahmanides) lives. His commentaries on the Bible take a mystical approach.   REL

1198–1216   The reign of Pope Innocent III marks the apex of the papacy's temporal power. Arguing that the pope has supreme political authority over lay rulers, Innocent intervenes in the public affairs of the Holy Roman Empire, England, France, and Italy. He excommunicates England's King John (1209) and Holy Roman emperor Otto IV (1210). He also promotes the Fourth Crusade (*see*

1202–1204, REL) and the Albigensian Crusade (*see* 1208, REL) and encourages the founding of the Dominican Order (*see* 1216, REL).   REL

1200s   Medieval scholastic philosophy is in its golden age, with Italian philosopher Thomas Aquinas (*see* 1254, PHIL) its greatest practitioner. Contributing to the age is the growth of universities, notably at Paris and Oxford, and the accessibility in Latin of the works of Greek philosophe Aristotle and the commentaries of Islamic philosophers Ibn Sina (Avicenna) and Ibn Rushd (Averröes). *See also* 1093–1109, PHIL.   PHIL

1200s   European alchemists include German scientist Albertus Magnus (*see* 1200–1280, PHIL) and English scientist Roger Bacon (*see* 1277, PHIL), who believe that there is only one elemental matter (*materia prima*), which can be obtained by the removal of impurities.   PHIL

1200s   Indian brahmin philosopher Madhva develops a dualistic version of Vaishnava theology known as Dvaita.   REL

1200s   In Maharashtra in India, religious teacher and poet Jñāneśvara founds the cult of devotion to Vithoba (Vishnu-Krishna) and his wife Rukmini. Jnanesvara and his successors up through the 17th century, known as the Maratha saints, will write devotional songs renowned for their beauty.   REL

1200s   Spanish Jewish scholar Moses de León writes *Sefer ha-Zohar* (*Book of Splendor*), a cabalistic mystical commentary on the Pentateuch, attributed to second-century scholar Simon ben Yohai.   REL

1200s   Italian prelate and writer Jacobus de Voragine publishes *The Golden Legend*, a widely read collection of saints' lives. With its emphasis on the fantastic and miraculous, it will remain popular for centuries.   REL

1200s   In Indonesia, Buddhism gradually begins to be displaced by Islam as the dominant religion.   REL

1200s   The Suhrawardiyya order of Sufi mystics is founded in Mesopotamia (Iraq).
                       REL

1200s   The secret criminal brotherhood known as the Mafia has its beginnings in Sicily. Over the centuries, its "families" will become active in the United States and South America.   SOC

c. 1200–1280 German philosopher and scientist Albertus Magnus lives. A Dominican, he attempts to combine Aristotelian thought and Christian theology in his unfinished *Summa theologiae*. He also writes commentaries on Aristotle and practices experimental science. Considered the greatest scholar of his day, he is the teacher of Thomas Aquinas. PHIL

1200   By now, Buddhism is virtually extinct in India, where it was founded in the sixth and fifth centuries B.C. REL

1200–1253   Japanese Buddhist philosopher Dōgen lives. He will be considered the founder of the Japanese Soto School of Zen, which emphasizes meditation rather than koans. REL

1202–1204   The Fourth Crusade is diverted from its original aim of fighting Muslims in the Holy Land, as the crusaders undertake European combat on behalf of Venice and seize Constantinople (Istanbul), establishing a Latin Kingdom there. REL

1206   The Sultanate of Delhi is established in India by Central Asiatic Turks. Over the next two centuries, most of India will come under Delhi's rule, providing ground for the spread of Islam. Itinerant Persian Sufi mystics play a major role in converting Hindus to the Islamic faith. REL

1208   Pope Innocent III declares the Albigensian Crusade to combat the dualistic heresy of the Albigenses (see 1100–1300, REL). REL

1209   Francis of Assisi founds the Franciscan order of monks. Wandering and preaching throughout Italy and abroad, they attempt to follow the example of their leader, who is notable for his devotion to poverty, love of humanity and nature, humility, and joyous spirit. REL

1212   The Children's Crusade takes place, in which thousands of children, led by French peasant boy Stephen of Cloyes, set out for Palestine to reconquer the holy places, only to be sold into slavery or die of hunger and disease. REL

1212   Following the example of Francis of Assisi, Clare of Assisi forms the Poor Clares, or Second Order of Saint Francis, a cloistered, contemplative order of women. REL

1215–1235   English theologian Robert Grosseteste publishes such scientific treatises as *On Light*. In these he is one of the first to stress the scientific need for care in isolating relevant factors. PHIL

1215   The Magna Carta, which outlines British constitutional law and basic civil liberties, is signed at Runnymede by King John. A central document of the English legal tradition, it affirms the right to trial by jury, *habeas corpus*, and freedom of worship. POL

1215	The Fourth Lateran Council, convened by Pope Innocent III, defines transubstantiation as an article of faith, confirms previous disciplinary canons, and establishes that confession once a year and communion at Easter time (Easter duty) are the minimum requirements for membership in the Roman Catholic Church. REL
1216	Castilian cleric Dominic founds the new preaching order, the Dominicans. Dominic is famed for his successful preaching to the heretical Albigenses in France and for introducing the rosary. REL
1217–1272	Christian warriors continue to fight unsuccessfully against Muslims for control of the Holy Land in the Fifth (1217–1221), Sixth (1228–1229), Seventh (1248–1254), Eighth (1270) and Ninth (1271–1272) Crusades. See also 1291, REL. REL
1224	Francis of Assisi miraculously receives the stigmata, the wounds of the Crucifixion, from which he will suffer for the remaining two years of his life. REL
1233	Pope Gregory IX founds the Papal Inquisition, a tribunal formed to fight the dualistic heresy of the Albigenses (see 1100–1300, REL). Its methods include judicial torture but not usually burning at the stake. The Inquisition later turns its focus on Protestantism. See also 1478, REL. REL
1245	The First Council of Lyon, France, convened by Pope Innocent IV and considered ecumenical by the Roman Catholic Church, declares Holy Roman emperor Frederick II deposed, but is without effect. REL
1250	Much medieval lore and legend about animals is recorded in what will be the only surviving Middle English bestiary, written anonymously. MISC
1253	Japanese Buddhist monk Nichiren founds the Nichiren sect, notable for its nationalism, syncretism, and emphasis on the Lotus Sutra. REL
1254	Italian philosopher Thomas Aquinas, known as the Angelic Doctor, begins his commentaries on the *Sentences* of Italian theologian Peter Lombard, Roman philosopher Boethius, and the Bible. Earlier, Aquinas was the student of German philosopher and scientist Albertus Magnus (see c. 1200–1280, PHIL). The greatest scholastic philosopher, Aquinas will synthesize Aristotelian thought and Christian theology as he demonstrates how faith and reason can exist in harmony. See also c. 1265–1274, PHIL. PHIL
1256	Italian philosopher Thomas Aquinas expounds his metaphysics in *On Being and Essence*. PHIL

1256   Mongol conqueror Hülegü destroys the power of the Assassin sect in Persia
               (Iran). Baybars, Mamluk sultan of Egypt, will do the same in Syria in 1270. *See
               also* c. 1090, REL.   REL

1259–1264   Italian philosopher Thomas Aquinas publishes *Summa contra gentiles*, in which
               he defends the truth of Catholic faith against paganism by showing that reason
               and faith are distinct but complementary realms, with God as the ultimate
               source of truth.   PHIL

1259   Italian scholastic philosopher Bonaventure, known as the Seraphic Doctor,
               publishes *The Mind's Road to God*, in which he argues that the goal of philoso-
               phy is to prepare the mind for contemplation of and mystic union with God.
               A reformer of the Franciscan order, Bonaventure emphasizes faith over reason,
               unlike his contemporary Thomas Aquinas. His other works include studies of
               the lives of Christ and Francis of Assisi.   PHIL

1260–1368   During China's Yüan dynasty, founded by Mongol leader Kublai Khan, Islam
               is promoted at the expense of neo-Confucian philosophy.   REL

1260–1368   During the Yüan dynasty in China, the heterodox Buddhist sect Bai-lian Jiao,
               or the White Lotus society, is one of several rebellious secret societies that
               speed the demise of Mongol rule. White Lotus teachings include belief in
               imminent deliverance by the future-Buddha Maitreya.   REL

c. 1265–1274   Italian philosopher Thomas Aquinas writes his most important work, *Summa
               theologica*. A monumental synthesis of Aristotelian logic and Christian theolo-
               gy, the work discusses God and the created universe, moral philosophy, and,
               in a third section completed after Aquinas's death in 1274 by his follower
               Reginald of Piperno, Jesus and the sacraments. In 1879 the system of Aquinas
               (known as Thomism) will be declared the official philosophy of the Roman
               Catholic Church.   PHIL

c. 1266–1308   Scottish philosopher John Duns Scotus, known as the Subtle Doctor, lives.
               Applying Aristotelian ideas in a Christian context, he founds the scholastic
               school called Scotism, which is opposed to Thomism (*see* c. 1265–1274, PHIL).
               His works include *On the First Principle* and two commentaries on the *Sentences*
               of Italian theologian Peter Lombard.   PHIL

1270   French philosopher Siger de Brabant flourishes. An interpreter of Greek
               philosopher Aristotle as understood by Islamic philosopher Ibn Rushd
               (Averroës), he is the author of the banned work *On the Necessity and
               Contingency of Causes*.   PHIL

1270–1343   Jewish scholar Jacob ben Asher lives and codifies Jewish law in *Arba´a turim*. REL

c. 1274   Spanish philosopher Ramon Lull, a Franciscan, publishes *Ars Magna*. He will also write the *Ars generalis ultima* (1308). His Neoplatonist philosophy is stated with a view to converting Muslims and Jews.   PHIL

1274   The Second Council of Lyon, France, convened by Pope Gregory X, proclaims the reunion of the Roman Catholic and Eastern Orthodox churches, but the declared reunion soon collapses. The council also formally defines the *Filioque*, the double procession of the Holy Spirit from the Father and the Son.   REL

1277   The work of English philosopher and scientist Roger Bacon is condemned by the Franciscan order to which he belongs. His studies show a great variety of influences, including Greek philosopher Aristotle and Neoplatonism, and treat many kinds of subject matter, including philosophy, optics, and mathematics. His major work is known as *Opus Majus* (*Greater Work*).   PHIL

1281   The word *kamikaze* (Japanese for "divine wind") is used to describe a powerful typhoon that destroys Kublai Khan's fleet of Mongol warships, which had been poised to invade Japan. During World War II (1939–1945), the Japanese will use the word to refer to pilots who take on suicide missions.   MISC

1283–1350 Japanese Buddhist monk and poet Yoshida Kenko lives. He writes *Essays in Idleness*, a miscellany of sketches, anecdotes, and thoughts.   PHIL

c. 1285–1349 English philosopher William of Ockham lives. His advocacy of nominalism, the view that universal concepts (*nomina*) have no objective existence outside the mind, contrasts with the realism of Italian philosopher Thomas Aquinas (*see* 1254, PHIL). He argues that reason is not competent in matters of faith but can be in other areas. He also expounds the principle of parsimony, or "Ockham's razor," stating that entities should not be multiplied in explaining phenomena. Ockham's views will be important in the development of materialism, empiricism, and the scientific method.   PHIL

1288–1344 Jewish philosopher Gersonides (Levi ben Gershom) lives. His book *The Wars of the Lord* takes a more strictly Aristotelian approach than Spanish-born Jewish philosopher Maimonides.   PHIL

1291   Acre (Akko), the last Christian stronghold in the Holy Land, falls to the Muslims, marking the end of the struggle that began with the First Crusade (*see* 1095, REL).   REL

c. 1293   Italian poet Dante Alighieri completes *La vita nuova*, a collection of poetry about his love for Beatrice, with prose commentary that will be considered to mark the beginning of literary criticism.   CRIT

c. 1295–1358   French scholastic philosopher Jean Buridan lives. He writes on logic in such works as *Consequentiae* and *Sophismata*.   PHIL

1300s   With the rise of scholasticism, classical liberal education is reconfigured. Logic, mathematics, and the scientific pursuit of knowledge gain prominence. The teaching of moral precepts, rhetoric, and the arts drop in importance.   EDUC

1300s   In India, the feudal system known as jagirdar develops. It allows authorities to collect monies from property owners rather than taking salaries. It will remain in use until India gains political independence.   POL

1300s   Freemasonry has its origins in medieval lodges of stonemasons with secret signs for recognition of members. The secret organization will claim even older roots, going back to ancient Egypt, Babylon, and Palestine. *See also* 1716, PHIL.   REL

1300s   By this time, popular veneration of the Virgin Mary has won acceptance in the official doctrines and learned discourse of the Catholic church.   REL

1300s   According to legend, the English hero Robin Hood and his gang rob from the rich and give to the poor. Robin Hood becomes a symbol of the noble, if illegal, redistribution of wealth.   SOC

c. 1300   Italian poet Dante Alighieri discusses the development of a work of art by coupling the two painters Cimabue and Giotto. He finds that a painting's realization is met in three stages: the artist's mind, the tool, and material.   CRIT

1300–1700   The Renaissance in Europe marks a time of great development in art, literature, science, and scholarship. It is also a time of dramatic political and religious change, including the Protestant Reformation and the rise of modern nation-states. The art and ideas of classical antiquity are revived, while humanistic thought is concerned with the capabilities of individuals.   MISC

1300–1600   Humanism is a powerful intellectual force in western Europe. By reading classical texts in the original languages, humanists seek to revive the spirit of Greek and Roman art and learning, with an emphasis on the dignity of human existence.   MISC

1300–1500   Following a period of corruption, the Yellow Hat sect, led by Tsongkhapa, reforms Tibetan Buddhism with a new emphasis on monastic discipline.   REL

1300–1600   In Indonesia, Arab traders and colonizers and Sufi preachers make Islam the dominant religion.   REL

1300	By now, most of the people of Kampuchea (Cambodia) are either Hindu Brahmins or Theravada Buddhists. Throughout the next century, Buddhism will gain in strength at the expense of Hinduism. **REL**
1302	Pope Boniface VIII issues the papal bull *Unam Sanctam*, which states that the pope has supreme authority in civic and spiritual affairs. A year later, he will be kidnapped by agents of French king Philip IV, with whom he had previously clashed. **REL**
c. 1304–1307	Italian poet Dante Alighieri writes *De vulgari eloquentia*, which argues for the literary use of the vernacular as opposed to Latin, and *Il convivio*, which comments on some of his own poetry. **CRIT**
1304–1374	Italian humanist and poet Petrarch lives. He helps to effect the resurrection of classically based humanism, based on the rhetoric of Roman orators Cicero and Quintilian, among others. He stands in conflict with the philosophers and logicians of the scholastic movement. **EDUC**
1305	The "Babylonian Captivity" begins as Pope Clement V moves the papacy from Rome to Avignon, France. Throughout this period of more than seven decades, the popes will reside at Avignon under the control of the French kings. *See also* 1377, **REL**. **REL**
1307–1321	Italian poet Dante Alighieri writes the epic that will come to be known as *The Divine Comedy*, an imaginative poetic synthesis of personal experience with medieval theology and philosophy. Originally titled *Commedia* (known as *Divina commedia* from the 16th century onward), the 100-canto work tells of the poet's journey through the worlds of the afterlife in three parts: *Inferno, Purgatorio,* and *Paradiso*. **PHIL**
1308	Franciscan missionary Giovanni da Montecorvino, working in Peking under the Mongols, becomes the first archbishop of the Latin Church of the Far East. The church will be expelled in 1369, following Chinese recapture of the city from the Mongols. **REL**
1313–1375	Italian writer Giovanni Boccaccio lives. With Petrarch, he will be considered one of the founders of Italian Renaissance humanism. His works include commentaries on Dante and *De genealogia deorum gentilium*, an encyclopedic interpretation of myth and legend that includes a defense of poetry. **CRIT**
1324	English philosopher William of Ockham, an exponent of nominalism (*see* c. 1285–1349, **PHIL**), is charged with heresy by Pope John XXII. In 1328 William will escape to the protection of Holy Roman emperor Louis IV. **PHIL**

1324   Italian scholar Marsilius of Padua publishes *Defensor Pacis* (*Defender of the Peace*), which argues that the people are the source of political legitimacy and opposes papal claims to temporal authority. His ideas will be condemned as heretical.   POL

1332–1406   Arab historian and statesman Ibn Khaldûn lives. He is known both for his history of the world, *The Book of Lessons and Archive of Early and Subsequent History*, and for its preface, which outlines his theories of history and society.   HIST

1337   Protectionism, which shelters a country's goods by levying taxes against those imported from a competing country, is practiced in England by Edward II. It marks one of the earliest occurrences of the practice.   ECON

c. 1340   Italian historian Giovanni Villani devotes a chapter of his *De origine civitatis Florentiae*, a book on famous Florentine citizens, to discussion of such painters as Cimabue and Giotto.   CRIT

1340–1412   Jewish philosopher Hasdai ben Abraham Crescas lives. In cosmology, he argues for an infinitely extended cosmos; in religious life, he argues for the role of emotion, in opposition to Maimonides's rationalism.   REL

c. 1350   Italian writer Benvenuto da Immola both honors and criticizes Giotto by writing a comparative judgment based on his own admiration for ancient art.   CRIT

c. 1350   Italian writer Giovanni Boccaccio compares Giotto's light-infused art and the dark art of the Middle Ages.   CRIT

1350   The anonymous mystical treatise *The Cloud of Unknowing* is written in England.   REL

1353   A Thai prince, educated by a Theravada Buddhist monk in Kampuchea (Cambodia), founds the state of Laos as a predominantly Buddhist country.   REL

1368–1644   Buddhist histories, family and local histories, and biographies appear in large numbers in China during the Ming dynasty. Most works are simply narratives, though there is some analysis in the form of textual criticism.   HIST

1368–1644   During the Ming dynasty in China, the White Lotus society (*see* 1260–1368, REL) adopts the worship of the Wusheng Laomu, or Eternal Mother.   REL

1370–1445   Italian writer Pier Paolo Vergerio lives. He writes *On the Upright Character and Liberal Studies of Youth*, which will become important in establishing the Renaissance educational tradition.   EDUC

1377   English cleric John Wycliffe is charged with heresy by Pope Gregory XI. Wycliffe argues that ecclesiastical and secular authority are forfeited when the possessor becomes guilty of mortal sin; that the clergy is corrupt and should practice poverty; and that Christian life should be based on the Bible. He will later deny the power of priests to absolve sin, the power of indulgences and penances, and the doctrine of transubstantiation. A forerunner of English Protestantism, he also begins the first complete translation of the Bible into English. His follow- ers, known as Lollards, will gain strength after his death in 1384, despite church condemnation of his works. *See also* 1400s, REL.   REL

1377   The Babylonian Captivity ends (*see* 1305, REL) as Pope Gregory XI moves the papacy back from Avignon to Rome.   REL

1378–1417   The Great Schism wracks the Roman Catholic Church upon the death of Gregory XI in 1378. Urban VI reigns as pope in Rome while the antipope Clement VII reigns in Avignon; both are the originators of two separate lines of popes. *See also* 1409 and 1414–1418, REL.   REL

1400s   Gypsies introduce tarot cards to western Europe as a means of foretelling the future. Illustrated with richly symbolic images, the cards in a tarot deck number 78.   PHIL

1400s   The Lollard movement founded by heretical English cleric John Wycliffe is gradually eradicated by persecution under the royal house of Lancaster. *See also* 1377, REL.   REL

1400s   In northern India, preacher Ramanand reforms the Vaishnava cult of devotion to the god Vishnu. He advocates communal meals and worship among fol- lowers from all castes.   REL

1400s   Indian mystic and poet Kabir attacks idolatry, empty ritual, and the caste sys- tem. His teachings influence and are remembered by Hindus and Muslims alike.   REL

1400s   Vietnam falls to the Chinese, who curtail the activities of the country's Buddhist monks and increase the influence of Confucian and Taoist beliefs.   REL

1400–1800   In Europe, the *querelles des femmes* is an ongoing debate among male and female thinkers on the place of women in the natural world. Questions about their humanity, educability, and inferiority are standard areas of discussion.   PHIL

1400–1700   Modern imperialism takes shape on the European continent, as countries attempt to build wealth through colonization and empire building. Important European colonial powers during the period include Portugal, Spain, Britain, France, and the Netherlands.   POL

1400   English mystic Julian of Norwich writes her prose work *A Revelation of Divine Love*.   REL

1405–1457   Italian humanist Lorenzo Valla lives. A critic of scholasticism, his works include *On Pleasure* and *On Free Choice*.   PHIL

1405   In *The Book of the City of Ladies,* French poet Christine de Pisan charts men's unequal treatment of women and argues the need to fight it. In so doing, she becomes the first woman to participate in the *querelles des femmes,* an ongoing debate about women's alleged moral deficiencies and lack of human qualities (*see* 1400–1800, PHIL).   PHIL

1409   In a failed attempt to heal the Great Schism (*see* 1378–1417, REL), the Council of Pisa unsuccessfully tries to depose Roman pope Gregory XII and Avignon antipope Benedict XIII while electing a second antipope, Alexander V, who is quickly succeeded by John XXIII. *See also* 1414–1418, REL.   REL

1414–1418   The Council of Constance ends the Great Schism in the Roman Catholic Church (*see* 1378–1417, REL) by persuading Pope Gregory XII to resign, elect-

---

Are Women Human? The Debate

In 1405, French poet Christine de Pisan forthrightly proclaimed the innate humanity of women: "There is not the slightest doubt that women belong to the people of God and the human race as much as men and are not another species or dissimilar race, for which they should be excluded from moral teachings." At the time, her belief was highly debatable.

For centuries, theologians and philosophers had pondered the question of the human qualities of the female sex. The 1400s saw the beginning of a formal European debate on the subject known as the *querelles des femmes.* A line of thinkers, beginning with Greek philosopher Aristotle and continuing with 12th-century Italian legal scholar Gratian and Italian philosopher Thomas Aquinas, believed that women were not only inferior to men, but of an entirely different race. In the 16th century, German religious reformer Martin Luther wrote, "[W]oman is a different animal to man, not only having different members, but also being far weaker in intellect." This alleged innate weakness could lead to moral failing, it was argued, and for that reason women must be subordinate. Warned Gratian, "Adam was beguiled by Eve, not she by him," and therefore he must shield himself from her "so that he may not fail a second time through female levity."

Beginning with Pisan, a number of early feminist writers countered these assertions. Pisan's *The Book of the City of Ladies* went further, suggesting better education and fairness in marriage for women. Thanks in part to Pisan and other feminist thinkers, male and female, the *querelles des femmes* officially ended by the end of the 18th century.

ing Pope Martin V in his place, and deposing the antipopes Benedict XIII and John XXIII. *See also* 1409, REL.   REL

1415   Czech religious reformer Jan Hus (or Huss), who has denounced corrupt church practices, is burned at the stake for heresy.   REL

1426   *The Imitation of Christ*, an enduring work of Christian devotional literature usually ascribed to Dutch ecclesiastic Thomas à Kempis, is published.   REL

1428   The Azteca-Mexica people conquer the central Mexican lake area, establishing a state religion that glorifies death in battle, death in childbirth, and death in human sacrifice.   REL

1432–1436   English mystic Margery Kempe writes the spiritual work *The Book of Margery Kempe*, one of the earliest autobiographies in English.   REL

1436   Italian artist and writer Leon Battista Alberti places the practice of the fine arts on a scientific level in his treatise on painting, *Della pittura*, which includes the first description of perspective.   CRIT

1436   In Thailand, the first recorded reference is made to the Emerald Buddha, a sacred statue made of green malachite. It will endure as a national symbol. REL

1437   Italian painter Cennino Cennini completes *Il libro dell'arte*, an artist's handbook that documents artistic theory and the traditions of training at the end of the 14th and the beginning of the 15th centuries.   CRIT

1438–1471   During the reign of Pachacuti Inca Yupanqui, the Inca empire in South America enjoys its greatest period of expansion and reform. The hierarchical society, which practices human sacrifice, worships the creator-and-destroyer god Viracocha along with such other deities as the sun god Inti and the rain god Apu Illapu.   REL

1440   Italian writer Micchele Savonarola coins the word "school" in his *De laudibus Patavii* to describe the most important painters from different regions who excelled at naturalism in their work.   CRIT

1440   German prelate and philosopher Nicholas of Cusa publishes *Of Learned Ignorance*. In this and other works, he proposes a negative theology, a belief in the unboundedness of space, and opposition to Greek philosopher Aristotle's law of noncontradiction.   PHIL

c. 1440–1480   Eware the Great rules as *oba*, or sacred king, of Benin, leading this African empire to prominence. The institution of *oba* is adopted from Yoruba culture.   POL

1444   Italian humanist Lorenzo Valla publishes *Elegantiae linguae latinae*, a defense
                of classical Latin as opposed to medieval and Church Latin. He is a prominent
                spokesperson for humanist learning and an opponent of scholasticism and
                monastic asceticism.   MISC

c. 1450   Florentine sculptor Lorenzo Ghiberti writes his *Commentarii* for the education
                of young artists. His treatise is notable for paying more attention to single
                works of art than to painters.   CRIT

c. 1450   Papal indulgences for the dead, which are believed to remit all or part of the
                temporal punishment due in purgatory for sins committed on earth, are intro-
                duced.   REL

1453   Constantinople, capital of the Byzantine empire, falls to the Ottoman Turks,
                marking the climax of Islam's military advance over formerly Christian lands.
                Constantinople will become the Turkish city of Istanbul.   REL

1454   German printer Johannes Gutenberg uses a movable metal type printing press
                of his own invention to publish a Latin edition of the Bible. Gutenberg's
                innovation launches the age of the modern printed book and, later, of mass-
                audience periodicals. In the coming centuries, the printed page will be the
                primary medium for dissemination of ideas. Film, television, radio, and com-
                puter networks will offer substantial competition in the 20th century. *See also*
                1990s, MISC.   MISC

1460–1464   Florentine architect and sculptor Filarete draws up vast schemes for palaces
                and ideal cities to be laid out according to elaborate astrological rules in his
                treatise *Trattato d'architettura*.   CRIT

1460–1491   Southern Burmese king Dhammaceti, formerly a monk, leads a national
                revival of Buddhism.   REL

c. 1465   Egyptian Sufi mystic al-Jazuli dies. He was the founder of the Shadhiliyya
                order of Sufis.   REL

1468–1534   Italian prelate Tommaso de Vio, known as Thomas Cajetan, lives. In *The
                Analogy of Names and the Concept of Beings*, he discusses the role of analogy in
                the development of knowledge and theology.   PHIL

1469–1539   In the Punjab region of northern India, Guru Nanak, the founder of Sikhism,
                lives. Breaking away from Hinduism, he preaches monotheism and the iden-
                tity of all religions. He also emphasizes meditation and opposes idolatry and
                the caste system.   REL

1478   Spanish monarchs Ferdinand and Isabella introduce the Spanish Inquisition, which is independent of the Papal Inquisition (*see* 1233, REL). Under such notorious leaders as Tomás de Torquemada, it will seek to find and punish Jews and Muslims whose conversion to Christianity is insincere. It will also be used freely to investigate and persecute all those suspected of heresy. Gaining a reputation for torture and ready execution, it will not be abolished until 1834.

REL

1484   Italian philosopher Marsilio Ficino publishes his translation of Greek philosopher Plato's dialogues. In his translations and commentaries, Ficino presents an interpretation that will dominate Western understanding of Plato until the 19th century.   PHIL

1485   English prose writer Sir Thomas Malory's *Morte d'Arthur* is published posthumously. This collection of Arthurian romances will be the principal vehicle through which the legends of King Arthur and his knights will be transmitted to future generations of English readers. Also influential are the Arthurian romances of 12th-century French poet Chrétien de Troyes. *See also* 1135, HIST.   MISC

1486   Italian humanist Giovanni Pico della Mirandola publishes his 900 theses on philosophical subjects. The work is prefaced by the Latin oration *On the Dignity of Man*. His emphasis on classical texts and human dignity will make him an example to other humanists, such as Desiderius Erasmus and Sir Thomas More. He is protected by the Medici in Florence after his 900 theses are condemned as heretical.   PHIL

1486   The book *Malleus Malificarum* (*Hammer of the Witches*) by clergymen Henry Kramer and Jacob Sprenger coalesces pervasive beliefs about the innate moral weakness of women, which, the authors believe, leads women to be lured by the Devil into the practice of witchcraft.   REL

1488–1575   Spanish-born Jewish rabbi Joseph Karo lives, spending most of his life in Asia Minor and Palestine. He publishes *Shulhan arukh* (*Prepared Table*), a codification of Jewish law that will become authoritative.   REL

1492   In Spain, the monarchs Ferdinand and Isabella conquer the Moorish stronghold of Granada, completing the Christian reconquest of Spain from the Muslims.   REL

1500s   Turkish historian Hoca Sadeddin writes *Tac üttevarih*, a history of the Ottoman empire that will become one of the most famous Turkish histories.   HIST

1500s–1700 English antiquarians such as Sir Robert Bruce Cotton, Thomas Hearne, John Leland, and Robert and Edward Harley collect and edit old manuscripts and documents, some of which will be preserved for centuries in museums and libraries. Several of these men also write histories themselves. HIST

1500s Several widely separated cultures exhibit a tendency toward greater literary, scholarly, and devotional use of the vernacular rather than sacred languages. In Europe, the language whose use declines is Latin; in India, Sanskrit; and in Burma, Pali. LING

1500s By the end of the century, Queen Catherine de Médicis of France popularizes the practice of enhancing female beauty with cosmetics. MISC

1500s Portuguese Catholics colonize Sri Lanka, threatening the country's Buddhist tradition. Subsequent domination by the Dutch (17th and 18th centuries) and British (19th and early 20th centuries) will further weaken the religion's hold on the country. *See also* 1890s, REL. REL

1500s In India, the Mughals, a Central Asiatic military elite, overthrow their fellow Muslims in the Delhi Sultanate. Mughal rule ensures the survival of Islam in India, though orthodox Islam is threatened by the introduction of more pantheistic forms of Sufism, the Islamic mystical tradition. REL

1500s The cult of Rama (an incarnation of the god Vishnu) flourishes in India. Hindu poet Tulsidas, a major figure in the movement, is noted for his version of the *Ramayana*. REL

1500s The *Popol Vuh*, a Mayan sacred document, is recorded in Guatemala. It recounts the mythology and history of the Quiché people. REL

c. 1500 The primary school has its beginnings in Europe. EDUC

1500–1800 Absolutist rule dominates Europe, as nation-states grow and their monarchs take more complete control, drawing power from the church and outside the nobility. An archetypal absolute monarch is French king Louis XIV (reigned 1643–1715), to whom is ascribed the quote, "L'état, c'est moi" ("I am the state"). POL

c. 1500 Indian religious leader Vallabha erects a shrine to the god Krishna. His teachings focus on Krishna's amorous adolescent sport with milkmaids, particularly Radha. REL

c. 1500 Hindu mystic Chaitanya spreads the cult of devotion to Krishna in Bengal in eastern India. REL

1501–1732 During the reign of the Safavid dynasty in Persia (Iran), the "Twelver" sect of Shiite Islam is the official religion. Twelver Shiism acknowledges 12 imams, of whom the last, the Imam Mahdi, is believed to be in hiding, ready to return in the last days. REL

1505 In his book *Libellus*, Johannes Butzbach credits Giotto alone for having restored to the art of painting the dignity of antiquity. CRIT

1505 German humanist Jacob Wimpheling devotes two chapters of his book, *Epitome rerum Germanicarum*, to German art; in particular, he praises the Strasbourg Cathedral as excelling over all European buildings. CRIT

1509 Dutch humanist Desiderius Erasmus publishes *Encomium moriae* (*The Praise of Folly*). Known for his classical learning and his skeptical but moderate and humane outlook, he is a critic of clerical abuse and lay superstition. He will initially show sympathy for Martin Luther (*see* 1517, REL) but, refusing to break with the Roman Catholic Church, will oppose the Protestant Reformation. *See also* 1524, REL. REL

c. 1511 In *De ratione studii*, Dutch humanist Desiderius Erasmus affirms that "all knowledge falls into one of two divisions: the knowledge of 'truths' and the knowledge of 'words.'" This distinction will inform later debates on the goals and possibilities for education. EDUC

1511 German humanist Johannes Reuchlin publishes *Augenspiegel*, in which he argues in favor of studying classical Hebrew works in the original Hebrew. A controversy results, with the Inquisition opposing Reuchlin, and Protestants such as German humanist Ulrich von Hutten supporting him. The Catholic church will suppress Reuchlin's writings in 1521. REL

1512–1517 The Fifth Ecumenical Council is convened by Popes Julius II and Leo X. It succeeds in countering the conciliar theory, the view that a council has supreme power, even over a pope. REL

1513 English writer Sir Thomas More writes *History of Richard III*, perhaps the first modern biography. Some will attribute this work, found among More's papers following his execution (*see* 1534, REL), to John Cardinal Morton. HIST

1513–1517 Italian political philosopher Niccolò Machiavelli composes the *Discorsi* (*Discourses*), political reflections on the first ten books of Roman historian Livy (*see* 59–17 B.C., HIST). Considered a pioneer of political science, Machiavelli draws on ancient and modern history to illustrate his republican principles. As the first major writer to promulgate the idea that history is cyclical, he will come to be seen as the founder of the philosophy of history. POL

1516 English writer Sir Thomas More publishes *Utopia*, his fictional portrait of an ideal state governed by reason. POL

1517   Italian political philosopher Niccolò Machiavelli composes *Il principe* (*The Prince*), a treatise for princes on how to gain and maintain power. His pragmatic approach, which sanctions ruthlessness and treachery when necessary, will be both controversial and influential.   POL

1517   German monk Johann Tetzel promotes the sale of indulgences (remissions of punishment due in purgatory for sin) in return for contributions for the building of Saint Peter's Church in Rome.   REL

1517   On October 31, German religious reformer Martin Luther nails his 95 Theses on the door of the castle church in Wittenberg. Prompted in part by Johann Tetzel's activities (*see* above), Luther protests the sale of indulgences and other Roman Catholic Church practices. His action marks the beginning of the Protestant Reformation.   REL

1517   The term "ghetto" is coined in Venice for the restricted areas in Christian Europe in which Jews are permitted to live. Anti-Semitism (hatred of or discrimination against Jews) has been prevalent in many parts of Christian Europe throughout the Middle Ages. It will persist into modern times, often

---

Is It Better to Be Loved or Feared?

The Prince, Niccolò Machiavelli's primer for princes on how to get and keep power, contains many crisp, concise bits of practical advice divorced from issues of private morality. Among the questions considered is whether it is better for a ruler to be loved or feared. Machiavelli responds: "The answer is, of course, that it would be best to be both loved and feared. But since the two rarely come together, anyone compelled to choose will find greater security in being feared than in being loved."

Machiavelli qualifies this advice by noting that the prince should not go so far as to be hated. Executing enemies now and then will win fear, but seizing citizens' property is a bad idea: "Men are quicker to forget the death of a father than the loss of a patrimony." Still, as long as a ruler is not hated, being feared is much safer than merely being loved: "I conclude that since men love as they themselves determine but fear as their ruler determines, a wise prince must rely upon what he and not others can control."

Machiavelli knew whereof he spoke. In 1513, four years before he wrote *The Prince*, the Italian statesman was imprisoned and tortured for allegedly conspiring to overthrow the Medici rulers of his native Florence. Found innocent and released, he was not moved to hate his rulers—however much he had learned to fear them. After all, princes must be princes. Indeed, he spent the remaining years of his life trying unsuccessfully to get a job from them.

erupting in persecutions and pogroms, and ultimately in the Nazi Holocaust (*see* 1933–1945, REL).   REL

1519   German religious reformer Martin Luther and theologian Johann Eck debate Luther's positions as stated in the 95 Theses (*see* 1517, REL). Eck forces Luther to take an open stand against the Roman Catholic church, including denying the authority of the papacy and church councils.   REL

1519   Swiss religious reformer Huldrych Zwingli delivers his lectures on the New Testament, marking the beginning of the Reformation in Switzerland. Zwingli, who adopts Martin Luther's doctrine of justification by faith alone (*see* 1520, REL), argues that scripture alone carries teaching authority. He opposes dispensing of indulgences, clerical celibacy, monasticism, papal authority, and numerous aspects of sacramental and liturgical life.   REL

1520   Italian political philosopher Niccolò Machiavelli completes *On the Art of War*. He will finish *Storia Fiorentina* (*History of Florence*) in 1525. While they will not become as well known as *The Prince*, these works will influence political leaders and thinkers from Machiavelli's day onward.   POL

1520   German religious reformer Martin Luther publishes *The Babylonian Captivity of the Church*, *Address to the Christian Nobility of the German Nation*, and *The Freedom of a Christian Man*. He argues that people are justified by faith alone, not works; that scripture alone, not tradition, is authoritative; and that priests have no claim to mediate between individuals and God. Proclaiming the "priesthood of all believers," he teaches that the sacraments are only aids to faith.   REL

1520–1566   The reign of Süleyman the Magnificent, Ottoman sultan, is marked by renewed expansion into the Balkans and Hungary. Ottoman expansion in this region from the 15th to 17th centuries will leave Muslim populations in a number of states, including Serbia, Albania, and Bulgaria.   REL

c. 1520   Reflecting commonly held beliefs about the position of women in a marriage, German religious reformer Martin Luther writes, "The rule remains with the husband, and the wife is compelled to obey him by God's command."   REL

1521   German religious reformer Martin Luther is excommunicated as a heretic. Appearing before the Diet of Worms in Germany, he refuses to retract his teachings, ending his defense with the words, "Here I stand. I can do no other. God help me. Amen." In the Edict of Worms that follows, Luther is declared an outlaw, but is shepherded away under the protection of Frederick III, elector of Saxony.   REL

1521   German religious reformer Philipp Melanchthon, an associate of Martin Luther, publishes *Loci communes*, the first systematic treatment of Reformation beliefs. Trained as a humanist, Melanchthon tends to be more conciliatory on doctrinal issues than Luther.   REL

1522   German religious reformer Martin Luther publishes his German translation of the New Testament. His Old Testament translation will follow in 1534.   REL

1524   Dutch humanist Desiderius Erasmus publishes *Freedom of the Will*, a work opposing German religious reformer Martin Luther's doctrine of predestination.   REL

1524–1526   The Peasants' Revolt erupts in Germany and Austria. Although the peasants fight primarily for such economic and political goals as abolition of serfdom and judicial impartiality, they are inspired by the reforming spirit of Martin Luther. Luther denounces the revolt, which is crushed militarily, but Swiss religious reformer Huldrych Zwingli endorses it.   REL

1524–1525   Radical German religious reformer Thomas Münzer sides with the rebels in the Peasants' Revolt (*see above*). Calling for the establishment of an egalitarian,

Native American Religion

Before Europeans brought Christianity to North America in the 16th and 17th centuries, the indigenous peoples of the continent had a rich pantheon of deities. Here are some Native American gods and goddesses little known today but once widely revered:

Agloolik—Inuit good spirit who lived under the ice and gave assistance to hunters and fishers.

Coyote—Trouble-making, clownish demon, believed by the Montana Sioux to have invented horses.

Ga-Oh—Iroquois god of the winds, known for his cannibalistic habits and penchant for uprooting trees.

Kitcki Manitou—Algonquin Great Spirit or Supreme Being. Most other Native American peoples also worshiped a Great Spirit.

Onatha—Iroquois goddess of wheat, abducted into the underworld and rescued by the sun.

Pah—Pawnee god of the moon, who mated with the sun to produce a son, while the morning star and evening star mated to produce a daughter. The son and daughter were the ancestors of humankind.

Pukkeenegak—Inuit goddess of childbirth and making clothes.

Thunder Bird—God of thunder worshiped by many peoples.

communistic society, he succeeds in setting up a theocracy in Mühlhausen, Germany. Upon the defeat of the peasants, Münzer is beheaded.   REL

1524–1583   Swiss Protestant theologian Thomas Lüber, known as Thomas Erastus, lives. A follower of Swiss religious reformer Huldrych Zwingli, he will be chiefly known for lending his name to Erastianism. This doctrine, which distorts his actual views, holds that the state should have complete dominance over the religious lives of its citizens—a view expressed in English philosopher Thomas Hobbes's *Leviathan* (1651).   REL

1525   In Zürich, Switzerland, religious reformer Huldrych Zwingli replaces the Catholic mass with a reformed service. Zwingli argues that the Lord's supper is only a commemorative feast.   REL

1525   Near Zürich, Switzerland, Anabaptists perform their first adult baptisms. The sect, also known as the Swiss Brethren, rejects the validity of infant baptism. Some, known as evangelical Anabaptists, will reject the use of violence, while others, the revolutionary Anabaptists, seek to bring about the New Jerusalem by force. Anabaptists of all varieties will be condemned and persecuted by both Catholics and Lutherans.   REL

The Man Behind the King James Bible

The King James Bible, the best-known translation of the Bible into English, was authorized by King James I of England and published in 1611. The committee of scholars who produced this Protestant version were honored for their efforts, and the translation's literary style has been a model for future generations. But the translator whose work was the original basis for the King James Bible enjoyed no such public admiration in his time. Indeed, he was strangled and burned at the stake as a heretic.

William Tyndale (c. 1494–1536) was an English Catholic priest whose life changed forever when he converted to the Lutheran faith. Struck by the notion that true doctrine could only be determined by the reading of scripture, he set out to translate the Bible into English. Unable to do his work safely in Catholic England, he published the first printed English edition of the New Testament in Germany in 1525. Several sections of the Old Testament followed, including the first five books, known as the Pentateuch.

Tyndale's translations were condemned and burned in England. He got into trouble when he—like many of his Catholic adversaries—publicly disapproved of King Henry VIII's divorce. In 1535, Henry's agents seized Tyndale in Antwerp and executed him the following year. Ironically, it was Henry who began the process that led to Tyndale's rehabilitation. Henry had already broken with the pope over the issue of divorce and founded the independent Church of England. The Church of England eventually commissioned the King James Bible, which adopted about 90 percent of Tyndale's translation.

1525   The printing of English humanist William Tyndale's English translation of the New Testament begins at Cologne. His translation of this and other parts of the Bible will be banned and he will be executed for heresy in 1536, but his work will form the basis for the King James, or authorized, version, published in 1611.

REL

1525–1572   Polish rabbi Moses Isserles lives. He amends the legal code *Shulhan arukh* (*see* 1488–1575, REL) to include the ritual and practice of the Ashkenazim, Jews of northern and eastern Europe, as well as the Sephardim, Jews of the Mediterranean region.

REL

1527   The Schleitheim Confession is an important statement of evangelical Anabaptist beliefs. *See also* 1525, REL.

REL

1528   Italian writer Count Baldassare Castiglione publishes *Il cortegiano* (*The Courtier*), a work in dialogue form concerning courtly manners and education. The book will be popular and influential across Europe.

EDUC

1528   The popular Renaissance view of women as an aberration of nature is expressed in *The Courtier*, by Italian writer Count Baldassare Castiglione. He writes, "Since nature always intends and plans to make things most perfect, she would consistently bring forth men if she could. . . . When a woman is born, it is a defect or mistake of nature and contrary to what she would wish to do."

PHIL

1529   The term "Protestant" originates in the *Protestatio* (protest) delivered by German religious reformer Martin Luther's supporters in opposition to the decision at the Diet of Speyer to legislate against Lutheranism.

REL

1529   At the Colloquy of Marburg, religious reformers Martin Luther and Huldrych Zwingli meet. Agreement is reached on 14 articles of faith, but not on the 15th, concerning the Eucharist. Luther believes in the real presence of Christ in the bread and wine (through consubstantiation) while Zwingli believes the sacrament is only symbolic.

REL

1530   The Augsburg Confession, written at the Diet of Augsburg by Martin Luther's associate Philipp Melanchthon, codifies Lutheran beliefs.

REL

1530   By now, Spanish conquistadors have heard the Latin American Indian legend of the golden city of El Dorado. The search for the mythical city will generate much new geographic knowledge but will not uncover the city itself.

REL

1531   On October 11, Swiss religious reformer Huldrych Zwingli is killed at the battle of Kappel, which results from religious disputes within Switzerland.

REL

1531   The Schmalkaldic League, an alliance of Protestant princes and free cities, is formed at Schmalkalden, Germany, in defense against the anti-Lutheran Holy Roman emperor Charles V. The league helps to spread Lutheranism throughout Germany. *See also* 1546–1547, REL.   REL

1533   English prelate Thomas Cranmer is made archbishop of Canterbury. He will preside over English king Henry VIII's establishment of the independent Church of England, placing the English Bible in churches and revising the Book of Common Prayer (*see* 1549, REL). He will be convicted of heresy and burned at the stake under English queen Mary I in 1556 (*see* 1553–1558, REL).   REL

1533   Fleeing the Mongols in Tibet, the people known as the Sherpas arrive in Nepal. There they will practic a form of Buddhism based on Tibetan Lamaism and including Tantric cults.   REL

1534   English king Henry VIII issues the Act of Supremacy, which declares him to be head of the Church of England. The culmination of centuries of conflict between the papacy and the English crown, the complete separation of the Anglican communion from the Roman Catholic Church is sparked by Pope Clement VII's refusal to annul Henry's marriage to Catherine of Aragon to permit a new marriage to Anne Boleyn. Excommunicated by the pope, Henry suppresses English monasteries.   REL

1534   English writer Sir Thomas More is beheaded on a charge of treason for refusing to assent to the Act of Supremacy, by which King Henry VIII is made head of the English church. More will be canonized as a saint by the Roman Catholic Church in 1935.   REL

1534–1535   Radical Dutch Anabaptist Jan Beuckelson, known as John of Leiden, leads a revolt that briefly establishes a theocracy in Münster, Germany. Property is made communal and polygamy is legalized before the revolt is suppressed and John of Leiden executed.   REL

1534–1572   Palestinian Jewish mystic Isaac Luria lives. With his pupil Hayyim Vital, he develops a mystical school within the cabalistic tradition.   REL

c. 1535   English biographer William Roper writes *Mirrour of Vertue in Worldly Greatness or the Life of Syr Thomas More*, a biography of his father-in-law (*see* 1513, HIST) that will circulate in manuscript form for many years before finally being published in 1626. English writer George Cavendish will publish *Life of Cardinal Wolsey*, a biography of the man Cavendish had served for many years as gentleman usher, in 1557. These books will be considered two of the first significant biographies in English.   HIST

1535   *Philosophy of Love*, by Portuguese Jewish philosopher Judah Abrabanel, is
              posthumously published.   PHIL

1535–1600   Spanish philosopher Luis de Molina lives. He is the author of *Concordia*, in
              which he proposes the *scientia media* (*middle knowledge*), the unique way in
              which God knows about future events.   PHIL

1535   In Zürich, Miles Coverdale publishes the first complete English translation of
              the Bible.   REL

1536   Moravian Anabaptist minister Jacob Hutter is burned at the stake. His follow-
              ers, known as the Hutterian Brethren, will continue to form brotherhoods
              practicing common ownership of property. Persecution will drive them from
              Germany to Russia and eventually to the United States.   REL

1536   Dutch religious reformer Menno Simons becomes the leader of the Dutch
              Anabaptists, a sect that becomes known as the Mennonites. Practicing adult
              baptism, nonviolence, and simplicity of dress and habits, the Mennonites will
              spread to Germany, France, Russia, and the United States.   REL

1536   French Protestant theologian John Calvin publishes the first edition of
              Institutes of the Christian Religion, which defines Christian doctrine in a way that
              differs from both Roman Catholicism and Lutheranism. His principles include
              the total depravity of man, unmerited salvation of an elect by grace alone, and
              predestination. Calvinism will be highly influential in Britain and the United
              States, affecting not only theology and devotion but social thought and eco-
              nomic activity.   REL

1536   German Protestant reformer Martin Bucer is active in establishing the
              Wittenberg Concord on the doctrine of the Eucharist.   REL

1539   English king Henry VIII authorizes the Great Bible, an English translation for
              use by the Anglican church, and the Six Articles are enacted to suppress
              Lutheranism.   REL

1540   Spanish cleric Ignatius of Loyola receives papal approval for the new Catholic
              order called the Jesuits, or Society of Jesus. The order is noted for its emphasis
              on education, foreign missions, and obedience to the pope. Well known as a
              spiritual director, Ignatius writes *Spiritual Exercises*, a classic of prayer and med-
              itation.   REL

1541   Basque missionary Francis Xavier, one of the first Jesuits, sets sail from Lisbon,
              Portugal, for India. In the 11 years that follow, until his death in 1552, he will
              be successful in establishing Roman Catholic missions and winning converts
              in India, Southeast Asia, and Japan.   REL

1541	After a period of banishment from Geneva, Switzerland, French theologian John Calvin returns there, reforms the church, and establishes a theocratic government founded on Calvinist principles. REL
1542	French theologian John Calvin publishes the *Little Treatise on the Lord's Supper*, in which he rejects both Roman Catholic transubstantiation and Lutheran consubtantiation, viewing the Eucharist as only a spiritual partaking in Christ's presence. REL
1543	Polish astronomer Nicolaus Copernicus publishes *On the Revolutions of Celestial Bodies*, which contradicts long-standing geocentric belief by claiming that Earth and the other planets travel around the sun. After much controversy, the Copernican hypothesis will come to be accepted. It is the first of several intellectual revolutions that tend to move humanity away from its presumed place of central importance in the natural order. *See also* 1859, MISC. MISC
1545–1563	The Council of Trent meets during three periods (1545–1547, 1551–1552, and 1562–1563) to formulate the official Roman Catholic response to the Protestant Reformation. The Council authorizes a thorough reform of church practices while clearly defining dogma in contradistinction to Protestant teachings. The doctrinal results will be published in *Catechism of the Council of Trent* or *Roman Catechism* (1566). The Council provides the basis for the Catholic Reformation. REL
1546–1547	In league with the pope, Holy Roman emperor Charles V conducts and wins the Schmalkaldic War, defeating the Lutheran states of the Schmalkaldic League. *See also* 1531, REL. REL
1547	English king Edward VI repeals the Six Articles (*see* 1539, REL) and favors Protestant influence in church services. REL
1549	The Anglican Book of Common Prayer, deriving principally from the Roman Catholic breviary and missal, is first issued. Archbishop of Canterbury Thomas Cranmer supervises its publication and its revision in 1552. REL
1549	Basque missionary Francis Xavier arrives in Japan and wins many converts, but the religion's advance will be hindered by anti-Christian legislation from Japanese ruler Hideyoshi in 1587. REL
1550	Italian painter and writer Giorgio Vasari writes his *Lives of the Artists*. Vasari employs for the first time a consistent use of the word "manner" to indicate a certain way of working. His biographies will serve as the earliest prototype of modern artistic criticism and will be expanded in 1568. CRIT
1551–1602	Muslim historian, soldier and theologian Abulfazl lives. Minister of state and adviser to Mughal emperor Akbar, he writes of the history of Akbar's reign

(1556–1605), providing a detailed description of the Mughal empire in India at its peak. His Persian text is among the greatest examples of Indian historical writing.   HIST

1552   English prelate Thomas Cranmer publishes the 42 Articles defining the Anglican faith.   REL

1553   Italian writer Ascanio Condivi discusses the work of Italian sculptor and painter Michelangelo (1475–1564), describing in detail the paintings of the Sistine Chapel ceiling, in his *Life of Michelangelo*.   CRIT

1553–1558   English queen Mary I, a Roman Catholic, reigns. Two decades after the establishment of an independent Anglican church (*see* 1534, REL), she reestablishes papal authority in England, persecuting Protestants and executing Thomas Cranmer, archbishop of Canterbury (*see* 1533, REL). Known as "Bloody Mary," she will be succeeded by Elizabeth I, who restores Anglicanism to England (*see* 1558, REL).   REL

1554   In Basel, Switzerland, Francisco Robertello publishes Longinus's first-century treatise *On the Sublime* (*see* 50, CRIT), which will prove highly influential among neoclassical critics of the 17th and 18th centuries.   CRIT

1554   English Protestant reformer John Foxe publishes the first part of his *History of the Actes and Monuments of the Church*, better known as *The Book of Martyrs*. Scottish religious reformer John Knox will write *History of the Reformation in Scotland* in the 1560s. These two popular, highly partisan works will effectively advance their writers' causes.   HIST

1555   The Peace of Augsburg allows each prince within the Holy Roman Empire to determine whether his state will be Lutheran or Roman Catholic, with dissenters allowed to emigrate.   REL

1556–1605   Mughal emperor Akbar reigns in India. During this time, Sufi mysticism tends to merge with Hindu bhakti (devotion) and the gnostic philosophy of the *Upanishads*. Akbar's grandson Prince Dara Shikoh is one of the proponents of this blend.   REL

1557   The first group of Scottish Covenanters is born with the signing of a covenant for defense of religion among Presbyterians in Scotland. Covenanters will support the Parliamentary cause in the English Civil War (*see* 1642–1649, POL).REL

1558   Italian composer and music theorist Gioseffo Zarlino publishes *Institutioni harmoniche*, a work on harmony in which he establishes the major and minor chords.   CRIT

1558   Spanish missionary and historian Bernardino de Sahagún and his assistants gather Aztec folklore and history by interviewing elderly Indians in Mexico. The resulting transcripts and illustrations preserve vast amounts of information that otherwise would have been lost.   HIST

1558   Queen Elizabeth I of England restores the Church of England as the state church. During her reign (1558–1603), the Book of Common Prayer is again revised and the Anglican church develops along a middle path between Catholicism and Calvinism. *See also* 1553–1558, REL.   REL

1559   The first edition of *A Mirror for Magistrates*, a collection of didactic poetry on fortune, wickedness, and the lives of great men, is published in England. Later editions of this work, directed to rulers, will follow through the early 17th century.   POL

1560   Scottish religious reformer John Knox leads the Protestant reformation in Scotland, helping to establish his country's Presbyterian Church.   REL

1561–1564   Florentine historian and politician Francesco Guicciardini's *Storia d'Italia*, a history of Italy from 1494 to 1532, is published. Unusually objective and analytical, it will come to be regarded as one of the major historical works of the Renaissance.   HIST

1562–1598   In France, the Wars of Religion (or Huguenot Wars) are fought between Catholics and Protestants. (French Protestants are known as Huguenots, from the German *Eidgenossen*, or sworn companions). *See also* 1572 and 1598, REL.   REL

1562   Spanish nun and mystic Teresa of Avila begins her reform of the Carmelite order. Her colleague in the reform, which emphasizes poverty, discipline, and mental prayer, is John of the Cross, whose mystical works include *The Dark Night of the Soul* and *The Living Flame of Love*. *See also* 1583, REL.   REL

1563   In England, the 39 Articles replace the 42 Articles (*see* 1552, REL) as the definition of Anglican doctrine.   REL

1565   English historian John Stow publishes *A Summarie of Englyshe Chronicles*, a work which, for its day, shows unusual concern for accuracy, treating source material skeptically.   HIST

1572   On August 24, the Saint Bartholomew's Day massacre of French Protestants (Huguenots) by French Catholics begins. By the time the massacres are over in October, some 70,000 people will have been killed. The massacres bring about the resumption of the Wars of Religion (*see* 1562–1598, REL) after a brief period of peace.   REL

1574   Persian historian 'Abd al-Qādir Bada'uni is appointed to the court of Mughal
               emperor Akbar. His works will include the *Kitâb al-Hadith*, a collection of
               Muhammad's sayings, and *Muntakhab ut Tavarikh (Selection from History)*, a
               history of the Mughal empire.   HIST

1575–1624   German mystic Jakob Böhme lives. The Quakers and German Romantics will
               be influenced by his opposition to formal doctrine and his view of God as the
               undifferentiated Absolute.   REL

1576   French political philosopher Jean Bodin publishes *Six Books of a Republic*. In
               this and *Method for the Easy Comprehension of History* (1566), he attempts to set
               forth a comprehensive theory of political society without reference to divine
               command.   POL

1577   English chronicler Raphael Holinshed publishes *Chronicles of England,
               Scotlande, and Irelande*, which will provide source material for many plays by
               English dramatist William Shakespeare, including *King Lear* (c. 1605) and
               Macbeth (c. 1606).   HIST

1577   Lutheran churches accept the credal formulations of the *Book of Concord*.   REL

1580   French essayist Michel de Montaigne publishes his first two books of *Essays*; a
               third will follow in 1588. Creator of the personal essay, Montaigne uses the form
               to consider a wide range of moral, political, and philosophical subjects. His
               method synthesizes reflection on personal experience with broad reading in his-
               tory and literature.   PHIL

1581   English Jesuit Edmund Campion is executed for his secret work as a Catholic
               missionary in Protestant England.   REL

1582   An English translation of the Latin Vulgate Bible (*see* 405, REL) is completed in
               France. With an Old Testament translation completed in Douay in 1609, it will
               be known as the Douay Version and will long serve as the authorized English
               Bible for Roman Catholics.   REL

1582   Italian Jesuit missionary Matteo Ricci travels to China to seek converts to
               Christianity.   REL

1582   English clergyman Robert Browne articulates the principles behind
               Congregationalism, a form of Protestant Christianity that regards each con-
               gregation as entirely autonomous. Congregationalism will spread to America
               through the Pilgrims (*see* 1620, REL) and will play a powerful role in the Great
               Awakening (*see* 1720, REL).   REL

1583   The contemplative works *The Interior Castle* and *The Way of Perfection* by Spanish nun and mystic Teresa of Avila are posthumously published.   REL

c. 1586   The Society of Antiquaries of London, probably the first formally organized historical society, is founded.   HIST

1586   English historian William Camden publishes *Britannia,* a pioneering topographical study of Great Britain. The work considers archaeological remains and discusses social customs of the past.   HIST

1588   French priest Thoinot Arbeau (pseudonym of Jehan Tabourot) writes *Orchésographie,* one of the first works on dance.   CRIT

1588–1590   In England, the Marprelate Controversy rages. A secret press publishes a series of anti-Anglican Puritan pamphlets written under the pseudonym Martin Marprelate. The Church of England responds by secretly hiring Robert Greene and Thomas Nash to write pamphlets in response. The controversy comes to an end when the Marprelate press is discovered and the printer executed.   REL

1590   A collection of essays on human nature and the soul, edited by Rudolf Goeckel, is the first to have the word *psychology* (*psychologia*) in the title.   PSYCH

c. 1590   In India, the Bohra Muslim community splits between two rival leaders, Dawud ibn Qutb Shah of India and Sulayman of Yemen.   REL

c. 1591–1643 American religious leader Anne Hutchinson lives. Disagreeing with New England Puritan leader John Cotton and colonist John Winthrop, she believes in a covenant of grace rather than a covenant of works. She is banished from Massachusetts Bay Colony in 1637 and moves to New Hampshire, where she and most of her family are killed by Native Americans in 1643. *See also* 1620, REL.   REL

1594   Published in Cologne, Germany, the periodical *Mercurius gallobbelgicus* is one of the first publications to use the printing press in the service of mass journalism.   JOURN

1594   English theologian Richard Hooker publishes the first four books of *Of the Laws of Ecclesiastical Polity* (Books I–IV, 1594, Book V, 1597). Books VI–VIII, which will be published posthumously in 1648–1661, are of dubious authenticity. The apology for the organization of the Church of England will be considered a theological masterpiece.   REL

1595   English poet Sir Philip Sidney's critical treatise *An Apologie for Poetrie* is published posthumously in two editions, one under the title of *The Defence of Poesie.*

Sidney writes in response to a Puritan attack on poetry by Stephen Gosson, *The School of Abuse* (1579).   CRIT

1597   The first edition of English philosopher Francis Bacon's *Essays* is published. Second and third editions will follow in 1612 and 1625, respectively. The aphoristic, witty essays concern philosophical, religious, moral, and political subjects.   PHIL

1597   Spanish theologian and philosopher Francisco Suárez publishes *Metaphysical Disputations.* Considered one of the greatest scholastic philosophers and Jesuit thinkers, he will influence many 17th-century philosophers.   PHIL

1598   English playwright Ben Jonson's comedy *Every Man in His Humour* is first performed. In his prologue to the play, Jonson attacks his rival English dramatist William Shakespeare's violations of the classical unities. In this and other critical writings, Jonson adopts a neoclassical poetic stance that will appeal to subsequent critics into the 18th century.   CRIT

1598–1600   English geographer Richard Hakluyt publishes *Principall Navigations, Voiages, Traffiques and Discoveries of the English Nation,* a three-volume work describing the expeditions of Sir Walter Raleigh (*see* 1614, HIST) and other English adventurers. Hakluyt draws on primary source material in several languages in writing what will come to be seen as a landmark work in the history of exploration.   HIST

1598   French king Henry IV issues the Edict of Nantes, granting freedom of religion to Protestants (Huguenots) and bringing an end to the Wars of Religion (*see* 1562–1598, REL). *See also* 1685, REL.   REL

1600s   Lingua Franca evolves in Algiers. The pidgin language combines European and African tongues into a simplified common speech; the name "Lingua Franca" will come to refer to all such trade languages.   LING

1600s   Late this century, the German-speaking Amish Church breaks away from the Mennonite Church (*see* 1536, REL). The Amish, who will emigrate from Europe to the United States, are among the most conservative of Mennonite offshoots, practicing nonviolence and austere simplicity.   REL

1600s   In Shiite Muslim domains such as Persia (Iran), a new school of Islamic law develops. The Akhbari school emphasizes literal adherence to the tradition of the imams and calls for limits on the use of analogical reasoning.   REL

1600s   In England, a number of factions known as Separatists attempt to distance themselves from the authority of the Church of England. The factions include the Baptists, Brownists, Pilgrims, and Society of Friends.   REL

1600–1800   Mercantilism is the dominant economic theory among Western nations. It calls for strict governmental regulation of industry and trade, the accumulation of precious metals, and the favoring of foreign over domestic trade. Its premises will be questioned by Scottish economist Adam Smith in *The Wealth of Nations* (1776).   ECON

1600   Italian hermetic philosopher Giordano Bruno is burned at the stake for heretical views, including his association with the Copernican theory that Earth revolves around the sun.   PHIL

1602   English poet and composer Thomas Campion argues against rhyme and for classical meters in the treatise *Observations on the Arte of English Poesie*. His arguments will be countered by Samuel Daniel in *Defence of Rime* (1603). CRIT

1602   The Bodleian Library opens at Oxford University.   MISC

1602   French prelate Francis de Sales becomes bishop of Geneva. A great preacher, he is an important figure in the Catholic Reformation who will bring about many conversions of Protestants. He will also be notable for his *Introduction to the Devout Life* (1608).   REL

1603–1867   A great deal of historical writing, much of it in Chinese and modeled after Chinese annalistic narratives, is produced in Tokugawa-period Japan.   HIST

1603–1867   In Tokugawa Japan, the dominant intellectual system is Sushigaku, a form of neo-Confucianism emphasizing feudal obligations and relying heavily on the teachings of Chinese scholar Chu Hsi (1130–1200).   PHIL

1603–1867   The Tokugawa shogunate rules in Japan. During most of this period, foreign cultural, religious, and economic influences are kept out. Buddhism is the official religion. *See also* 1853, POL.   POL

1603   Dutch Reformed theologian Jacob Harmensen, known as Jacobus Arminius, argues for a modified Calvinism, one in which divine sovereignty is compatible with human freedom. Known as Arminianism, his views will be adopted by English church leaders John and Charles Wesley and most Methodist churches (*see* 1729, REL). *See also* 1618–1619, REL.   REL

1603–1604   Punjabi religious leader Guru Arjun, leader of the Sikhs, compiles the principal Sikh scripture, the *Adi Granth* ("First Volume").   REL

1604   Dutch painter and writer Karel van Mander writes *Het Schilderboeck* to encourage young painters to study classical antiquity and the Italian masters. He judges paintings based on the demand for clear contours and the preference for allegories.   CRIT

1604   English king James I convenes the Hampton Court Conference, which fails to resolve areas of doctrinal disagreement between Protestants and Catholics. REL

1605   English philosopher Francis Bacon publishes *The Advancement of Learning,* a treatise that begins the project he calls *Instauratio Magna,* an encyclopedia of all knowledge. Bacon proposes a program of educational and scientific reform based on the idea that true knowledge depends on experiment and observation, not the speculative generalizing characteristic of scholasticism. Bacon's philosophy contributes to the development of the scientific method. *See also* 1620, PHIL.   PHIL

1608   French aristocrat Catherine d'Angennes, marquise de Rambouillet, founds the first literary salon as she begins to receive Paris intellectuals in her home. Widely imitated and open to both women and men, the conversation and opinions at her salon exert a strong influence on French literature of the day. CRIT

1608   In Holland, English clergyman John Smith founds the Baptist denomination, which believes in baptism of adult believers only, by total immersion. REL

1609   English philosopher Francis Bacon publishes the Latin work on classical mythology *De Sapientia Veterum* (*The Wisdom of the Ancients*).   PHIL

1610–1695   Chinese scholar Huang Zongxi lives. As a historian (e.g., *History of the Ming*), he values objective treatments of recent events. As a political theorist (e.g., *A Plan for the Prince*), he critiques the Chinese dynastic system. He also compiles collections of neo-Confucian philosphy and argues for universal education.   MISC

1610   English metaphysical poet John Donne publishes his most important prose work, *Pseudo-Martyr,* which encourages English Roman Catholics to become Anglicans. In 1615, Donne, once a notorious rake and writer of love poems, will become an Anglican minister and will devote himself to religious verse and prose works, including sermons.   REL

1611   The King James, or authorized, version of the Bible is published. Commissioned by England's King James I and much esteemed for the eloquence and beauty of its style, it becomes the definitive English translation for Protestants. *See also* 1525, REL.   REL

1611   English clergyman John Smith founds the first Baptist church in London (considered "General Baptists"; *see* 1633, REL).   REL

1614   English courtier, navigator, historian, and poet Sir Walter Raleigh publishes the first volume of his *History of the World,* the only volume he will be able to complete while captive in the Tower of London following his fall from political favor.   HIST

1614   The existence of a Rosicrucian society is first noted in the work *Fama fraternitas*, possibly by Johan Valentin Andrea. Persisting for centuries, the esoteric occult order will influence the work of 20th-century Irish poet William Butler Yeats. The movement will eventually splinter into several different societies.   REL

1615   English historian William Camden publishes *Annals of the Reign of Elizabeth to 1588*. In researching this work, he was permitted access to official state papers, an uncommon thing at the time. He will be seen as the greatest historian of his period. *See also* 1586, HIST.   HIST

1618   The Maurists, a congregation of Benedictine monks, is founded in France. The group will produce, particularly in the late 1600s and early 1700s, a vast amount of ecclesiastical history of a very high quality.   HIST

1618–1680   Bohemian-born English philosopher Elizabeth of Bohemia lives. She is known for her correspondence with French philosopher René Descartes.   PHIL

1618–1619   The Remonstrants, Dutch adherents of the modified Calvinism of Jacobus Arminius (*see* 1603, REL), are legally suppressed by the Dutch Reformed Church in the Netherlands. Their persecution will end in 1625.   REL

1618–1648   The Thirty Years War rages in Europe between German Protestant princes and their allies (including England, France, Sweden, Denmark, and the United Provinces of the Netherlands) against the Holy Roman Empire and Catholic German princes. Beginning with a Protestant uprising in Prague, Bohemia, the war devastates Germany and greatly weakens the Holy Roman Empire. Catholic France emerges as the greatest power on the continent.   REL

1620   German composer and music historian Michael Praetorius completes *Syntagma musicum*, a three-volume work containing information on the musical instruments and practices of the early 17th century.   CRIT

1620   English philosopher Francis Bacon writes the Latin work *Novum Organum* (*New Instrument*), which forms the second part of his projected *Instauratio Magna* (*see* 1605, PHIL). In it, Bacon adds inductive reasoning to the tools of deductive inquiry outlined in Greek philosopher Aristotle's treatises of logic known as the *Organum* (*Instrument*).   PHIL

c. 1620   In North America, five tribes form the Iroquois Confederacy to provide a united front in warfare and politics. The tribes include the Mohawk, Seneca, Onondaga, Oneida, Cayuga, and beginning around 1722, the Tuscarora. They will split loyalties between the British and the Americans during the American Revolution.   POL

1620	Leaders of the newly settled Plymouth Colony in Massachusetts write the Mayflower Compact, a social contract that attempts to form the basis for a "civil Body Politick." POL
1620	The Pilgrims, a community of English Puritans, found a theocratic colony at Plymouth Rock, Massachusetts. They usher in a long tradition of Calvinist religion and Calvinist-inspired thought in what will become the United States. REL
1621	English writer Robert Burton publishes *The Anatomy of Melancholy*, a serio-comic, paramedical study of melancholy, with many erudite digressions on religion, politics, and many other matters. PHIL
1622	English philosopher Francis Bacon publishes *History of Henry VII*, a scholarly work which is perhaps the finest historical biography published so far. HIST
1622	The Congregation for the Propagation of the Faith, a Catholic missionary organization, is founded by Pope Gregory XV. REL
1624	English philosopher Francis Bacon publishes *Apophthegmes New and Old*. PHIL
1624	French philosopher and mathematician Pierre Gassendi publishes *Exercises Against the Aristotelians*, in which he develops a philosophical position of mitigated skepticism and openness to scientific investigation. PHIL
1624–1669	Dutch philosopher Arnold Geulincx lives. He takes an occasionalist position, arguing that there is no causal link between mind and body. PHIL
1625	French mathematician Marin Mersenne publishes *The Truth of Science Against the Skeptics or Pyrrhonians*, in which he argues against the Skepticism that began with Greek philosopher Pyrrho. PHIL
1625	Dutch scholar Huigh de Groot, known as Hugo Grotius, publishes *The Laws of War and Peace*, a work that will earn him the reputation of the father of modern international law. POL
1627	*The New Atlantis*, an unfinished Utopian fiction in Latin by English philosopher Francis Bacon, is published posthumously. PHIL
1628–1632	In his *Didactica Magna*, Moravian educator and theologian Johann Amos Comenius advocates the systematization of knowledge, teaching in the vernacular language, and the opening of educational opportunities to women. EDUC
1628–1700	Japanese scholar Tokugawa Mitsukuni lives. He founds the Mito school, which encourages Japanese nationalism through historical studies documenting the

legitimacy of the Japanese emperor. The school's major historical work is *Dai Nihonshi* (*History of Japan*). HIST

1630–1650   American religious and colonial leader William Bradford writes *History of Plimouth Plantation*, probably the first history of an American colony. HIST

1630   While a thousand Puritans sail to the the new land of America from England, their leader, John Winthrop, presents "A Model of Christian Charity," which details their covenant of love and tolerance. Their godly reward for upholding the covenant will be that the settlement will be considered a hallowed "city on a hill," due respect and emulation. The phrase will come to represent an idealized America. POL

1632   The Dordrecht Confession of Faith, issued in Holland, codifies Mennonite beliefs. *See also* 1536, REL. REL

1633   *The Temple*, a collection of religious poetry by English priest and Metaphysical poet George Herbert, is published posthumously. REL

1633   In England, the Particular Baptists are founded. Unlike General Baptists (*see* 1611, REL), they are Calvinists who believe the atonement of Christ is efficacious only for elect individuals, not all people generally. REL

1633   Italian scientist Galileo Galilei, called before the Inquisition in Rome on charges of heresy, recants his support for the Copernican heliocentric hypothesis (*see* 1543, MISC). The spectacle of scientific discovery being forced to bow to religious dogma will long remain a paradigm for conflicts between religion and science. REL

1636   Harvard, the first American college, is founded. EDUC

1636   American clergyman Roger Williams establishes Providence, later the capital of Rhode Island, as a haven for religious dissenters following his banishment from Massachusetts Bay Colony by the Puritans. In 1639, he will found the first American Baptist Church. REL

1637   French philosopher René Descartes, who will be known as the father of modern philosophy, publishes *Discourse on Method*. In this and other works (*see* 1641 and 1649, PHIL), he expounds his theory of knowledge, which begins with universal doubt, and develops the assertion *Cogito ergo sum* (I think, therefore I am). His metaphysics poses a dualistic separation between mind and matter, presenting a mind-body problem that will bedevil philosophers indefinitely. Other aspects of his thought, such as his belief in the validity of "clear and distinct ideas" and his proofs of God's existence, will also provide a framework for future philosophers, including those who adamantly oppose him. PHIL

1638
English theologian William Chillingworth publishes *The Religion of Protestants a Safe Way to Salvation*, a defense of the Protestant belief in the sole authority of the Bible and the legitimacy of individual interpretation. REL

1639–1723
American clergyman Increase Mather lives. He will influence the establishment of Puritanism as a dominant American tradition. His books include *Cases of Conscience Concerning Evil Spirits* (1693), about the Salem Witch Trials. He is the father of American clergyman Cotton Mather. REL

1640
English writer Izaak Walton publishes *The Life of John Donne*, the first in his "Brief Lives" series of short biographies. Walton gives a vivid impression of what each of his subjects was like by drawing on their own writings (especially letters) as well as on anecdotes contributed by others. HIST

1640
The treatise *Augustinus* by Dutch Catholic theologian Cornelis Jansen is posthumously published. Advocating greater personal sanctity, discouraging frequent communion, and taking an extreme stand on predestination, the book becomes the basis for a movement (known as Jansenism) that will be attacked by the church in papal bulls in 1705 and 1713. REL

1641
French philosopher René Descartes publishes *Meditations on First Philosophy* and *Objections and Replies*. The latter contains objections by his contemporaries, including Johan de Kater, Mersenne, Hobbes, Arnauld, and Gassendi, and Descartes's responses. More objections, from Jesuit philosopher Pierre Bourdin, will follow in the second edition (1642). PHIL

1641
The Mongol prince who rules Tibet grants temporal and spiritual control of the Buddhist region to the fifth grand lama ("superior one"), known as the Dalai Lama. While the Dalai Lama will retain temporal control, spiritual authority will reside in the Panchen Lama, chief abbot of the Zhaxilhünbo monastery. Direct reincarnation is believed to be the vehicle for succession to either position. REL

1641
English poet John Milton publishes three pamphlets supporting the Presbyterian cause by attacking the Anglican church's episcopal form of government: *Of Reformation Touching Church Discipline in England*, *Of Prelatical Episcopacy*, and *Animadversions Upon the Remonstrant's Defence Against Smectymnuus*. REL

1642–1649
The English Civil War is fought. Parliament's victorious struggle for power against King Charles I is an important step in the development of constitutional restraints on monarchical authority. It also confirms the growing economic power of the middle class and will contribute to increased toleration for Protestant dissenters. Generally, Puritans and Presbyterians favor the Parliamentary side; Anglicans and Catholics the royal side. POL

1642	English physician and writer Sir Thomas Browne publishes *Religio Medici* (*A Doctor's Faith*), a prose masterpiece in which the author examines his own religious beliefs. REL
1643	English poet John Milton publishes a series of pamphlets arguing that divorce on grounds of incompatibility is legitimate. He writes these shortly after his wife abandons him; she will later return. SOC
1644	English poet John Milton publishes *Areopagitica*, a classical oration in favor of freedom of the press, and the treatise *Tractate of Education*. JOURN
1644–1911	During the Ch'ing (Manchu) dynasty in China, many encyclopedias, compendia, and works of literary and philological scholarship are composed. MISC
1644	French philosopher and mathematician Pierre Gassendi publishes *Disquisitio Metaphysica*, an expanded version of his objections to Descartes's *Meditations*. PHIL
1645	English theologian John Biddle publishes *Twelve Arguments Drawn Out of Scripture*, in which he rejects the Christian doctrine of the trinity. Biddle is the father of Unitarianism, which states that God exists in one being and which affirms reason, conscience, universal brotherhood, and religious toleration. REL
1646	English statesman and historian Edward Hyde, earl of Clarendon, begins writing *History of the Rebellion and Civil Wars in England*, a well-crafted work that covers events in which he himself has participated. HIST
1646	English physician and writer Sir Thomas Browne publishes *Pseudodoxia Epidemica* (*Vulgar Errors*), a compendium of delusive beliefs with accompanying refutations. PHIL
1646	English Calvinist philosopher Nathanael Culverwel publishes *An Elegant and Learned Discourse of the Light of Nature*. PHIL
1646	In England, the Long Parliament establishes Presbyterianism as the official religion, which it will remain until the restoration of the monarchy in 1660. REL
1647	In Massachusetts, a law is passed requiring towns with a population of 50 or more to maintain schools. These schools provide lessons in reading, writing, and counting, and studies in classical languages and literature. EDUC
c. 1647	English religious reformer George Fox founds the Society of Friends (Quakers), a quietist, pacifist movement that teaches revelation through the "inner light" available to each person. REL

1647   The Westminster Confession of Faith is set forth. It will be widely accepted by
            Presbyterians around the world.   REL

1648–1649   Ukrainian Cossacks, led by Bohdan Khmelnytsky, torture and kill vast num-
            bers of Jews, whom they view as collaborators with the Polish masters of the
            Ukraine. The Khmelnytsky massacres usher in waves of persecution against
            Polish Jews that will last until the next century, culminating in more massacres
            in 1768. In one ten–year period (1648–1658), an estimated 100,000 Jews are
            killed.   REL

1648   Jewish mystic Shabbetai Tzevi proclaims himself the Messiah and claims that the
            millennium will come in 1666. After attracting many followers, he will be cap-
            tured in Constantinople (Istanbul) in 1666, when he will convert to Islam to
            avoid death.   REL

1649   Spanish painter Francisco Pacheco publishes *The Art of Painting*, a work pro-
            viding important information on the careers of Spanish painters.   CRIT

1649   French philosopher René Descartes publishes *The Passions of the Soul*.   PHIL

1649   English poet John Milton publishes *The Tenure of Kings and Magistrates* and
            Eikonoklastes, pamphlets attacking monarchy and justifying the execution that
            year of English king Charles I.   POL

1651   English philosopher Thomas Hobbes publishes *Leviathan*, which offers a ratio-
            nalistic basis for the establishment of governments. Hobbes claims that peo-
            ple willingly submit to absolute authority to protect themselves from each
            other's aggression and greed. With this work, Hobbes will become recognized
            as one of the fathers of political science.   POL

1653   English writer Izaak Walton publishes *The Compleat Angler*, a treatise on fishes
            and fishing that is also a meditation on peace and simple virtue.   PHIL

1653   In India, the Sthanakavasis, a Jainist reform movement, condemns image wor-
            ship and temple worship.   REL

1654   Swedish queen Christina abdicates. In the years until her death in 1689, she
            will be known as an atheist, an ethical philosopher, and a correspondent of
            French philosopher René Descartes and Dutch scholar Hugo Grotius.   PHIL

1656   English historian Sir William Dugdale publishes *Antiquities of Warwickshire*, a
            local history that will serve as a model for British county and shire historians
            for centuries to come. In 1673, he will complete publication, with the assis-
            tance of Roger Dodsworth, of *Monasticon Anglicanum*, a massive history of
            medieval English religious life.   HIST

1656	Dutch Jewish philosopher Baruch Spinoza is condemned as a heretic for his pantheistic views and banished from the synagogue. *See also* 1677, PHIL. PHIL

1656–1680   Native American holy woman Kateri Tekakwitha lives. The daughter of a Mohawk chief, she converts to Roman Catholicism in childhood and is rejected by her tribe. After moving to a Canadian mission, she becomes known for her piety and asceticism.   REL

1658   Moravian educator and theologian Johann Amos Comenius emphasizes the presentation of educational material in accordance with a child's developmental stages. He also introduces the planned school year and group instruction formats.   EDUC

1658   English physician and writer Sir Thomas Browne publishes *Hydriotaphia: Urne-Buriall*, a discussion of funeral practices that develops into a meditation on life and death, and *The Garden of Cyrus*, a treatise on the quincunx, a particular kind of five-spot pattern.   PHIL

1658–1707   Mughal emperor Aurangzeb lives. During his reign, Hindu scholars lead a conservative reaction against unorthodox forms of Hinduism.   REL

1659   Spanish philosopher Antonio Diana, known as the "prince of casuists," publishes *Resolutiones morales*, in which he analyzes 20,000 moral cases or situa-

Thomas Hobbes

In his best-known work, *Leviathan* (1651), English philosopher Thomas Hobbes pits "every man against every man" in a life that is "nasty, brutish and short." Yet Hobbes lived a long and distinguished life of 91 years. He was a stellar student at Oxford, after which he entered into nearly lifelong employment with William Cavendish, third earl of Devonshire. His association with Cavendish led him to travels that introduced him to the leading figures of the time, including Bacon, Harvey, Galileo, and Ben Jonson. He published widely, including the trilogy *Elements of Philosophy* (*De cive*, 1642; *De corpore*, 1655, *De homine*, 1658). Although the 1651 publication of *Leviathan* brought the specter of prosecution by Charles II for its challenge to the divine right of kings and the call for religious independence, he lived without incident (except for shocking some of his friends) long afterward.

He spent the last years of his life at the home of the earl of Devonshire, working primarily on translations. Despite his successes, he remained guarded about expressing pleasure at a long, fruitful life, allegedly saying only that he was "91 years finding a hole to go out of this world, and at length found it."

tions. Casuistry is an ethical approach that holds that the circumstances of cases affect the application of general principles. PHIL

1660s The quick delivery of news has its beginnings with the regular publication of newspapers in Europe. JOURN

1660 In protest of the impending restoration of the English monarchy, English poet John Milton publishes the pamphlet *The Ready and Easy Way to Establish a Free Commonwealth.* After the crown is restored this year, Milton's works are publicly burned and Milton is imprisoned and fined. POL

1660 With the restoration of the English monarchy under Charles II, the episcopacy is restored in England. REL

1661 English philosopher Joseph Glanvill publishes *The Vanity of Dogmatizing,* in which he distinguishes between ideal science and actual understanding. PHIL

1661–1665 In England, the Clarendon Codes are enacted, strictly suppressing the Catholic and Presbyterian denominations in favor of the Church of England. The Act of Uniformity (1662) requires all Christians to follow the Book of Common Prayer. REL

1662 English clergyman Thomas Fuller's *The History of the Worthies of England* is published by Fuller's son. English antiquary Anthony à Wood will publish *Athenae Oxonienses: an Exact History of All the Writers and Bishops Who Have Had Their Education in the University of Oxford from 1500 to 1690* in 1691 and 1692. Biographical collections are popular in 17th-century England, and these books are exemplary works of the genre. HIST

1662–1722 In China, during the reign of K'ang-hsi (Hsüan-yeh), the last of a monumental series of dictionaries is produced. LING

1662 A new revision of the Book of Common Prayer is made compulsory in England by an Act of Uniformity. The book had been suppressed under the Commonwealth and Protectorate (1645–1660). REL

1663 The Académie des Inscriptions is founded in France. It will develop a collection of classical and national antiquities. HIST

1663 English philosopher Edward Herbert, first baron of Cherbury, posthumously publishes an early work of comparative religion, *On the Religion of the Gentiles.* Herbert will be known as the father of deism, the view that there is a natural religion available to reason, and that this religion gives assurance of God's existence while excluding any need for revelation or dogma. *See also* 1696, REL. REL

1666	English Nonconformist preacher and writer John Bunyan publishes his spiritual autobiography, *Grace Abounding to the Chief of Sinners*. REL
1666–1708	In the Punjab, Sikh leader Govind Singh lives. The last of the line of ten gurus beginning with Sikh founder Nanak (*see* 1469–1539, REL), Singh organizes the Sikhs to oppose Islam militarily and introduces the practices of wearing turbans and not cutting the hair. REL
1667	English writer Margaret Lucas publishes *The Life of William Cavendishe, Duke of Newcastle*, a colorful biography of her husband, an English soldier and royalist. Around this time, Lucy Hutchinson will write a biography of her husband, John, a Puritan leader and English statesman, which will challenge prevalent stereotypes about Puritans. They are among the first women in England to write history. HIST
1667	English poet John Milton publishes his masterpiece *Paradise Lost*, a blank-verse epic on the Fall of Man and the expulsion of Adam and Eve from Eden. The work proposes to "justify the ways of God to men." An expanded edition will appear in 1674; a companion work, *Paradise Regained*, on the temptations of Christ, will appear in 1671. REL
1667–1677	In Nepal, the Sherpa temples of Pangboche, Thami, and Rimijung are founded. REL
1668	English poet and dramatist John Dryden publishes the critical work *Essay of Dramatic Poesy*. CRIT
1668	English prelate Thomas Sprat publishes *An Account of the Life and Writings of Mr. Abraham Cowley*, the first English-language biography of a significant literary figure. CRIT
1668	English poet Abraham Cowley's *Several Discourses by Way of Essays, in Verse and Prose*, is published posthumously. PHIL
1670	Dutch Jewish philosopher Baruch Spinoza publishes *A Treatise on Religious and Political Philosophy*. PHIL
1670	German theologian Philipp Jacob Spener holds devotional meetings that mark the foundation of German Pietism. Originating in the Lutheran church, this movement deemphasizes doctrine in favor of Bible study and genuine faith. REL
1670	*Pensées*, a devotional work by French scientist and philosopher Blaise Pascal, is published posthumously. The work introduces the view known as Pascal's wager, which argues that nothing is lost by believing in God but potentially

much is gained. Pascal is also known for founding probability theory and for defending Jansenism (*see* 1640, REL) in *Provincial Letters* (1656).   REL

1672   Italian art historian Giovanni Pietro Bellori writes *The Idea of the Painter, Sculptor and Architect*, a critical study of art that asserts the antique as a model for value judgment. The book will greatly influence French academic theory and become the theoretical foundation of neoclassicism as developed by German archaeologist and art critic Johann Winckelmann (*see* 1764, CRIT). CRIT

1672   German philosopher and historian Samuel von Pufendorf publishes *Of the Law of Nature and Nations*.   PHIL

1672   English rationalist philosopher Richard Cumberland publishes *Of the Laws of Nature*, in which he tries to refute English philosopher Thomas Hobbes's theory of law.   PHIL

1673   French philosopher Simon Foucher, a critic of French philosopher René Descartes, publishes *Critique de la recherche de la vérité*.   PHIL

1673   English poet John Milton publishes *Of True Religion, Heresy, Schism, and Toleration*.   REL

1674   French critic and poet Nicolas Boileau-Despréaux publishes the didactic poem *L'Art poétique*, in which he expresses and helps define the aesthetics of 17th-century French classicism. An arbiter of poetic taste in his day, Boileau translates Longinus's treatise *On the Sublime* and often uses the phrase *je ne sais quoi* to refer to the distinctive quality of a great work of art.   CRIT

1674–1675   French philosopher Nicolas de Malebranche publishes *On the Search for Truth*, which builds on and extends Cartesian theory.   PHIL

c. 1675   Italian writer G. B. Passeri describes the personal merits of painters who died between 1641 and 1673 in terms of manner, taste, knowledge, and expression in his *Vite*.   CRIT

1677   *Ethics*, the major work of Dutch Jewish philosopher Baruch Spinoza, is published posthumously. Highly respected by many philosophers of his day, Spinoza adopted a rationalist, monist, pantheistic approach. He argued that mind and body are two different aspects of a single substance that can be considered God or Nature. Though denying the possibility of free will, he advanced an ethics founded in the "intellectual love of God."   PHIL

1678   English philosopher Ralph Cudworth publishes *The True Intellectual System of the Universe*. He is a leader of the Cambridge Platonists, who also include Henry

More and Benjamin Whichcote, and who return to Platonic thinking to develop mystical and ethical themes.   PHIL

1678   English preacher and writer John Bunyan publishes his masterpiece, *The Pilgrim's Progress*, a Christian allegory written during his imprisonment for Nonconformist preaching.   REL

1679   French prelate Jacques Bossuet writes *Discours sur l'histoire universelle*, in which he views history as being invariably governed by Providence. *Discours* is one of the first philosophies of history.   HIST

1679–1714   Scottish prelate and historian Gilbert Burnet publishes his three-volume *History of the Reformation*. His *History of His Own Time* will appear posthumously (1724–1734). Burnet displays his strong anti-Catholic bias in his writing, a bias also reflected in his religious and political activism.   HIST

1679   French philosopher and theologian Antoine Arnauld is forced into exile in Belgium for his controversial Jansenist views (*see* 1640, REL). He is the author of the *Port-Royal Logic* and *On True and False Ideas*. The latter attacks French philosopher Nicolas de Malebranche's representationalist views.   PHIL

1680s   In England, the Tory party forms, composed largely of supporters of Catholic monarch James II. The rural, conservative party of foreign nonintervention will break up during the reign of George I (1660–1717) but will be rebuilt in 1789 and will take and hold power until 1830.   POL

1680   Based on notes made at the Academie, French writer Henri Testelin publishes *Opinions of the Most Skilled Painters on the Practice of Painting and Sculpture Put into a Table of Rules*, a systematic outline concerning composition, line, color, and the expression of emotion. His rules will become guides to quality for both artists and critics.   CRIT

1681   French scholar Jean Mabillon completes *De re diplomatica*, in which he sets out standards for determining the authenticity and date of historical documents. Mabillon will come to be viewed as the greatest of the Maurist scholars (*see* 1618, HIST) and the founder of Latin paleography.   HIST

1681–1682   English poet and dramatist John Dryden critiques contemporary religion, poetry, and politics in such poetic works as *Absalom and Achitophel* (1681), *Mac Flecknoe* (1682), and *Religio Laici* (1682).   MISC

1682   French Jesuit Claude-François Menestrier writes the first history of the ballet.   CRIT

1682   French king Louis XIV presents the Gallican Articles, which definitively outline the aims of the French Catholic Gallican movement to separate itself from the pope and the powers of the church. Gallicanism has been an active force since the 14th century.   REL

c. 1684   Persecuted in New England, a group of Baptists move from Maine to Charleston, South Carolina.   REL

1685   French architect and writer André Félibien's *Entretiens* provides one of the first theories of connoisseurship. He promotes the examination of a number of works of art to acquire thorough critical judgment.   CRIT

1685   French king Louis XIV revokes the Edict of Nantes (*see* 1598, REL), thereby formally depriving French Protestants of freedom of religion. The edict had already been weakened by years of continuing persecution.   REL

1688   French philosopher Nicolas de Malebranche publishes *Dialogues on Metaphysics and Religion*.   PHIL

1688   The Glorious Revolution takes place in England as King James II is deposed and William III and Mary II take his place. The revolution ensures that the royal throne will not be held by Roman Catholics and, with the passage of the Bill of Rights in 1689, assures that Parliament will have power over the monarchy.   POL

1689   In Britain, the Act of Toleration gives rights to dissenters from the Church of England, and English philosopher John Locke publishes *Letter on Toleration*, which espouses religious toleration (though not for Roman Catholics).   REL

1690   *The New England Primer*, which will become a popular children's textbook in the American colonies, is published.   EDUC

1690   In *Essay Concerning Human Understanding*, English philosopher John Locke opposes belief in innate ideas, arguing instead that the mind at birth is a "blank slate" that acquires all knowledge from experience (empiricism). Locke's ideas will influence British empiricist philosophers David Hume and George Berkeley and form the basis for the 20th-century American psychological school of behaviorism.   PHIL

1690   English philosopher John Locke publishes *Two Treatises on Civil Government*, a seminal work of political science. Locke argues that people are born equal, free, and with certain inalienable rights, and that they form a "social contract" to guarantee those rights. His views will influence centuries of democratic theory and practice, particularly in the American Declaration of Independence (1776) and Constitution (1789).   POL

1692   The notebooks of vitalist philosopher Lady Anne Finch Conway are published posthumously under the title *The Principles of the Most Ancient and Modern Philosophy*. Conway's work will influence German philosopher and mathematician Gottfried Wilhelm Leibniz's theory of monads (*see* 1710, PHIL).   PHIL

1693   English critic John Dennis writes *The Impartial Critick*. In this and other works, such as *The Grounds of Criticism in Poetry* (1704), he argues for the observance of classical rules as a way of fulfilling the moral purpose of art.   CRIT

1695–1697   French skeptical philosopher Pierre Bayle publishes *A General Dictionary, Historical and Critical*, in which he reviews the lives of religious and philosophical figures from a satirical, skeptical standpoint.   PHIL

1696   English philosopher Damaris Masham, a friend of English philosopher John Locke and German philosopher and mathematician Gottfried Wilhelm Leibniz and a proponent of education for women, publishes *A Discourse Concerning the Love of God*. Her other works include *Occasional Thoughts in Reference to a Christian Life* (1694).   PHIL

1696   Irish-born British philosopher John Toland publishes the deist work *Christianity not Mysterious*, in which he asserts that human reason is capable of comprehending God; the book will be burned in Ireland the following year. Deism, however, will remain influential throughout the 18th century. *See also* 1663, REL.   REL

1698   The Church of England founds the Society for Promoting Christian Knowledge as a missionary and educational arm. The Society for the Propagation of the Gospel in Foreign Parts will follow in 1701.   REL

1699   French writer Florent Le Comte writes *Cabinet des Singularitez*, which seeks to distinguish great works of art from average ones by following French architect and writer André Félibien's methods of connoisseurship (*see* 1685, CRIT). He counts three schools of quattrocento Italian painting and four different manners of Greek art.   CRIT

1699   Sikh leader Govind Singh (*see* 1666–1708, REL) organizes the Khalsa, a Sikh order combining religious, military, and social aspects.   REL

1700s   Biographical dictionaries that attempt comprehensiveness are published in England, including *Biographia Britannica* (1747–1760). Literary biographical dictionaries include *The Lives of the Poets of Great Britain and Ireland* (1753), Horace Walpole's *A Catalogue of the Royal and Noble Authors of England, Scotland and Ireland* (1758), and David Rivers's *Literary Memoirs of Living Authors of Great Britain* (1798).   HIST

1700s
An increasing interest in the development of science and medicine is reflected in the publication of such specialized British biographical dictionaries as John Aikin's *Biographical Memoirs of Medicine in Great Britain* (1780) and Benjamin Hutchinson's *Biographia Medica* (1789).   HIST

1700s
The period known as the Enlightenment comes into full flower in Europe and America during this century. Also known as the Age of Reason, it is characterized by liberal, rationalist, scientific ideals, with faith in progress and a mistrust of traditional religious and political institutions.   MISC

1700s
In Japan, new schools of thought critique the reigning philosophy of Sushigaku (*see* 1603–1867, PHIL) and emphasize Japanese nationality. They include the Yōmeigaku school, which teaches an individualist form of Confucianism, and the National Learning, or Kokugaku, school, which urges restoration of pure Japanese culture.   PHIL

1700s
The political philosophy of liberalism gains popularity on the European continent. It is fueled by the ideal of change as a path to perfection, and has as its basic stances the need for limited government interaction and increased individual rights. The economic disparity that will be brought on by the Industrial Revolution will transform the movement by the 20th century.   POL

1700s
In Shiite Muslim domains such as Persia (Iran), the Usuli school of law is revived, while a new movement, the Shaykhiyya, emphasizes mystical interpretation of sacred texts.   REL

1700s
The Asante (or Ashanti) people of Ghana are unified under king Osei Tutu. Legend has it that his throne was a "golden stool" that came down from heaven. The stool—made of wood covered with gold leaf and ornaments—will survive to modern times as a sacred relic used during the installation of kings.   REL

1700
English poet and dramatist John Dryden publishes his last major work, *Fables, Ancient and Modern*, which is prefaced by a much-respected critical essay.   CRIT

1700
French writer Roger de Piles publishes his *Idée*, a work that defines for the first time in art history the Middle Ages as a period from 611 until 1450.   CRIT

1700
French dancer and choreographer Raoul-Auger Feuillet publishes *Choreography, or the Art of Describing Dance*, a system of dance notation.   CRIT

c. 1700–1750
In Japan, the Ancient Learning (Kogaku) school rejects the metaphysical claims of neo-Confucianism for the more empirical approach of the ancient Chinese classics. The school's rational spirit is embodied in the teachings of Itō Jinsai and Ogyū Sorai.   PHIL

1700–1760	Polish rabbi Israel ben Eliezer, known as the Ba´al Shem Tov (Master of the Good Name), lives. Reputedly a miracle healer, he is the founder of the Hasidic movement, which advocates striving for communion with God through a spirit of joyfulness in all activities. The movement attracts many followers, especially in eastern and central Europe. REL
1702	The daily newspaper debuts in England with the publication of *The Daily Courant*. JOURN
1702	English dramatist and philosopher Catherine Clarke publishes a defense of English philosopher John Locke; she will also publish a defense of English philosopher Samuel Clarke (1747). PHIL
1702	English journalist and novelist Daniel Defoe publishes the satirical pamphlet *The Shortest Way with the Dissenters*, for which he is fined, imprisoned, and pilloried. REL
1702	American clergyman Cotton Mather writes *Magnalia Christi Americana*, a history of the Church in New England that sparks a religious renaissance in the colonies. REL
1703–1762	Indian Muslim theologian Shah Wali Allah lives. He argues for purification of Islam, including stricter limits on Sufism. REL
1703–1792	Arab religious reformer Muhammad ibn Abd al-Wahhab lives. Advocating a return to traditional Islam and a rejection of many Sufi innovations, he helps to found a state (the Wahhabi state) based rigorously on the shariah, or Islamic law. REL
1704–1776	*The Boston News-Letter* is the first newspaper published in the American colonies to have an extended life. JOURN
1704	Clergyman and writer Jonathan Swift publishes *The Battle of the Books* and *A Tale of a Tub*, two satires on intellectual corruption. Born in Dublin of English parents, he was educated in Ireland and will work in both England and Ireland; although he will become an Irish patriot in his later years, he will be traditionally identified as English. PHIL
1704–1705	English philosopher Samuel Clarke delivers lectures purporting to demonstrate the existence of God and to derive morality from reason alone. PHIL
1705	Dutch-born English moral philosopher Bernard Mandeville publishes the first edition of *The Fable of the Bees*, which will be revised until reaching its final form in 1729. Arguing that public benefits, such as employment, can grow out

of private vices, such as vanity, the work will influence Scottish economist Adam Smith.   ECON

1706   Irish-born American clergyman church leader Francis Makemie founds the Presbyterian Church in America.   REL

1709–1711   English essayists Sir Richard Steele and Joseph Addison publish the thrice-weekly periodical *The Tatler*, which offers urbane, reasoned opinions on poetry, entertainment, and society.   JOURN

1709   Irish philosopher George Berkeley publishes *An Essay Towards a New Theory of Vision*, in which he agrees with English philosopher John Locke (*see* 1690, PHIL) that all knowledge comes from experience and depends on human perception.   PHIL

1710   Irish philosopher George Berkeley publishes *A Treatise Concerning the Principles of Human Knowledge*, which will be followed in 1713 by *Three Dialogues Between Hylas and Philonous*. Berkeley's radical idealism represents a challenge to empiricists such as English philosopher John Locke.   PHIL

1710   German philosopher and mathematician Gottfried Wilhelm Leibniz publishes *Theodicy*. In these and other works, including *Discourse of Metaphysics* (1685) and *Monadology* (1714), he develops a rationalist system in which he identifies "monads," immaterial individual unities, as the basic constituents of the cosmos. He is also known for the principle of sufficient reason, with the related view that this world is "the best of all possible worlds." *See also* 1759, PHIL, and 1765, PSYCH.   PHIL

1711   English poet Alexander Pope publishes *Essay on Criticism*, a didactic poem in the manner of Roman poet Horace.   CRIT

1711   English historian Thomas Madox publishes *History and Antiquities of the Exchequer of the Kings of England*, a pioneering study of British legal history.   HIST

1711–1712   English essayists Joseph Addison and Sir Richard Steele publish the daily periodical *The Spectator*, the successor to *The Tatler* (*see* 1709–1711, JOURN). Addison will revive it briefly in 1714.   JOURN

1711   English moral philosopher Anthony Ashley Cooper, third earl of Shaftesbury, publishes *Characteristiks of Men, Manners, Opinions, Times*, which includes "Inquiry Concerning Virtue," written in 1699. The latter work introduces the phrase the "moral sense," which becomes central to the doctrine of sentimentalism, the view that ethics is founded on human sentiment or emotion. Cooper and Scottish philosophers Francis Hutcheson and David Hume will all promote this view.   PHIL

1711   British churchman and satirist Jonathan Swift publishes the ironic *Argument Against Abolishing Christianity.*   REL

1712   By enacting a stamp tax on newspapers, England curtails the dissemination of knowledge to the lower classes.   JOURN

1713   In Britain, the Scriblerus Club is formed, an association of Tory writers and intellectuals, including Alexander Pope, Jonathan Swift, John Gay, Thomas Parnell, and John Arbuthnot.   CRIT

1713   English writer Anthony Collins publishes *Discourse of Freethinking Occasioned by the Rise and Growth of a Sect Called Freethinkers.* The work popularizes the ideas of those people who reject supernatural authority, relying instead on reason to reach conclusions about morality and religion. Freethinking will be an important movement of the Enlightenment, linked with deism in England and the United States and with anti-Christianity in France.   REL

1716   The Grand Lodge of England, the first modern freemasonry organization, is founded (*see* 1300s, REL). Its bylaws will be set down as *Anderson's Constitutions* (1723). The organization, which will expand worldwide, is marked by a vow of secrecy taken by all members, elaborate rituals and symbolism, and complex degrees of membership. In England, the United States, and continental Europe, freemasonry will long be associated with social prestige. It will be condemned by the Roman Catholic Church and totalitarian societies.   PHIL

1718   English critic Charles Gildon advocates strict neoclassicism in *The Complete Art of Poetry.*   CRIT

1719   English writer Jonathan Richardson describes in *Two Discourses* the methods of distinguishing hands of different painters simply by observing the works of art themselves.   CRIT

1719   German philosopher Christian von Wolff publishes *Rational Thoughts on God, the World, and the Souls of Men.* A popularizer of the philosophy of his compatriot Gottfried Wilhelm Leibniz (*see* 1710, PHIL), Wolff will be satirized as Dr. Pangloss in French philosopher Voltaire's *Candide* (1759).   PHIL

1720   In New Jersey, the American movement known as the Great Awakening begins, as revivalist sermons of Theodore Frelinghuysen arouse Protestant fervor. In the next two decades, various denominations across the colonies will be spiritually reinvigorated by fiery, mesmerizing speakers, notably Americans Jonathan Edwards, James Davenport, and Gilbert Tennent, and visiting English evangelist George Whitefield. The Great Awakening movement shifts American religion toward more emotion and direct experience. It will be associated with anti-intellectualism, a strain that will persist in America.   REL

1720–1797   Lithuanian Jewish leader Elijah ben Solomon lives. He opposes the spread of Hasidism in Lithuania and Poland because he believes the new groups may weaken the Jewish community. He is known for his commentaries on the Bible and Talmud.   REL

1721   Irish philosopher George Berkeley attacks English physicist Isaac Newton's philosophy of space in *On Motion*. He will revisit the topic in *The Analyst* (1734).   PHIL

1721   French political philosopher Charles-Louis de Secondat, baron de Montesquieu, publishes *The Persian Letters*, a satire on French social and political institutions.   POL

1722–1726   French composer Jean-Philippe Rameau publishes two influential treatises on harmony in which he introduces the theory of chord inversion.   CRIT

1724   Spanish painter Antonio Palomino publishes *El museo pictórico y escala óptica*, an important work on Spanish painting.   CRIT

1724   Regis chairs of history are established at Oxford and Cambridge universities by English king George I.   HIST

1724   British churchman and satirist Jonathan Swift publishes the *Drapier Letters*. The public letters urge the populace not to accept debased coinage from England, earning Swift a reputation as an Irish patriot.   POL

1725   Scottish philosopher Francis Hutcheson proposes a theory of the moral sense in *Inquiry into the Origins of Our Ideas of Beauty and Virtue*.   PHIL

1726   German writer Johann Friedrich Christ publishes *Leben Cranach*, the first analysis of the life of a single artist, German painter Lucas Cranach. Christ stresses that art criticism must be based on periods since a work of art and its purpose can only be judged in connection with the period in which it was made.   CRIT

1726   English theologian Joseph Butler publishes *Fifteen Sermons*, in which he develops a system of ethics based on his theory of human nature.   PHIL

1726   British churchman and satirist Jonathan Swift satirizes human society in his masterpiece, *Gulliver's Travels*, the fantastic tale of Dr. Lemuel Gulliver's adventures in Lilliput, Brobdingnag, Laputa, and Houyhnhnmland.   SOC

1728   English poet Alexander Pope publishes the mock-epic satire *The Dunciad*, in which he excoriates his literary enemies, particularly playwright and critic Lewis Theobald and playwright Colley Cibber. An expanded edition will appear in 1742.   CRIT

1728   Scottish scholar Ephraim Chambers publishes *Cyclopaedia, or An Universal Dictionary of Arts and Sciences*.   CRIT

1728   Italian goldsmith and sculptor Benvenuto Cellini's *Autobiography* is published. His book will become one of the most famous autobiographies ever written and an important source of information about life in Renaissance Italy.   HIST

1729   American statesman and scientist Benjamin Franklin takes over the periodical *The Pennsylvania Gazette*, imprinting it with his views and making it a success. The weekly will stay in print until 1815.   JOURN

1729–1786   German Jewish philosopher Moses Mendelssohn lives. He writes on religious, aesthetic, and other topics.   PHIL

1729   British churchman and satirist Jonathan Swift publishes the satirical pamphlet *A Modest Proposal*, which ironically advocates that the English eat the Irish.   POL

1729   English religious leader John Wesley, along with his brother Charles and English evangelist George Whitefield, founds the Methodist movement, so-called for its methodical devotion to religious study and duty. In 1738, Wesley will begin preaching intensively, emphasizing personal conversion and holiness. In his lifetime, Wesley will be said to have preached 40,000 sermons and traveled 250,000 miles. Methodism will later become independent from the Church of England (*see* 1784, REL).   REL

1730s   With the success of American statesman and scientist Benjamin Franklin, the Age of Franklin begins its decades-long span in American thought. It will be defined by reason and humanitarianism, and the rise of Philadelphia as an intellectual center of the colonies. *See also* 1732–1757, JOURN.   MISC

1730   The first American masonic lodge (*see* 1716, PHIL) is founded in Philadelphia; Benjamin Franklin is among its members.   PHIL

1730–1788   German philosopher and theologian Johann Georg Hamann lives. Arguing against the Enlightenment's emphasis on reason, he advocates a union of reason and emotion.   PHIL

1731   French writer Voltaire (François-Marie Arouet) publishes *Histoire de Charles XII*. He will publish *Le Siècle de Louis XIV* in 1751 and *L'Essai sur les moeurs* (*Essay on Morals*), a world history, in 1756. These three carefully researched books—critical of the people, institutions and events that they consider—will come to be seen as exemplary works of Enlightenment history.   HIST

1732   German organist and composer Johann Gottfried Walther publishes *Musicalisches Lexicon*, one of the first musical dictionaries.   CRIT

1732–1757   American statesman and scientist Benjamin Franklin publishes *Poor Richard's Almanack*, an annual compendium of practical information and plain thinking.
                                                                                    JOURN

1732–1734   German philosopher Baron Christian von Wolff develops rational psychology, a subdivision of empirical psychology that depends more on reason than experience.
                                                                                    PSYCH

1732–1791   Yemenite scholar Muhammad al-Murtadā lives. He writes an Arabic lexicon and commentaries on al-Ghazali and the Hadith.
                                                                                    REL

1733–1804   British clergyman and chemist Joseph Priestley lives. His scientific and philosophical writings provide a model to educational reformers for reshaping liberal education to encompass the sciences and the free pursuit of knowledge as well as classical liberal arts.
                                                                                    EDUC

1733   English poet Alexander Pope publishes the four poetic epistles of his *Essay on Man*, establishing himself as a philosophical and ethical poet.
                                                                                    PHIL

1734   French writer Voltaire publishes *Letters Concerning the English Nation*, which helps spur French interest in English philosophy, science, and liberal political ideas. Voltaire will be known for his tragedies, novels, and histories as well as his philosophical works, which express empiricist and deist views.
                                                                                    PHIL

1736   English theologian Joseph Butler publishes the theological work *The Analogy of Religion*.
                                                                                    PHIL

1739   Scottish philosopher David Hume publishes his major work, *A Treatise of Human Nature*, in which he carries empiricism to its logical conclusion of thorough skepticism. Arguing that all knowledge is based on sense impressions, he refutes the ideas of causation and substance. His skepticism will be highly influential, motivating both followers and opponents.
                                                                                    PHIL

1740   Italian violinist and composer Francesco Geminiani publishes *The Art of Playing on the Violin*, an important source for performance of late Baroque music.
                                                                                    CRIT

1740   English playwright Colley Cibber's autobiography contains much information on the theater of his time.
                                                                                    CRIT

1740   English evangelist George Whitefield breaks with the Arminian views of English church leader John Wesley to establish the Calvinist Methodist Church. *See also* 1603, REL.
                                                                                    REL

1740–1741   American Presbyterian clergyman Gilbert Tennent makes an evangelical tour of New England, during which he firmly establishes himself as a leading spokesman of the country's Great Awakening (*see* 1720, REL).   REL

1741   American theologian Jonathan Edwards publishes his sermon *Sinners in the Hands of an Angry God*, in which he describes the inadequacy of humankind and the absolute need for salvation by God. The work vividly describes the horrors of hell that await the unrepentant.   REL

1742–1744   English lawyer and writer Roger North publishes *Lives of the Norths*, biographies of his brothers Francis, Dudley, and John. The insight and vividness of North's writing help make these books one of the greatest biographical series of the 18th century.   HIST

1742   Scottish philosopher David Hume publishes *Essays Moral and Political*.   PHIL

1742–1799   German philosopher and scientist Georg Cristoph Lichtenberg lives. His notebooks, written throughout his adult years, contain aphorisms that will be much studied by later philosophers.   PHIL

1744   English writer and lexicographer Samuel Johnson publishes the first of his critical biographies, the life of his late friend, poet Richard Savage. Later biographies will include those of Sir Thomas Browne (1758) and Roger Ascham (1761). A collection of Johnson's *Lives of the Poets* will be published in 1779–1781.   CRIT

1744   Italian philosopher and historian Giambattista Vico publishes the third edition of his *The New Science*, in which he argues that the study of history is different from scientific and other forms of inquiry and that the historian should focus on the beliefs and feelings, the general outlook and spirit, prevalent in the period being studied.   HIST

1744   Irish philosopher George Berkeley writes on his philosophy of nature in *Siris*.   PHIL

1745   French writer A. J. Dezaillier provides a more exact definition of connoisseurship and distinguishes three larger schools, Italian, Flemish, and French, in *Abrégé des vies des peintres*.   CRIT

1745   French philosopher Julien de La Mettrie publishes *The Natural History of the Soul*. This and other works, among them *Man as Machine* (*see* 1748, PHIL), espouse an atheistic, materialistic philosophy.   PHIL

1746   French philosopher and encyclopedist Denis Diderot publishes *Pensées*.   PHIL

1746   French empiricist philosopher Étienne Bonnot de Condillac publishes *Essai sur l'origine des connaissances humaines* (*An Essay on the Origin of Human Knowledge*). His other works will include *Traité des sensations* (1754).   PHIL

1746   American theologian Jonathan Edwards publishes *A Treatise Concerning Religious Affections,* one of the first books on psychology (in relation to religion) written by an American. Edwards believes there is no free will and that all choices are made by God.   PSYCH

1747   Scottish philosopher Francis Hutcheson publishes *A Short Introduction to Moral Philosophy.*   PHIL

1748   French philosopher Julien de La Mettrie pioneers French materialism in *L'homme machine* (*Man as Machine*), in which he argues that body and soul are mortal and that life and thought result from the mechanical action of the nervous system.   PHIL

1748   Scottish philosopher David Hume publishes *An Enquiry Concerning Human Understanding.*   PHIL

1748   French political philosopher Charles-Louis de Secondat, baron de Montesquieu, publishes *On the Spirit of the Laws.* Montesquieu sympathizes with liberal ideals, in combination with aristocratic privilege, and takes an approach to law that might later be considered positivist.   POL

1749   English writer and lexicographer Samuel Johnson publishes a poetic meditation on ephemerality, *The Vanity of Human Wishes.*   PHIL

1749   French philosopher and encyclopedist Denis Diderot publishes *Lettre sur les aveugles,* in which he develops his materialistic philosophy while examining how the blind learn. This year he also publishes *Lettre sur les sourds et les muets,* a study of the deaf and mute that is also an aesthetic inquiry.   PHIL

1749   English philosopher and physician David Hartley publishes *Observations on Man, His Frame, His Duty, and His Expectations.* He is the founder of associationist psychology, which argues that there are discoverable laws governing the ways in which one conscious idea connects to another.   PSYCH

1749–1756   Swedish theologian and philosopher Emanuel Swedenborg publishes *Arcana Coelestis,* one of several works in which he propounds an influential system of mysticism and theosophy. After his death in 1772, his followers will found the New Church or New Jerusalem Church. English poet William Blake will be remembered for attacking Swedenborgian doctrines (*see* 1790, PHIL).   REL

1750s	In Pennsylvania, Quakers are encouraged to free their own slaves and to work for the emancipation of all slaves. SOC
1750–1758	German aesthetician Alexander Gottlieb Baumgarten publishes *Aesthetica Acroamatica*, in which he builds on a modified Leibnizian foundation. CRIT
1750	French philosopher and writer Jean-Jacques Rousseau attacks science and art as tools of the rich that undermine morality in his *Discours sur les arts et sciences*. CRIT
1750–1752	British writer and lexicographer Samuel Johnson publishes over 200 moral essays and commentaries for the twice-weekly periodical the *Rambler*. Later essays will be published under the title *The Idler*. JOURN
c. 1750	In Japan, interest in Western learning is fostered by the Rangaku (Dutch Studies) school, which focuses on study of European medical science, astronomy, weaponry, and technology. MISC
c. 1750	The Baule people, led by Queen Awura Pokou, emigrate from Ghana to the Ivory Coast, where they will remain. Their religious beliefs are symbolized by wooden masks, such as the *kple-kple* mask, representing Guli, spirit of the dead. REL
c. 1750–1800	In Africa, Gèlèdé masquerades begin among the Yoruba people. Involving wooden headpieces, dances, songs, and costumes, the ceremonies pay homage to women and to the cosmic forces they represent. REL
1751–1772	French philosopher and encyclopedist Denis Diderot and others compile the 28-volume *Encyclopédie ou Dictionnaire raisonné des sciences, des arts et des métiers*. The work is remarkable for its rational, secular, scientific approach. A five-volume supplement and two-volume index will be added by 1780. The "preliminary discourse" to the *Encyclopédie* (1751) is written by French philosopher and mathematician Jean Le Rond d'Alembert, coeditor of the work. MISC
1751	Scottish philosopher David Hume publishes *An Enquiry Concerning the Principles of Morals*. PHIL
1753	German composer Carl Philipp Emanuel Bach publishes the first part of *Essay on the True Art of Playing Keyboard Instruments*, an influential work essential to an understanding of 18th-century music. CRIT
1753–1825	Islamic historian Abd al-Rahman al-Jabarti lives. His chronicle includes biographies of both political and scholarly figures. HIST

1754–1762   Scottish philosopher David Hume publishes his multivolume *History of England*, a work that is highly regarded in its author's day but which, unlike Hume's philosophical writing, will not prove an enduring classic.   HIST

1754   French philosopher and writer Jean-Jacques Rousseau publishes *Discourse on the Inequalities of Men*, an innovative expression of his political thought, which will be developed further in *The Social Contract* (*see* 1762, POL).   POL

1754   The Albany Congress accepts American statesman and scientist Benjamin Franklin's Plan of Union to unite the American colonies during the French and Indian War. However, this early attempt at federal government is rejected by colonial legislatures and the British crown.   POL

1755   English writer and lexicographer Samuel Johnson publishes *A Dictionary of the English Language*, a lexicographical milestone compiled entirely by himself over the course of eight years.   LING

1755   The Separate Baptist church is founded in Sandy Creek, North Carolina, by Shubael Stearns and Daniel Marshall, who have migrated there from New England.   REL

1756   Irish-born British statesman and orator Edmund Burke publishes *A Philosophical Enquiry into the Origin of Our Ideas of the Sublime and Beautiful*, in which he explores the emotional basis of aesthetic response.   CRIT

1756–1767   French archaeologist Anne-Claude-Philippe de Tubières-Grimoard, Count of Caylus, publishes *Recueil d'antiquités*, a collection of reproductions of ancient works of art accompanied by detailed descriptions. He considers Egypt the real source of art and underscores a connection between history and fine art.   CRIT

1757   In his essay "Of the Standard of Taste," Scottish philosopher David Hume applies empiricist principles to aesthetic theory. This year he also publishes *The Natural History of Religion*. His *Dialogues Concerning Natural Religion* will be published posthumously in 1779.   CRIT

1758   French philosopher Claude-Adrien Helvétius publishes what will become his best-known work, *De l'esprit*, in which he rejects religion as a basis for morality, upholding the public interest instead. His views anticipate those of 19th-century utilitarian philosophers Jeremy Bentham and James Mill but are condemned in their time by the Sorbonne and the pope. The book will be publicly burned in 1759.   PHIL

1758   Croatian mathematician and scientist Ruggiero Boscovich publishes *A Theory of Natural Philosophy Reduced to a Single Law of the Actions Existing in Nature*. His work will influence the development of field theories in physics.   PHIL

1758   Welsh philosopher Richard Price publishes *A Review of the Principal Questions in Morals*, which counters prevailing empiricist views by taking a rationalist position.   PHIL

1759   Irish-born British playwright, poet, and novelist Oliver Goldsmith critiques contemporary scholarship and poetry in *An Inquiry into the Present State of Polite Learning in Europe*.   CRIT

1759–1781 French philosopher and encyclopedist Denis Diderot establishes the literary genre of art criticism with his essays *Salons*.   CRIT

1759   English poet Edward Young publishes *Conjectures on Original Composition*, in which he argues that originality is essential to literary genius.   CRIT

1759   Scottish historian William Robertson publishes *History of Scotland 1542–1603*. He will publish *History of the Reign of the Emperor Charles V* in 1769. These works will be considered two of the best 18th-century histories, perhaps to be surpassed only by Gibbon's *The History of the Decline and Fall of the Roman Empire* (*see* 1776–1788, HIST).   HIST

1759   Scottish economist Adam Smith publishes *The Theory of the Moral Sentiments*, which draws on Stoicism to emphasize self-command and sympathy in relation to ethics.   PHIL

1759   English writer and lexicographer Samuel Johnson publishes the philosophical romance *Rasselas*.   PHIL

1759   The term "optimism" is first used in English, to refer to the work of German philosopher and mathematician Gottfried Wilhelm Leibniz (*see* 1710, PHIL). The term "pessimism" will first be used by English poet and critic Samuel Taylor Coleridge in 1795.   PHIL

1759   French philosopher Voltaire writes the satirical novel *Candide, ou L'Optimisme*, an attack on the view of German philosopher and mathematician Gottfried Wilhelm Leibniz that this is the "best of all possible worlds." Dr. Pangloss, the pedantic tutor of the naive title character, is based on Leibniz and on German philosopher Christian von Wolff, who popularized Leibnitz's works (*see* 1710 and 1719, PHIL).   PHIL

1760s   English agriculturist Arthur Young uses questionnaires to survey the country's population. Questionnaires and case studies (also developed in this century) will become essential instruments of social science.   SOC

1760–1762 Dutch anatomist Pieter Camper publishes *Demonstrationum anatomico-pathologicarum*, a work comparing the anatomy of human races.   ANTH

1760	French dancer and choreographer Jean-Georges Noverre publishes the influential *Letters on the Dance and on Ballet in France*. CRIT
1760–1825	French social reformer Claude-Henri de Rouvroy, Comte de Saint-Simon lives. Considered one of the founders of socialism, he emphasizes the clash of economic classes, particularly in his journal *L'Industrie*. POL
1762	English prelate Richard Hurd publishes *Letters on Chivalry and Romance*, in which he praises the poetic qualities of the "Gothic" medieval imagination. CRIT
1762	German writer C. L. von Hagedorn publishes *Betrachtungen*, a work for young painters showing the history of art and featuring Jan van Eyck, Holbein, and Cranach. CRIT
1762	In *Émile*, French philosopher and writer Jean-Jacques Rousseau argues that women fulfill themselves through motherhood and that they should devote their lives to it. PHIL
1762	French philosopher and writer Jean-Jacques Rousseau publishes *The Social Contract*. In this and his other works of political theory (*see* 1754, POL), he argues that human nature is noble, civilization corrupts, the general will of the people is for the common good, and governments are established by social contract in an attempt to ensure the common good. POL
1762–1796	The Dukhobors, a newly formed Russian Christian sect, experiences persecution under Russian empress Catherine the Great. Like the Quakers, they believe in direct communication with God and reject priesthood and sacraments. They practice communal ownership of property and refuse military service. REL
1762	Irish-born British playwright, poet, and novelist Oliver Goldsmith publishes *Letters from a Citizen of the World*, a collection of satirical essays on British society from the point of view of a Chinese visitor. SOC
1762	French philosopher and encyclopedist Denis Diderot publishes *Rameau's Nephew*, a novelistic satire on contemporary society and the arts. SOC
1763–1764	*An Essay Towards Solving a Problem in the Doctrine of Chances* by English mathematician Thomas Bayes is published posthumously. It introduces Bayes's theorem, an important proposition in probability theory. PHIL
1764	German archaeologist and art critic Johann Winckelmann publishes the landmark *History of Art*, a mixture of theory and history with original interpretation of ancient works of art. He is the first art historian to replace the word "manner" with the term "style" to indicate the highest artistic achievement in a cer-

tain period. He declares Athens to be the birthplace of all art and the origin of good taste and ideal beauty. His works will be extremely influential in the development of neoclassicism.   CRIT

1764   French writer Voltaire publishes the satirical *Philosophical Dictionary*. Other works include *Essays on the Manners and Spirit of Nations* (1758).   PHIL

1764   Scottish philosopher Thomas Reid publishes *Enquiry into the Human Mind on the Principles of Common Sense*. He is the founder of the Scottish common-sense school of philosophy. Other works will include *Essays on the Intellectual Powers of Man* (1785) and *Essays on the Active Powers of Man* (1788).   PHIL

1764   Scottish philosopher Thomas Reid, objecting to empiricism and association-ism, founds the Scottish school of psychology. Reid's theory, which will become known as faculty psychology, argues that the mind is an organized unity that can perform activities such as self-preservation, desire, self-esteem, pity, and gratitude.   PSYCH

1765   English writer and lexicographer Samuel Johnson publishes his eight-volume edition of English dramatist William Shakespeare's plays; this edition will be noted for its critical preface.   CRIT

1765   French monk Abbot Laugier publishes *Observations sur l'architecture*, a trea-tise on the significance and beauty of French Gothic architecture.   CRIT

1765–1769   English jurist Sir William Blackstone publishes his *Commentaries on the Laws of England*, which will have a lasting influence on English jurisprudence.   POL

1765   *New Essays on Understanding*, completed in 1704 by German philosopher and mathematician Gottfried Wilhelm Leibniz, is published posthumously. Disputing English philosopher John Locke's empiricist view of knowledge (*see* 1690, PHIL), and taking what is called a nativist position, Leibniz argued that the human mind has innate intelligence, ideas, truths, dispositions, habits, and potentials.   PSYCH

1765   The term *Yankee* is being used as a term of derision toward colonists in New England. The term, probably derived from the Dutch *Janke* (diminutive of Jan) or *Jan* and *kees* (John Cheese), will have become a moniker of pride by the American Revolution.   SOC

1766   German dramatist and critic Gotthold Lessing presents his aesthetic theories in *Laocoön*, which compares plastic art as a static form with poetry as a dynamic form. Other works include *Letters, Concerning the Most Recent Literature* (1759–1765) and *Hamburg Dramaturgy* (1767–1769).   CRIT

1766   German philosopher Immanuel Kant publishes *Dreams of a Spirit-Seer*, in which he attacks metaphysical speculation, especially that of German philosophers Christian August Crusius and Christian von Wolff.   PHIL

1767   English critic William Duff publishes *An Essay on Original Genius*, expressing the growing consensus of critics of the importance of originality over imitation of the classics. *See also* 1759, CRIT.   CRIT

1767   Russian empress Catherine the Great outlines her political plans and views in a paper, the *Document of Catherine the Great*. Her views, influenced by French thinker Montesquieu, are meant to lead to political reform.   POL

1769–1790   Sir Joshua Reynolds, English portrait painter and president of the newly founded Royal Academy, delivers the lectures published as *Discourses on Art*. His exposition of neoclassical style, favoring idealized generalization over observed particulars, is highly influential.   CRIT

1769   French philosopher and encyclopedist Denis Diderot writes *Le Rêve de d'Alembert* (published in 1830), a dramatic dialogue in which he discusses the physical universe, morality, and society.   PHIL

1769   The Gurkha state conquers the Kathmandu Valley of Nepal, becoming the country's preeminent ethnic and cultural group. Gurkha religious belief combines Buddhism, Hinduism, and Tantrism.   REL

1770s   The *Sturm und Drang* literary movement in Germany, a major precursor to romanticism, stresses natural feeling, Promethean individualism, and social reform. Its adherents include Johann Wolfgang von Goethe and Johann von Schiller.   CRIT

1770   German educator Christoph Dock publishes the first book on the practice of teaching.   EDUC

1770   French philosopher Paul-Henri d'Holbach, publishes *The System of Nature*. An atheist and materialist, he is host to many French Enlightenment intellectuals at his Paris salon.   PHIL

1771   English orientalist Sir William Jones discovers relationships among Latin, Greek, and Sanskrit that will lead to reconstruction of the Indo-European language (spoken 3300–2500 B.C.) from which numerous ancient and modern languages are believed to descend.   LING

1772   German philosopher and theologian Johann Gottfried von Herder publishes *Treatise upon the Origin of Language*.   LING

1772	German physician Franz Anton Mesmer argues that mental power (magnetism) can exert a powerful influence on the human body. He will later call this power "animal magnetism" and claim it has medicinal value. This popular form of hypnotism (also known as mesmerism) will later fall into disrepute. MISC
1773	American statesman and scientist Benjamin Franklin publishes *Edict by the King of Prussia*, a satire directed against England and Germany that reflects the author's stance against the taxation measures known as the Townshend Acts. POL
1773	Pope Clement XIV abolishes the Society of Jesus (the Jesuits), under pressure from Europe's Bourbon monarchies. *See also* 1814, REL. REL
1773	On December 16, the Boston Tea Party occurs in Boston Harbor as colonists disguised as Native Americans destroy hundreds of chests of tea in protest against taxes levied on tea by the English Parliament. The action symbolizes the growing conflict between the colonies and England, and more generally, is an early example of the persistent strain of antitax sentiment in America. SOC
1774–1781	English critic Thomas Warton publishes *The History of English Poetry*, a much-honored example of literary history. As a critic, Warton emphasizes the "sublime" and the "pathetic" as the chief characteristics of great poetry. CRIT
1774–1789	The Continental Congress serves as the legislature for the 13 American colonies during the American Revolution and before the ratification of the U.S. Constitution. POL
1775–1850	Romanticism is widespread in Europe and America. The literary, artistic, and intellectual movement emphasizes the emotions, belief in innate human goodness, heroic individualism, and imagination. It develops in reaction to the rationalism and classicism of the Enlightenment. Romanticism is associated with German poets Johann Wolfgang von Goethe and Johann von Schiller, American transcendentalists Ralph Waldo Emerson and Henry David Thoreau, Scottish historian Thomas Carlyle, English poets Samuel Taylor Coleridge and William Wordsworth, French writers Victor Hugo and Alexandre Dumas père, and Russian writers Aleksandr Pushkin and Mikhail Lermontov, among others. MISC
1775–1783	American colonists who defend the English position during the American Revolution are known as Loyalists. POL
1775	In a March speech, American patriot Patrick Henry says, "Give me liberty or give me death." The call to take arms in the revolution against England stirs colonists and over the decades will come to symbolize national determination to preserve the country's freedom. POL

1775–1783   The conflict between Britain and the American colonies known as the American Revolution occurs. The victory of the colonies results in the establishment of the United States, a new country based on democratic ideals (*see* 1776, POL). The revolution's success will inform future attempts at democratic revolution in France and throughout Europe and will inspire other colonies struggling for independence.   POL

1775–1850   In many predominantly Christian countries such as France, Britain, the United States, and Germany, religious liberty for Jews increases as measures are taken to abolish or reduce institutional anti-Semitism.   REL

1776   German anthropologist Johann Blumenbach publishes *On the Natural Varieties of Mankind*, in which he distinguishes the American Indian, Caucasian, Ethiopian, Malayan, and Mongolian races. He argues that Caucasians were the original race from which the others arose through "degeneration" under different environmental demands.   ANTH

1776   English writer John Hawkins begins publication of the five-volume *A General History of the Science and Practice of Music*.   CRIT

Gibbon's Idea

One of the questions most often asked of writers is, "Where do you get your ideas?" Ever the chronicler, English historian Edward Gibbon was able to answer that question precisely with regard to his greatest work, *The History of the Decline and Fall of the Roman Empire* (1776–1788). "It was at Rome, on the 15th of October 1764, as I sat musing amid the ruins of the Capitol, while the barefooted friars were singing vespers in the temple of Jupiter, that the idea of writing the decline and fall of the city first started to my mind."

The circumstances of Gibbon's brainstorm are telling. A skeptical deist who regarded most religious beliefs with suspicion, Gibbon was convinced that the Roman empire's slide into barbarism was linked to the spread of Christianity. While maintaining a seemingly detached demeanor, Gibbon's chapters on the early church are in fact a scathing critique of what he regarded as Christian intolerance and irrationality. The publication of those chapters in 1776 aroused a furor among devout Christians, including Scottish writer James Boswell, who called Gibbon "an infidel puppet." Alluding to the American Revolution then taking place, Gibbon wrote that he was withstanding "as hot a cannonading as can be pointed at Washington."

Despite the criticism, Gibbon's monumental six-volume work became one of the acknowledged world classics of history. On completing the writing, Gibbon noted his melancholy at taking "an everlasting leave of an old and agreeable companion."

1776   English composer and music historian Charles Burney publishes the first vol-
            ume of *General History of Music*. A total of four volumes will be completed by
            1789.   CRIT

1776   Scottish economist Adam Smith publishes *An Inquiry into the Nature and
            Causes of the Wealth of Nations*, the founding text of classical economics. Smith
            proposes a *laissez-faire* market approach, in which individuals pursuing their
            own interest improve the condition of society as a whole. However, he also
            argues that it may be necessary for the state to provide tax-funded public ser-
            vices, including education.   ECON

1776–1841   German philosopher and educator Johann Herbart lives. In his *Application of
            Psychology to the Science of Education*, he becomes the first to call pedagogy
            a science.   EDUC

1776–1788   English historian Edward Gibbon publishes the monumental six-volume work
            The History of the Decline and Fall of the Roman Empire. Given the high quality
            of its scholarship and storytelling, the work will be seen as one of the greatest
            histories of all time.   HIST

1776   German philosopher Adam Weishaupt founds the Illuminati, a secret society
            dedicated to the advancement of Enlightenment ideals. Its members will include
            German poets Johann Wolfgang von Goethe and Johann von Schiller.   PHIL

1776   The Declaration of Independence, written by American statesman Thomas
            Jefferson and adopted by the Continental Congress, puts forth the country's
            intellectual and ethical premises. Inspired by the theories of English
            philosopher John Locke and French philosopher Jean-Jacques Rousseau,
            among others, it states in part, "We hold these truths to be self-evident, that
            all men are created equal, that they are endowed by their Creator with cer-
            tain unalienable Rights, that among these are Life, Liberty, and the pursuit
            of Happiness."   POL

1776   In his pamphlet *Common Sense*, American political philosopher Thomas Paine
            argues that the American colonies have established themselves outside of
            British rule and should seek political independence. In this and the 16 addi-
            tional pamphlets in his collection *Crisis* (1776–1783), he generates strong
            support for the patriot position.   POL

1777   English critic Maurice Morgan publishes *An Essay on the Dramatic Character of
            Sir John Falstaff*. Influenced by English empiricist philosopher John Locke, he
            argues that a literary work consists of a series of sense impressions creating a
            whole experience.   CRIT

1777	Scottish historian Willam Robertson publishes *History of America,* the first major chronicle of European settlement in the New World. *See also* 1759, HIST. HIST
1779	American statesman Thomas Jefferson proposes the idea for a state-paid, voluntary school system in the United States. The idea will take several decades to be put into widespread practice. EDUC
1780s	The ideas of American statesman Thomas Jefferson affect a wide spectrum of American thought. His political beliefs help to define American liberalism; his devotion to classical architecture fosters an American architectural sensibility; and his belief in free education for all will shape public education in the next two centuries. SOC
1780–1850	Japanese holy man Kurozumi Munetado, founder of the Shinto sect of Kurozumikyo, lives. REL

Renaissance Man of the Enlightenment

As statesman, Thomas Jefferson left his legacy to America on paper and in law. As the primary author of the Declaration of Independence, he made the pursuit of life, liberty, and happiness a cornerstone of American political philosophy. Before he was elected president, he fought in the Virginia state legislature for religious freedom and separation of church and state. He also served as the first secretary of state and founded the Democratic Republican Party, the early form of the Democratic Party. During his presidency (1801–1809), he brought about the Louisiana Purchase (1803), which vastly increased American territory, and worked to restrict American involvement in the Napoleonic Wars.

In addition to these contributions, however, Jefferson was active in the fields of agriculture, architecture, and education. Throughout his life he made a successful living as a planter, on the family estate, Monticello, which he designed himself. Believing an educated populace central to the growth of the new American republic, he helped to create an important center for higher education, the University of Virginia (1819). He also dabbled in archaeology and helped to found the Library of Congress. For the final 15 years of his life, he kept an illuminating correspondence with his former political enemy, John Adams. With such an accomplished, unsated mind, it is not surprising that President John Kennedy once told a group of visiting Nobel Prize winners, "I think this is the most extraordinary collection of talent, of human knowledge, that has ever been gathered together at the White House, with the possible exception of when Thomas Jefferson dined alone."

1781–1787   Swiss educational reformer Johann Pestalozzi publishes the four-volume work *Leonard and Gertrude*, in which he outlines his educational theories. They are grounded in the belief that education must be shaped for each individual child, disagreeing with the then-popular system of rote memorization. His ideas will be influential among 19th- and 20th-century educational reformers. His other works include *How Gertrude Teaches Her Children*.   EDUC

1781–1788   French philosopher and writer Jean-Jacques Rousseau's *Confessions* is published posthumously. It will come to be seen as one of the greatest autobiographies ever written.   HIST

1781–1848   Austrian philosopher Bernhard Bolzano lives. His epistemology and socialist, utopian moral philosophy are influential.   PHIL

1781   German philosopher Immanuel Kant publishes *The Critique of Pure Reason*, in which he begins to expound a system of critical philosophy that will decisively influence future Western philosophical thinking. Kant finds a middle way between total skepticism and unrestrained rationalism by defining the limits of reason and certifying its authority through the "transcendental deduction." Kant distinguishes between objects of experience (the phenomenal) and "things in themselves" (the noumenal); the latter he considers unknowable.   PHIL

1781   Named for the paper on which they are printed, "blue laws" are established to regulate commerce and entertainment on the Sabbath in New England. Over the decades, blue laws will become widespread across the United States; by the end of the 20th century, however, many of them will have been rescinded.   SOC

1782   French-born American writer J. Hector St. John de Crèvecoeur publishes *Letters from an American Farmer*, which discusses agrarian life and the American character.   SOC

1783–1785   American lexicographer Noah Webster publishes *Grammatical Institute of the English Language*. Its first part, *The American Spelling Book* not only standardizes spelling but for several decades is a widely used basic reader.   EDUC

1784   German philosopher Immanuel Kant writes his essay *Idea for a Universal History*, one of the works in which he applies his critical philosophy to the subject of history.   HIST

1784–1791   German philosopher and theologian Johann Gottfried von Herder publishes *Outlines of a Philosophy of the History of Man*. Herder emphasizes the role of history in shaping human language, and the role of language in shaping thinking.   PHIL

1784   English religious leader John Wesley approves legal status for Methodist soci-
            eties in England and America, making them organizationally separate from
            the Church of England. Formal independence from the Church of England
            will be enacted in 1791.   REL

1785   The public school system in the United States pushes forward with the passage
            of the U.S. Land Ordinance, which sets aside land for public schools.   EDUC

1785   French social philosopher and mathematician Marie-Jean de Caritat, marquis
            de Condorcet publishes *Essay on the Application of Analysis to the Probability of
            Majority Decisions*, in which he applies mathematical methods to the social
            sciences.   SOC

1787–1832   Danish philologist Rasmus Kristian Rask lives. He publishes influential works
            on the relationship of Indo-European languages and compiles the first usable
            Anglo-Saxon and Icelandic grammars.   LING

1787   American statesman Alexander Hamilton leads the founding of the Federalist
            Party, the first political party in the United States. It supports a strong federal
            government that largely follows the precepts of *The Federalist*, a series of essays
            on government written by Hamilton and American statesmen James Madison
            and John Jay (*see below*).   POL

1787–1788   A series of 85 political essays known as *The Federalist* are written by
            American statesmen Alexander Hamilton, James Madison, and John Jay.
            Published under the pseudonym "Publius," they discuss the problems of
            republican government and offer federalism as an effective alternative for
            preserving state and individual rights. The first 77 of the essays first appear
            in New York newspapers.   POL

1787   The Virginia and New York plans for structuring a government are presented at
            the U.S. Constitutional Convention. The plans vary widely in their commit-
            ment to a strong federal government and structure of political representation.
            The Connecticut Compromise, which integrates portions of both plans, is
            passed on July 16.   POL

1788   German philosopher Immanuel Kant publishes *Critique of Practical Reason*, in
            which he develops a system of ethics based on the concept of the categorical
            imperative: "Act as if the maxim from which you act were to become through
            your will a universal law." He discerns a practical need to believe in a God who
            upholds the moral order.   PHIL

1789   The French Revolution begins, unleashing tremendous social change. Its ideas
            and events, including the Reign of Terror (1793–1794), the French
            Revolutionary Wars (1792–1802), and the Napoleonic Wars (1803–1815),

will generate an enormous amount of excellent historical writing and arguably give birth to the modern field of history. Its causes, course, and consequences will continue to engage historians hereafter. *See also* 1833–1867, 1837, 1847, 1856, 1862, 1910, and 1995, HIST.   HIST

1789   English philosopher Jeremy Bentham publishes *Introduction to the Principles of Morals and Legislation.* Considered the founder of utilitarianism, he proposes the view that action should aim at achieving the greatest happiness of the greatest number of people. He is also the founder of the influential *Westminster Review* and University College, London.   POL

1789   The Supreme Court of the United States is established, under provisions in Article 3 of the Constitution.   POL

1789   Drafted and signed two years earlier at the Constitutional Convention in Philadelphia, Pennsylvania, the Constitution of the United States is ratified. It will become a model for representative democracies throughout the world, with its balancing of federal and state sovereignty, separation of powers among three branches of government, bicameral legislature, and system for electing officials. POL

1789–1799 The French Revolution stretches over a decade, beginning with the overthrow of the monarchy and the dissolution of the *ancien regime*, encompassing the mass executions of the Reign of Terror (1793–1794), and ending with the establishment of Napoleon as dictator. Though unsuccessful in many of its aims, the revolution opened the way for the eventual development of liberal democracies in Europe. Rooted in the intellectual milieu of the Enlightenment, it produced the catch phrase, "Liberty, Equality, Fraternity."   POL

1789–1799 In France, radical supporters of the French Revolution are known as the "sans-culottes," meaning "without knee breeches," the short pants associated with the hated aristocracy.   POL

1789   The Protestant Episcopal Church is founded in the United States as the independent American branch of the Anglican communion. The church adopts its first revision of the Book of Common Prayer.   REL

1790   German philosopher Immanuel Kant publishes *The Critique of Judgment,* in which he examines the problems involved in attempts at objective aesthetic evaluation.   CRIT

1790   English artist and poet William Blake publishes the prose work *The Marriage of Heaven and Hell,* in which he sets forth his dualistic notion of Contraries and attacks contemporary Protestant and Swedenborgian thinking (*see* 1749–1756, REL).   PHIL

1790   Irish-born British statesman and orator Edmund Burke publishes *Reflections on the Revolution in France*, a landmark in conservative political thought.   POL

1791   Scottish writer James Boswell completes *The Life of Samuel Johnson LL.D.*, perhaps the best-known biography in English.   HIST

1791   The Massachusetts Historical Society is founded. Many other state historical societies, dedicated to preserving and promoting the study of local history, will be founded in the 1800s, including the Historical Society of Pennsylvania (1824), and the Maryland Historical Society (1844), and the New York State Historical Association (1899). (The New-York Historical Society, dedicated to early American and New York history, will be founded in New York City in 1804.)   HIST

1791–1792   American political philosopher Thomas Paine, writing in response to Edmund Burke's conservative treatise *Reflections on the Revolution in France* (*see* 1790, POL), defends revolution in *The Rights of Man*.   POL

1791   The Bill of Rights, comprising the first ten amendments to the U.S. Constitution, is ratified. The amendments apply to the federal government and are largely concerned with preserving the rights of individuals, including those of freedom of speech and religion, the right to bear arms, and the guarantee of "due process of law."   POL

1791   French playwright and reformer Olympe de Gouges (born Marie Gouze) writes *The Declaration of the Rights of Woman and the Female Citizen*, a treatise calling for universal equality for the sexes. The work is based on the Declaration of the Rights of Man and Citizen, which is embodied in the French constitution as a preamble this year. Gouges will be beheaded for her beliefs in 1793.   POL

1791   French writer Donatien-Alphonse-François de Sade (better known as the Marquis de Sade) publishes the novel *Justine ou les Malheurs de la vertu*. In this and other works, often banned as pornography, de Sade explores the nature of sexuality and perversity. He will eventually be considered a predecessor to such thinkers as German philosopher Friedrich Nietzsche and Austrian psychoanalyst Sigmund Freud.   PSYCH

1792–1796   Italian archaeologist and antiquary Luigi Lanzi contributes to the study of different painting styles in *Storia pittorica dell'Italia*, a work that presents Florentine artist Giotto as the father of modern painting. He boldly distinguishes 14 schools of painting in Italy alone and up to three or four periods according to changes in tastes.   CRIT

1792   German philosopher Johann Gottlieb Fichte publishes *Critique of All Revelation*. In this and other works, he lays out his idealist philosophy, which posits the moral law as the ground of cognition, and consciousness as the ground for experience. Fichte will often be seen as a transitional thinker between German philosophers Immanuel Kant and Georg Wilhelm Friedrich Hegel.   PHIL

1792   American statesman Thomas Jefferson founds the Democratic Republican Party, which forms the basis for the modern-day Democratic Party. It will officially become known as the Democratic Party following the election of American president Andrew Jackson in 1828. Supporting the interests of the small farmer, it originally supports low tariffs and limited government intervention.   POL

1792   English writer Mary Wollstonecraft publishes the feminist polemic, *A Vindication of the Rights of Women*, the first work to call for the removal of the legal, educational, and cultural barriers to women's advancement in society.   POL

1793   *The Farmer's Almanac* begins publication under American publisher Robert Bailey Thomas. Still in publication two centuries later, it will eventually be called *The Old Farmer's Almanac*.   JOURN

1793   English philosopher and writer William Godwin publishes *Enquiry Concerning Political Justice*.   POL

1793   The first of two federal fugitive slave laws is passed in the United States, calling for the return of escaped slaves to their owners. The second fugitive slave law will be passed as part of the Compromise of 1850. Both acts will be repealed by Congress in 1864, 18 months after President Abraham Lincoln's Emancipation Proclamation, which will free only those slaves in Confederate states still engaged in fighting the Civil War, not those slaves in territory that will have been reconquered by Union forces nor those in slave states loyal to the Union. Slavery will be abolished in the United States in 1865 by the 13th Amendment to the Constitution.   POL

1793–1795   English artist and poet William Blake sets forth his visionary mysticism and private mythology in such "prophetic books" of poetry as *The Gates of Paradise* (1793), *The Visions of the Daughters of Albion* (1793), *The Song of Los* (1795), and *The Book of Los* (1795).   REL

1794–1795   German poet and playwright Johann von Schiller publishes *Letters on the Aesthetic Education of Mankind* (1794–1795) and *On Naive and Sentimental Poetry* (1795). In these works he argues that aesthetics is the fundamental and supreme exercise of human freedom. His work helps to provide a philosophical basis for romantic literary works.   CRIT

1794   French activist François Babeuf founds a journal that supports what will become basic socialist ideals of economic and political equality. He will be caught in a plan to overthrow the French government and will be executed.   SOC

1795   In a contest held by the American Philosophy Society, American writers Samuel Knox and Samuel H. Smith write the winning essays on "the best system of liberal Education and literary instruction adapted to the genius of the Government of the United States." In their essays, they take the enlightened view of pursuing modern sciences as well as the traditional pursuits of the classical languages and instilling civic-mindedness.   EDUC

1795–1817   American clergyman and educator Timothy Dwight assumes the presidency of Yale College. During his tenure, he redirects the school in light of his theocratic and federalist beliefs, many of which have their origins with his grandfather, theologian Jonathan Edwards. His activities at Yale may be said to mark a new religious movement, the Second Great Awakening (see 1800s, REL).   EDUC

1795   French mathematician, philosopher, and revolutionary Marie-Jean de Caritat, marquis de Condorcet, writes *Sketch of an Historic Scene of the Progress of the Human Spirit*, a work calling for equality for all, including women.   POL

1795   German physician Franz Joseph Gall begins writing on phrenology. He argues that personality can be judged by physical characteristics, especially bumps and ridges of the skull over specific brain regions.   PSYCH

1795   The London Missionary Society, an Anglican and Nonconformist Protestant group, is founded.   REL

1796   The novel *Jacques le fataliste* by French philosopher and encyclopedist Denis Diderot is published posthumously. Among the topics raised in its digressive narrative is the problem of freedom versus determinism.   PHIL

1796   French writer Anne-Louise-Germaine de Staël publishes *A Treatise on the Influence of the Passions on the Happiness of Individuals and of Nations.*   PHIL

1796   In his farewell address, American president George Washington cautions against easy friendship among nations, citing the need to desist from "permanent alliances" with foreign countries. His caution lays a foundation for American isolationist sentiment, which will remain strong throughout U.S. history.   POL

1796   French emperor Napoleon conquers the Papal States. They will be restored to the pope in 1815.   REL

1796–1805   In China, the White Lotus society wages an unsuccessful millenarian rebellion against Manchu rule.   REL

1797   German poets Johann Wolfgang von Goethe and Johann von Schiller cowrite the essay "On Epic and Dramatic Poetry." Goethe will write further on literary theory in his own journal, *The Propylaea* (1798–1800).   CRIT

1798   German historian Johann Dominicus Fiorillo publishes *Geschichte der Zeichnenden Kunste*, a general history of the art of painting that is critical of 16th-century Italian art historian Giorgio Vasari. Fiorillo is the first art historian to discuss miniature painting.   CRIT

1798–1800   German poet Friedrich Hölderlin writes the series of unfinished essays known as the Homburg writings. In these and other works, he outlines a poetic theory that analyzes the dialectical forces influencing the "poetic spirit."   CRIT

1798   English economist Thomas Robert Malthus publishes *Essay on the Principle of Population*, in which he observes that population tends to increase in geometric progression but food supply in arithmetic progression. He concludes that population tends to outstrip food supply until reduced by famine, war, or disease.   ECON

1798   Four laws known as the Alien and Sedition Acts are passed by the U.S. Congress. The Alien Acts increase the number of years of residence required to gain naturalization from 5 to 14 and grant the president the power to deport or imprison aliens involved in suspect activity. The Sedition Act severely limits public criticism of government. The laws are designed largely to disable Thomas Jefferson and the Republican Party.   POL

1799–1888   American teacher and writer Bronson Alcott lives. He propounds his progressive child-centered educational philosophy at his Temple School, which he founds in Boston in 1834, as well as in his positions with the Concord public schools and Concord School of Philosophy. He becomes a spokesman for American transcendentalism with his writings for the *Dial*.   EDUC

1799   American historian Hannah Adams, the first woman to become a professional writer in the United States, publishes *A Summary History of New England*.   HIST

1799   In France, the national commitment to reason leads to the adoption of the metric system as a rational system of weights and measures.   MISC

1799   German theologian Friedrich Schleiermacher publishes *Religion: Speeches to Its Cultured Despisers*, in which he presents religion as absolute dependence on God attained through intuition rather than dogma.   REL

1800s   Mass education, the construction of major libraries, and the opening of government and private archives all contribute to a great increase in historical writing.   HIST

1800s   Such Russian scholars as A. D. Gradovski, V. I. Sergeyevich, and N. M. Korkunov write Russian legal history, using solid source material and displaying strong interpretive skills.   HIST

1800s   The finer Victorian biographies follow Scottish writer James Boswell's (*see* 1791, HIST) approach of combining sympathy for the subject with rigorous research. Examples include John Lockhart's seven-volume *Memoirs of the Life of Sir Walter Scott* (1837–1838) and Sir George Trevelyan's *The Life and Letters of Lord Macaulay* (1876). In other biographies of the era, however, laxness in research and an overriding concern for propriety compromise the quality of the work.   HIST

1800s   Western historians who had lived and worked in India write histories that are respectful of Indian ideas and customs. Examples include James Grant Duff's three-volume *History of the Mahrattas* (1826) and Mountstuart Elphinstone's two-volume *History of India* (1841).   HIST

1800s   French socialist Pierre Joseph Proudhon and Russian revolutionary Mikhail Bakunin, among others, develop the tenets of modern political anarchism. Proudhon promotes anarchism as a nonviolent evolutionary movement in society; Bakunin defends violence against existing government as a means for achieving anarchy. Anarchists will be connected to several high-profile acts of violence, including the Haymarket Square riot in Chicago (*see* 1886, SOC) and the assassination of American president William McKinley in 1901.   POL

1800s   The term "enlightened despot" comes into usage, representing absolute rulers who base their leadership principles on reason.   POL

1800s   The political philosophy of socialism has its beginnings in the writings of French social reformer Claude-Henri de Rouvroy and Welsh socialist Robert Owen. Both write in reaction to the perceived injustices of the Industrial Revolution.   POL

1800s   The Second Great Awakening revives and infuses American religion with a new force as its believers move west. Its leaders, including Timothy Dwight, Lyman Beecher, and Charles Grandison Finney, infuse their sermons with emotion and diminish dependence on erudition and intellect (*see also* 1795–1817, EDUC).   REL

1800s   During the end of the 18th and the beginning of the 19th century, under the first chief justice John Marshall, the Supreme Court decides a variety of cases that establish the supremacy of national over state laws.   SOC

1800s   Unmarried women are treated as social outcasts, commonly referred to by pejoratives such as "spinsters," "old maids," and "tabbies."   SOC

1800s   Throughout the 19th century, physical violence against women is considered acceptable and at times necessary in light of women's alleged moral weakness and subordinate position in the household.   SOC

1800	English poets William Wordsworth and Samuel Taylor Coleridge publish the second edition of the poetry collection *Lyrical Ballads*; the first appeared in 1798. The new edition of this founding work of British romanticism contains a famous critical preface written by Wordsworth. CRIT
1800–1802	German writer and critic Friedrich von Schlegel lectures in Jena (1800) and Paris (1802) on language, literature, and history. A major founder of German romanticism, he also cofounded and coedited, with his brother August Wilhelm, the periodical *Athenaeum* (1798–1800), an important organ of romanticism. PHIL
1800	German philosopher Johann Gottlieb Fichte publishes *The Vocation of Man*. PHIL
1800	German philosopher Friedrich von Schelling publishes *System des transzendentalen Idealismus*, which, in its focus on force, striving, and dynamic spirit, expresses the spirit of German romanticism. Schelling argues that art is the sphere in which nature and history are reconciled. PHIL
c. 1800	Sikh leader Ranjit Singh founds a Sikh kingdom over most of the Punjab. It will become a province of British India in 1849 and be partitioned between India and Pakistan in 1947. REL
1800–1850	In Europe and Russia, the Jewish Haskalah (Enlightenment) movement advocates cultural assimilation and the writing in Hebrew of works imitating contemporary literature. REL
1800–1900	Reform Judaism develops in Germany, characterized by a liberal attitude toward Jewish law, whereas Orthodox Judaism considers all the particulars of the law to be binding. The proponents of Reform Judaism include rabbis Abraham Geiger and Samuel Holdheim. REL
1800	In the United States, Seneca prophet Ganioda'yo, or Handsome Lake, begins preaching the religion of Gaiwiio, or Good Message. Also known as the Longhouse religion, it blends traditional beliefs and Christianity and helps to revitalize the Iroquois. REL
1800–1850	Over the first half of the 19th century, the United States experiences a variety of attempts at social reform, in such areas as education, criminal rehabilitation, treatment of the insane, and restriction of liquor consumption. SOC
1800	Welsh socialist Robert Owen moves to New Lanark, Scotland, where he and others establish an experimental mill community that treats workers well and also earns profits. The town becomes a standard for other social reformers and will be central to Owen's later ventures, including the founding of a cooperative community in New Harmony, Indiana (*see* 1825, soc). In Britain, he will be central to the passage of the Factory Act of 1819. SOC

1802   English theologian and philosopher William Paley publishes *Natural Theology*, in which he attempts to prove God's existence through an elaborate version of the argument from design. Paley is also the author of *A View of the Evidences of Christianity* (1794).   PHIL

1803   German philosopher Friedrich von Schelling publishes *Vorlesungen über die Methode des akademischen Studiums*, in which he proposes his "philosophy of identity." He presents the concept of an Absolute in which mind and nature are unified. After 1809, Schelling's philosophy will become increasingly mystical and personal.   PHIL

1803–1815   In the Napoleonic Wars, French emperor Napoleon Bonaparte (Napoleon I) leads France against Britain, Russia, and much of the European continent. In 1815, Bonaparte is defeated at the Battle of Waterloo and exiled to the island of Saint Helena; Louis XVII takes power.   POL

1804   English artist and poet William Blake publishes the long mystical poems *Jerusalem* and *Milton*.   REL

1804–1808   In the Sudan, Islamic religious reformer Usman dan Fodio leads a jihad, or holy war, against the Hausa states. The revolution succeeds in establishing a militant Islamic state called the Fulani empire.   REL

1804–1815   During the First French Empire, French soldier Nicolas Chauvin's zealous dedication to French emperor Napoleon gives rise to the term chauvinism, an excessive and aggressive devotion to a cause, nation, or group.   SOC

1805   German anthropologist Johann Blumenbach founds the science of physical anthropology.   ANTH

1805–1823   French archaeologist and politician Antoine Chrysostome, Quatremère de Quincy, publishes a series of writings which includes *Dictionnaire de l'architecture*. He rejects the study of medieval art and considers only the art of the age of Phidias, the fifth-century B.C. Greek sculptor, to be models of perfection, beauty, and truth.   CRIT

1805   Swiss educational reformer Johann Pestalozzi uses his newly founded school as the basis for experiments on discipline and learning processes.   EDUC

1807–1808   The irreverent journal *Salmagundi* is published by American writers Washington Irving, his brother William, and James Paulding, and it establishes itself as an important periodical of the post-Enlightenment years. The word *salmagundi* means "hash."   JOURN

1807   German philosopher Georg Wilhelm Friedrich Hegel publishes *The
                 Phenomenology of Mind*. In this and other works (*see* 1812–1816, HIST; 1816, PHIL;
                 and 1820–1830, CRIT), he develops an absolute idealist philosophical system, in
                 which the process of cosmology and history is equated with absolute thought
                 or spirit. Hegel will influence thinkers in many fields, including German polit-
                 ical philosopher Karl Marx, Danish philosopher Søren Kierkegaard, and
                 American philosopher John Dewey. Hegel's discussion of such concepts as
                 dialectic, alienation, becoming, and self-consciousness will become lasting ele-
                 ments of the Western intellectual heritage.   PHIL

1807–1808   German philosopher Johann Gottlieb Fichte's *Addresses to the German Nation*
                 are among the first works to develop a nationalist totalitarian ideology.   POL

1807   The political thought of German philosopher Georg Wilhelm Friedrich Hegel
                 emphasizes the interdependence of individuals in a rationally organized state or
                 community. His belief that history expresses the progress of humankind toward an
                 ideal condition will influence many social and political movements, including the
                 Young Hegelians, who seek German unification, and Marxist communists.   POL

1808   English poet and critic Samuel Taylor Coleridge delivers 18 lectures "On
                 Poetry and the Principles of Taste" at the Royal Institute, the first of his many
                 lecture series.   CRIT

1808   French writer F. X. de Burtin publishes *Traité théorique*, which details the
                 steps of correct art appreciation with regard to schools, state of preserva-
                 tion, originality, price, and description.   CRIT

1808   English essayist and poet Leigh Hunt begins editing the radical weekly *The
                 Examiner*, which introduces English poets John Keats and Percy Bysshe Shelley
                 to the public.   JOURN

1808   German writer and critic Friedrich von Schlegel publishes *On the Language and
                 Wisdom of India*, an influential study of Sanskrit, Indian civilization, and the
                 nature of wisdom.   PHIL

1808   French social philosopher Charles Fourier publishes *Théorie des quatre mouve-
                 ments et des destinées générales*, in which he outlines his propositions for an
                 ideal society that can be based on the natural abilities and interests of its
                 inhabitants. Community size is based on the phalanx, a unit of 1,620 people.
                 His philosophy, which prophesies the shortcomings of the machine age, will
                 spur the creation of a number of utopian communities, including Brook Farm
                 (*see* 1841–1847, SOC).   SOC

1810s   The secret Italian society known as the Carbonari is active in the kingdom of
                 Naples, attempting to oppose foreign control. In the next decade, groups form

in Spain and France. In the 1830s, it will be subsumed by the drive for the unification of Italy.   POL

1810   German physician Samuel Hahnemann, founder of homeopathy, expounds his medical beliefs in *Organon of the Rational Art of Healing*. His belief that like cures like—that a disease can be cured by inducing similar symptoms with small amounts of a substance—will generally be rejected by modern medicine but nevertheless builds a sizable following.   PHIL

1810–1819   German physician Franz Joseph Gall (*see* 1795, PSYCH) and his student Johann Spurzheim publish a five-volume work on phrenology, in which they try to develop a perfect knowledge of human nature based on measurements of the skulls and brains of multiple species. They theorize that brain functions are localized in the cerebral cortex and that the brain is a bundle of individual organs governing all aspects of human behavior.   PSYCH

1810   The interdenominational American Board of Commissioners for Foreign Missions is founded in the United States.   REL

1811–1832   German historian Barthold Niebuhr publishes *The History of Rome*, his greatest work. He revolutionizes historiography by developing a critical approach to source material that much more effectively separates fact from fiction.   HIST

General Ludd's Army

In Nottingham, England, in 1811, groups of militant men made a vain attempt to save their jobs by burning a newly modernized textile factory and smashing a spinning jenny in a nearby house. Their cause was just: they were trying to rescue families from poverty and restore humanity to a mechanized workplace. They signed their pamphlets boldly, but with the name of an imaginary leader—King Ludd, General Ludd, or simply, Ned Ludd. They were the Luddites.

For five years, the Luddites continued their attacks, expanding into the communities of Derbyshire, Lancashire, Leicestershire, and Yorkshire, protesting rising food prices as well as the threat of industrialization. Although supported in part by the public, the Luddites were considered enemies by the British government. In 1813, the government hanged 13 of the protesters; by 1816, its violent phase was over, and the movement dissipated.

Although a Luddite-influenced action to protest new machinery took place at a Paterson, New Jersey, silk plant in 1813, as did other isolated incidents, the movement never regained its original strength. The Industrial Revolution had won. The term Luddite, however, endured; broadly, it refers to one who opposes technological progress.

1811	In England, disaffected workingmen called Luddites attempt to destroy the textile industry through physical violence. The Luddites will vandalize textile factory equipment until 1816, although government sanctions will be placed on them from 1812. **POL**
1811	English poet Percy Bysshe Shelley and his friend Thomas Jefferson Hogg publish the pamphlet *On the Necessity of Atheism*, resulting in their expulsion from Oxford University. **REL**
1812–1816	German philosopher Georg Wilhelm Friedrich Hegel publishes *Science of Logic*, in which he views history as a dialectical process—thesis leads to antithesis, which is followed by a higher-level synthesis combining the elements of both. **HIST**
1812	French astronomer Pierre-Simon de Laplace proposes a mechanistic model of the universe—one in which the entire history of the cosmos could theoretically be established by knowing the mass, position, and velocity of every particle. German physicist Werner Heisenberg's uncertainty principle (*see* 1927, PHIL) will provide a strong argument against this view. **PHIL**
1812	South American revolutionary Simón Bolívar writes *The Cartagena Manifesto*, his first political statement. His *Letter from Jamaica* will soon follow, outlining his plan for liberating Latin America from Spain and establishing a federation of republics. He will win military victory and independence throughout much of Latin America by 1824, though the new republics will fail to unify according to his vision. **POL**
1813	German philosopher Arthur Schopenhauer publishes *Fourfold Root of the Principle of Sufficient Reason*, in which he defines the roots cited in the title as causality (or becoming), knowing, being, and acting. **PHIL**
1814	The Society of Jesus (Jesuits) is restored as a Catholic religious order, more than 40 years after its abolition (*see* 1773, REL). **REL**
1815–1831	German jurist Friedrich Karl von Savigny publishes *Roman Law in the Middle Ages*. Savigny, who will come to be seen as 19th-century Germany's greatest jurist, will later publish *System of Roman Law* (1840–1849). **HIST**
1816	American critic Edward Tyrell Channing urges American writers to create a distinctly American literature in the essay "On Models in Literature." **CRIT**
1816	American lawyer and linguist John Pickering writes an early study of the American language, *A Vocabulary, or, Collection of Words and Phrases Which Have Supposed to Be Peculiar to the U.S. of America*. **LING**

1816   German philosopher Georg Wilhelm Friedrich Hegel publishes *Encyclopedia of the Philosophical Sciences in Outline*.   PHIL

1816   The African Methodist Episcopal Church is founded in Philadelphia as an independent Methodist denomination, with founder and former slave Richard Allen as its first bishop.   REL

1816   American clergyman Robert Finley and others found the American Colonization Society, an organization aimed at effecting the transport of black freedmen to Africa. The work of this organization will lead in part to the founding of Liberia.   SOC

1817   English poet and critic Samuel Taylor Coleridge publishes *Biographia Literaria*, an idiosyncratic compendium of critical theory, philosophy, and autobiography.   CRIT

1817   English writer William Hazlitt establishes himself as England's leading critic with the publication of *Characters of Shakespeare's Plays*. Other works include the moral-philosophical treatise *An Essay on the Principles of Human Action* (1805), *Lectures on the English Poets* (1818), and *The Spirit of the Age* (1825).   CRIT

1817   In *The Principles of Political Economy and Taxation*, English economist David Ricardo develops important theories on the determination of wages and value.   ECON

1817–1818   Scottish philosopher, historian, and economist James Mill publishes his six-volume *History of British India*, a major study of colonial India that is critical of both the Indians and the British.   HIST

1817–1824   The American presidency of James Monroe comes to be known as the Era of Good Feelings for its lack of political rancor among parties and general public interest in returning to everyday life following the War of 1812 (1812–1815). The era sees the decline of the Federalist Party and the rise of the Democratic Republican Party.   POL

1818   French philosopher Victor Cousin coins the phrase "art for art's sake." It will become the central doctrine of aestheticism, the late 19th-century British movement that regards works of art only in terms of beauty, not moral or social purpose. Prominent aesthetes will include English essayist Walter Pater and Irish playwright Oscar Wilde.   CRIT

1818   English historian Henry Hallam publishes *Europe during the Middle Ages*. He will be known for his great commitment to accuracy—and for the mediocrity of his prose.   HIST

1818   German philosopher Arthur Schopenhauer publishes *The World As Will and Idea*, in which he identifies will as German philosopher Immanuel Kant's "thing in itself" (*see* 1781, PHIL). Drawing on Buddhist thought, he argues that conformity to will leads only to pain and suffering, but that aesthetic contemplation can offer escape.   PHIL

1820s   French writer Charles-Augustin Sainte-Beuve begins a celebrated career that will last until his death in 1869. His copious criticism, collected in such works as *Portraits littéraires* (1862–1864) and *Portraits contemporains* (1869–1871), will examine literary works in the biographical, psychological, historical, and social context in which they were written.   CRIT

1820s   German historian Isaak Markus Jost publishes one of the first histories of the Jews since biblical times.   HIST

1820s   In England, a group known as the "philosophical radicals" espouse utilitarian social and political views. They include James Mill, John Austin, and David Ricardo.   POL

1820–1830   German philosopher Georg Wilhelm Friedrich Hegel delivers a series of lectures on the *Philosophy of Fine Art*. They will be compiled and published posthumously in the book *Logic*.   CRIT

1820–1821   The early conflict between slaveholding and free American states is epitomized in the passage of the Missouri Compromise. The federal law allows for the admission of Missouri to the Union as a slave state, Maine as a free state, with slavery prohibited in land acquired in the Louisiana Purchase north of Arkansas. The legislation allows for the equal apportioning of free to slave states in the United States.   POL

1820   Indian religious leader Raja Rammohun Roy, known as the "Father of Modern India," publishes *The Principles of Jesus: The Guide to Peace and Happiness*. Though sympathetic to Christianity and committed to social reform, he is loyal to Hinduism.   REL

1820–1826   American clergyman Lyman Beecher publishes a series of six sermons on intemperance, which become widely popular. Over the coming decades, his simplified Protestant theology and use of revivals will put him at odds with his Congregational church. Among his 13 children are Harriet Beecher (Stowe), Henry Ward Beecher, and Catharine Beecher.   SOC

1820–1913   American abolitionist Harriet Tubman lives. She is instrumental to the formation of the Underground Railroad, which transports American slaves to freedom in the North.   SOC

1821   English poet Percy Bysshe Shelley writes what will be considered his best-known prose work, the essay *The Defence of Poetry* (published posthumously in 1840). CRIT

1821   American secondary education has its beginnings with the opening of the first high school, in Boston. EDUC

1821–1822   German theologian Friedrich Schleiermacher publishes his major work *The Christian Faith*, a systematic treatment of his earlier ideas. *See also* 1799, REL. REL

1822   German poet Johann Wolfgang von Goethe publishes *Maxims and Reflections*, in which he develops a mature theory of allegory and symbolism. CRIT

1822   German philologist and folklorist Jacob Grimm introduces Grimm's law, a principle of relationships in Indo-European languages dealing with shifts in consonants in the development of English and other Germanic languages. LING

1823   French art historian J. B. L. G. Seroux d'Agincourt's *Histoire de l'art par les monuments* marks a new step in art history writing by treating separately three branches of art—architecture, sculpture, and painting—in one volume. CRIT

1823   U.S. president James Monroe, on the advice of Secretary of State John Quincy Adams, articulates the Monroe Doctrine: that the United States would not allow European nations to extend their political power in the Western Hemisphere, nor would the United States interfere with existing European colonies in the Americas. In various forms, the doctrine will become a permanent part of U.S. foreign policy. POL

1824   U.S. Speaker of the House Henry Clay proposes a wide-ranging plan for domestic improvement called the "American System." Among its features are federal aid programs for agriculture and road and canal construction, and increased tariffs to promote domestic manufacturing. POL

1824   English reformer Richard Martin founds the Society for the Prevention of Cruelty to Animals. His efforts will help bring about anticruelty laws in England (in 1849 and 1854), continental Europe, and the United States. SOC

1824–1898   English reformer Samuel Plimsoll lives. A member of Parliament, he fights to improve working conditions for sailors and helps secure the passage of maritime reforms. SOC

1825   Scottish historian and essayist Thomas Carlyle publishes *The Life of Schiller*. He will publish *Life of John Sterling* in 1851. These two works will establish Carlyle as a great biographer as well as a great historian. HIST

1825	In Russia, revolutionaries known as the Decembrists attempt to stop the accession of Nicholas I to the throne following the death of Tsar Alexander. Although the uprising fails and brings about the execution of five Decembrists, the movement will stir future revolutionary activity. **POL**
1825	Japanese scholar Aizawa Seishisai writes *Shinron* (*New Proposals*), in which he proposes his doctrine of *kokutai*, a nationalist theory of state emphasizing the supremacy of the emperor. **POL**
c. 1825–1850	In Japan, two schools of thought advocate contrary approaches to relations with the West. The Kaikoku ("open the country") school argues that Western technology is needed at home; the Jōi ("expel the barbarians") school urges a complete ban on contact with foreigners. **POL**
1825	French social reformer Claude-Henri de Rouvroy publishes *The New Christianity*, detailing his views of the relationship of religion and the Enlightenment. Rouvroy is the first thinker to treat society as an independent unit for analysis. **SOC**
1825	Welsh socialist Robert Owen (*see* 1800, **SOC**) applies his communistic principles to New Harmony, Indiana. The cooperative community will be the site of the nation's first kindergarten and first free public school and library. **SOC**
1826	The first volume of *Monuments Germaniae Historica*, a series founded by Prussian statesman Carl Stein, is published. It marks the beginning of a period of great German historical writing. **HIST**
1826	The Anti-Masonic Party, the first American third party, is formed in New York. It works to unseat President Martin Van Buren and to undermine the efforts of Jacksonian Democrats. In Baltimore in 1831, the Anti-Masonic Party will hold the first nominating convention in U.S. history. This will become the model for future nominating conventions for all parties. **POL**
1827	German art historian Karl Friedrich von Rumohr publishes *Italienische Forschungen*, a critical study of artistic sources. He criticizes 16th-century Italian art historian Giorgio Vasari and concludes that the Gothic style in architecture originated only in the 13th century. **CRIT**
1827	In a vision, American religious leader Joseph Smith claims to receive golden plates that he translates as *The Book of Mormon*. Smith becomes the founder of the Mormon religion, or the Church of Jesus Christ of Latter-Day Saints. *See also* 1847, **REL**. **REL**
1827–1831	German poet Heinrich Heine publishes *Reisebilder* (*Travel Pictures*), a work combining poetry and prose. A leading figure of the "Young Germany" revo-

lutionary literary movement, he is also a satirist and critic of contemporary society and politics. His other works include *On the History of Religion and Philosophy in Germany* (1833).   soc

1828   French historian and politician François Guizot publishes *Histoire de la civilisation en Europe*. He will publish *Histoire des origines du gouvernement représentatif* in 1851. Guizot will be the leading proponent in France of focusing the study of history on social structure and international relations.   HIST

1828   Indian religious leader Raja Rammohun Roy founds the Brahmo Samaj, a community of Hindus who meet for scripture readings and services similar to those of Protestants. Reconstituted in 1843 by Debendranath Tagore, the group will inspire the formation of similar bodies across India.   REL

1829–1833   The term "Kitchen Cabinet" refers to the group of unofficial advisors to American president Andrew Jackson during his first term. The group is composed of leading politicians and journalists, including Francis P. Blair and Martin Van Buren.   POL

1829   Scottish philosopher, historian, and economist James Mill publishes *An Analysis of the Phenomena of the Human Mind*, a work of associationist psychology that adds muscle sensation (kinesthesis), disorganized sensation (itching or tickling), and gastrointestinal tract sensations to Greek philosopher Aristotle's classic five senses. He claims these eight varieties of sensation are the basis of ideas and consciousness.   PSYCH

1829   The Catholic Emancipation Act repeals most remaining discriminatory restrictions against Roman Catholics in Britain. It is a successor to an act of 1791 that had repealed many other restrictions against Catholics.   REL

1830   The first women's magazine in the United States, *Godey's Lady's Book*, is founded by American publisher Louis Antoine Godey. Although limited in its views, it is the first popular magazine to give voice to the aesthetic concerns of women.   JOURN

1830–1842   French philosopher Auguste Comte, regarded as the father of positivism, publishes *Cours de philosophie positive*.   PHIL

1830   In Washington, D.C., the U.S. Capitol is completed. The domed building housing the U.S. Senate and House of Representatives becomes a symbol of democracy.   POL

1830   To allow for U.S. expansion, the Indian Removal Act is passed, forcing the evacuation of all Native Americans living east of the Mississippi. Other forms

of displacement occur over the coming decades, notably through the establishment and eradication of the Indian Territory (1834–1907).   soc

1831–1865   American abolitionist William Lloyd Garrison fights for an end to slavery
through his newspaper *The Liberator*.   JOURN

1831–1832   The political term "spoils system," referring to gifts bestowed upon political
victors, has its origins in a remark by U.S. Senator William Learned Marcy, who
says about political patronage, "to the victor belong the spoils of the enemy."   POL

1831   Unwritten rules of American society are revealed in the Eaton affair, in which
Secretary of State John Eaton is forced to resign his office because the
Washington social world rebuffed his new wife, recent middle-class widow
Margaret O'Neale.   soc

1832   English jurist John Austin publishes *The Province of Jurisprudence Determined*,
in which he expounds his imperativist view of law.   POL

1832   English philosopher Jeremy Bentham coins the phrase "bicameral system" to
refer to a two-part form of government, such as that of the U.S. Congress, with
its upper chamber of the Senate and lower chamber of the House of
Representatives. The bicameral system dates back to the 14th century, with the
division of the English Parliament into the House of Lords and the House of
Commons.   POL

1832–1928   In Britain, a number of reform bills increase the pool of eligible voters. The
1832 bill increases the electorate 50 percent by increasing representation in
large towns and by adapting requirement rules. Later bills, in 1867, 1884,
1918, and 1928, deal with parliamentary redistribution, bring about nearly
universal male and female suffrage, and lower the voting age.   POL

1832   Following the Reform Bill of 1832, the Liberal Party is founded in Britain. A
major party for much of the 19th and part of the 20th century, it will champion social reform and free trade. Among its prime ministers will be William
Gladstone and David Lloyd George.   POL

1832   The Conservative Party forms in Britain following the collapse of the Tory
Party and the passage of the Reform Bill of 1832. It will control the nation's
government intermittently.   POL

1832   Scottish phrenologist George Combe continues the work of German physi-
cians Franz Joseph Gall and Johann Spurzheim (*see* 1810–1819, PSYCH), but
turns phrenology into more of a faddish cult than a science. He will help
establish more than 45 regional phrenological societies that will flourish

through the early 20th century, despite evidence presented as early as 1843 that the claims of phrenology are false.   PSYCH

1832   The American Baptist Home Mission Society is organized.   REL

1832   German Jewish scholar Leopold Zunz publishes *Die gottesdienstlichen Vorträge der Juden,* a pioneer effort to apply modern critical methods to Jewish history and literature. The work shows the antiquity of the practice of vernacular synagogue sermons. Zunz also will write on Jewish liturgy and synagogal poetry. REL

1833   Oberlin College admits women and becomes the first coeducational institution of higher learning in the United States.   EDUC

1833   The Société de l'Histoire de France is founded. It will play a significant role in the development of historiography in Europe.   HIST

1833–1867 French historian Jules Michelet publishes his massive 24 volume *Histoire de France.* The greatest of the historians of the French romantic school, Michelet will also publish the seven-volume *Histoire de la Révolution Française* (1847–1853).   HIST

1833   The *New York Sun* is founded. It represents a kind of mass-market, illustrated periodical that becomes possible with the reduced costs of printing.   JOURN

1833–1834 Scottish historian and essayist Thomas Carlyle publishes *Sartor Resartus,* a spiritual, satirical, and philosophical work of wide-ranging import strongly influenced by German romanticism.   PHIL

1833   The Abolition Act of 1833 is passed in England, abolishing slavery throughout the British empire. Laws ending the trading of slaves had been passed in 1807. POL

1833   In England, the Oxford movement is begun by Anglican clergy who want to revive some Roman Catholic doctrines and practices. The movement's leaders include John Keble, Richard Hurrell Froude, and John Henry Newman. Its beliefs will be expounded in *Tracts for the Times,* earning its followers the name "Tractarians."   REL

1833   A sign of the growing interest in the abolitionist movement, the American Antislavery Society is formed. Among the movement's leaders are reformer Theodore Dwight Weld and businessmen brothers Arthur and Lewis Tappan, among others. They are spurred by Christian teachings, and consider the debate over slavery a question of good versus evil.   SOC

1834   English writer Thomas De Quincey publishes *Recollections of the Lakes and the Lake Poets.*   CRIT

1834   American playwright and historian William Dunlap publishes two volumes of
              History of the Rise and Progress of the Arts of Design in the United States.   CRIT

1834   Russian critic Vissarion Belinsky publishes *Literary Reveries*. By the 1840s, the
              period known as the golden age of the Russian intelligentsia, Belinsky will be
              his country's most admired critic. His criticism advocates realistic representa-
              tion with the aim of spurring social reform; these ideas form the basis of
              Russia's "natural school."   CRIT

1834–1836   German historian Leopold von Ranke publishes his *History of the Popes in the
              16th and 17th Centuries*, perhaps his greatest work. Ranke uses original docu-
              ments as his source material and attempts to write accurately and objectively.
              He will come to be viewed as the founder of the modern school of history and
              a major influence on most of the historians who follow him.   HIST

1834–1848   American historian Jared Sparks supervises publication of and helps write the
              25-volume *Library of American Biography*. Providing 60 biographies, the *Library*
              will be the most prominent 19th-century American biographical series.   HIST

1834–1874   American historian George Bancroft publishes his ten-volume *History of the
              United States*, a work focused on the colonial and Revolutionary periods.
              Bancroft, both romantic and nationalistic in his approach, will be seen as the
              first great American historian.   HIST

1834   In the United States, the Whig Party is founded by politician Henry Clay. In sup-
              port of tariffs, westward development, and a regulated currency, it will divide
              over the issue of slavery and align itself with the Republican Party in 1854.   POL

Taxes on Knowledge

One way to discourage a free press is to make sure the price is not free. Beginning in
1712, the English government exacted numerous taxes and duties on paper, printing,
advertisements, and publications—especially newspapers. The result was that regular
reading was affordable only for the well-to-do.

   In the 1830s, underground newspapers began to circulate widely. Illegal because
they lacked the fourpence stamp required on each copy of a newspaper, they also
tended to be politically radical in editorial content. The publisher of the *Poor Man's
Guardian*, Henry Hetherington, was among those imprisoned in the ensuing crack-
down. The newspaper tax was repealed in 1836, and other "taxes on knowledge" soon
fell to continuing pressure from reformers. The repeal of the last of the taxes gave
mass periodicals the chance to thrive. Such low-priced publications as the *Penny
Magazine* made information affordable to the poorest readers.

1834   German philosopher and educator Johann Herbart defines psychology as a science based on experience, mathematics, metaphysics, and experimentation.   PSYCH

1835   German philosopher Georg Wilhelm Friedrich Hegel publishes *Aesthetics: Lectures on Fine Art.*   CRIT

1835   American clergyman Charles Grandison Finney publishes *Lectures on Revivals of Religion*, which encapsulates his influential strain of Protestant revivalism. The largely self-educated Finney is central in establishing the dominance in American Protestantism of local revivalists over highly educated New England–based clerics.   REL

1835–1840   In his book, *Democracy in America*, French writer Alexis de Tocqueville observes, among other things, American self-reliance, social freedom, dismissal of traditional class boundaries, and affiliation with the businessman as exemplar of society. His ideas will influence American social thought for years to come.   SOC

1836   American philosopher of language Alexander Byron Johnson publishes *Treatise on Language.*   PHIL

1836   American essayist and poet Ralph Waldo Emerson publishes *Nature.* Informed by Swedish theologian and philosopher Emanuel Swedenborg and German romanticism, he outlines his transcendentalist philosophy, which focuses on the relation between nature, man, and spiritual truth. Emerson will be the leader of the New England–based transcendentalist movement, which takes a pantheistic view of nature and emphasizes reliance on direct experience.   PHIL

1837–1859   German art historian C. F. Waagen publishes a series of essays criticizing historians who neglect the connection of art to the historical circumstances of its creation. He is the first writer to trace the progress of painting in France and England from the 9th to the 15th century, with emphasis on the idea of continuous development, and to make regular use of the concept of "influence."   CRIT

1837   German art historian Franz Kugler publishes *History of Painting.* He will be considered the first "modern" art historian and be appointed professor of the history of art at the Academy of Art in Berlin. He will later publish *Handbook of the History of Art.*   CRIT

1837–1901   European literary criticism in the Victorian era tends to emphasize the historical context of literary works rather than the texts themselves. Encyclopedic histories of national literatures are compiled by such authors as Francesco De Sanctis, Hippolyte Taine, Julian Schmidt, Leslie Stephens, Henry Hallam, and William John Courthope.   CRIT

1837   With the opening of Mount Holyoke in Massachusetts, the women's college
              has its beginnings in the United States.   EDUC

1837   Part of a statewide investigation of education in Massachusetts, American edu-
              cator Horace Mann recommends that the state provide a complete education
              for its youth in order to train it for productive citizenry. Although eventually
              accepted nationwide, his ideas are originally rejected as an unnecessary tax
              burden and invitation for social unrest among the masses.   EDUC

1837   In Bad Blankenburg, Germany, German educator Friedrich Froebel opens the
              first kindergarten, founding the pre-school education movement. Although
              the kindergarten will be banned in Germany from 1851 to 1860, it will be res-
              urrected and will eventually spread throughout the industrialized world. Like
              his colleague Johann Pestalozzi (see 1781–1787, EDUC, and 1805, EDUC), he
              believes in the complete training of the child, taking into account the child's
              physical and spiritual training and need for pleasure.   EDUC

The Philosophy of Childhood

When childhood became an intense area of study and adulation in Britain during the
Victorian era (1837–1901), reformers and artists were inspired by the conflicting ideas of
philosophers from the two previous centuries—John Locke and Jean-Jacques Rousseau.

Utilitarians (like Jeremy Bentham and James Mill) and Evangelicals (like Hannah
More) ushered in the Victorian era with the idea of children as beings requiring rigorous
educational and moral training to sharpen their reasoning skills and ameliorate their
state of original sin. These practices had their origins in English philosopher John Locke's
Essay Concerning Human Understanding (1689). In it, he posits that an infant's mind is a
tabula rasa, or blank slate, ready to be shaped by outside forces. Under the training of
utilitarians and Evangelicals, a child would be erudite and chaste.

Even more influential in the Victorian era was the image of childhood as a golden
age of innocence. Crystallizing that idea was French philosopher Jean-Jacques
Rousseau's *Émile* (1762), in which the title character is educated according to the principles of nature. Such education, according to Rousseau, preserves the child's innocence and evokes his natural moral instincts. Rousseau's views on child development
would inform child psychologists, educational reformers, and artists throughout the
Victorian era and for much of the 20th century.

Perhaps the only stronger image of the child in the 19th century came from someone
who followed neither the Utilitarian nor the romantic view—Charles Dickens. His views of
children in *Oliver Twist, David Copperfield,* and *Great Expectations* created an image of the
innocent yet worldly-wise child that came to represent Victorian childhood in its own age
and beyond.

1837   Scottish philosopher and essayist Thomas Carlyle publishes the history *The French Revolution*. Carlyle focuses sympathetically on the plight of French commoners.   HIST

1837   American essayist and poet Ralph Waldo Emerson delivers his address "The American Scholar" to the Phi Beta Kappa Society at Harvard University. In it, he calls for independence in American thought and cites the responsibility of the American thinker in establishing a national creative identity separate from European influence.   PHIL

1837   English writer Harriet Martineau publishes *Society in America*, a systematic look at life in the United States. The work is a contemporary of French writer Tocqueville's *Democracy in America* (*see* 1835–1840, soc). Martineau is also the translator of French philosopher Auguste Comte.   SOC

1838   American historian William Prescott publishes *History of the Reign of Ferdinand and Isabella the Catholic*. He will publish *History of the Conquest of Mexico* in 1843. Prescott's writing, focused mostly on the history of Spain and its empire, will be known for its fine literary style and its skillful organization of very large amounts of material, and it will influence the United States in its dealing with Mexico in the 1840s.   HIST

1838   English mathematician and logician Augustus De Morgan publishes *Essay on Probabilities*. In this and other works, such as *Formal Logic* (1847), he expounds on aspects of logic, including its connections to algebra.   PHIL

1838–1848   The Chartist movement is active among workingmen in England. Its aims, set forth in the People's Charter by William Lovett, include universal male suffrage and reform of the Poor Laws.   POL

1838   American essayist and poet Ralph Waldo Emerson presents "The Divinity School Address" to the Harvard Divinity School. His comments on the divinity of Christ generate controversy among church and divinity school officials.   REL

1838   Japanese holy woman Nakayama Miki is possessed by a *kami* (supernatural power), leading her to found the Shinto sect Tenrikyo (the Religion of Heavenly Wisdom). Devoted to the *kami* of the Moon (*Tsuki*) and Sun (*Hi*), the sect emphasizes joyous living and voluntary labor done in a spirit of gratitude to God. The sect's scriptures will include *Ofudesaki* (1869–1882) and *Mikagura-uta* (1866–1882).   REL

c. 1838   In the United States, a clandestine program known as the Underground Railroad is developed to transport slaves in the South to free regions in the Northern states and Canada.   SOC

1838   French philosopher Auguste Comte coins the term *sociology*. Considered the
              father of this discipline and of the philosophical school of positivism, Comte
              argues that the only real (or positive) knowledge is that gained by observation
              and experiment.   SOC

1838–1842   American clergyman Orestes Brownson founds and edits the *Boston Quarterly
              Review*. In 1842, he also founds and edits the *Democratic Review* (1842–1844).
              In his work on these magazines as well as through his own church, the Society
              for Christian Union (1836), he is a leading spokesman against social injustice
              and for reform through the leading high-minded avenues of the day.   SOC

1839   In Britain, English politician and economist Richard Cobden and others found
              the Anti-Corn Law League to repeal the duties on corn, which have kept bread
              prices artificially high. The Corn Laws will be repealed in 1846.   POL

1839–1897   Muslim religious reformer Jamāl ad-Dīn al-Afghānī lives. He advocates both a
              revolutionary rejection of foreign hegemony and adoption of aspects of mod-
              ern culture, including devotion to reason and progress.   REL

1840s   The invention of the telegraph improves reporting speed and is instrumental
              in the creation of national and international news agencies, like the Associated
              Press (1848) and Reuters (1851).   JOURN

1840s   American religious leader John Thomas founds the Christadelphians, a reli-
              gious denomination that rejects the Trinity and emphasizes reliance on
              Scripture and belief in the Second Coming of Christ.   REL

1840s   In his writings, German political philosopher Karl Marx resurrects the term *pro-
              letariat* to describe the working class, who are supported only by their labor. In
              ancient Rome, the proletariat referred to its unmoneyed citizenry, who consti-
              tuted the lowest level of society.   SOC

1840   German art historian E. Kolloff outlines the development of modern art in *Die
              Entwicklung der modernen Kunst*. He criticizes German archaeologist and art
              critic Johann Winckelmann for ignoring the art of the Middle Ages and under-
              scores the power of Christianity in modern art history.   CRIT

1840   American essayist and poet Ralph Waldo Emerson and social reformer
              Margaret Fuller begin publication of the transcendentalist periodical the
              Dial.   JOURN

1840   English philosopher William Whewell publishes *The Philosophy of the Inductive
              Sciences*, in which he takes a Kantian approach that emphasizes the inventive-
              ness of scientific discovery. He also published *History of the Inductive Sciences*
              (1837).   PHIL

1840   French journalist Pierre-Joseph Proudhon publishes *What Is Property?* One of the founders of anarchism, Proudhon can be seen as advocating a form of libertarian socialism.   POL

1840–1850   American reformers Susan B. Anthony and Elizabeth Cady Stanton present public statements in support of a woman's rights to her property, wages, and children.   POL

1840   The unorthodox life of French novelist George Sand (pseudonym of Aurore Dudevant) spurs the pejorative term "George Sandism," which is used in Europe and Russia to describe lifestyles open to free love, divorce, and questioning of gender rules.   SOC

1841   Scottish historian and essayist Thomas Carlyle publishes *On Heroes, Hero Worship and the Heroic in History*, a collection of lectures promoting benevolent autocracy as the best form of government. *On Heroes* reflects a major shift to the right in Carlyle's views. In 1845, he will publish *Oliver Cromwell's Letters and Speeches*, a work which will lead people to view the Puritan leader much more favorably.   HIST

1841   American essayist and poet Ralph Waldo Emerson publishes *Essays: First Series*, which includes his philosophical works "The Over-Soul" and "Self-Reliance."   PHIL

1841   Scottish surgeon James Braid witnesses demonstrations of mesmerism (*see* 1772, MISC). By experimenting with the process, he proves the existence of hypnosis (of which he is considered the discoverer) and helps to take the phenomenon out of the realm of magic and into that of modern psychology.   PSYCH

1841   American reformer Dorothea Dix begins campaigning for reform of the care of mentally ill patients and poor people in almshouses.   SOC

1841–1847   An example of the 19th-century urge to form utopian societies, Brook Farm is founded in Wext Roxbury, Massachusetts, by American minister and transcendentalist George Ripley. Meant, in Ripley's words, to "substitute a system of brotherly cooperation for one of selfish competition," its inhabitants and visitors include American writer Nathaniel Hawthorne and social reformer Margaret Fuller. In 1844, it adopts Fourierist principles (*see* 1808, SOC). Following a fire in 1846, Brook Farm will close.   SOC

1842   In his speeches and book *A Discourse of Matters Pertaining to Religion*, American clergyman Theodore Parker makes a case for making religion a movement for social change. "A Christian church should be the means of reforming the world," he writes. Dismissed as extreme at the time, his ideas will come to be widely accepted.   REL

1843	English writer and politician Thomas Babington Macaulay publishes the essay collection *Critical and Historical Essays*. CRIT

1843   English writer and politician Thomas Babington Macaulay publishes the essay collection *Critical and Historical Essays*.   CRIT

1843–1860 English art critic and writer John Ruskin, known for his religious and moral aesthetic, publishes the series *Modern Painters*.   CRIT

1843   German art historian Carl Schnaase begins writing *Geschichte der Bildenden Kunst*, a work that compresses the whole history of art in one volume. He finds that "modern" art history starts about 1420 with the Renaissance as a rebirth of the classics. His work will be published posthumously in 1879.   CRIT

1843   Scottish historian and essayist Thomas Carlyle publishes *Past and Present*. PHIL

1843   Danish philosopher Søren Kierkegaard publishes *Either/Or* and *Fear and Trembling*. A forerunner of 20th-century existentialism, he posits the freedom of the will and the need for a "leap of faith" in establishing a relationship with God. His views will influence much of later Protestant theology. Other works will include *Concluding Unscientific Postscript* (1846) and *The Sickness Unto Death* (1849).   PHIL

1843   English philosopher John Stuart Mill publishes *System of Logic*, in which he defines rules for inductive thinking.   PHIL

1843   American religious leader William Miller predicts from a study of biblical prophecies that the world will end this year. When the Second Coming of Christ fails to occur, the predicted apocalypse is moved to 1844. Unbowed by its nonoccurrence in that year, Miller will found the Seventh-Day Adventist church in 1845.   REL

1844–1906 Austrian physicist Ludwig Boltzmann lives. He tries to integrate physics and philosophy and contributes to the developing concept of time's arrow.   PHIL

1844   The Democratic slogan "54°40' or fight" is used to refer to the latitude of the Oregon Territory that some Americans are attempting to bring from joint British-American to complete American control. The slogan aids in the presidential election of James Polk.   POL

1844   The American Psychiatric Association is founded.   PSYCH

1844   Persian religious leader Mirza Ali Mohammad of Shiraz proclaims himself the Bab (gate) and founds the sect of Babism. Growing out of Shiite Islam and including Sufi and Gnostic beliefs, the religion preaches the coming of a Promised One. The sect will break completely from Islam in 1848. In 1863 Babists will be expelled from Persia (Iran). *See also* 1863, REL.   REL

c. 1845–1855   In correspondence, French novelist Gustave Flaubert outlines his aesthetics, which favor precise style, realistic representation, and authorial impersonality.   CRIT

1845   German political philosopher Karl Marx writes, in collaboration with German socialist Friedrich Engels, *The German Ideology*, a presentation of his dialectical-materialist view of history. It will be published posthumously.   POL

1845   The Know-Nothing Party becomes a national U.S. political party. It gains popularity in the Northeast with its platform of curtailing immigration.   POL

1845   The Southern Baptist Convention, which will become the largest body of Baptists, is established.   REL

1845   American social reformer Margaret Fuller publishes the feminist work *Woman in the 19th Century*, which will be followed the next year by *Papers on Literature and Art*.   SOC

1845   German socialist Friedrich Engels publishes *The Condition of the Working Class in England*.   SOC

1845   African-American writer and activist Frederick Douglass describes his slave years in *Narrative of the Life of Frederick Douglass*. A prominent abolitionist, he will be a civil rights leader after the Civil War.   SOC

1846   In "The Old Manse," the preface to *Mosses from an Old Manse*, American writer Nathaniel Hawthorne argues that the roots of his creativity lie in American history and social institutions rather than the American natural landscape. Hawthorne will reflect on his art in several prefaces, including "The Custom House," the preface to *The Scarlet Letter* (1850).   CRIT

1846   American poet and writer Edgar Allan Poe writes on poetic composition in "The Philosophy of Composition." Other critical works will include the essay "The Poetic Principle" and reviews of the works of English writer Charles Dickens and American writer Nathaniel Hawthorne.   CRIT

1846   German philosopher Ludwig Feuerbach publishes *The Essence of Christianity*, in which he argues that religion is a projection of humanity's emotional needs. German political philosopher Karl Marx, Austrian psychoanalyst Sigmund Freud, and others will incorporate the idea into their thinking.   REL

1847   The French poet who inspired the Symbolist movement, Charles Baudelaire, publishes his only novel, the autobiographical *La Fanfarlo*. His literary criticism will be collected posthumously with his art criticism under the titles of *Art Romantique* and *Curiosites Esthetiques* (1868–1869).   CRIT

1847   French poet Alphonse de Lamartine publishes *History of the Girondists*. In 1851–1852, he will publish *History of the Restoration*. Both are major histories of the French Revolution.   HIST

1847   English mathematician George Boole publishes *The Mathematical Analysis of Logic*. In this and *An Investigation of the Laws of Thought* (1854), he develops a set of symbols and algebraic manipulations that express logical arguments. His system will become known as Boolean algebra or symbolic logic.   PHIL

1847   After years of persecution culminating in the 1844 slaying of Mormon founder Joseph Smith (*see* 1827, REL), the Mormons under Brigham Young move to Utah and found Salt Lake City, which will remain the world center of the religion.   REL

1847   Spiritualism, a religious movement emphasizing contact with the spirits of the dead, is founded when American spiritualist Andrew Jackson Davis publishes *Nature's Divine Revelations*. By the late 19th century, séances led by mediums attempting to contact the dead will be widely practiced in America and Europe.   REL

1848   English writer and politician Thomas Babington Macaulay publishes the first two volumes of his *History of England from the Accession of James II*. The next two volumes will appear in 1855 and an unfinished fifth volume will be published in 1861. Macaulay's *History* is perhaps the most thorough study of a period and the most popular historical work written to date, though problems with accuracy and interpretation will be detected later.   HIST

1848   German political philosopher Karl Marx and his colleague Friedrich Engels publish *The Communist Manifesto*, elaborating their view that class conflict is the prime moving force of history and that it will lead inexorably to the triumph of the working class. *See also* 1867–1894, POL.   POL

1848   Russian anarchist Mikhail Bakunin publishes *Appeal to the Slavs*. His *Revolutionary Catechism* (1865) will be the manifesto of the International Brotherhood.   POL

1848   Across Europe the Revolutions of 1848 occur, reflecting strong levels of economic and political dissent. In France, the February Revolution results in the abdication of King Louis-Philippe and the establishment of a provisional republican government. Division over labor and rights reforms leads to the downfall of the government and the election of Prince Louis-Napoléon (the future Napoleon III). In Germany, uprisings bring about the short-lived national parliament known as the Frankfurt Parliament. In 1849, the new government will be crushed and replaced by the former parliament. Some countries of the Hapsburg empire (Austria, Hungary, and Bohemia) seek more autonomy, but are suppressed by the empire's military forces. Similarly, Italy's fight for internal unification and independence from Austria is broken by the Austrian military. The revolutions, though limited in success, are crucial to the founding of modern parliamentary governments and unification movements.   POL

1848   American reformers Lucretia Mott and Elizabeth Cady Stanton formally introduce the idea of legal equality for women at the first women's rights convention, in Seneca Falls, New York.   POL

1849–1872   American historian George Ticknor, known as an inventive professor of languages, writes his monumental *History of Spanish Literature*.   HIST

1849   Following his participation in the revolutions of 1848, French journalist Pierre-Joseph Proudhon publishes *Confessions of a Revolutionary*.   PHIL

1849   American writer Henry David Thoreau publishes the essay "Civil Disobedience," in which he advocates breaking unjust laws as a form of protest. The essay recounts his own imprisonment for refusing to pay a tax that would help finance the Mexican War. Thoreau's concept of civil disobedience will inspire future political dissenters, including Indian nationalist Mohandas Gandhi and American civil rights leader Martin Luther King Jr.   POL

1849–1905   Egyptian religious reformer Muhammad Abduh lives. An Islamic modernist, he argues for the place of reason, science, and social change.   REL

1850s   American transcendentalist and writer John Sullivan Dwight establishes himself as a music critic, one of the first in the nation.   CRIT

1850s   English reformer Harriet Taylor Mill (wife of English philosopher John Stuart Mill) campaigns for women's suffrage and rights at women's conventions in the United States and England, asserting in one of her many essays that "what is wanted for women is equal rights, equal admission to all social privileges; not a position apart, a sort of sentimental priesthood."   POL

c. 1850s   In Brazil, the Afro-Brazilian religion called Macumba flourishes. Combining African religious traditions and Roman Catholicism, it originated among Africans brought to the country as slaves. The most important sects are Candomblé and Umbanda.   REL

1850s   The end of the "peculiar" institution of slavery becomes the focus of American reformers such as politician William Henry Seward, who claims, "there is a higher law than the Constitution, which regulates our authority over the domain, and devotes it to the same noble purposes."   SOC

1850	German art historian F. Mertens publishes *Die Baukunst des Mittelalters*, a serious study of medieval architecture that argues Gothic architecture had its origin in France with Abbé Suger as its inventor. CRIT

1850   English poet William Wordsworth's 14-book blank-verse poem, *The Prelude*, is published posthumously. Begun in 1798, the autobiographical work represents a meditation on time, memory, nature, politics, and other matters.   PHIL

1850   American essayist and poet Ralph Waldo Emerson publishes the essay collection *Representative Men*.   PHIL

c. 1850   In Russia, a controversy ensues between Westerners, who believe Russia should imitate Western social, cultural, and political models, and Slavophiles, who argue that Russia should remain true to its native, Orthodox roots. Prominent Westerners include Vissarion Belinsky, Aleksandr Herzen, and Ivan Turgenev; Slavophiles include Aleksey Khomyakov, Ivan Kireyevsky, and Konstantin and Ivan Aksakov.   POL

1850   The U.S. Congress passes a series of laws known as the Compromise of 1850, which are meant to address the states' conflicts over slavery and to preserve the faltering Union. The compromise will be disrupted by the 1854 passage of the Kansas-Nebraska Act. *See* 1854, POL.   POL

c. 1850   German Jewish bibliographer Moritz Steinschneider publishes catalogues of and articles on Hebrew works in European libraries.   REL

1850   By now, after centuries of decline, the lands of the great Islamic empires of the past have fallen under Christian European hegemony or outright colonization. These include the Ottoman Turkish empire, the Mughal empire of India, and the Persian empire of Iran.   REL

c. 1850-1890 The peyotist movement spreads among more than 50 Native American tribes in the United States and Canada. Beginning in Oklahoma among the Kiowa and Comanche tribes, it combines Christian teachings and Native American rituals, including use of the hallucinogenic drug peyote to induce visions. The movement is the basis for what will be called the Native American Church.   REL

1851–1853   British art critic and writer John Ruskin publishes *The Stones of Venice*, a seminal work linking artistic and social criticism. His examination of architecture in Venice in relation to the city's moral and artistic decline does much to spur the Gothic revival in arts and architecture. Ruskin's works include *The Seven Lamps of Architecture* (1849) and *Lectures on Art* (1870).   CRIT

1851   German architect Gottfried Semper discusses how artifacts and architecture take
                on meaning from the purposes they serve in *Die Vier Elemente der Baukunst.*
                                                                                          CRIT

1851   English philosopher John Stuart Mill publishes *Principles of Political Economy,*
                which will remain a basic economic text for several decades.   ECON

1851   The *New York Times* is first published, under the editorship of American jour-
                nalist Henry Raymond. *See also* 1896, JOURN.   JOURN

1851   German philosopher Arthur Schopenhauer publishes *Parerga and Paralipomena*
                (*Comments and Omissions*), a collection of aphorisms.   PHIL

1851–1854   French philosopher Auguste Comte publishes *The System of Positive Polity.* PHIL

1851   English philosopher Herbert Spencer publishes *Social Statics,* in which he
                advocates extreme libertarian political views.   POL

1851–1868   Mongkut reigns as Rama IV in Siam, modernizing the nation under Western
                technological lines. Previously, as a Buddhist scholar and abbot, he intro-
                duced reforms and contemporary reinterpretations of Buddhist doctrine.
                He also founded a reformed school of the Sangha (monastic community)
                known as the Dhammayutika.   REL

1851   American reformer Amelia Jenks Bloomer invents and wears a cotton pantaloon
                called "bloomers." The clothing grants more freedom of movement and ushers
                in a century-long redefinition of the purpose of women's clothing.   SOC

1852   School attendance is made mandatory in Massachusetts. It is the first state to
                require it.   EDUC

1852   English physician and scholar Peter Mark Roget publishes *Thesaurus of English
                Words and Phrases.*   LING

1852   American novelist Harriet Beecher Stowe publishes the antislavery novel
                Uncle Tom's Cabin. One of the best-selling books of the century, it helps
                promote abolitionist sentiment, hastening the American Civil War. Its
                many dramatic renditions will increase its appeal.   POL

1852   Argentine statesman and philosopher Juan Bautista Alberdi publishes *Bases
                and Starting Points for the Political Organization of the Argentine Republic,* which
                influences the development of his nation's constitution.   POL

1853–1876   German historian Heinrich Graetz publishes his monumental *History of the
                Jews.*   HIST

1853	The visit of U.S. Commodore Matthew Perry to Japan reopens that nation to foreign influence and trade after more than two centuries of isolation (*see* 1603–1867, POL). POL
1853–1855	French diplomat Joseph-Arthur de Gobineau publishes *Essai sur l'inégalité des races humaines* (*The Inequality of Human Races*), which argues for the superiority of Nordic peoples. His ideas will contribute to the Nazi belief in a superior Aryan race. SOC
1854	Influential Austrian music critic Eduard Hanslick develops a formalist theory of music in *The Beautiful in Music*. CRIT
1854–1856	German historian Theodor Mommsen publishes his three-volume *History of Rome*. He will publish *The Roman Provinces* in 1885. These will be seen as the greatest works of an enormously prolific historian. As recipient of the Nobel Prize for literature in 1902, he will be one of the few historians to receive this award. HIST
1854	The Astor Library, a precursor to the New York Public Library system, begins operation with 80,000 volumes in its collection. MISC
1854	American writer Henry David Thoreau publishes *Walden*, a work of transcendentalist philosophy woven around the author's attempt to "live deliberately" at Walden Pond near Concord, Massachusetts. PHIL
1854	In the United States, the Republican Party is formed by antislavery forces, notably Whigs. Its second presidential candidate, Abraham Lincoln, will be elected in 1860. POL
1854	The passage of the Kansas-Nebraska Act by the U.S. Congress introduces the concept of popular sovereignty, which grants to localities the power to legalize slavery. The bill overrides provisions of the Missouri Compromise (1820) and becomes another factor leading to the Civil War. POL
1854	Pope Pius IX defines the dogma of the Immaculate Conception, according to which the Virgin Mary was conceived free of original sin. REL
1854	In Mali, Africa, Islamic conqueror al-Hājj Umar encounters resistance from a people he calls the Bambara, meaning "infidel." Their beliefs, including acknowledgment of a creator-god, are symbolized in distinctive masks and carvings. REL
1854	English novelist Elizabeth Gaskell publishes *North and South*, which, like other "social-problem novels" of the day, discusses industrialized England. SOC

1854   American novelist Timothy Shay Arthur publishes *Ten Nights in a Barroom and*
           What I Saw There, which gives fictional voice to the antiliquor movement.
           William Pratt will write a long-lived stage adaptation in 1858.   SOC

1855   In the preface to his *Leaves of Grass*, American poet Walt Whitman articulates
           the principles behind his attempt to write "the great poem of the republic."
                                                                                    CRIT

1855   The New York *Daily News* is founded.   JOURN

1855   *Leslie's Illustrated Newspaper* is founded by American publisher Frank Leslie. It
           is notable for its titillating stories and ample use of illustrations.   JOURN

1855   In Britain, the *Daily Telegraph* is founded. In the next two decades, it will become
           the world's best-selling newspaper.   JOURN

1855   English philosopher Herbert Spencer publishes *Principles of Psychology*. It will
           later be recast in the series *System of Synthetic Philosophy* (*see* 1860, PHIL).   PSYCH

1855   Hindu mystic Ramakrishna becomes a devotee of the goddess Kali. Through years
           of spiritual practice in the Hindu Yoga, Christian, and Islamic traditions, he
           reaches the conclusion that all religions are one and that they share in common
           the goal of union with God. The message of universal religion will spread
           throughout India and, largely through his disciple Vivekenanda (*see* 1886, REL), to
           the West.   REL

1855   The Amana Church Society, a group of seven colonies, is established in east-
           ern Iowa by the Ebenezer Society, a German Pietist group fleeing religious per-
           secution. The cooperative villages, one of the most successful of such experi-
           mental communities, will continue to thrive into the 20th century. They will
           be known for their fine woolens and long-lived farms.   SOC

1856   French writer Alexis de Tocqueville publishes *L'Ancien Régime et la Révolution*,
           the first volume of a work that he will not complete. He views the French
           Revolution as having been the inevitable result of several factors; a historical
           trend toward increasingly centralized government being perhaps the most
           important.   HIST

1856   American historian John Lothrop Motley publishes *The Rise of the Dutch*
           Republic. He will publish *The History of the United Netherlands* in the 1860s, and
           he will be considered a leading writer on the Dutch movement for freedom.   HIST

1856–1857   In the Dred Scott Case, the United States Supreme Court rules against Scott, a
           slave who moves to a free territory and claims that he is a free man. Because
           he is a slave, the Court does not recognize his right to present his case; further,

it questions federal rights to alter slavery practices in the territories and deems the Missouri Compromise (1820) unconstitutional. The decision stirs conflict between North and South before the American Civil War.   POL

1856–1920   Indian nationalist Bal Gangadhar Tilak lives. His commentary on the *Bhagavad-Gita* argues that political action and violence are legitimate means toward divinely sanctioned ends.   REL

1857–1867   In Britain, exiled Russian writer and revolutionary Aleksandr Herzen publishes the weekly journal *Kolokol*, which is banned in Russia. He is the author of *My Past and Thoughts* (1855).   POL

1857   A number of English writers and activists, including Bessie Raynor Parker, Mary Howitt, and Anna Jameson begin a movement to gain legal rights for women following the defeat of a women's property rights petition to Parliament. The group present their ideas through their periodical, *The Englishwoman's Journal*, and a Ladies Institute study center. Feminists who will later join the group include physician Elizabeth Garrett and printer Emily Faithfull.   POL

1857–1858   The Indian Mutiny, or Sepoy Rebellion, takes place in India, as Hindus and Muslims alike take up arms against their British rulers, who they believe are undermining their religious principles.   REL

1857   Christian missionaries in Nigeria encounter the Igbo people, whose traditional religion entails the worship of the creator God Chukwu, spirits, and ancestors.   REL

1858   The phrase "King Cotton" is introduced in a speech in the U.S. Senate by Senator James Hammond. The term refers to the vast economic power of the South's primary crop and the accompanying belief that the cotton industry will support the region if it secedes from the Union.   ECON

1858–1865   Scottish historian and essayist Thomas Carlyle publishes *The History of Friedrich II of Prussia*, a major military and political history and arguably Carlyle's finest historical work.   HIST

1858   American jurist Oliver Wendell Holmes publishes *The Autocrat of the Breakfast Table*, a collection of his *Atlantic Monthly* essays and poetry on social, scientific, and philosophical topics. Several sequels will follow until 1890.   PHIL

c. 1858   The secret nationalist group known as the Fenians is organized in Ireland. It aims at gaining complete independence for Ireland from England, and will be active in Ireland, Britain, and the United States during the 1860s and 1870s.   POL

1858   The United Presbyterian Church of North America is formed. The Presbyterian
            Church in United States, or Southern Presbyterian Church, will split from that
            body (c. 1861) over the issue of slavery.   REL

1859   French anthropologist Pierre-Paul Broca founds the *Société d'Anthropologie*.
                                                                                   ANTH

1859   Emphasizing the growing belief that women as well as men should achieve a
            certain level of education to function in society, English reformer Jessie
            Boucherette founds the Society for Promoting the Employment of Women, in
            London. By the end of the 19th century, most industrialized nations will open
            some public education to females.   EDUC

1859   English naturalist Charles Darwin publishes *The Origin of Species*, an exposi-
            tion of his theory of evolution by natural selection. This controversial theory
            will eventually revolutionize the life sciences. It also has numerous implica-
            tions for theology, social philosophy, history, and other fields of thought. The
            theory is embraced by Social Darwinists, who apply it to human society. It is
            attacked by Christian theologians who are unable to reconcile Darwin's views
            with a literal interpretation of the scriptural account of creation. More gener-
            ally, *The Origin of Species* follows the tradition of Polish astronomer Nicolaus
            Copernicus (*see* 1543, MISC) in seeming to displace humanity from a place of
            central importance in the universe.   MISC

1859–1860   Scottish philosopher William Hamilton publishes *Lectures of Metaphysics and
            Logic*.   PHIL

1859   Over 20 American abolitionists, led by John Brown, attempt a raid on an arse-
            nal at Harpers Ferry, Virginia. The raid, which aims to capture the area to use
            as the base for a new state that would be a refuge for slaves, fails; Brown and
            six others are killed. However, the event crystallizes antislavery sentiment and
            pushes the country toward the Civil War.   POL

1859   English philosopher John Stuart Mill publishes *On Liberty*, a classic statement
            of liberal political theory. In this and other works, such as *Utilitarianism*, he
            modifies the utilitarian views of his father James Mill.   POL

1859   During the unification of Italy, the papacy loses control of most of the Papal
            States. *See also* 1870, REL.   REL

1859   After the French capture of Saigon this year, Buddhism in Vietnam will come
            under increasing restriction, losing ground to Catholicism though not vanishing
            completely. Buddhism will begin a gradual revival in the early 20th century. REL

1859   Japanese holy man Konko Daijin declares himself an *ikigami* (one in union with the divine), the intermediary of the supreme *kami* (deity). The Shinto sect he founds is called Konkokyo (the Religion of Metal Luster).   REL

1859   Czech-born Jewish theologian Zacharias Frankel publishes *Darke ha-Mishnah* (*Introduction to the Mishnah*). Frankel will be considered the founder of Conservative Judaism, which takes a middle way between Orthodox and Reform Judaism, emphasizing a positivist-historical approach to Jewish tradition. *See also* 1800–1900, REL.   REL

1859   The song "Dixie," by American songwriter Daniel Decatur Dennett, is written. It will become the anthem of the Confederacy during the American Civil War, and will contribute to the use of the term "Dixie" to refer to Southern states. Other sources for "Dixie" may be the Mason-Dixon line, which divides Northern and Southern states, or a past slaveholder named Dixie.   SOC

1860s   In Russia, the agrarian socialist group the Narodniki forms to effect socialist reforms to Russian society. In 1876, they will form the secret Land and Liberty society aimed at encouraging a revolution. The movement will become further consumed by another faction, the terrorist People's Will, which will assassinate Tsar Alexander II in 1881.   POL

The Unwed Philosophers

Although a few philosophers, like John Stuart Mill, were greatly influenced by their wives, many of the world's great thinkers never knew wedded bliss. Among such confirmed bachelors were:

Thomas Aquinas (1225–1274)—The Italian scholastic philosopher whose works united Aristotelian reason with Christian faith never entered into a union himself. He joined the Dominican order before he was 21.

Gottfried Wilhelm Leibniz (1646–1716)—Between entering college at 15, developing a metaphysics based on his theory of monads, and exploring the question of evil and the possibilities for optimism, the German philosopher and mathematician never married.

Immanuel Kant (1724–1804)—Not only did Kant write the *Critique of Pure Reason* and grapple with the categorical imperative without the help of a helpmeet, the German philosopher never left his hometown of Konigsberg, Germany.

Søren Kierkegaard (1813–1855)—After a period of youthful debauchery, the Dane who laid the groundwork for 20th-century existentialism was a scholarly hermit.

1860s	In the United States, the Radical Republican faction forms. Under the leadership of Charles Sumner, Thaddeus Stevens, and others, it fights for the rights of black Americans and urges harsh measures against the defeated Confederacy. POL
c. 1860–1900	Many late-Victorian biographies overwhelm the reader with a flood of unimportant detail about their subjects' lives and times. David Masson's massive *The Life of John Milton: Narrated in Connexion with the Political, Ecclesiastical and Literary History of His Time* (1859–1890) is a prime example. HIST
1860	French journalist and politician Charles-Forbes-René de Montalembert, a strong proponent of religious and political freedom during the postrevolutionary period, begins his seven-volume *The Monks of the West*. HIST
1860	Swiss historian Jakob Burckhardt publishes *The Civilization of the Renaissance in Italy*, his finest work. Burckhardt, one of the first historians of culture, uses original source material to carefully recreate the periods he studies. HIST
1860	English philosopher Herbert Spencer announces a projected series, *System of Synthetic Philosophy*, which will apply evolutionary principles to all branches of knowledge, including biology, psychology, sociology, and ethics. He will continue working on it until his death in 1903. PHIL
1860	American novelist and critic William Dean Howells publishes *Lives and Speeches of Abraham Lincoln and Hannibal Hamlin*, a book about the recent presidential campaign. POL
1860–1960	The Tammany organization controls New York politics for nearly a century. It becomes known for its power and corruption, particularly under the rule of William Marcy "Boss" Tweed, in the late 19th century. POL
1860	English art critic and writer John Ruskin publishes *Unto This Last*, a collection of essays on political economy that stresses the social responsibility of employers toward employees. SOC
1860–1870	The Irish-American social reform and terrorist group known as the Molly Maguires is active in coal-mining regions of Pennsylvania. Until the group is broken by Pinkerton detectives, they kill coal mining executives and perform other criminal acts. SOC
1861	English philosopher Herbert Spencer publishes the influential work *Education*, in which he argues for natural development of intelligence through interesting activities in a curriculum that includes science. EDUC
1861	Russian Tsar Alexander II issues the Edict of Emancipation, granting serfs individual freedom and allotments of land. The breakdown in the land-grant

process, which was to be completed in 49 years, will be the underlying reason for the Russian Revolution. At the time of the edict, serfs comprise one-third of Russia's population.   POL

1861–1865   The American secessionist government of the Confederacy is composed of Southern states that have separated from the Union over the issue of slavery. The Confederacy comprises the states of Alabama, Arkansas, Florida, Georgia, Louisiana, Mississippi, North Carolina, South Carolina, Tennessee, Texas, and Virginia. Its president is Jefferson Davis. Division over the issue of slavery and states' rights, among other issues, has led to the American Civil War. It pits Northern, largely antislavery, states against Southern states, whose economy is built on the use of slave labor. The war is the most costly American conflict to date, taking some 600,000 lives. It also brings about the end of slavery in the country, ushering in a century of political and social turmoil over civil rights.   POL

1861   The German book *The Housewife*, which details the myriad duties a woman of the house must either do or have done to maintain a proper home, reflects the increased responsibilities expected of middle- and upper-class women of the Industrial Age. These new expectations arose as the advances of the Industrial Age began to ease women's domestic chores.   SOC

1862   In order to move away from colleges centering on classical and theological studies, the U.S. Congress passes the Morrill Act, which allots public lands for schools of higher education in agriculture and the mechanical sciences. These schools will be known as land-grant colleges.   EDUC

1862   French socialist Louis Blanc completes *Histoire de la Révolution française*, a chronicle of the French Revolution from a strongly Republican viewpoint.   HIST

1862   Russian writer Ivan Turgenev is the first to use the term *nihilist* for one who believes in nothing.   PHIL

1862   In the United States, the Homestead Act passes. It grants 160 acres of public land to settlers who live on the land for five years. The ruling is popular in the expanding American west.   POL

1862–1865   Japanese philospher Nishi Amane is sent to Europe to study Western social sciences. On his return to Japan, he will introduce to his country positivism, utilitarianism, and European concepts of natural and international law.   SOC

1863   French poet Charles Baudelaire publishes "The Painter of Modern Life." In this and other essays on aesthetics, he presents his doctrine of correspondences, or the interrelatedness of the senses that must be represented in order to achieve the modern poet's task of capturing fleeting moments.   CRIT

1863   English historian Samuel Gardiner publishes the first installment of his *History
           of England from the Accession of James I to the Restoration*, a work which will con-
           tinue to influence historians of the Stuart period.   HIST

1863   On November 19, American president Abraham Lincoln delivers the
           Gettysburg Address. In fewer than 300 words, spoken at the dedication of a
           military cemetery at the site of the Battle of Gettysburg in Pennsylvania,
           Lincoln enduringly expresses American dedication to the ideals of freedom,
           democracy, and union.   POL

1863   In his Emancipation Proclamation, American president Abraham Lincoln
           abolishes slavery in Confederate states and territories. Two years later, the 13th
           Amendment to the Constitution will end slavery throughout the nation.   POL

1863   Persian religious leader Mīrzā Huseyn Alī Nūrī declares himself the Promised
           One of Babism (*see* 1844, REL). Known as Bahā Allāh or Bahaullah, he founds
           the religion of Baha'ism, which preaches the unity of all religions, universal
           education, world peace, international government, and gender equality. Bahā
           Allāh writes the fundamental Baha'i text, *Kitabi Ikan* (*The Book of Certitude*).   REL

1863   In the United States, the Seventh-Day Adventists are formally organized, based
           on the apocalyptic teachings of William Miller (*see* 1843, REL).   REL

1864   German political philosopher Karl Marx organizes the First International as the
           International Workingmen's Association, which will dissolve in 1876.   POL

1864   Pope Pius IX promulgates the *Syllabus of Errors*, which opposes religious mod-
           ernism, socialism, secular education, civil marriage, and other aspects of the
           modern world.   REL

1864   English theologian John Henry Newman publishes *Apologia pro Vita Sua* (which
           will be revised 1865), a defense of his conversion from Anglicanism to Roman
           Catholicism. The work is both a spiritual autobiography and a masterful apolo-
           getic. Newman will be made a cardinal in 1879.   REL

1864   Swiss philanthropist Jean-Henri Dunant founds the Red Cross, which provides
           aid to wounded soldiers. He will win the first Nobel Prize for peace in 1901.
                                                                                            SOC

1865   English anthropologist Edward Burnett Tylor publishes *Early History of Mankind*.
                                                                                            ANTH

1865   English poet and critic Matthew Arnold publishes *Essays in Criticism: First
           Series*, with its acclaimed introduction, "The Function of Criticism at the
           Present Time." The Second Series will appear posthumously in 1888.   CRIT

1865–1869   French philosopher, critic, and historian Hippolyte Taine publishes *La Philosophie de l'art*. His work presents a view of art, literature, and history influenced by scientific determinism.   CRIT

1865   American historian Francis Parkman publishes *The Pioneers of France in the New World*. He will publish *The Old Régime in Canada* in 1874, as well as many other histories, and he will be regarded as the leading chronicler of French dominion in America.   HIST

1865   English mathematician and writer Lewis Carroll (pseudonym of Charles Lutwidge Dodgson) publishes the children's book *Alice's Adventures in Wonderland*, which takes a humorous approach to logical paradoxes, word play, and social commentary.   MISC

1865–1935   Syrian religious reformer Muhammad Rashid Rida lives. A follower of Muhammad Abduh (*see* 1849–1905, REL), he defends Islam's essential religious doctrines while seeking changes in Islamic law.   REL

1865–1866   A series of Black Codes are passed by the former Confederate states of the United States. While allowing some personal freedoms (to marry, own property), they call for segregation in public places and place restrictions on types of employment.   SOC

1866   American writer Alexander Wheelock Thayer publishes the first volume of *The Life of Beethoven*. It will be translated into German with two more volumes published in 1872 and 1879.   CRIT

1866   American reformer Henry Bergh founds the American Society for the Prevention of Cruelty to Animals (ASPCA).   SOC

1866   In Baltimore, the eight-hour workday becomes a goal of a labor union, when it is adopted as a central goal by the newly founded National Labor Union.   SOC

1867   French novelist Émile Zola, founder of the Naturalist movement, defends Édouard Manet's controversial painting style in *Review of the 19th Century*. CRIT

1867   English logician John Venn publishes *The Logic of Chance*, which examines the frequency theory of probability.   PHIL

1867–1894   *Das Kapital*, by German political philosopher Karl Marx, is published: volume I in 1867; volumes II-III posthumously in 1885–1894, edited by German socialist Friedrich Engels following Marx's death in 1883. The work is a systematic exposition of the economic and political philosophy that will become known as Marxism, which places class struggle at the center of history and predicts the overthrow of the capitalist class by the exploited workers. By inspiring communist revolution and threatening the status quo, Marx's work will have a powerful influence on subsequent world history. By providing an all-embracing explanatory framework, it will influence not only social, economic, and political thought, but also such intellectual fields as literary studies and historical analysis.   POL

1867   The National Grange of the Patrons of Husbandry is founded to protect the interests of U.S. farmers.   POL

1867   In a sign of incipient interest in women's voting rights, English philosopher John Stuart Mill submits Britain's first national suffrage bill to Parliament. It is defeated.   POL

1867   The bishops of the worldwide Anglican Communion meet for the first time in the Lambeth Conference, which will be held every ten years and presided over by the Archbishop of Canterbury.   REL

1867   The secret American organization known as the Ku Klux Klan is founded in Tennessee by General Nathan Bedford Forrest to suppress Reconstruction and uphold white supremacy. Although it will be nearly banned by the U.S. Congress in the 1870s, it will later reorganize (*see* 1915, soc), becoming a powerful social force to promote hatred and violence against blacks, Catholics, and Jews. The KKK will also be active in the 1950s and 1960s, directing most of its energy against the civil rights movement.   SOC

1868   The Royal Historical Society is founded in Britain. The Historical Association, also a British group, will be founded in 1906.   HIST

1868   American statesman and scientist Benjamin Franklin's *Autobiography* is published in complete, accurate form for the first time. It is considered one of the greatest American autobiographies.   HIST

1868   The Meiji restoration in Japan brings an end to more than two centuries of rule by the Tokugawa shogunate (*see* 1603–1867, POL). Feudalism is abolished and Westernization and modernization begin.   POL

1868   After the Meiji restoration this year in Japan, folk chants and magic dances develop and new religious movements gain ground, often tied to a wish for social reform.   REL

1869   English poet and critic Matthew Arnold publishes *Culture and Anarchy*, a collection of essays setting forth his belief in the power of literature, art, and humanistic studies to improve individuals and society.   CRIT

1869   Italian-French economist Enrico Cernuschi is the first to use the term *bimet-allism* to denote a monetary system based on two metals, most often gold and silver. The practice was commonplace in many countries from the 18th to the mid-19th century.   ECON

1869   American educator Charles Willam Eliot becomes president of Harvard. Over his 40-year tenure at Harvard, he will become known for redefining liberal education to allow more academic freedom. He will define liberal studies as those "which are pursued in the scientific spirit for truth's sake." His two articles in *Scientific American*, on "The New Education: Its Organization," are important to debate on curriculum and instrumental to his rise to the presidency of Harvard.   EDUC

1869–1944   French philosopher Léon Brunschvicg lives. He synthesizes the ideas of German philosophers Immanuel Kant and Georg Wilhelm Friedrich Hegel in the philosophical view known as critical idealism.   PHIL

1869   American reformers Susan B. Anthony and Elizabeth Cady Stanton found the National Woman's Suffrage Association as a centralized force in the growing movement for women's voting rights.   POL

1869   English philosopher John Stuart Mill publishes the essay, "The Subjection of Women," which defends "the claim of women, whether in marriage or out of it, to perfect equality in all rights with the male sex." He is said to have been influenced by the beliefs of his wife, English reformer Harriet Taylor Mill, who died in 1859.   POL

1869–1870   The First Vatican Council, convened by Pope Pius IX, defines the dogma of papal infallibility when the pope speaks *ex cathedra* on matters of faith and morals. The Council ends when Italian troops seize Rome (*see* 1870, REL).   REL

1869   The term *agnostic*, referring to one who believes neither in the existence nor in the nonexistence of God, is coined by English biologist Thomas Henry Huxley. Agnosticism will be espoused by many leading 19th- and 20th-century thinkers, including English philosopher Herbert Spencer.   REL

1869   The first major American labor union, the Knights of Labor, is founded. Unlike other organizations, it admits all workers, not simply craft workers. Its aim is the overthrow of the capitalist system and its replacement with workers' cooperatives. It will abandon secrecy in 1881, but its association with violent labor activities will lead to its demise in 1917.   SOC

1870s   In speeches and writings, English poet and critic Matthew Arnold elucidates his concept of liberal education, which, as he will explain during an 1883 U.S. lecture tour, captures "the best which has been thought and said in the world."

He believes that such elements, drawn from classical texts, are the basis not only for curricula, but culture and personality. He will engage in decades-long conflict with English biologist Thomas Huxley, who defends the teaching of natural sciences in a liberal education.   EDUC

1870s   In Japan, the *keimo*, or "enlightenment," scholars urge their country to adopt Western philosophical and social doctrines. The scholars include Nishi Amane (*see* 1862–1865, SOC), Tsuda Mamichi, Nishimura Shigeki, and Fukuzawa Yukichi.   MISC

1870s   English philosopher John Stuart Mill proposes post hoc analysis: examination of childhood experiences and their effect on moral character development. In the 20th century, developmental psychologists will use this procedure in longitudinal studies of children.   PSYCH

1870s   Capturing the image of the United States as a brash, still fledgling country in the shadow of Europe, American writer Henry James writes, "It's a complex fate, being an American, and one of the responsibilities it entails is fighting against a superstitious valuation of Europe."   SOC

1870   Building on his studies of the Seneca people, American ethnologist Lewis Henry Morgan correlates kinship terminology with cultural traditions of marriage and descent.   ANTH

1870–1900   In France, the Symbolist movement takes shape as a force in poetry and aesthetics, emphasizing rich, evocative, mysterious symbols rather than logical sequence and realistic description. Prominent Symbolists include Arthur Rimbaud, Paul Verlaine, and Stéphane Mallarmé.   CRIT

1870–1871   Italian critic Francesco De Sanctis publishes *History of Italian Literature*, which develops a critical theory combining historicity and universality.   CRIT

1870   English prelate and historian William Stubbs publishes *Select Charters*. He will publish his three-volume *The Constitutional History of England* between 1873 and 1878. Stubbs will be seen as the founder of the study of English medieval constitutional history.   HIST

1870–1920   Neo-Kantian philosophy flourishes in Germany, led by Kuno Fischer, who invented the slogan "back to Kant" in 1860.   PHIL

c. 1870–1871   The irredentist movement becomes active in Italy. It is a nationalist force that attempts to gain for Italy all Italian-speaking provinces that were not included in the unification of Italy. The term derives from the Italian *Italia irredentia*, or "unredeemed Italy." Over the years, irredentism will come to apply generally to countries seeking to incorporate land linked by geography or ethnicity.   POL

1870–1924	Russian Communist leader Lenin (born Vladimir Ilich Ulyanov) lives. As dictator of Russia from 1917 following the October Revolution, he enacts his plans for an organized, nonimperialist Communist state. POL
1870	Italian troops seize the last vestiges of the Papal States, including Rome. The pope considers himself a prisoner and refuses to accept Italy's proposed settlement. The status of papal sovereignty (the Roman Question) is not resolved until the Lateran Treaty in 1929. REL
1870	English theologian John Henry Newman publishes *The Grammar of Assent*, an argument for Roman Catholic religious belief. REL
1870–1875	German Chancellor Otto von Bismarck enacts Kulturkampf, his program to undermine the power of the Roman Catholic Church in Germany. Among his actions are his denial of papal infallibility (1870); the expulsion of Jesuits from Germany (1870–1872); the Falk Laws, which circumscribe church powers; and the mandating of civil marriage (1875). REL
1871	English anthropologist Edward Burnett Tylor publishes *Primitive Culture*, in which he analyzes animistic religion and presents methods for making cultural comparisons. ANTH
1871	English economist William Stanley Jevons, known for introducing the marginal utility theory of value, publishes *The Theory of Political Economy*. ECON
1871–1944	Japanese religious leader Makiguchi Tsunesaburo lives and founds Soka Gakkai (Scholarly Association for the Creation of Value), a pragmatic, utilitarian religious movement within the Nichiren Buddhist tradition. REL
1871	American poet Walt Whitman publishes his prose work of social criticism, *Democratic Vistas*. He attacks the corruption and excesses of the Gilded Age and challenges Americans to renew their democratic ideals. SOC
1872	German philosopher Friedrich Nietzsche publishes *The Birth of Tragedy from the Spirit of Music*, in which he identifies the Apollonian and Dionysian strands of ancient Greek culture, and shows a preference for the dark, dynamic pattern of the latter. He decries the emphasis on "Apollonian" reason and stasis associated with the neoclassical tradition beginning with 18th-century German archaeologist and art critic Johann Winckelmann. CRIT
1872	English writer Samuel Butler satirizes ethics in the fantasy *Erewhon*. A sequel, *Erewhon Revisited*, will be published in 1901. PHIL

1872   Russian anarchist Mikhail Bakunin clashes doctrinally with German political philosopher Karl Marx and is expelled from the First International (International Workingmen's Association). The First International will dissolve in 1876 as a result of the schism.   POL

1872   English naturalist Charles Darwin analyzes emotions from an evolutionary standpoint in *The Expression of the Emotions in Man and Animals*.   PSYCH

1872   In Australia, Ernest Giles is the first European to see Ayers Rock or "Uluru." This ancient oval monolith with caves at its base has long been sacred to the regional Aborigines.   REL

1873   English essayist and critic Walter Pater publishes *Studies in the History of the Renaissance*.   CRIT

1873   The Chautauqua Movement, a traveling program that offers adult education and exposure to the arts, becomes popular in the United States.   EDUC

1873   The title of the novel *The Gilded Age*, by American writers Mark Twain (pseudonym of Samuel Langhorne Clemens) and Charles Dudley Warner, becomes the moniker for the approximately two-decade period in U.S. history following the Civil War. The period is categorized by confidence, high spending, and growth in business.   SOC

1874   English historian John Richard Green publishes *Short History of the English People*, the first complete history of Great Britain to take into account social forces, economics, and geography.   HIST

1874   German philosopher Rudolf Hermann Lotze publishes *Logik; Metaphysik* will follow in 1879. His views represent a form of idealism modified by empiricism.   PHIL

1874   English philosopher Henry Sidgwick publishes *Methods of Ethics*. He defines these methods as intuitive common sense, calculation of self-interest, and general utilitarianism. He is also known for supporting women's education and for his involvement in the Society for Psychical Research.   PHIL

1874   German philosopher Franz Brentano publishes *Psychology from an Empirical Standpoint*.   PSYCH

1874   The Old Catholic denomination is founded in Germany by Roman Catholics who break with the church over the Vatican Council's decrees, particularly papal infallibility (*see* 1869–1870, REL).   REL

1874   Fleeing persecution in Russia, groups of Hutterian Brethren and Russian Mennonites begin emigrating to the United States.   REL

1874	In Cleveland, Ohio, the Woman's Christian Temperance Union is founded. It is central to the passage of laws enacting Prohibition. **SOC**
1875–1876	English poet, essayist, and historian John Addington Symonds publishes his six-volume *Renaissance in Italy*. **HIST**
1875	Hindu religious reformer Dayananda Sarasvati founds the Arya Samaj (Society of Nobles) a movement to reform Hinduism, reject Western cultural dominance, and bring modern technology to India, in Bombay. Giving exclusive legitimacy to the Vedas, he reinterprets these and condemns non-Vedic practices such as idol worship, low status of women, and untouchability. **REL**
1875	American religious leader Mary Baker Eddy publishes *Science and Health*, the founding work of the Christian Science religion. It sets forth her belief that physical illness as well as sin can be healed by spiritual means. *See also* 1879, REL. **REL**
1875–1947	English poet Aleister Crowley lives. Calling himself the "wickedest man in the world," he helps to popularize Satanism, with an emphasis on sex as a form of magic. **REL**
1875	In New York, Helena Petrovna Blavatsky founds the Theosophical Society, which popularizes theosophy, a system of mystical philosophy drawing heavily on such Eastern beliefs as reincarnation and karma. **REL**
1875	Indian reformer Sir Sayyid Ahmad Khan founds a college at Aligarh to serve his aim of educational and social rehabilitation for Indian Muslims. Sir Sayyid accepts the value of Western science and scholarship while instilling his followers with a sense of ethnic and religious consciousness. **REL**
1875	American sociologist William Graham Sumner, who has been strongly influenced by his English colleague Herbert Spencer, teaches the first American course in sociology at Yale University. **SOC**
1875–1900	Owing to the growing availability of contraceptives and an increased standard of living, the practice of infanticide in Europe virtually ceases. **SOC**
1876	Johns Hopkins University opens in Baltimore. Modeled on the European university, it emphasizes graduate research and study over undergraduate education. It will influence the concerns of other American universities founded in the 19th century, among them the University of Chicago. **EDUC**
1876	The *Harvard Lampoon* magazine is founded by a group of Harvard students, including Ralph Curtis and Samuel Sherwood. **JOURN**

1876   American educator Felix Adler founds the Society for Ethical Culture, which emphasizes ethical action without espousing a particular ethical or religious system. The Ethical Culture movement will spread across the United States and England.   PHIL

1876   English absolute idealist philosopher Francis Herbert Bradley publishes *Ethical Studies*, in which he criticizes utilitarianism and empiricism. His other works will include *Principles of Logic* (1883).   PHIL

1876   Scottish psychologist Alexander Bain founds the periodical *Mind*, the first general psychological journal. At about this time, psychology begins to develop as a discipline distinct from philosophy and physiology.   PSYCH

1876–1896   English philosopher Herbert Spencer publishes *Principles of Sociology*, in which he applies concepts from Darwinian evolution to the study of human society. He describes the process of individual differentiation from a group and its effect on individual freedom.   SOC

1876   Italian criminologist Cesare Lombroso publishes a pamphlet stating his theory that criminal behavior is rooted in physiology and associated with certain facial features, such as slanting eyes and a receding brow. The treatise will be expanded into *L'uomo delinquente* (*Criminal Man*). Though many of Lombroso's ideas will be discredited, he will be regarded as the father of scientific criminology.   SOC

1877   American ethnologist Lewis Henry Morgan publishes *Ancient Society*, which argues that human societies undergo evolutionary stages, from savagery to barbarism to civilization.   ANTH

1877   American educator Felix Adler publishes *Creed and Deed*. Founder of such institutions as the Workingman's Lyceum, the Workingmen's School, and the Society for Ethical Culture (*see* 1876, PHIL), he stresses ethical action in this and other books such as *An Ethical Philosophy of Life* (1918).   PHIL

1877   Russian physiologist Ivan Pavlov begins studies on dogs' digestion. He will become known for these studies on conditioned response. *See also* 1926, PSYCH.   PSYCH

1877   The American Humane Association for the protection of animals and children is organized. The first Society for the Prevention of Cruelty to Children appeared in the United States in 1875, nine years after a similar society for animals was formed (*see* 1866, SOC).   SOC

1878   American physicist Charles Sanders Peirce coins the term *pragmatism*, which refers to his theories about analyzing ideas in terms of their potential consequences. His major works will be collected in *Chance, Love, and Logic* (1923). *See also* 1907, PHIL.   PHIL

1878   German socialist Friedrich Engels publishes *Anti-Dühring*, in which he develops the philosophy of dialectical materialism, which will be central to Marxist political thought.   PHIL

1878   A constitutional amendment granting suffrage to women is introduced for the first time into the U.S. Congress, where it will be rejected annually for the next four decades (*see* 1919, POL).   POL

1878   The Salvation Army, a Christian evangelical and philanthropic organization, is founded by English religious leaders William and Catherine Booth. Adopting a military structure, it includes ministers called "soldiers" and cites its purpose as "warfare against evil." The group often practices street-corner evangelism.   SOC

1878   In *The Law of Population*, English theosophist Annie Besant outlines the reasons for population control through contraception, ideas she has put into practice for the past several years and for which she has already been convicted by the British courts.   SOC

1879–1894   German historian Heinrich von Treitschke publishes *History of Germany in the Nineteenth Century*, his greatest work. A supporter of authoritarian government and German unification, Treitschke writes from an ardently nationalistic viewpoint, and he criticizes Ranke (*see* 1834–1836, HIST) for his advocacy of objectivity.   HIST

1879   The first journalism course is offered at the University of Missouri, setting the stage to make it a field of professional study.   JOURN

1879   German mathematician and philosopher Ludwig Gottlob Frege publishes *Begriffsschrift* (*Concept Writing*), in which he develops the first formal system of modern logic. Frege will be considered the founder of analytical philosophy, which focuses on analysis of the logical structure of concepts. *See also* 1884 and 1893–1903, PHIL.   PHIL

1879   German psychologist Wilhelm Wundt founds the world's first psychological research laboratory at the University of Leipzig, Germany.   PSYCH

1879   Pope Leo XIII proclaims the system of Italian philosophy of Saint Thomas Aquinas (*see* 1254, REL) to be the official Catholic philosophy. Neo-Thomist philosophy flourishes afterward, notably in the work of such scholars as Étienne Gilson and Jacques Maritain.   REL

1879   American religious leader Mary Baker Eddy founds the Church of Christ, Scientist. Her religious denomination is also known as Christian Science. *See also* 1875, REL.

                                                                                        REL

1879   In India, Hindu religious leader Keshub Chunder Sen, director of the Brahmo Samaj, creates a schism when he claims to have received a "New Dispensation" from God that supersedes earlier religions.

                                                                                        REL

1879–1950   Hindu teacher Ramana Maharishi lives. His beliefs emphasize asceticism and attract a strong following.

                                                                                        REL

1880s   Half-tone reproductions are used in newspapers, increasing the immediacy of newspaper reporting.

                                                                                        JOURN

1880s   American psychologist and philosopher William James and his Danish colleague Carl Lange independently develop the theory that emotion is a consequence of physiological stimulus.

                                                                                        PSYCH

1880s   The term "civilized morality" enters the American lexicon to refer to the moral and ethical precepts accepted in the United States. The way of life is largely Protestant in its sensibilities, representing the majority religion in the country.

                                                                                        SOC

1880s   In Europe, feminists working for women's equality join with socialists to effect a broader social revolution against the capitalism of the Industrial Age. Feminist leaders of the time include German socialist Clara Zetkin and French socialist Louise Michel, who says in 1885, "When the Revolution comes, you and I and all humanity will be transformed."

                                                                                        SOC

1880   French novelist Émile Zola publishes *The Experimental Novel*, in which he explains his theory and method for writing naturalistic fiction. Naturalism emphasizes objective narration, minute depiction of social reality, and a concern with social injustice and the plight of the lower classes. The movement is important in Europe from the mid-19th century and in the United States from the late 19th century.

                                                                                        CRIT

1880   English biologist Thomas Huxley delivers the speech, "Science and Culture," in which he attacks Matthew Arnold's (*see* 1870s–1880, EDUC) ideas on liberal education. To Huxley, liberal education should be based on "an unhesitating faith that the free employment of reason, in accordance with scientific method, is the sole method of reaching truth."

                                                                                        EDUC

1880   American political scientist John Burgess helps found a separate school of political science at Columbia College (later to become Columbia University), an event considered to mark the birth of political science as a field of study distinct from political economy and political philosophy.   POL

1880   Austrian physician Josef Breuer begins treating the hysterical patient he calls "Anna O." Her case study will be considered the founding case of psychoanalysis. *See also* 1895, PSYCH.   PSYCH

1880   In Ireland, the term *boycott* is coined when town locals shun an estate manager named Charles Boycott for not lowering rents for those affected by famine.   SOC

1880–1968   American writer and lecturer Helen Keller lives. Her activism and writings are instrumental in generating more understanding and acceptance of the deaf and blind in society. Keller is deaf and blind from early childhood.   SOC

1880–1890   The philosophy of Social Darwinism, which applies the idea of "survival of the fittest" to everyday life, gains popularity as a business and social construct. Major proponents include English philosopher Herbert Spencer and American sociologist William Graham Sumner.   SOC

1881   African-American educator and orator Booker T. Washington founds and becomes president of the Tuskegee Normal and Industrial Institute in Alabama, which quickly becomes one of the leading educational institutions for black Americans.   EDUC

1881   American historian Herbert Baxter Adams establishes the first graduate historical seminar at Johns Hopkins University. Adams will inaugurate the *Johns Hopkins Studies in Historical and Political Science* series in 1882. He will also help organize the American Historical Association in 1884, playing a major role in the professionalization of historical study in the United States. His students will include Woodrow Wilson (*see* 1902, HIST) and Frederick Jackson Turner (*see* 1893, HIST).   HIST

1881–1902   With Elizabeth Cady Stanton and M. J. Gage, American reformer Susan B. Anthony publishes the multivolume *History of Woman Suffrage*.   HIST

1881   English logician John Venn publishes *Symbolic Logic*, which extends the algebraic approach to logic begun by English mathematician George Boole. Among other contributions, Venn introduces the Venn diagram, in which intersecting circles are used to represent logical statements.   PHIL

1881   American clergyman Charles Taze Russell founds the religious group called Jehovah's Witnesses. Their formal organization will be known as the Watchtower Bible and Tract Society.   REL

1882   American philologist Francis J. Child publishes his exhaustive work, *The English and Scottish Popular Ballads*.   CRIT

1882   Ecuadorean writer Juan Montalvo publishes *Siete tratados* (*Seven Treatises*), essays on moral, political, and literary subjects.   PHIL

1882–1891   German geographer Friedrich Ratzel publishes *Anthropogeography*. In this and *Political Geography* (1897) he helps to develop the two disciplines named in the titles and introduces the idea of *Lebensraum*, the "living space" occupied by a population, as an important determinant of history.   POL

1882   Russian anarchist Mikhail Bakunin espouses his anarchist views in *God and the State*.   POL

1882   American psychologist Granville Stanley Hall founds the first formal psychological laboratory in the United States at Johns Hopkins University.   PSYCH

1882   The Society for Psychical Research is founded in London.   PSYCH

1882   The Knights of Columbus, a fraternal order of Roman Catholic laymen, is founded.   REL

1882   The Japanese government divides all Shinto organizations into either state shrines or sects. The state shrines are closely supervised by the government, with the emperor considered its chief priest and a descendant of the sun-goddess. Shinto sects, in contrast, follow many different paths, some highly syncretistic.   REL

1882–1955   Japanese holy man Okada Mokichi lives and breaks away from the Shinto sect of Omoto to found Sekaikyuseikyo (the Religion of World Messianity).   REL

1882   The word *feminism* is popularized in France, used first by French writer Hubertine Auclert, who applies it to the granting of legal rights to women. The meaning of the term *feminism* differs throughout Europe. In Germany and England, it refers to "the possession of womanly qualities." The first English usage of the term will occur in 1894.   SOC

1883   English scientist Sir Francis Galton coins the term *eugenics* for the study of ways to improve the human species through selective breeding.   ANTH

1883   American anthropologist Franz Boas begins doing field work among the Central Eskimos. He will become the most influential figure in American anthropology, training or inspiring such colleagues as Alfred Kroeber, Margaret Mead, Ruth Benedict, and Edward Sapir. Boas and his followers stress the impact of culture and language on human behavior. His strict methodology and careful research help bring respect to the discipline of cultural anthropology.   ANTH

1883   English historian Sir John Seeley publishes *The Expansion of England*, a landmark work of imperial history that will influence many scholars.   HIST

1883–1927   American historian John McMaster publishes his nine-volume *The History of the People of the United States*, the first major social history to include an examination of the country's westward expansion.   HIST

1883   *Prologomena to Ethics* by English absolute idealist philosopher Thomas Hill Green is published posthumously.   PHIL

1883   German philosopher Wilhelm Dilthey publishes *Introduction to the Human Sciences*, in which he is concerned with separating the natural sciences from such "human sciences" as the study of history.   PHIL

Nietzsche in Love

The greatest work of German philosopher Friedrich Nietzsche was born as a result of his greatest disappointment: his unconsummated love affair with the intellectual beauty Lou Salomé. In March 1882, at age 21, she met the 37-year-old philosopher through their mutual friend Paul Rée. On meeting her, Nietzsche's first words are said to have been, "What stars have sent us orbiting towards each other?"

Refusing both Nietzsche's and Rée's proposals of marriage, Salomé suggested a platonic ménage-à-trois. Her hold on the two men as they traveled together through Europe that year is symbolized by a comic photograph in which Salomé pretends to be driving a cart, whip in hand, with Nietzsche and Rée hauling her. For Nietzsche, having lived long in solitude, this was a time of emotional awakening. "I don't want to be lonely any more," he wrote to her. "I want to learn to be human again. Alas, in this field I have almost everything still to learn!"

The triangular relationship was too unstable to last, and when it came time to choose, she did not choose him. In November 1882, Rée and Salomé left Nietzsche without arranging to meet him again, and he was once again alone. In despair he wrote, "This last mouthful of life was the toughest I have ever had to chew. . . . Unless I can learn the alchemist's trick of turning this filth into gold, I am lost."

That January, he learned the trick. In ten feverish days, he wrote the first part of *Also sprach Zarathustra* (*Thus Spake Zarathustra*), often considered his greatest work. Its final sentence was completed in 1885: "Thus spoke Zarathustra and left his cave, glowing and strong, like a morning sun emerging from behind dark mountains."

1883   Austrian physicist and philosopher Ernst Mach publishes *The Science of Mechanics*, in which he takes a radically empirical view of scientific theory. His other works will include *The Analysis of Sensations* (1906).   PHIL

1883–1892   German philosopher Friedrich Nietzsche publishes *Thus Spake Zarathustra*, in which he rejects Christian morality and develops the idea of the *Übermensch*, or Superman. Among Nietzsche's other influential ideas, expressed in aphoristic style in such works as *The Gay Science* (1882) and *Beyond Good and Evil* and *The Genealogy of Morals* (both 1887), are the existence of an unconscious will to power and joyful acceptance of eternal recurrence.   PHIL

1883   Karl Kautsky, German Marxist theorist and leader of the German Social Democratic Party establishes *Neue Zeit*, a leading review of Marxist thought which will be published until 1917. He will later write the Erfurt Program, which the Socialist Party will adopt in 1891 and which will be attacked by Russian Communist leader Lenin for its rejection of revolutionary Marxism in favor of gradualism.   POL

1883   The Pendleton Civil Service Act is passed by the U.S. Congress, making merit rather than patronage the criterion for hiring civil servants in the United States. The Civil Service Exam is to measure job aptitude.   POL

1883   The Socialist reform association known as the Fabian Society is formed by Englishmen Frank Podmore and Edward Pease. They advocate working within the existing government to promote Socialist principles. Appealing to many writers, artists, and reformers, the movement attracts such notable members as English writers Sidney and Beatrice Webb and Irish-born British playwright George Bernard Shaw.   SOC

1884   American writer Henry James publishes the essay "The Art of Fiction," which explains his aesthetics of writing.   CRIT

1884   Greek poet Jean Moréas (pseudonym of Yánnis Papadiamantópoulos) publishes *Les Syrtes*, a work that contains the first definition of Symbolism.   CRIT

1884   German mathematician and philosopher Ludwig Gottlob Frege publishes *The Foundations of Arithmetic*, in which he analyzes basic mathematical concepts, thereby reducing arithmetic to fundamentally logical operations.   PHIL

1884   German socialist Friedrich Engels attacks the subordination of women in patriarchal family structure in *The Origin of the Family, Private Property, and the State*.   SOC

1885   English scientist Sir Francis Galton observes that each individual's fingerprints
        are unique and develops a system for classifying them. His work will become
        important in law enforcement.   ANTH

1885   American economist John Bates Clark founds the American Economic
        Association. His most respected work will be *The Distribution of Wealth* (1899).   ECON

1885   English absolute idealist philosopher Bernard Bosanquet publishes *Knowledge
        and Reality*. His other works will include *Essentials of Logic* (1895).   PHIL

1885   American philosopher Josiah Royce, an absolute idealist, publishes *The Religious
        Aspects of Philosophy*. He will publish *The World and the Individual* in 1901. PHIL

1885   Polish economist and sociologist Ludwig Gumplowicz publishes *The Outlines
        of Sociology*. His ideas on pressure groups and political conflict will heavily
        influence Arthur Bentley and other political scientists in the 20th century.   POL

1885   German psychologist Hermann Ebbinghaus, who will be regarded as the
        father of memory research, publishes the first experimental research on
        memory. By 1905, he will also develop the sentence completion test, the
        first successful test of higher mental abilities, and the nonsense syllable,
        which will greatly contribute to the study of learning and association. PSYCH

1885   African-American educator and orator Booker T. Washington delivers his
        "Atlanta Exposition Address," in which he argues that economic equality is a pre-
        requisite for social equality for blacks and that vocational training is important
        for self-esteem and economic advancement. This speech will form chapter 14 of
        his autobiography, *Up from Slavery* (*see* 1901, HIST).   SOC

1886   Teodor de Wyzewa, a Polish critic and leading theorist of the Symbolist move-
        ment, publishes his essay "L'Art Wagnérien: la peinture" in *La Revue Wagnérienne*.
        His thoughts anticipate the development of abstract art and later formalist the-
        ories.   CRIT

1886   Following the death this year of Hindu mystic Ramakrishna (*see* 1855, REL), his
        disciple Vivekenanda, traveling India as a wandering monk, becomes a major
        exponent of his teachings. Vivekenanda founds the Ramakrishna Mission, a
        monastic order whose missionaries travel throughout India and the West. REL

1886   Although the Haymarket Square riot in Chicago is largely incited by the govern-
        ment, it nonetheless generates antilabor sentiment across the nation. Unions fail
        in their attempts to use it as a rallying point.   SOC

1886   The American Federation of Labor is founded in the United States to strength-
        en a number of local and national craft unions. Under the leadership of labor

reformer Samuel Gompers, the AFL will bring a number improvements to the lives of workingmen. In 1955, the AFL will merge with the Congress of Industrial Organizations (CIO).

SOC

1887   In an attempt to ease communication among nations, Polish inventor Ludwik Zamenhof develops an artificial language known as Esperanto. Influenced by Indo-European and Slavonic languages, it will gain only limited acceptance over the years.

LING

1887   The Dawes Act attempts to assimilate Native Americans into the dominant American culture by offering grants of land to those who renounce tribal affinities.

POL

1887   French sociologist Émile Durkheim teaches the first course in sociology at the University of Bordeaux. One of the founders of sociology, he will be known for developing scientific methods for the discipline and stressing the importance of collective beliefs and values for social cohesion.

SOC

1887   German sociologist Ferdinand Tönnies publishes *Gemeinschaft and Gesellschaft*, describing how societies shift from primary, family-based associations, to those dominated by contractual relationships.

SOC

1887   Liberian educator Edward Wilmot Blyden publishes the essay collection *Christianity, Islam and the Negro Race*. Credited with the phrase "Africa for the Africans," he is an advocate of Pan-Africanism and of a unified West African nation.

SOC

1888   German historian Adolf Goller publishes *Die Entstehung der architektonischen Stilformen*, a work that offers a theory of the historical transformations of motifs in terms of an artist's motivations and interpretations.

CRIT

1888–1890   German philosopher Richard Avenarius publishes *Critique of Pure Experience*, in which he expounds the positivist doctrine known as empirio-criticism. PHIL

1888   English historian and jurist James Bryce publishes his three-volume *The American Commonwealth*. Its detailed descriptions of local and national political institutions will influence the development of the field of comparative government.

POL

1888   The Hermetic Order of the Golden Dawn is founded in Britain. The mystical secret society, with an emphasis on the occult, includes as its members the writers William Butler Yeats and Algernon Blackwood and poet Aleister Crowley. *See also* 1905, REL.

REL

1888	The Lambeth Conference of bishops of the Anglican Communion affirms the Chicago-Lambeth Quadrilateral, first proposed two years earlier by the Protestant Episcopal Church of America. It extends principles for reunion of Christian churches. <div align="right">REL</div>
1888	Native American religious leader Wovoka founds the Ghost Dance religion, which will be adopted by many Northern Plains Indians. The religion preaches the imminent restoration of former tribal ways and the elimination of white people from the country. Ghost Dance fervor will end with the massacre of Native Americans at Wounded Knee (*see* 1890, soc). <div align="right">REL</div>
1888	American writer Edward Bellamy publishes the novel *Looking Backward*, a vision of how the coming century might be corrupted by economic inequality. <div align="right">SOC</div>
1889–1891	American historian Henry Adams publishes the nine-volume *History of the United States of America During the Administrations of Jefferson and Madison.* <div align="right">HIST</div>
1889–1896	Theodore Roosevelt, who will become the 26th president of the United States and a prolific writer, publishes *The Winning of the West*. Roosevelt's historical writing reflects his nationalistic and expansionistic views. <div align="right">HIST</div>
1889	German philosopher Friedrich Nietzsche goes insane, a condition in which he will remain until his death in 1900. <div align="right">PHIL</div>
1889	Formerly an outspoken atheist and socialist, English reformer Annie Besant becomes a theosophist. After moving to India, she will fight for Indian home rule, becoming president of the Indian National Congress in 1917. <div align="right">REL</div>
1889–1914	The school known as the Cambridge Ritualists brings a new approach to the study of religion, particularly Greek and Roman myth and ritual, emphasizing evolutionary trends and the meaning of universal symbols. The school's members include Jane Ellen Harrison, Gilbert Murray, Francis MacDonald Cornford, and Arthur B. Book. James George Frazer's work is associated with the school, although Frazer himself is not a member. <div align="right">REL</div>
1889	With the opening of Hull House, a settlement house in Chicago, American social reformer Jane Addams epitomizes progressivist beliefs in direct improvement of society. <div align="right">SOC</div>
c. 1890s	Chinese historians, under Western influence, call into question the validity of source material from premodern China. Their skepticism will disappear during the 1930s when archaeological research will show that most of the records they had been using are indeed accurate. <div align="right">HIST</div>

c. 1890s   Japanese historians adopt Western attitudes toward history and Western methods of historical writing. They focus particularly on economic history and on the history of various lands—Korea, Manchuria, part of China—occupied at different times by Japan.   HIST

1890s   Social theorists known as legalists are active, including Léon Duguit, Maurice Hauriou, and Georg Jellinek. They help establish political science as a separate academic discipline. *See also* 1880, POL.   POL

1890s   A Buddhist revival begins in Sri Lanka, which is under British rule. Meditation practices are renewed in monasteries and retreats, as is study of the Pali literature. The interest of Western orientalist scholars helps stimulate the revival.   REL

1890s   In the United States, strikes become popular methods of protest among workers for higher wages and improved conditions. In Europe, strikes defending political beliefs become popular.   SOC

1890   Scottish anthropologist James George Frazer publishes *The Golden Bough*, a massive comparative study of folklore and religion.   ANTH

1890   English economist Alfred Marshall, founder of neoclassical economics, publishes the influential text *Principles of Economics*.   ECON

1890–1940   Histories are published, primarily by Western scholars, describing the European colonization of Africa. Examples include J. S. Keltie's *Partition of Africa* (1893), Harry Hamilton Johnston's *Colonization of Africa* (1899), P. T. Moon's *Imperialism and World Politics* (1926), William Leonard Langer's *The Diplomacy of Imperialism* (1935), and R. Coupland's *Exploitation of East Africa* (1939).   HIST

1890   The Daughters of the American Revolution (DAR) is founded in Washington, D.C., for women who are descendants of those who fought in or otherwise aided the cause of the American war for independence.   HIST

1890   The current events periodical *Literary Digest* is founded in New York City by Isaac Kauffman Funk. Continuing in publication until 1938, it will be subsumed by the newsmagazine *Time*.   JOURN

1890   American naval officer and historian Alfred Thayer Mahan publishes *The Influence of Sea Power upon History, 1660–1783*. In this and a companion volume, *The Influence of Sea Power upon the French Revolution and Empire, 1793–1812* (1892), he argues that naval power is the decisive factor in international politics. Widely influential, his views will help motivate naval buildups in the United States and Germany.   POL

1890–1891   American political scientist John Burgess publishes *Political Science and Comparative Constitutional Law*, an early classic in the field. An abridged version will be published as *The Foundations of Political Science* in 1933.   POL

1890   Leading a movement toward national suffrage, Wyoming becomes the first state to grant women the right to vote. Two decades previously, in 1869, it had been the first territory to offer woman suffrage.   POL

1890   American psychologist and philosopher William James publishes *The Principles of Psychology*. Known as the dean of American psychologists, he develops the school of functionalism (understanding the conscious aspects of mental life). He is also known for his pragmatic philosophy and research on religious experience.   PSYCH

1890   In Japan, the doctrine known as Tennoism is embodied in an imperial decree that the practice of state Shinto is nonreligious and required by all Japanese citizens.   REL

1890   French sociologist Jean-Gabriel de Tarde publishes *The Laws of Imitation*, an attempt to explain social behavior and change through the widespread imitation of leaders by the masses.   SOC

1890   On December 29, on the South Dakota Pine Ridge Indian Reservation at Wounded Knee, approximately 200 Sioux are massacred by the U.S. calvary. The incident at Wounded Knee will come to symbolize barbarous treatment of Native Americans by white settlers.   SOC

1891   American novelist and critic William Dean Howells argues in favor of the "new realism" in *Criticism and Fiction*. He believes it will be more successful than romanticism in broadening sympathy and challenging tradition.   CRIT

1891   Irish poet, dramatist, and critic Oscar Wilde publishes *Intentions*, which includes several of his critical essays, including "The Critic as Artist." His aesthetic principles include the autonomy of art and the separation of art from morality.   CRIT

1891   English philosopher Henry Sidgwick publishes *The Elements of Politics*, the most comprehensive book on English politics up to this time.   POL

1891   General and Particular Baptists are united into a single denomination, the Baptist Union.   REL

1891   English poet and artist William Morris advocates a medieval-based socialism in the utopian novel *News from Nowhere*.   SOC

1892   The Populist Party is formed in Omaha, Nebraska. It largely represents farm-
                ers' concerns, such as free silver and a nationalized railroad, which had pre-
                viously been championed by social organizations like the Grange movement
                and the Farmers' Alliances. It will be active in the 1892 and 1896 presiden-
                tial elections.   POL

1892   Japanese holy woman Deguchi Nao is possessed by a *kami* (deity) and writes
                Ofudesaki. With her son-in-law Onisaburo, who writes *Stories of the Spirit
                World*, she founds the Omoto religion.   REL

1892   American sociologist Albion Small becomes chair of the sociology department
                at the University of Chicago. Under his leadership, the department will dom-
                inate the American sociological scene for decades. Small will also found the
                American Journal of Sociology and serve as its first editor.   SOC

1892   A bloody steelworkers' strike in Homestead, Pennsylvania, becomes a symbol
                of the partnership between big business and government to act against the
                labor movement. The strike is brought to an end through a combination of
                executive order and company strongarm tactics, including the use of a private
                police force of "Pinkerton men" from the Pinkerton detective agency.   SOC

1893   Austrian art historian Alois Riegl publishes *Stilfragen* in Berlin, an influential
                history of ornamentation from ancient Egyptian to Arabian art that rejects the
                traditional art-historical distinction between "fine art" and the "minor" or
                "decorative" arts.   CRIT

1893   German art historian Aby Warburg draws on Nietzschean concepts in an essay
                on Botticelli's *Birth of Venus* and *Primavera* that places the classical tradition in
                Dionysian as well as Apollonian terms. *Gesammelte Schriften*, a collection of 40
                of Warburg's essays, will be published posthumously in 1932.   CRIT

1893   American historian Frederick Jackson Turner delivers his paper "The
                Significance of the Frontier in American History" at the Chicago World's Fair,
                espousing the radical view that American democracy stems more from the
                country's frontier experience than from its European heritage. He will further
                develop this idea in his books *Rise of the New West* (1906) and *The Frontier in
                American History* (1920).   HIST

1893–1906   American historian James Rhodes publishes *A History of the United States from
                the Compromise of 1850*, one of the best works on America from the years lead-
                ing up to the Civil War through Reconstruction. He is the first major historian
                to be harshly critical of the North's behavior during Reconstruction.   HIST

1893–1903	German mathematician and philosopher Ludwig Gottlob Frege publishes *The Basic Laws of Arithmetic*, in which he formalizes his logical analysis of mathematics and presents the first formal theory of classes. *See also* 1901, PHIL. PHIL
1893–1976	Chinese Communist leader Mao Zedong lives. In leading the revolution against the Kuomintang and creating the People's Republic of China in 1949, he acts on his political philosophy of Maoism. A version of revolutionary Communism, it differs from Russian Communism in its involvement of the peasant, not proletariat, classes. In 1958, Mao launches the economic program known as the Great Leap Forward (*see* 1958–1960, ECON). He later leads the Cultural Revolution (*see* 1966–1969, POL). POL
1893	New Zealand becomes the first country to grant woman suffrage. It will take five decades for industrialized nations to grant universal suffrage, with France not giving women the vote until 1944. POL
1893	The World Parliament of Religions, a gathering of representatives from many faiths, is held in Chicago. REL
1893	French sociologist Émile Durkheim publishes *The Division of Labor*. SOC
1893	The Anti-Saloon League is founded in Oberlin, Ohio, to combat the sale of liquor. Two years later, it will become a national organization; it will prove central to the passage of the 18th Amendment and the National Prohibition Act (*see* 1919, SOC). SOC
1894	Lithuanian-born American art critic Bernard Berenson publishes *Venetian Painters of the Renaissance*, which helps to establish his reputation as an authority on classical art. Among his later works will be *Central Italian Painters of the Renaissance* (1897), *Northern Italian Painters of the Renaissance* (1907), and *Rumor and Reflection* (1952). CRIT
1894	During a year rife with labor strikes in the United States, especially by railroad workers, Congress establishes Labor Day as a legal holiday on the Monday after the first Sunday in September. ECON
1894	Radcliffe College for women, established in 1879, is chartered as an institution affiliated with Harvard University. EDUC
1894	United Daughters of the Confederacy is founded to preserve the memory of the Southern states' secessionist movement. HIST
1894–1895	The first Sino-Japanese war results in the emergence of Japan as an imperial power. Its status as a world power will be cemented with its victory in the Russo-Japanese war of 1904–1905. POL

1894   While reporting on the Dreyfus affair in France (the court martial of a Jewish
            army captain that fuels anti-Semitism), Hungarian Jewish journalist Theodor
            Herzl becomes convinced of the necessity of establishing a Jewish state. Two
            years later he will explicate his Zionist views in his pamphlet *Der Judenstaat* (*The
            Jewish State*). *See also* 1897, REL.   REL

1894   The women's movement gains strength internationally with the founding of the
            Federation of German Women's Associations, the Greek Union for the
            Emancipation of Women, and the British Women's Industrial Council.   SOC

1895   French writer Paul Valéry publishes *Introduction à la méthode de Leonard da Vinci*,
            in which he develops his theory of the processes of the creative mind.   CRIT

1895   English historian Frederic Maitland and English jurist Sir Frederick Pollock
            publish *History of English Law before the Time of Edward I*. Maitland is a pio-
            neering and brilliant English legal historian.   HIST

1895   American newspaper publisher William Randolph Hearst purchases the New
            York *Morning Journal*. It is the first of dozens of papers he will own and stamp
            with his brand of loosely factual reporting aimed at readers' emotions. Other
            important Hearst papers will include the Chicago *American* and the Boston
            American. For decades, his journalism will be hugely popular and influential. JOURN

1895   The London School of Economics and Political Science is established, signal-
            ing the acceptance of political science as an independent discipline.   POL

1895   Austrian physician Josef Breuer and psychoanalyst Sigmund Freud publish
            Studies on Hysteria, the first book on psychoanalysis. Breuer contributed the
            case history of Anna O. (*see* 1880, PSYCH) and some theoretical portions.   PSYCH

1895–1896   Austrian psychoanalyst Sigmund Freud identifies the phenomenon of projec-
            tion, a defense mechanism in which a person attributes his or her own feelings
            or wishes to another person, group, or thing.   PSYCH

1895   French sociologist Gustave Le Bon publishes *The Crowd*, a famous early study
            of mass behavior. Le Bon posits that crowds possess properties that cannot be
            reduced to the attributes of the individuals they comprise.   SOC

1896   African-American writer, editor, and educator W. E. B. Du Bois publishes "The
            Suppression of the African Slave-Trade to America," the first monograph in the
            Harvard Educational Series. Du Bois will draw on history, sociology, and other
            disciplines in such popular and influential works as *The Souls of Black Folk*
            (1903), *The Negro* (1915), and *The World and Africa* (1947).   HIST

1896–1903   Russian politician and historian Pavel Milyukov publishes *Outlines of Russian Culture*. Besides writing social and cultural history, Milyukov will serve as a leader of anti-tsarist opposition groups.   HIST

1896   American newspaper publisher Adolph Ochs purchases the *New York Times* (*see* 1851, JOURN) and establishes it as a periodical of accurate reporting and cultural commentary. It will contrast with most popular newspapers of the day.   JOURN

1896   French philosopher Henri Bergson publishes *Matter and Memory*. His view of evolution as the product of a creative, driving force will be further expounded in *Creative Evolution* (1907).   PHIL

1896   English philosopher John M'Taggart publishes *Studies in the Hegelian Dialectic*. His ideas combine Hegelian absolute idealism with beliefs about the immortality of the soul and the nonexistence of matter, space, and time.   PHIL

Yesterday's Rhetoric

The burning issues of a given day tend to become historical curiosities on the following day. Such was the debate in the 1890s over whether American currency should be based on the gold standard or on bimetallism (both gold and silver). Though the terms of the argument seem abstruse today, they were a call to battle for the readers of William Hope Harvey's best-seller *Coin's Financial School* (1894). In the midst of a national depression, Harvey argued that only London bankers and wealthy East Coast financiers wanted a gold standard, because it would maintain the high value of their investments. Debt-laden farmers and other impoverished Americans would do much better if allowed to pay their debts with the cheaper metal, silver.

Nebraska politician William Jennings Bryan rode this issue to national prominence with his "Cross of Gold" speech at the 1896 Democratic National Convention at Chicago. Having never met an emotion to which he didn't like to appeal, he argued that the gold-standard men were not only selling out America's farmers but delivering the nation back to British tyranny. "We are fighting," he boomed, "in the defense of our homes, our families, and posterity." He ended with, "You shall not press down upon the brow of labor this crown of thorns, you shall not crucify mankind upon a cross of gold."

The speech won Bryan his first of three chances as the Democratic candidate for president. He lost every time. As for the gold standard, it prevailed, but not for long: Eventually, other means of determining the value of money were worked out. Today's system of controlled floating exchange rates is based on the relative supply and demand of particular currencies in the world market. It renders moot the heated rhetoric of a century ago.

1896   Italian political scientist Gaetano Mosca publishes *The Ruling Class*, in which
            he argues that all societies are governed by elites.   POL

1896   At the Democratic National Convention in Chicago, American politician
            William Jennings Bryan delivers his "Cross of Gold" speech, in which he
            champions the free silver movement and establishes himself as a national
            political figure.   POL

1896   In *Plessy v. Ferguson*, the U.S. Supreme Court upholds the right to establish
            "separate but equal" public facilities. Until the passage of civil rights laws fol-
            lowing World War II, the ruling allows for legal segregation of the races in
            many areas.   POL

1896   American evangelist Billy Sunday begins drawing large crowds to his religious
            revivals.   REL

1897   German architect and designer August Endell publishes his essay "The Beauty
            of Form and Decorative Art" in *Dekorative Kunst*. He advances the idea of a
            new visual art which would be both abstract and expressive.   CRIT

1897   Russian anarchist Pyotr Kropotkin publishes *Mutual Aid*, in which he reinter-
            prets English naturalist Charles Darwin's theory of evolution to show that
            altruism and communal life are natural to human beings, and that a society of
            small voluntary communities is most congenial to human nature. He will also
            publish *Fields, Factories, and Workshops* (1901).   POL

1897   Hungarian Jewish journalist Theodor Herzl organizes the first Zionist World
            Congress in Basel, Switzerland. He will remain its president until his death in
            1904. Herzl is considered the founder of modern Zionism, the movement to
            reestablish a Jewish state in Palestine.   REL

1897   French sociologist Émile Durkheim publishes *Suicide: A Study in Sociology*, one
            of the first rigorous statistical studies in sociology. Two years earlier, Durkheim
            had published *Rules of the Sociological Method* (1895).   SOC

1898   American poet Sidney Lanier publishes *Music and Poetry* which argues for
            music education and chairs of music at universities.   CRIT

1898   Russian novelist Leo Tolstoy writes *What Is Art?*, claiming that his earlier works,
            as well as those by English dramatist William Shakespeare, German composer
            Richard Wagner, and others, are invalid because they do not improve humani-
            ty's moral, spiritual, or social condition.   CRIT

1898   In *Women and Economics*, American writer Charlotte Perkins Gilman becomes one
            of the first to equate women's emancipation with economic independence. She

also cites the need for other changes in society to effect social equality, including outside care for children.   ECON

1898   American psychologist and philosopher William James introduces the philosophical term *pragmatism* to audiences at the University of California.   PHIL

1898   During the Hundred Days Reform in China, many reform edicts are issued, aimed at modernizing industry, education, and other institutions along Western lines. The reforms embody the teachings of scholar Kang Youwei, who regards Confucius as a reformer who supported the rights of the people as a check on the ruler's authority. The edicts are soon repudiated.   POL

1898   English physician Havelock Ellis publishes the first of seven volumes on sexuality, which collectively will be titled *Studies in the Psychology of Sex*. He is the first to discuss sex in psychological terms, and his works will be subject to controversy and litigation.   PSYCH

1898   A year after its young author's death, *Historie d'une âme*, the spiritual autobiography of Thérèse de Lisieux, is published. Perennially popular, it describes the "little way" of achieving holiness by performing humble duties. Thérèse, a French Carmelite nun, is also known as the Little Flower.   REL

1898   After over a century of intermittent persecution in Russia (*see* 1762–1796, REL), the Christian sect the Dukhobors emigrates to Canada to settle in Saskatchewan. The move is aided by sympathetic Russian novelist Leo Tolstoy.   REL

1898   Following the lead of Britain's Fabian Society, Germans popularize the Revisionist School of Socialism, which also calls for peaceful rather than violent political pursuit of their goals.   SOC

1899   American anthropologist Franz Boas is appointed first professor of anthropology at Columbia University. He is the founder of the "American historical school," which emphasizes historical research into folklore and belief.   ANTH

1899   French painter Paul Signac defines neoimpressionism in his book, *D'Eugène Delacroix au néo-impressionnisme*.   CRIT

1899   Russian art critic and impressario Sergey Pavlovich Diaghilev establishes the periodical *World of Art*.   CRIT

1899   The first Hague Conference, also known as the International Peace Conference of 1899, discusses arms limitations. Held at the Hague, in the Netherlands, its conclusions include the banning of poison gas and expanding (or dumdum) bullets. A second Hague Conference, the International Peace Conference of 1907, will reach conclusions on land and sea warfare and the banning of sub-

marine mines. The two conferences will be important to the founding of the
League of Nations (*see* 1919, POL).   POL

1899   Austrian psychoanalyst Sigmund Freud publishes *The Interpretation of Dreams*,
the first major presentation of his psychoanalytic theories following his break
with Josef Breuer (*see* 1895, PSYCH). Freud's belief that human behavior is pow-
erfully driven by unconscious wishes rooted in repressed childhood sexuality
will be highly controversial but also influential in many fields of learning,
including philosophy, history, and literary studies. Many of his key concepts,
such as the Oedipus complex and the organization of the mind into id, ego,
and superego, will become part of the next century's common stock of ideas.
His basic method of "talk" psychotherapy will be practiced by therapists of
many schools, including those not avowedly Freudian.   PSYCH

1899   The American economist Thorstein Veblen publishes *The Theory of the Leisure
Class*, a critique of American society that introduces the phrase "conspicuous
consumption."   SOC

1899   The Veterans of Foreign Wars is founded in the United States to protect veterans' rights, particularly for those veterans of the recent Spanish-American War. SOC

1900s   In the United States, academics disagree on whether higher education should
remain focused on the general enculturation of young men and women or
move toward specialized study in defined fields.   EDUC

1900s   A great deal of history of Latin America is published by historians both from
the region and from other places. Examples include J. F. da Rocha Pombo's
ten-volume *História do Brasil* (1906–1910), Ricardo Levene's *A History of
Argentina* (1937), Anita Brenner's *The Wind That Swept Mexico: The History of
the Mexican Revolution, 1910–1942* (1943), Ysabel F. Rennie's *The Argentine
Republic* (1945), G. Freyre's *The Masters and the Slaves* (1946), Oscar Efrén
Reyes's *Breve Historia General del Ecuador* (1949), and J. A. Caruso's *Liberators of
Mexico* (1954).   HIST

1900s   Biography becomes increasingly psychological, focusing more on the inner life
of the subject. This trend reflects the growing influence of Austrian psychoanalyst Sigmund Freud and his followers. Examples of such work include Gamaliel
Bradford's biographies (*see* 1912, HIST), Katharine Anthony's *Margaret Fuller*
(1920), and Van Wyck Brooks's *The Ordeal of Mark Twain* (1920) and *The
Pilgrimage of Henry James* (1925).   HIST

1900s   Early this century, a philosophical reaction sets in against Hegelian idealist meta-
physics. Known as "new realism," this movement includes Bertrand Russell and
George Edward Moore in England and Frederick James Woodbridge and Ralph
Barton Perry in the United States.   PHIL

1900   African-American educator and orator Booker T. Washington organizes the
                National Negro Business League, which is devoted to helping black Americans
                achieve economic independence.   EDUC

1900–1960   Historians of the "Dunning School," students and followers of American
                historian William Dunning, produce studies of the post–Civil War South
                that present Reconstruction as having been an unwise, corrupt experiment
                that could not possibly have succeeded. The problem, they posit, was not
                only exploitation by the North but also what they believe to be the innate
                inferiority of blacks.   HIST

1900   Uruguayan essayist and philosopher José Enrique Rodó publishes *Ariel*, in
                which he urges Latin America to retain its cultural values in the face of pres-
                sure from the materialistic culture of the United States. In other works, Rodó
                also writes on the philosophy of ethics and other topics.   PHIL

1900   German mathematician David Hilbert presents the address "Mathematical
                Problems," in which he describes several unsolved problems, including that of
                proving the consistency of mathematics. Gödel's theorems (*see* 1931, PHIL) will
                show that this problem is unsolvable.   PHIL

1900–1913   German philosopher Edmund Husserl publishes the three-volume *Logical
                Investigations*. Husserl is considered the founder of modern phenomenology,
                which focuses on the nature of consciousness.   PHIL

1900   American political scientist Frank Goodnow, who will help to found the American
                Political Science Association in 1903, publishes *Politics and Administration*. This
                work will influence American public administration for several decades and help
                stimulate government reforms.   POL

1900   In Britain, the Labour Party forms, rooted in a group of labor unions and sup-
                ported by the Fabian Society. Among its leaders will be James Ramsay
                MacDonald, its first prime minister, and Clement Atlee, whose reforms will
                include the nationalization of the railroad and a national health plan.   POL

1901   American anthropologist Alfred Louis Kroeber founds the anthropology
                department at University of California–Berkeley.   ANTH

1901   African-American educator Booker T. Washington publishes *Up from Slavery*,
                an autobiography which will be translated into many languages and be much
                acclaimed. His *My Larger Education*, a sequel, will appear in 1911.   HIST

1901   French mathematician and historian of ideas Louis Couturat publishes an inter-
                pretation of the work of German philosopher and mathematician Gottfried
                Wilhelm Leibniz entitled *La Logique de Leibniz*.   PHIL

1901   British mathematician and philosopher Bertrand Russell states what will
                become known as Russell's paradox, an apparent contradiction in German
                philosopher and mathematician Ludwig Gottlob Frege's theory of classes (*see*
                1893–1903, PHIL). Frege is unable to respond in a satisfactory way.   PHIL

1901–1909   American president Theodore Roosevelt uses the phrase "speak softly and
                carry a big stick" to characterize his foreign policy, which involves establish-
                ing negotiating power through a strong naval and military presence.   POL

1901–1920   French psychologist Pierre-Marie-Félix Janet uses hypnosis to study ego states.
                His production of dissociative states, such as are found in multiple personali-
                ty disorder, creates a deeper understanding of the ego's role in personality.   PSYCH

1901   Pentecostal Christian prayer meetings, which emphasize mystical experi-
                ences and speaking in tongues, begin to spread in the United States.   REL

1901–1903   American novelist Frank Norris writes *The Octopus* (1901) and *The Pit*
                (1903), two muckraking novels of a projected trilogy about the social ram-
                ifications of modern wheat production. The first explores the conflicts
                between the railroad industry and wheat farmers; the second the conflicts
                between farmers and wheat traders.   SOC

1901–1945   The first international trade union, eventually known as the International
                Federation of Trade Unions, forms in Europe. Internal conflicts bring about its
                end in 1945. At its height, it represents half of the world's union members.   SOC

1902   The American Anthropological Association is founded.   ANTH

1902   Danish explorer and ethnologist Knud Johan Victor Rasmussen begins his
                decades of study of the Eskimo. His works will include *Across Arctic America*
                (1927).   ANTH

1902   Woodrow Wilson, a historian who will become the 28th president of the
                United States, publishes *A History of the American People*, a work which
                includes both political and nonpolitical history.   HIST

1902   American writer and lecturer Helen Keller publishes *The Story of My Life*, per-
                haps the first autobiography of a disabled person. *The World I Live In* will
                appear in 1908, and other autobiographical works will follow.   HIST

1902   Italian philosopher and historian Benedetto Croce publishes *Estetica*. In this
                and *Logica* (1909), he develops his "philosophy of the spirit," which draws on
                the works of German philosopher Georg Wilhelm Friedrich Hegel to explain
                how aesthetics and logic together bring about understanding and spiritual
                development.   PHIL

1902   German Jewish philosopher Herman Cohen publishes *The Logic of Pure Intelligence*. In this and other works, he develops the system of thought that is the basis for the Marburg School of neo-Kantianism. He is also known for his essays in response to anti-Semitic attacks.   PHIL

1902   French mathematician Jules-Henri Poincaré discusses the nature of science and mathematics, particularly geometry, in *Science and Hypothesis*.   PHIL

1902   Russian political scientist Moisey Ostrogorsky publishes *Democracy and the Organization of Political Parties*, a pioneering work in the comparative study of political parties and their tendency toward oligarchy.   POL

1902   Russian revolutionary leader Lenin publishes *What Is to Be Done?*, which sets out his program for Marxist revolution. Lenin modifies German political philosopher Karl Marx's thought with such ideas as the role of the intelligentsia in forming a professional revolutionary vanguard, and an explanation of why a nonindustrialized nation such as Russia can nevertheless experience communist revolution.   POL

1902   American psychologist and philosopher William James publishes *The Varieties of Religious Experience*, a seminal work in the psychology of religion. Related works include *The Will to Believe* (1897).   REL

1902   American clergyman Walter Rauschenbusch is named professor of church history at Rochester Theological Seminary. With Washington Gladden, he is one of the leaders of the Social Gospel movement, which preaches the basic goodness of humanity and seeks to apply Christian teachings to the solution of the social problems of industrial society. *See also* 1907, REL.   REL

1902   In Thailand, the Buddhist Sangha (monastic community) becomes independent of the secular government.   REL

1902   American sociologist Charles Horton Cooley publishes *Human Nature and the Social Order*, which will be best known for its idea of the "looking-glass self." Cooley maintains that the individual's self is formed and adjusted in the course of viewing others' reactions to it.   SOC

1903   American photographer and editor Alfred Stieglitz, the founder of the Photo-Secession, founds the quarterly magazine *Camera Work*.   CRIT

1903–1908   French historian and statesman Gabriel Hanotaux publishes *Histoire de France contemporaine*, which will be considered one of the great works on modern French history.   HIST

1903   English philosopher George Edward Moore, a founder of modern analytical
                philosophy, publishes *Principia Ethica*, which will be famed for its precision in
                analyzing ethical problems. Moore will also be known for his defense of common
                sense.   PHIL

1903   Onozuka Kiheiji, considered to be the founder of Japanese political science,
                publishes *Principles of Political Science.*   POL

1903   Russian Bolshevism is established as revolutionary leader Lenin breaks from
                the Russian socialist movement. Bolshevism becomes the basis for the Russian
                Communist movement.   POL

1903   In his essay collection *The Souls of Black Folk,* African-American writer, editor,
                and educator W. E. B. Du Bois challenges the positions of Booker T. Washington
                on race (*see* 1895, EDUC, and 1901, HIST). Du Bois argues that Washington's
                emphasis on vocational education and economic advancement has merely
                served to appease the white establishment; therefore, Du Bois asserts, political
                and social equality can only be achieved via a demand for complete civil rights,
                especially in the areas of education and voting.   SOC

1904   German art historian Julius Meier-Graefe publishes *Moderne Kunst,* a pioneer-
                ing work that will help decide the terms of reference for subsequent modern
                art historians.   CRIT

1904–1921   Five volumes of lectures by Russian historian Vasily Klyuchevsky are pub-
                lished. They focus on Russian social and political history, taking into account
                class structure. Many will regard the lectures as comprising the greatest inter-
                pretation of Russian history.   HIST

1904–1905   Japan emerges victorious from the Russo-Japanese war, its status as a world
                power cemented.   POL

1904   American psychologist Edward Titchener founds an organization committed
                to what will be called existential psychology or existentialism. This school
                emphasizes subjectivity, personal decision, free will, and individuality.   PSYCH

1904–1905   German sociologist Max Weber publishes *The Protestant Ethic and the Spirit of
                Capitalism,* in which he relates Protestant ideals to the development of capi-
                talist society and takes issue with Marxist economic determinism. A revised
                edition will follow in 1920. In the course of his career, Weber will develop
                methodologies for cross-cultural studies and argue that sociology should
                be value-free.   SOC

1904	American journalist Lincoln Steffens publishes *The Shame of the Cities*, a collection of muckraking studies on the corruption and degradation in the nation's urban areas. SOC
1905	The group of writers, artists, and thinkers known as the Bloomsbury Group begins to meet in the Bloomsbury section of London. The group, which includes Virginia and Leonard Woolf, Vanessa and Clive Bell, Lytton Strachey, and Edward Morgan Forster, will continue to exist until Virginia Woolf's suicide in 1941. CRIT
1905	French scholar Charles Bally publishes *Précis de stylistique*, an influential work of stylistics, which will become a distinct branch of modern linguistics. LING
1905–1906	Spanish-born American philosopher George Santayana publishes *The Life of Reason*, in which he takes a naturalistic, psychological approach to his subject. PHIL
1905	Dutch mathematician Luitzen Brouwer publishes *Life, Art, and Mysticism*, which gives a philosophical account of the bases of logic and mathematics. PHIL
1905	English mathematician and philosopher Bertrand Russell publishes the paper "On Denoting," in which he states the theory of definite descriptions, a theory that will become central to analysis of propositions in the work of Russell and others. At about this time, Russell also formulates his theory of types, which is an attempt to deal with Russell's paradox, a paradox in the foundations of set theory that Russell himself discovered in 1901. PHIL
1905	Britain's attempted partition of colonial Bengal into Muslim and Hindu provinces brings to the fore an extreme nationalist Hindu movement that advocates anarchy and assassination. POL
1905	French psychologist Alfred Binet publishes the first batteries of tests purported to measure intelligence. He introduces the phrase "intelligence quotient," or "I.Q.," for a score representing an individual's intelligence as quantified against a standard. PSYCH
1905	The Baptist World Alliance is founded, an organization uniting Baptists around the world. REL
1905	German Jewish theologian Leo Baeck publishes *The Essence of Judaism*, in which he refutes the claim that Christianity is historically unconnected to Judaism. REL
1905	English poet Aleister Crowley founds the occult society the Argenteum Astrum after being expelled from the Hermetic Order of the Golden Dawn in 1900 (*see* 1888, REL). Crowley is accused of practicing black magic as opposed to the white magic advocated by the society. *See also* 1875–1947, REL. REL

1905   Indian nationalist Gopal Krishna Gokhale founds the Servants of India
                Society, an organization dedicated to social reform and home rule.   soc

1905   The Industrial Workers of the World (IWW), also known as the Wobblies, is
                founded in Chicago to promote the overthrow of the capitalist system and its
                replacement by union rule. Some of its leaders include Eugene Debs and
                William "Big Bill" Haywood; its best-known activist is Joe Hill. The union's
                motto is "One Big Union," representing its syndicalist position.   soc

1906   English anthropologist William Halse Rivers Rivers introduces the genealog-
                ical method into social science research in *The Todas*.   ANTH

1906   American archaeologist and historian James Henry Breasted publishes *Ancient
                Records of Egypt*, a five-volume work that transcribes every known hieroglyphic
                inscription. Breasted will establish the Oriental Institute at the University of

The I.Q. and Imbecility

In 1905, French psychologist Alfred Binet and physician Théodore Simon developed tests they believed would measure the intelligence of children. But it was American educational psychologist Lewis Madison Terman who in 1918 revised the Binet-Simon test and made it easier to be used widely, on children and army recruits, among others. The Stanford psychology professor also introduced the term that would be associated both with an intellectual measurement and social controversy—intelligence quotient, or I.Q.

Even in the 1920s, the newly revised Stanford-Binet test—along with other intelligence tests—was being used for ends other than as a measure of intellect. Since the late 19th century, social scientists had linked low intelligence, or "feeblemindedness" with criminality, sociopathological behavior, and future generations of the same. "The best material out of which to make criminals, and perhaps the material from which they are most frequently made, is feeblemindedness," said American psychologist Henry Herbert Goddard.

This prevailing belief among social scientists, public officials, and the public informed the 1927 Supreme Court case *Buck v. Bell*. In it, the Supreme Court upheld the constitutionality of a Virginia law allowing the involuntary sterilization of residents of state institutions tested as mentally deficient—such as the namesake of the case, Carrie Buck. Wrote Justice Oliver Wendell Holmes in his majority opinion, "It is better for all the world, if instead of waiting to execute degenerate offspring for crime, or let them starve for their imbecility, society can prevent those who are manifestly unfit from continuing their kind. . . . Three generations of imbeciles are enough."

Chicago in 1919 and will be considered the founder of American Egyptology.

HIST

1906   French physicist and philosopher Pierre-Maurice-Marie Duhem publishes *The Aim and Structure of Physical Theory*, in which he argues that science is a device for calculating, not representing, essential reality.

PHIL

1906   The Octobrists, a conservative political party, forms in Russia. It aims at reform in terms named in the limited October Manifesto issued by Tsar Nicholas II, following the Russian Revolution of 1905. The party will disband during the Russian Revolution of 1917.

POL

1906–1914   English suffragists Millicent Garrett Fawcett and Emmeline Pankhurst are among the leaders of continuing efforts in Britain to win the vote for women.

POL

1906   The All-India Muslim League is founded in India by Aga Khan III to preserve Muslim rights. Later known as the Muslim League, it will be central to the founding of Pakistan in 1947.

REL

1906   American novelist and socialist Upton Sinclair publishes the novel *The Jungle*, whose graphic depiction of an immigrant worker's life in the Chicago stockyards results in the reform of federal food inspection laws.

SOC

1907   In England, the Fabian Arts Group, aided financially by Irish-born playwright George Bernard Shaw, begins publication of the modernist journal the *New Age*, which will publish work by Ezra Pound, Edwin Muir, Thomas Ernest Hulme, and Katherine Mansfield.

CRIT

1907   Austrian art historian Alois Riegl describes his theory of Kunstwollen (the "will-to-art"), a specific artist's or period's creative impulse to solve artistic questions, in *Die Entstehung der Barockkunst in Rom*.

CRIT

1907   French painter Maurice Denis publishes his essay "Cézanne," which recognizes French impressionist Paul Cézanne's art as the essential form of modern painting.

CRIT

1907   The open teaching methods of Italian educator and physician Maria Montessori are practiced at her day-care center in Italy. Her pedagogical methods, which will gain a lasting following, become known as the "Montessori method." EDUC

1907   American psychologist and philosopher William James publishes *Pragmatism*. With American physicist Charles Sanders Peirce, he is the founder of pragmatism, a school of thought that measures the truth of a statement by its experimental and practical results.

PHIL

1907   Austrian psychologist and philosopher Alexius Meinong publishes *On
                Assumptions*. He is known for his experimental psychology and his philosophy
                of mind and meaning.   PSYCH

1907   In the encyclical *Pascendi*, Pope Pius X condemns religious modernism, calling
                it the "synthesis of all heresies." Modernist thinkers apply modern critical
                methods to the study of the Bible, question the literal truth of dogma, and take
                a psychological approach to the nature of spiritual experience.   REL

1907   In *Christianity and the Social Crisis*, American clergyman Walter Rauschenbusch
                reenvisions Christian theology as a force for social change. With this book and
                Christianizing the Social Order (1912), he establishes himself as a major theolo-
                gian of the progressive era and pre–World War I years. *See also* 1902, REL.   REL

1907   American sociologist William Graham Sumner publishes *Folkways*, in which
                he analyzes the power of folkways and mores. Sumner introduces the concept
                of ethnocentrism, the belief that one's own culture is superior to others.   SOC

1908   English writer Ford Madox Ford founds the journal *The English Review*, which
                publishes work by Thomas Hardy, Henry James, David Herbert Lawrence, and
                Wyndham Lewis.   CRIT

The Montessori Method

When Italian medical student Maria Montessori was graduating from the University
of Rome in 1894, she was concerned about starting her first job, not revolutioniz-
ing the early childhood educational process. But the position, as assistant doctor at
the University of Rome, led her to a calling that would result in accomplishments
far beyond that of being the first woman in Italy to earn a medical degree.

In her work with retarded children, she developed a successful educational program
that involved interaction with simple materials that encouraged self-teaching and creativity.

After years of additional study and testing, she came to believe that her approach
could also spur children of normal intelligence. She believed children would thrive
if they were freed of the confines of the classroom, which trapped them, "like but-
terflies mounted on pins, [and] fastened, each to his place."

In Rome in 1907, she opened her first Casa dei Bambini, or "Children's Room,"
which introduced the Montessori method and led to the opening of Montessori
schools across Europe and the United States. For the next several decades, Montessori
devoted her life to her educational principles, training teachers, and writing books (*The
Montessori Method*, 1912).

1908   German art historian Wilhelm Worringer publishes *Abstraktion und Einfuhlung*, an influential book that furnishes theoretical support for the modernist tendency to look to primitive art for modern forms of abstraction.   **CRIT**

1908   American scholar Irving Babbitt publishes *Literature and the American College*, in which he presents the principles of new humanism, a movement for spiritual and ethical reform, classically based education, and morally based literary criticism. Other prominent new humanists will include Paul Elmer More, Stuart Pratt Sherman, and Norman Foerster. Other Babbitt works will include *Towards Standards* (1929).   **CRIT**

1908   German historian Friedrich Meinecke publishes *Cosmopolitanism and Nation-State*. He will publish *The Origin of Historicism* in 1936. Meinecke is one of the first modern historians to take a philosophical approach to the study of social problems.   **HIST**

1908   The International Order for Ethics and Culture is formed at Bern, Switzerland, with the aim of investigating ethics without reference to theology or metaphysics.   **PHIL**

1908   German mathematician Ernst Zermelo axiomatizes set theory, which is central to 20th-century analytic philosophy. A. A. Fraenkel will refine the theory with the axiom of replacement, producing the classical set theory called ZF.   **PHIL**

1908   English political scientist Graham Wallas publishes *Human Nature in Politics*, in which he urges a greater emphasis on studying the psychological aspects of political behavior.   **POL**

1908   French socialist Georges Sorel publishes *Reflections on Violence*. This widely translated work examines the role of violence and social myth in revolutionary movements. Some of his ideas will influence Benito Mussolini and the Italian fascist movement.   **POL**

1908   American political scientist Arthur Bentley, one of the first to call for a value-free, empirical study of politics, publishes *The Process of Government*. This seminal work develops themes that will heavily influence political science from the 1930s through the 1950s. Bentley focuses on group processes and actual political behavior rather than the formal, legalistic workings of government institutions.   **POL**

1908   In the Danbury Hatters' Case, the United States Supreme Court rules that hatters who have boycotted nonunion manufacturers are in restraint of trade. This ruling marks the first time the Sherman Anti-Trust law is applied to a labor action.   **POL**

1908   American psychologist William McDougall publishes his controversial theory
            of instincts, which claims that instincts such as hunger, sex, escape, self-asser-
            tion, and curiosity motivate all behavior.   PSYCH

1908   Austrian psychoanalyst Abraham Arden Brill becomes Sigmund Freud's trans-
            lator into English. Brill coins the term *id* by substituting the Latin word mean-
            ing "it" for Freud's German word for the unconscious, *Es* ("it").   PSYCH

1908   The German sociologist Georg Simmel publishes his major work, *Sociology:
            Investigations on the Forms of Sociation*, a collection of writings that describe the
            basic forms of human interaction. His work on the properties of groups as well
            as the nature of conflict are among his principal contributions.   SOC

1909   Italian Symbolist poet and founder of futurism Emilio Filippo Tommaso
            Marinetti publishes the essay "The Foundation and Manifesto of Futurism."
            The first English translation will appear in 1912 in conjunction with the futur-
            ist exhibition at the Sackville Gallery, London.   CRIT

1909   French writer André Gide founds *La Nouvelle Revue française*, an influential
            review of literature and the arts.   CRIT

1909–1913   Dollar diplomacy is practiced during the presidency of William Howard Taft.
            Through it, the United States supports American businesses abroad in an
            attempt to increase foreign trade.   ECON

1909   Italian philosopher and historian Benedetto Croce publishes *Philosophy of the
            Practical*. Later works will include *Theory and History of Historiography* (1917).
            After 1925, he will lead the intellectual opposition to fascism in Italy.   PHIL

1909   Austrian psychoanalyst Otto Rank publishes *The Myth of the Birth of a Hero*, a
            classic in the psychology of myths.   PSYCH

1909   The National Association for the Advancement of Colored People (NAACP) is
            established the United States. Originally organized in response to the practice
            of lynching blacks, it will become an important advocacy organization for
            legal and social change. Its first leader is African-American writer, editor, and
            educator W. E. B. Du Bois.   SOC

1910   Scottish anthropologist James George Frazer publishes *Totemism and Exogamy*,
            a work that will influence Austrian psychoanalyst Sigmund Freud's *Totem and
            Taboo* (*see* 1913, PSYCH).   ANTH

1910   French philosopher and sociologist Lucien Lévy-Bruhl publishes *How Natives Think*.
            In this and other works, such as *Primitive Mentality* (1922), he emphasizes empiri-
            cal investigation of the minds of members of "primitive" societies.   ANTH

c. 1910   The theory of poetry called imagism develops in England and the United States. Adherents include English philosopher and poet Thomas Ernest Hulme and American poet, critic, and editor Ezra Pound. The school emphasizes poems that are short, precise, free-verse presentations of a single image.   CRIT

1910   Austrian psychoanalist Sigmund Freud publishes *Leonardo da Vinci and a Memory of His Childhood*, a controversial attempt to explain paintings in terms of the artist's mind and childhood.   CRIT

1910   English painter and critic Roger Eliot Fry organizes the first postimpressionism show at Grafton Galleries in London to celebrate modern French painting. His academic theory champions the new aesthetic of postimpressionism, which rejects finish or decoration. His influential articles and lectures will be collected in *Vision and Design* (1920) and *Transformations* (1926).   CRIT

1910   French Cubist painter Jean Metzinger publishes the essay "Note on Painting," which establishes Cubism as the decisive modern art movement and Spanish painter Pablo Picasso and French painter Georges Braque as its leaders.   CRIT

1910   African-American writer, editor, and educator W. E .B. Du Bois and writer A. G. Dill publish *The College-Bred Negro American*.   EDUC

1910   French historian François Aulard publishes *Histoire politique de la Révolution française*, a work about the French Revolution that emphasizes the quest for more democratic government.   HIST

1910   American philosopher Ralph Barton Perry poses the egocentric predicament, the confinement of each person to his or her own world of perception.   PHIL

1910–1913   English mathematicians and philosophers Bertrand Russell and Alfred North Whitehead publish *Principia Mathematica*, an exhaustive attempt to root mathematics in logic and build it up systematically.   PHIL

1910   University of Frankfurt psychologists Max Wertheimer, Kurt Koffka, and Wolfgang Köhler reject the associationism then prevailing in German psychology. They found Gestalt psychology, which seeks to restore the mental balance of patients by heightening awareness, emphasizing present experiences rather than memories of the past.   PSYCH

1910   The first World Missionary Conference (for Anglican and Nonconformist Protestant denominations) is held at Edinburgh, Scotland. It will result in the formation of the International Missionary Council in 1921.   REL

1910   American social reformer Jane Addams publishes her autobiography *Twenty Years at Hull House*, about her life and work at Chicago's Hull House Settlement.   SOC

1910   *Crisis*, the journal of the National Association for the Advancement of Colored People (NAACP), begins publication under the editorship of African-American writer, editor, and educator W. E. B. Du Bois.   soc

1911   American ethnologist Alice Cunningham Fletcher publishes a monograph on American Indian culture, *The Omaha Tribe*.   ANTH

1911   American anthropologist Franz Boas publishes *The Mind of Primitive Man*.   ANTH

1911   Russian painter Wassily Kandinsky publishes his treatise *Concerning the Spiritual in Art*. He develops a program for abstract painting conceived as an index of social and spiritual progress.   CRIT

1911   American historian James Robinson publishes *The New History*, a collection of essays arguing that history should be much more than just political history—that it must include intellectual, social, cultural, economic, and scientific developments. Robinson is perhaps the foremost American advocate of this increasingly popular revisionist approach.   HIST

1911   Hungarian Marxist philosopher György Lukács publishes *The Soul and Its Forms*. He will be known for his views on literary theory as well as the philosophy of history. Other works will include *History and Class Consciousness* (1923).   PHIL

1911   German philosopher Hans Vaihinger publishes *The Philosophy of "As If,"* in which he argues that the human mind invents and uses fictions, or ideas known to be false, including many religious and philosophical concepts, such as God and freedom.   PHIL

1911   Swiss psychiatrist Eugen Bleuler introduces the terms *schizophrenia* and *ambivalence* into psychiatry.   PSYCH

1911   French psychologist Alfred Binet and French physician Théodore Simon develop the Binet-Simon scale for use with a series of graded intelligence tests to measure a person's intelligence quotient (I.Q.). *See also* 1905, PSYCH.   PSYCH

1911   German sociologist and economist Robert Michels publishes *Political Parties: A Sociological Study of the Oligarchical Tendencies of Modern Democracy*, in which he develops his famous "iron law of oligarchy." This theory states that even the most democratically spirited organizations become oligarchies dominated by elites because they need full-time leaders with specialized knowledge.   soc

1912   American editor Harriet Monroe founds the influential literary magazine *Poetry*.   CRIT

1912   French poet Guillaume Apollinaire publishes *The Cubist Painters*, a work that defines Cubism in both art and literature.   CRIT

1912   Indian historian R. K. Mukherji publishes *Indian Shipping*. He will publish *Local Government in Ancient India* in 1919. His works are examples of modern Indian historians' interest in the Hindu period and in showing that precolonial Indian achievements were comparable to Western ones.   HIST

1912   American biographer Gamaliel Bradford publishes *Lee the American*, a work that seeks to find its subject's "inner soul." Bradford's other "psychographs" will include *Portraits of Women* (1916), *Damaged Souls* (1923), and *Darwin* (1926).   HIST

1912   A separate chair of politics is established at Oxford.   POL

1912   The Chinese political party known as the Kuomintang (KMT) is formed after the Chinese Revolution (1911). The Nationalist Party, led by Sun Yat-sen, will join and then break with the Communist Party before assuming control of the government by 1927. It will retain power until 1949, when Communists will take control.   POL

1912   In the United States, the Republican Party splinters to form the Progressive, or Bull Moose, Party. It means to counter the conservative Republican policies of President William Howard Taft. Its nomination of Theodore Roosevelt for president in 1912 splits the Republican vote and facilitates the election of Democrat Woodrow Wilson.   POL

1912   French sociologist Émile Durkheim publishes *Elementary Forms of Religious Life*, a major work in the development of cultural anthropology.   SOC

1913   Italian philosopher and historian Benedetto Croce publishes his *Guide to Aesthetics*, a work inspired by German philosopher Georg Wilhelm Friedrich Hegel that represents a revival of idealism as applied to art and history.   CRIT

1913   American economist Wesley Clair Mitchell publishes his major work of statistical investigation, *Business Cycles*.   ECON

1913   American writer Henry Adams publishes *Mont-Saint-Michel and Chartres*, a study of the unity of the medieval world as seen through Chartres cathedral and the Abbey Church at Mont-Saint-Michel.   HIST

1913   American historian Charles Beard publishes *An Economic Interpretation of the Constitution of the United States*, a landmark work arguing that economic interests were behind the framing of the Constitution. Beard will express similar deterministic views in *The Economic Origins of Jeffersonian Democracy*

(1915). Beard will later help found the New School for Social Research in New York City (1919). *See also* 1927, HIST.   HIST

1913   Spanish philosopher Miguel de Unamuno publishes his major work, *The Tragic Sense of Life in Men and Nations,* expressing his existentialist belief in radical solitude, the absurdity of life, and in faith itself.   PHIL

1913   German philosopher Edmund Husserl, founder of the phenomenological method for analyzing consciousness, publishes *Phenomenology.*   PHIL

1913   Indian poet Rabindranath Tagore publishes the philosophical work *Sadhana: The Realization of Life.*   PHIL

1913   American editor Max Eastman founds and edits the radical periodical *The Masses* (through 1918); he will later found *The Liberator* (1919–1922).   POL

1913   English socialists Sidney and Beatrice Webb found the influential political periodical *The New Statesman.*   POL

1913   Austrian psychoanalyst Sigmund Freud publishes *Totem and Taboo,* a work investigating similarities between modern neuroses and "primitive" cultural practices.   PSYCH

1913   Swiss psychologist and psychiatrist Carl Gustav Jung breaks with his mentor, Sigmund Freud, and develops his own theories. *See also* 1921, PSYCH.   PSYCH

1913   German psychiatrist and philosopher Karl Jaspers publishes his first book, *General Psychopathology,* a medical text that also treats the existential theme of humans in extreme situations.   PSYCH

1913   American psychologist John Broadus Watson explains his theory of behaviorism in the article "Psychology as the Behaviorist Views It." *See also* 1919, PSYCH.   PSYCH

1913   Austrian social philosopher Rudolph Steiner breaks away from the theosophical movement to form the Anthroposophical Society. Influenced by German poet Johann Wolfgang von Goethe, Steiner believes in the power of art in spiritual development. His ideas are embodied in the Goetheanum, a temple of arts and sciences in Dornach, Switzerland, that serves as the society's headquarters.   REL

1913   French physician, philosopher, and theologian Albert Schweitzer founds Lambaréné Hospital in French Equatorial Africa.   SOC

1914   English anthropologist W. H. R. Rivers publishes *History of Melanesian Society,* based on his research in the South Pacific.   ANTH

1914   English critic Clive Bell publishes *Art*, which includes his seminal essay, "The Aesthetic Hypothesis." He develops a highly formalist theory of art which argues that the significance of a work of art lies in its form rather than its content. A major modernist thinker and member of the Bloomsbury group (*see* 1905, CRIT), he will publish *Civilization* in 1928.   CRIT

1914   Russian-born American choreographer Michel Fokine, considered the "father of modern ballet," outlines his theory of choreography in a letter to the London *Times*.   CRIT

1914–1923   American journalist and writer Henry Louis Mencken gains a national reputation as he and George Jean Nathan coedit the periodical the *Smart Set*.   JOURN

1914   Spanish philosopher José Ortega y Gasset publishes *Meditations on Quixote*, in which he argues for a middle way between idealism and realism. His essays and teaching help revitalize intellectual life in Spain.   PHIL

1914   English philosopher Charlie Dunbar Broad publishes *Perception, Physics, and Reality*, in which he adopts an analytic approach to the philosophy of sense perception.   PHIL

1914   English mathematician and philosopher Bertrand Russell publishes *Our Knowledge of the External World*. In this and other works, he emphasizes logical analysis of objects of belief and argues that knowledge depends on original experience. His works will influence Viennese-born British philosopher Ludwig Wittgenstein and the logical positivists, including German-born American philosopher Rudolph Carnap. He will also be known for his pacifism and liberal views on social, political, and sexual matters.   PHIL

1914   On June 28 in Sarajevo, Bosnia, Serbian nationalist Gavrilo Princip shoots Austrian archduke Francis Ferdinand, triggering World War I (lasting until 1918). The war's devastation will feed pessimism and skepticism among Western thinkers; wartime deprivation in Russia will set the stage for Communist revolution (*see* 1917, POL); and postwar depression will assist the rise of the Nazi Party (*see* 1921, POL).   POL

1914   French socialist Jean Jaurès, who has recommended arbitration to avert war in Europe, is assassinated.   POL

1914–1922   Pope Benedict XV succeeds Pope Pius X upon the latter's death. Benedict keeps the Vatican neutral during World War I, organizes relief work, and strives to restore peace.   REL

1914   The Assemblies of God, the largest Pentecostal organization in the United States, is founded at Hot Springs, Arkansas.   REL

1914   The World Alliance for International Friendship through the Churches is
            founded with the aim of preventing war.   REL

1914   Jamaican-born American newspaper editor, orator, and social reformer Marcus
            Garvey founds the Universal Negro Improvement Association (UNIA) in
            London to promote racial pride. Two years later he will move to Harlem, New
            York City, where he will open an American branch of the UNIA. Among the
            most important black nationalists of the early 1920s, he will be remembered
            for advocating a "back to Africa" movement whose goal is the establishment
            of an autonomous black state in Africa.   SOC

1915–1918   English anthropologist Bronislaw Malinowski does field research with
            Trobriand Islanders. He will found the theory of functionalism with his ethno-
            graphies in the 1920s and 1930s.   ANTH

1915   Swiss art historian Heinrich Wölfflin publishes *Principles of Art History* in
            Munich, an influential work of formal analysis.   CRIT

1915–1918   Russian historian and politician Mikhail Pokrovsky publishes *An Outline
            History of Russian Culture*. He will publish *Sketches of the History of the
            Revolutionary Movement in Russia in the 19th and 20th Centuries* in 1924. His
            works will provide the first major Marxist interpretation of Russian history. HIST

1915   In the United States, the Ku Klux Klan is reorganized (*see* 1867, soc). The racist
            organization, associated with nativist, fundamentalist, anti-Semitic, and anti-
            Catholic ideas, will gain great strength by the 1920s, creating terror in both the
            North and South.   SOC

1915   American labor leader and songwriter Joe Hill, active in the Industrial Workers
            of the World (IWW), or the Wobblies, is executed for murder based on cir-
            cumstantial evidence. He will become a legendary martyr of the labor
            movement.   SOC

1915   American nurse and reformer Margaret Sanger is indicted for distributing birth
            control information through the mail. The following year, in Brooklyn, she
            will open the first birth control clinic in the United States.   SOC

1915   The growing popularity of female emancipation is symbolized, reports the
            London *Daily Mail*, by the "extraordinary short skirt" of the day, which falls
            above the ankles and allows more freedom of movement than floor-length
            clothing. The trend toward similarly unencumbered clothing will continue
            throughout the century.   SOC

1916–1922   The Russian formalist movement in literary criticism, led by Roman Jakobson,
            Viktor Shklovsky, Osip Brik, and others, produces *Studies in the Theory of Poetic*

Language in six volumes. Their work emphasizes the distortions of poetic language and applies linguistic tools to close analysis of the formal structures of literary texts. The movement will flourish throughout the 1920s, until it is repressed by Stalinism.   CRIT

1916   German art critic Hermann Bahr publishes *Expressionism*, a book that will be associated with *Der Blaue Reiter* through its concern for the spiritual function of art.   CRIT

1916   Romanian-born French poet Tristan Tzara founds the Dada group in Zurich and becomes editor of the periodical *Dada*. He will later publish his own Dada works, including *Vingt-cinq poèmes* in 1918 and the play *Le Coeur à Gaz* in 1923. CRIT

1916   German-born American psychologist Hugo Münsterberg publishes *The Film: A Psychological Study*. The first major work in film theory, it attempts to define the features of the silent "photoplay" by contrasting it with the theater. He argues that the cinema should not try to imitate nature since its concern is a display of the inner workings of the mind.   CRIT

1916   Through his teachings and his book *Democracy and Education*, American philosopher and educator John Dewey presents his belief in the need to reform educational methods. He states the need to abandon authoritarian methods for a pragmatic pedagogy that serves a democratic culture. This and other works by Dewey, including *Logic* (1938), serve as a basis for 20th-century progressive education.   EDUC

1916   *Cours de linguistique générale* (*Course in General Linguistics*), by Swiss linguist Ferdinand de Saussure, is published posthumously. A founding work of modern structural linguistics, it will also influence the development of semiotics. Saussure argues that language sounds are arbitrary signs, while language itself is a systematic structure linking sign and signified.   LING

1916   German physicist Albert Einstein proposes the general theory of relativity. By dethroning Newtonian physics and eliminating the notion of absolute reference points, Einstein exerts a lasting influence in many areas of thought, notably epistemology and the philosophy of science.   MISC

1916   American philosopher Roy Wood Sellars publishes *Critical Realism*, in which he develops a doctrine that combines an appreciation of the independent, objective, real nature of the world with an understanding that the mind knows this world only through sensory perception and thought.   PHIL

1916–1922   In Ireland, the Irish Republican Army forms to fight for the creation of a unified nation-state. It will oppose the dominion status conferred in 1922 by the creation of the Irish Free State. Over the decades, it will become known for its use of terrorist violence to promote its aims.   POL

1916   German philosopher and writer Martin Buber publishes *The Spirit of Judaism*.   REL

1916   Russian mystic Grigory Yefimovich Rasputin, famed for combining religious zeal, sexual excess, and political manipulation, is assassinated by a party of nobles on suspicion that he and Tsarina Alexandra Feodorovna are planning to make peace with Germany.   REL

1916   In Nepal, the Sherpas found the Tengboche monastery, initiating a local tradition of celibate Buddhist monasticism.   REL

1916   Italian economist and sociologist Vilfredo Pareto publishes his monumental *Trattato di sociologia generale* (*Mind and Society*) in which he develops his idea of the "circulation of elites." This theory holds that while society is always dominated by an elite, the composition of this elite changes as the ablest members of the lower classes work their way into the upper echelons of business and industry. Pareto will be considered a forerunner of Italian fascism.   SOC

1917   Russian novelist and critic Viktor Shklovsky outlines his theory of "defamiliarization," an unconventional view of the nature of art in his essay "Art as Technique."   CRIT

1917   French poet Guillaume Apollinaire coins the term *surrealism* in his review of the ballet *Parade*, by French composer Erik Satie and French poet, novelist, playwright, and artist Jean Cocteau, choreographed by Russian dancer Léonide Massine and designed by Spanish painter Pablo Picasso.   CRIT

1917   Sri Lankan scholar Ananda Kentish Coomaraswamy establishes the first subdepartment of Indian art in an American museum at the Museum of Fine Arts in Boston. His writings throughout the 1920s and 1930s will emphasize the communicative aspect of Ceylonese culture and portray Indian art as a form of knowledge.   CRIT

1917   After this year, many historians, particularly Russian scholars in exile following the Bolshevik Revolution, adopt a Eurasian approach to the study of Russia's past, emphasizing the importance of both Asian and European influence on Russia's development and taking Russia's enormous size and great ethnic diversity into account. Historians remaining in Russia following the Revolution are forced to work under the supervision of the Communist government. Initially, they will focus upon comparing Soviet institutions favorably to those of the tsarist years. After the 1930s, however, they will put more emphasis on the achievements of pre-Revolutionary leaders in an attempt to show the historic roots of their country's greatness.   HIST

1917   On the night of November 6 (October 24 Old Style, according to the Julian calendar), the October Revolution begins in Russia. The Bolshevik Party, led by Lenin, overthrows Aleksandr Kerensky's provisional government in Petrograd (St. Petersburg until 1914, then Leningrad from 1924 to 1991, then St. Petersburg again). On November 7 (October 25 Old Style), Lenin institutes the world's first national government founded explicitly on the Communist principles of Karl Marx and Friedrich Engels (see 1848, POL). The ideas of Marx and Engels, as modified by Lenin, will dominate Russia until the Soviet Union's collapse in 1991.   POL

1917   In the United States, the Espionage Act is passed, making it illegal to speak, write, or demonstrate against the draft or U.S. participation in World War I. Now and in the following year, thousands are prosecuted for antiwar and antidraft activities, including pacifists, IWW members (see 1905, SOC), and socialists such as Eugene Debs.   POL

1917   Austrian psychoanalyst Sigmund Freud publishes *Introduction to Psychoanalysis*.   PSYCH

1917   Urged by the Zionist movement, the British government issues the Balfour Declaration, promising the establishment of a Jewish national homeland in Palestine. *See also* 1948, REL.   REL

1917   The revised Roman Catholic Code of Canon Law is promulgated.   REL

1918   Swiss architect Le Corbusier (pseudonym of Charles Jeannert) and French painter Amédée Ozenfant publish *Après le cubisme*, a work that launches their theory of purism. In 1920 they will establish the review *L'Esprit nouveau* to promote a return within the avant-garde to principles of classical order.   CRIT

1918   Swedish economist Gustav Cassel publishes *Theory of Social Economy*.   ECON

1918   In *The Higher Learning in America*, American economist Thorstein Veblen attacks the growing move toward "marketable" research in universities as having a "corrupting effect" on scholars, tempting them to seek only "'practical' results" rather than engage in pure research.   EDUC

1918–1922   German writer Oswald Spengler publishes *The Decline of the West*, in which he presents a cyclical view of the growth and decay of cultures. Though he will never become a Nazi himself, Spengler's work will greatly influence the Nazis.   HIST

1918   English writer Lytton Strachey publishes *Eminent Victorians,* a book of sketch-
            es of four major Victorian figures which will be seen as a landmark in biogra-
            phy. Modern biographies will be greatly influenced by Strachey's brevity and
            selectivity, his use of irony and wit and the irreverence he displays toward his
            subjects and their times. He will publish the highly regarded *Queen Victoria* in
            1921.   HIST

1918   American historian Henry Adams publishes *The Education of Henry Adams,* an
            ironic examination of his own life as well as a search for a unified vision of the
            age. The chapter "The Dynamo and the Virgin" will be regarded as an exem-
            plary comparison between the unity of the past and the confusing multiplici-
            ty of modern times. Often considered the greatest American autobiography, it
            had been privately printed in 1907.   HIST

1918   German philosopher Moritz Schlick, who will found the logical positivist group
            called the Vienna Circle, publishes *General Epistemology. See also* 1924, PHIL.   PHIL

1918   American philosopher Clarence Irving Lewis, considered the founder of modal
            logic, publishes *A Survey of Symbolic Logic.* Other works will include *Mind and
            the World-Order* (1929).   PHIL

1918   American president Woodrow Wilson presents the 14 Points, a proposal for
            peace following World War I. Its suggestions for a just and generous peace will
            be largely set aside by the forthcoming Treaty of Versailles; the last point will
            be central to the founding of the League of Nations.   POL

1918–1919   Stanford University psychologist Lewis Madison Terman adapts the Binet-
            Simon Intelligence Scale (*see* 1911, PSYCH) for use in English, leading to the pub-
            lication of the Stanford-Binet Scale, the first standardized individual intelli-
            gence test in the United States.   PSYCH

1918   Austrian psychiatrist Alfred Adler publishes *The Theory and Practice of Individual
            Psychology.* Adler argues that people are motivated by expectations of the future
            and strive toward three life goals: physical security, sexual satisfaction, and
            social integration.   PSYCH

1918   The Russian Orthodox church is stripped of all legal rights by the Communist
            government.   REL

1918   The United Lutheran Church is founded in the United States.   REL

1918   Charles Horton Cooley, a pioneer in American sociology, publishes *Social
            Process.*   SOC

1918–1921   The American sociologist William Isaac Thomas collaborates with his Polish colleague Florian Znaniecki on the five-volume *The Polish Peasant in Europe and America*, an ethnographic account that portrays the relation of wider social values to individual attitudes.   SOC

1919   American-born English poet and critic T. S. Eliot publishes "Tradition and the Individual Talent," a poetic manifesto in which he argues that modern poets must draw creatively on tradition, write impersonal, detached verse, and focus on technique.   CRIT

1919   English novelist Virginia Woolf publishes the critical essay *Modern Fiction*.   CRIT

1919   Leading Italian futurist painter Carlo Carrà rejects the avant-garde and promotes the "Metaphysical School" of Italian painters in his essay "Our Antiquity," published in his book *Pittura Metafisica*.   CRIT

1919   Russian painter Kazimir Malevich publishes "Non-Objective Art and Suprematism" in the catalog to the tenth State Exhibition in Moscow to explain his celebration of the color white as the color of infinity.   CRIT

1919   English economist John Maynard Keynes argues against the reparations levied on Germany for its role in World War I in *The Economic Consequences of the Peace*.   ECON

1919   Dutch historian Johan Huizinga publishes *The Waning of the Middle Ages*.   HIST

1919   American journalist and Communist John Reed publishes *Ten Days That Shook the World*, on the October Revolution in Russia, which he witnessed (*see* 1917, POL).   HIST

1919   American journalist and writer H. L. Mencken publishes *The American Language*, a pioneering reference work on the differences between the English and American tongues. Supplements will be published in 1945 and 1948.   LING

1919   In China, the "May 4 movement" (*see* 1919, POL) urges adoption of a vernacular Chinese language. Scholar and educator Hu Shi, one of the movement's leaders, is inspired by the pragmatic philosophy of American John Dewey.   LING

1919   French philosopher Henri Bergson publishes *L'Energie spirituelle (Mind-Energy)*.   PHIL

1919   German philosopher Ernst Cassirer publishes *The Problem of Knowledge: Philosophy, Science, and History Since Hegel*. He will also publish *The Philosophy of Symbolic Forms* in 1923–1929.   PHIL

1919   German social philosopher Hermann Alexander Keyserling publishes *Travel Diary of a Philosopher*.   PHIL

1919   English physician Havelock Ellis publishes *The Philosophy of Conflict.*   PHIL

1919   Indian political and spiritual leader Mohandas Gandhi (known as Mahatma, "great-souled") organizes a nonviolent resistance movement against British rule in India. His philosophy of *satyagraha* ("firmness in truth") is rooted in a religious outlook that is Hindu in origin but ecumenical in spirit. He regards commitment to nonviolence as both a moral requirement and a means of political change. Gandhi will inspire resistance and reform movements throughout the world, including the African-American civil rights movement. *See also* 1955–1956, soc.   POL

1919   Britain introduces the political system of dyarchy to India, in which India retains control of local government, while Britain continues to rule the country as a whole. The system will not be satisfactory to Indian nationalists, who seek complete independence.   POL

1919   Russian revolutionary leader Lenin founds the Third Communist International, or Comintern, intended to dominate Communist organizations throughout the world. Non-Communist socialists in the West will henceforth tend to distinguish themselves as democratic socialists.   POL

1919   On May 4, students in Beijing, China, protest and riot to oppose grants of land to Japan. The protests grow into a broad-based nationalist movement, known as the "May 4 movement," that is opposed to foreign imperialism but open to Western concepts of individualism and liberalism.   POL

1919   In *Schenk* v. *United States*, the Supreme Court introduces the concept of "clear and present danger" in permitting restraint of free speech in wartime as embodied in the Espionage Act (*see also* 1917, POL).   POL

1919   Following two decades of arrests for voicing their views on government and birth contol, American anarchists Emma Goldman and Alexander Berkman are deported to the Soviet Union. The two represent a small but significant group of early 20th-century thinkers who believe the overthrow of the capitalist U.S. government is necessary to achieve social and economic equality. Disappointed with Soviet government, Goldman will later write *My Disillusionment in Russia* (1923).   POL

1919   Isolationism gains new popularity in the United States following World War I. A sign of its strength is the failure of the Senate to approve admission of the United States to the League of Nations. U.S. isolationism will subside with the

Japanese attack on Pearl Harbor in Hawaii and Americans' subsequent entry into World War II.											POL

1919		The League of Nations, an international peacekeeping organization, is founded after World War I. Though its principal architect is U.S. president Woodrow Wilson, the United States fails to join. Following years of increasing ineffectuality before and during World War II, in 1946 the organization will disband and be replaced by the United Nations.											POL

1919		After 41 years of attempted passage, the U.S. Congress passes the 19th Amendment, which grants women the right to vote. The amendment will be ratified in 1920.											POL

1919		American psychologist John Broadus Watson publishes *Psychology from the Standpoint of a Behaviorist*. Behavioral psychology, the school of which he is the founder, restricts itself to objectively observable behavior explained in terms of stimulus and response. Watson is also the author of *Animal Education* (1903), *Behavior* (1914), and *Psychological Care of Infant and Child* (1928).											PSYCH

1919		Swiss theologian Karl Barth publishes *Commentary on Romans*, a seminal work of Protestant dialectical theology. Barth challenges faith in human progress, seeking a return to revelation and the principles of the Reformation.											REL

1919		African-American religious leader and activist George Baker, or Father Divine, founds a commune in Sayville, Long Island. Following a jail sentence for disturbing the peace, his "Peace Mission" will move to Harlem in 1933. His enthusiastic preaching and emphasis on social justice will appeal to many African-Americans during the Great Depression.											REL

1919		The National Prohibition Act (also known as the Volstead Act), which allows for enforcing the18th Amendment, is passed by the U.S. Congress. The act prohibits the manufacture and distribution of alcoholic beverages. The desire for alcohol will create a black market run by bootleggers and gangsters. Prohibition will be repealed by the 21st Amendment, in 1933.											SOC

1920s		Harvard and Columbia Universities take different approaches to anthropology, with Harvard specializing in archaeology and physical anthropology and Columbia in ethnology and linguistics.											ANTH

1920s		Little magazines such as *Poetry*, *Story*, and *Transition* are popular vehicles for introducing and nurturing new literary talent and gain a wide readership.											CRIT

1920s		The Fugitives (or Agrarians), a group of poets and critics associated with Vanderbilt University, flourishes. They hold conservative political views, emphasizing southern agrarianism as an ideal. Their criticism takes a formal approach to literary texts, which are seen as autonomous verbal structures; these views will influence New Criticism (*see* 1941, CRIT). Members of the Fugitives include John Crowe Ransom, Allen Tate, Robert Penn Warren, and Cleanth Brooks. CRIT

1920s   The Paris home of American writer Gertrude Stein becomes the center for such fellow literary expatriates as Ernest Hemingway, F. Scott Fitzgerald, and Sherwood Anderson. Stein coins the phrase the "lost generation" for this group. Her critical works include *Lectures in America* (1935), *Picasso* (1938), and her memoir of the Parisian art colony, *The Autobiography of Alice B. Toklas* (1933).   CRIT

1920s   The centuries-old belief in the innate knowledge of the mother concerning child-rearing is replaced by pronouncements by "experts" in education and child psychology.   MISC

1920s   The modern pastoral counseling movement begins, incorporating aspects of traditional theological guidance and psychiatric treatment.   PSYCH

1920s   Austrian psychoanalyst Otto Rank stresses the therapeutic importance of individual will. His "will" therapy is the forerunner of assertiveness training and reality therapy.   PSYCH

1920   American-born English poet and critic T. S. Eliot publishes *The Sacred Wood*, a collection of critical essays that establishes his reputation as a modernist critic. He will become the foremost literary arbiter of his day.   CRIT

1920   English critic Jessie L. Weston publishes *From Ritual to Romance*, a study of the Holy Grail romances that will inspire T. S. Eliot's poem *The Waste Land* (1922).   CRIT

1920   German-born French art dealer and writer Daniel-Henri Kahnweiler publishes *Der Weg zum Kubismus*, a pioneering study of Cubism. He will write the first major monograph on Spanish artist Juan Gris in 1943 and be the first to publish the work of French writers Guillaume Apollinaire, Max Jacob, and André Masson.   CRIT

1920   English economist Arthur Cecil Pigou publishes *The Economics of Welfare*. An adherent of the view that society is responsible for the economic waste due to poverty, he contributes to the development of welfare economics.   ECON

c. 1920   Pre-primary school education in the United States has its beginnings with the opening of the first nursery school in the country. Early education is expected to better prepare children for primary school.   EDUC

1920   English writer H. G. Wells publishes the widely popular *Outline of History*.
                                                                                                             HIST

1920   English mathematician and philosopher Alfred North Whitehead publishes *The Concept of Nature*. In this and other works, such as *Enquiry Concerning the Principles of Natural Knowledge* (1919), he develops a metaphysics based on overlapping sets of processes ultimately ordered by God.   PHIL

1920   French philosopher Jacques Maritain publishes *Art et scolastique*.   PHIL

1920   English philosopher Samuel Alexander publishes *Space, Time, and Deity*.   PHIL

1920   American philosopher and educator John Dewey publishes *Reconstruction in Philosophy*, which presents his philosophy of pragmatism and its applications in society.   PHIL

1920   *Essays in Critical Realism* is published. Including articles from American philosophers Arthur Oncken Lovejoy and George Santayana, it develops the theory of knowledge known as critical realism (*see* 1916, PHIL).   PHIL

1920   A belief in the need to protect individual constitutional rights leads to the formation of the American Civil Liberties Union. Founding members include Jane Addams, Clarence Darrow, Felix Frankfurter, Helen Keller, and Norman Thomas.   POL

1920   On August 26, American women are officially granted the right to vote, as Tennessee becomes the final state to ratify the 19th Amendment to the Constitution.   POL

1920   Believing in the importance of getting information to newly enfranchised voters, American suffragist Carrie Chapman Catt organizes the League of Women Voters to further that end.   POL

c. 1920   Swiss psychologist Jean Piaget performs research in genetic epistemology, showing how intelligence varies qualitatively and quantitatively with age. He identifies stages in the development of a child's mental faculties and urges schools to provide developmentally appropriate education.   PSYCH

1920   American psychologist Robert Sessions Woodworth develops the Woodworth personal data sheet, a military screening device to identify emotional instability. It will become the prototype for personality questionnaires.   PSYCH

1920   Pope Benedict XV canonizes 15th-century French martyr Joan of Arc.   REL

1920   American attitudes toward immigrants and political dissent are revealed in the Sacco-Vanzetti case. In South Braintree, Massachusetts, two Italian immigrants, Nicola Sacco and Bartolomeo Vanzetti, are arrested for the murder of a factory paymaster. Despite years of worldwide protest, the two will be executed in 1927. SOC

1921   American-born English poet and critic T. S. Eliot publishes "The Metaphysical Poets," in which he reshapes the canon of English poetry, giving primacy to the 17th-century poets who he claims united thought and sensual imagery.   CRIT

1921   American historian Herbert Bolton publishes *Spanish Borderlands*. He will publish *Outpost of Empire* in 1931 and *Coronado on the Turquoise Trail* in 1949. He includes the contributions of the Spanish as well as those of the English and the French in discussing the development of the American West.   HIST

1921   Viennese-born British philosopher Ludwig Wittgenstein publishes his first major work, *Tractatus logico-philosophicus*, in which he argues that philosophical problems can best be handled through a critical method of linguistic analysis. His work will have a profound impact on the development of logical positivism.   PHIL

1921–1927   English neo-Hegelian philosopher John M'Taggart publishes *The Nature of Existence*.   PHIL

1921   English economist John Maynard Keynes publishes the philosophical work *Theory of Probability*, a landmark in confirmation theory, which deals with how to measure the degree to which any theory is supported by evidence.   PHIL

1921   British mathematician and philosopher Bertrand Russell publishes *The Analysis of Mind*. *The Analysis of Matter* will follow in 1927.   PHIL

1921   German politician Adolf Hitler becomes president of the National Socialist German Workers' Party, known as the Nazi Party. With their blend of racist pseudoscience, anti-Semitism, anti-Communism, nationalism, militarism, and fascism, the Nazis will dominate Germany and conquer other nations from 1933 until their defeat by Allied forces in 1945.   POL

1921   In Italy, fascism establishes itself with leader Benito Mussolini's formation of the Fascist Party.   POL

1921   Swiss psychiatrist Carl Gustav Jung publishes *Psychological Types*, in which he outlines the concepts of extroversion and introversion. Jung also develops the theory that certain ideas, called archetypes, are inherited from the distant past and reside in every person's unconscious (the collective unconscious).   PSYCH

1921   Swiss psychiatrist Hermann Rorschach publishes his major work, *Psycho-diagnostik*, introducing the inkblot test as an aid in diagnosing mental disorders.   PSYCH

1921   African religious leader Simon Kimbangu begins preaching and healing in what will become Zaire. Later arrested for sedition by the colonial Belgian government and imprisoned for life, he will be revered by the nationalist religious movement called Kimbanguism.   REL

1922   English anthropologist Bronislaw Malinowski publishes *Argonauts of the Western Pacific*, which becomes a model for anthropological monographs based on participant observation.   ANTH

1922   Russian designer, artist, and theorist Alexey Gan publishes *Constructivism*, an extensive exposition of the principles of constructivism.   CRIT

1922   French art historian Émile Male preserves the 19th-century iconological tradition of French art history in his book *Religious Art in France: The 12th Century*.   CRIT

1922   The American periodical *Reader's Digest*, edited by DeWitt and Lila Acheson Wallace, begins publication. In each issue, it disseminates to a wider audience a collection of current articles condensed from prominent periodicals.   JOURN

1922   German logical positivist philosopher Rudolf Carnap publishes *The Space*. PHIL

1922   French philosopher Étienne Gilson, an exponent of Thomism, publishes *Le Thomisme* and *La Philosophie au Moyen-Age*.   PHIL

1922   English philosopher George Edward Moore publishes *Philosophical Studies*. PHIL

1922–1923   American philosopher Arthur Oncken Lovejoy, with colleagues George Boas and Gilbert Chinard, form the History of Ideas Club at Johns Hopkins University. They develop history of ideas as an interdisciplinary field of study dedicated to the tracing of "unit-ideas" in many different areas of culture. The *Journal of the History of Ideas* will be founded in 1940; in 1948, Lovejoy will publish *Essays in the History of Ideas*. *See also* 1936, PHIL.   PHIL

1922   American journalist and political analyst Walter Lippmann publishes his most famous book, *Public Opinion*. He argues that the complexity of modern life makes citizens incapable of making rational judgments about public issues and that the mass media encourages sloganeering rather than thoughtful analysis.

POL

1922–1939   Pope Pius XI succeeds Benedict XV upon the latter's death. During his papacy, Pius opposes fascism, racism, and anti-Semitism. He criticizes both Communism and laissez-faire capitalism, calling for social reform, protection of native cultures, and increased lay participation in religious life (known as Catholic Action).   REL

1922   Armenian spiritualist George Ivanovich Gurdjieff founds the Institute for the Harmonious Development of Man in Fontainebleau, France. His occult philosophy, which purports to offer a way of attaining higher consciousness, will attract many followers among the European avant-garde. His works include *All and Everything: Beelzebub's Tales to His Grandson* and *Meetings with Remarkable Men*.   REL

1922   *Methodology of the Social Sciences,* by German sociologist Max Weber, is published posthumously.   SOC

1922   American writer Emily Post completes her first edition of *Etiquette,* which will become a standard reference work on manners.   SOC

1922   American sociologist William Ogburn publishes *Social Change,* arguing that technology plays an essential role in change in the wider society. A member of the University of Chicago faculty, he coins the phrase "cultural lag" to describe the tendency for technological development to outpace social response to it.   SOC

1922   German sociologist Max Weber's epochal work on bureaucracy is published posthumously. It is the starting point for all subsequent sociological treatments of the issue.   SOC

1923   Russian critic Osip Brik writes the essay "The So-Called 'Formal Method',", which establishes the revolutionary credentials of Constructivist practices. CRIT

1923   German architect Walter Gropius writes "The Theory and Organization of the Bauhaus" to promote modern design principles within industrial manufacturing. CRIT

1923   French writer André Maurois (pseudonym of Émile Herzog) publishes *Ariel, ou la vie de Shelley.* He will publish *Voltaire* in 1935 and *À la recherche de Marcel Proust* in 1949. He will be known for presenting the complexity and idiosyncracy of his subjects in highly engaging works that read like novels.   HIST

1923   English diplomat and writer Sir Harold Nicolson, a member of the Bloomsbury Group, publishes the biography *Tennyson.* His *Byron* will appear in 1924 and his *Swinburne* in 1926.   HIST

1923   The weekly newsmagazine *Time* is founded by American editors Henry Luce and Briton Hadden. It will form the basis for a publishing empire and set a standard for weekly news periodicals.   JOURN

1923   American publisher Frank Gannett founds the Gannett Company, uniting four upstate New York newspapers; it will come to encompass dozens more.   JOURN

1923   English linguist Charles Kay Ogden and scholar Ivor Armstrong Richards develop a "science of meaning," which will later be called semantics, in *The Meaning of Meaning.*   LING

1923	In *Kulturphilosophie* (*The Philosophy of Civilization*), French physician, philosopher, and theologian Albert Schweitzer develops an ethical philosophy based on the concept of reverence for life. <div align="right">PHIL</div>
1923	Spanish philosopher José Ortega y Gasset publishes *El tema de nuestro tiempo*. PHIL
1923–1927	Indian educator Sarvepalli Radhakrishnan presents a modernized Hindu philosophy in *Indian Philosophy*. <div align="right">PHIL</div>
1923	English socialists Sidney and Beatrice Webb publish *The Decay of Capitalist Civilization*. <div align="right">POL</div>
1923	The Institute for Social Research is founded in Frankfurt, Germany. It will become the center of the Frankfurt School of Marxist theory, which will flourish in the 1920s and 1930s and include such thinkers as Max Horkheimer, Theodor Adorno, Walter Benjamin, and Herbert Marcuse. The school will critique both contemporary capitalism and Stalinist Marxism, focusing particularly on the ways in which aesthetics and popular culture combine to perpetuate oppression. The school will influence the New Left in the 1960s and Marxist literary theory and cultural studies. <div align="right">POL</div>
1923	Japanese anarchist and feminist Itō Noe, founder of the socialist women's group Sekirankai, is executed by the military police in a purge of leftist activists. <div align="right">POL</div>
1923	Austrian psychoanalyst Sigmund Freud publishes *The Ego and the Id*. PSYCH
1923	Turkey, long the center of the Ottoman empire, becomes a parliamentary republic. Led by President Mustafa Kemal Atatürk, the new republic abolishes the Ottoman sultanate and state religion. The last caliph, titular head of Islam, will be expelled in 1924. <div align="right">REL</div>
1923	German philosopher and writer Martin Buber publishes *I and Thou*, which will influence both Jewish and Christian theologians. <div align="right">REL</div>
1923	Swedish Lutheran theologian Nathan Söderblom publishes *Christian Fellowship*. <div align="right">REL</div>
1923	Syrian writer Kahlil Gibran publishes the inspirational work of poetry *The Prophet*. Blending Eastern and Western mysticism, it will be translated and reprinted many times. <div align="right">REL</div>
1923	American nurse and reformer Margaret Sanger popularizes the idea of birth control at the first birth control conference in the United States. Two years later, she will organize the first international birth control conference. <div align="right">SOC</div>

1924   *Speculations*, by English philosopher and poet Thomas Ernest Hulme, is published
            posthumously. In distinguishing classicism from romanticism, and favoring the for-
            mer, his earlier work laid the foundations for the modernist aesthetics of American-
            born English poet and critic T. S. Eliot and American poet and critic Ezra Pound.CRIT

1924   English novelist David Herbert Lawrence publishes *Studies in Classic American
            Literature*. Other prose works of his include the political-philosophical essay
            collection *Reflections on the Death of a Porcupine* (1934), *Pornography and
            Obscenity* (1930), and two statements of his philosophy, *Psychoanalysis and the
            Unconscious* (1921) and *Fantasia of the Unconscious* (1922).   CRIT

Sage of Baltimore, Bane of Main Street

In America during the 1920s, the doughboys had long ago returned from the battles of
the Great War. Business was booming, people were secure in their position as American
citizens. But away from the tidy storefronts, discord stewed. The intelligentsia—writers,
artists, reformers, radical thinkers—feared that the country had grown complacent.
Literary works like Sinclair Lewis's *Babbitt* exposed the middlebrow moral rigidity and
devotion to money that postwar thinkers believed they had to fight. No voice was more
virulent, idiosyncratic, or influential than the Sage of Baltimore, hometown journalist
Henry Louis Mencken.

As writer for the Baltimore *Evening Sun* and coeditor (with critic George Jean
Nathan) of the *American Mercury* (founded in 1924), Mencken had a national platform
for his plans to "track down some of the worst nonsense prevailing and do execution
on it." His targets included religion, capitalism, and small towns, all of which were
stomping grounds for the limited middlebrow American he termed the "booboisie."

In part, Mencken's pitting of his superior individual morality against the
Herdenmoral (the beliefs of the mob) had its origins in his attraction to the work of the
German philosopher Friedrich Nietzsche. By the time he became a nationally known
journalist Mencken had also established himself as an American popularizer of
Nietzsche. He had written a favorable biography, *The Philosophy of Friedrich Nietzsche*
(1908), and had edited a collection of his writings, *The Gist of Nietzsche* (1910). The
effect of the summoner of the Übermensch on the future foil of the booboisie was
unmistakable.

It also made him wildly popular. In 1927 journalist Walter Lippmann called
Mencken "the most powerful personal influence on this whole generation of educated
people." By the Great Depression, however, Mencken's brand of barbed social satire
had run its course. The survival of the country, not its faults, became the central question. And as the Nazi Party gained power in Germany in the 1930s, the writer influenced by Nietzsche found Nietzschean ideas unwelcome.

1924–1933   American journalist and writer H. L. Mencken edits the *American Mercury*, cofounded with George Jean Nathan. Mencken's acid, perspicacious essays are collected in *Prejudices* (six volumes, 1919–1927).   JOURN

1924   German philosopher Moritz Schlick founds the Vienna Circle, a group of logical positivists that will last until Schlick's death in 1936; its members will include Friedrich Waismann, Otto Neurath, Rudolf Carnap, Herbert Feigl, Victor Kraft, and Kurt Gödel. Also known as scientific empiricism, logical positivism holds that philosophy should focus on clarifying scientific language; that science consists of logical truths coupled to statements about sense experience; that metaphysics is nonsense; and that value statements are purely emotive. For 20th-century philosophy in general, it will mark a long-term shift toward analytical philosophy and away from speculative philosophy.   PHIL

1924   Italian philosopher Giovanni Gentile becomes first president of the National Fascist Institute of Culture. Known for developing the theory of the spirit as pure act, he will be assassinated during World War II for his support of fascism.   PHIL

1924   Soviet political leader Joseph Stalin, who will combine systematic repression and terror with Marxist-Leninist ideology, succeeds Lenin as leader of the Soviet Union. His totalitarian approach, driven by a "cult of personality" centered on himself, allows for nearly complete dictatorship.   POL

1924   Indian political leader Bhimrao Ramji Ambedkar founds the Depressed Classes Institute, aimed at improving the lot of the Harijan caste, or "untouchables," to which he belongs. From 1947 to 1951, as independent India's first law minister, he will help outline the Hindu Code, which outlaws discrimination against untouchables.   POL

1924   American political scientists Charles Merriam and Harold Gosnell publish *Non-voting, Causes and Methods of Control*, one of the first important works in political science to use survey data and sampling techniques.   POL

1924–1939   The 12-volume *Collected Writings* of Austrian psychoanalyst Sigmund Freud is published.   PSYCH

1924   Austrian psychoanalyst Otto Rank publishes *Das Trauma der Geburt* (*The Trauma of Birth*), which departs from his mentor Freud's views in arguing that anxiety neurosis results from the trauma of birth.   PSYCH

1924   Swiss theologian Karl Barth publishes *The Word of God and the Word of Man*.   REL

1924   Indian political and spiritual leader Mohandas Gandhi fasts for 21 days to protest
                violence between Hindus and Muslims.   REL

1924   American scholar Irving Babbitt publishes *Democracy and Leadership*.   SOC

1924   American sociologist Franklin Giddings publishes *The Scientific Study of
                Human Society*, an early statement about the use of quantitative methods in
                sociological research.   SOC

1925   French anthropologist Marcel Mauss publishes *The Gift*, which studies the
                social bond of debt created by gift-giving.   ANTH

1925   English novelist Virginia Woolf publishes the collection of essays *The Common
                Reader*, which will be followed in 1932 by *The Second Common Reader*.   CRIT

1925   American critic Alain Locke publishes the anthology *The New Negro*, which
                collects scholarship and creative writing from prominent writers of the
                Harlem Renaissance. Locke's title essay discusses the "common conscious-
                ness" of African-Americans as a progressive force.   CRIT

1925   Dutch painter Theo van Doesburg (pseudonym of Christian Küpper) pub-
                lishes his theoretical treatise *Principles of Neo-Plastic Art* for the Bauhaus to
                articulate the principles of the *De Stijl* movement.   CRIT

1925   American philosopher and educator John Dewey publishes *Experience and
                Nature*, a work that explains his pragmatic view that ideas are instruments of
                action. He will publish *Art as Experience* in 1934.   CRIT

1925   English critic Ivor Armstrong Richards publishes *Principles of Literary Criticism*.
                In this work and others, including *Science and Poetry* (1926) and *Practical
                Criticism* (1929), he develops the theory and techniques of "close reading" that
                will be characteristic of the Cambridge critics (*see* 1930, CRIT) and new criticism
                (*see* 1941, CRIT). Richards will be considered the father of new criticism.   CRIT

1925   Belgian historian Henri Pirenne publishes *Medieval Cities*, a pioneering work
                of urban and economic history. His seven-volume *Histoire de Belgique*
                (1900–1932) will lead to his being known as the father of Belgian history.   HIST

1925–1929   Russian historian Simon Dubnow publishes his ten-volume *World History of
                the Jewish People*, a landmark work of Jewish history.   HIST

1925   English philosopher Charles Dunbar Broad publishes *Mind and Its Place in
                Nature*.   PHIL

1925   Austrian philosopher Hans Kelsen publishes *General Theory of Law and State*, which presents a strictly positivist view of law.   PHIL

1925–1927   German politician Adolf Hitler publishes *Mein Kampf* (*My Struggle*). The anti-Semitic work, dictated while in prison for leading the unsuccessful revolt called the "Beer Hall Putsch" (1923), becomes a key document of the Nazi Party (*see* 1921, POL).   POL

1925   English political scientist Harold Laski publishes *Grammar of Politics*.   POL

1925   American political scientist Charles Merriam publishes *New Aspects of Politics*, in which he calls for more use of quantitative methods and suggests drawing on the field of psychology to inform the study of politics.   POL

1925–1933   In his essays "Some Psychic Consequences of the Anatomical Distinction Between the Sexes" (1925) and "Femininity" (1933), Austrian psychoanalyst Sigmund

---

Religion and Self-Help Books

In the first half of the century, self-help books did not depend on multistep programs or charmingly named syndromes. A large number of them were driven by God. In them, readers learned that faith in religion could lead them to wealth, business success, and popularity.

Bruce Barton's *The Man Nobody Knows* (1925) foresaw good fortune for anyone who understood, as he did, "the real Jesus." To Barton, an advertising consultant, Jesus was the businessman who "picked up 12 men from the bottom ranks of business and forged them into an organization that conquered the world" and "followed every one of the principles of modern salesmanship." One would do well to imitate this version of the life of the Savior.

Similar claims were made in other books of the day. One called God "a 24-hour station" and suggested, "All you need to do is plug in." Another said that God was a "powerhouse" ready for us to "plug into." Even popular theologians linked faith in God to personal success. In *A Guide to Confident Living* (1948), Norman Vincent Peale promised, "Power and efficiency are available to you if you will believe." But for the strongest link of God and business, few books top the 1936 best-seller *The Return to Religion*, by psychologist Henry C. Link. To him, religion is "an aggressive mode of life by which the individual becomes the master of his environment, not its complacent victim." The book is a far cry from a later generation's paltry diagnoses of whether someone is or is not "O.K."—and further still from a biblical promise that the meek "shall inherit the earth."

Freud posits that women develop less fully than men as psychological beings. He argues that women must accept their lot of having been "castrated."   PSYCH

1925   Tennessee schoolteacher John Thomas Scopes goes on trial for violating a state law prohibiting the teaching of the theory of evolution. Defended by Clarence Darrow against prosecutor William Jennings Bryan, Scopes is convicted but later acquitted on a technicality. The trial is a milestone in the struggle between American Christian fundamentalist faith and the Darwinian theory of evolution.   REL

1925   The Japanese religious movement Reiyukai (Soul-Friend Association) grows out of the Nichiren Buddhist sect.   REL

1925   The Presbyterian, Congregational, and Methodist churches of Canada join together as the United Church of Canada.   REL

1925   The World Conference on Life and Work is held to apply Christian thinking and activity to social issues.   REL

1925   American writer Bruce Barton publishes *The Man Nobody Knows*, a best-selling self-help book that uses the life of Jesus to answer the needs and concerns of everyday businessmen.   REL

1925   American sociologist Robert Park and his associates publish *The City*, an early and influential study of the structure of urban settlements. Using Chicago as its research site, the authors conceive of the city as a set of concentric circles, each containing a zone of activity.   SOC

1926   The International Institute of African Languages is established to promote anthropological and linguistic research in Africa.   ANTH

1926   American critic George S. Schuyler publishes "The Negro-Art Hokum," in which he emphasizes national culture rather than race. Writer Langston Hughes responds later this year with "The Negro Artist and the Racial Mountain," in which he argues that the African-American artist's cultural integrity is weakened by fleeing from race.   CRIT

1926   Russian critic Osip Brik writes the essay "Photography versus Painting," arguing that photography is in a position to eclipse painting as a means of representing reality.   CRIT

1926   Russian filmmaker Vsevolod Pudovkin publishes his theoretical pamphlets as *Film Technique and Film Acting*, in which he celebrates the art of montage and recognizes American director D. W. Griffith as its true discoverer and leading contributor to the development of a cinematic language. In 1928 Pudovkin will join fellow Russian filmmakers Sergey Eisenstein and Grigory Alexandrov in a manifesto advocating audiovisual counterpoint as a basic technique in sound films. CRIT

1926   English economist Dennis Robertson publishes *Banking Policy and the Price Level*. During his lifetime, he will be both an associate and critic of English economist John Maynard Keynes. ECON

1926   The Scholastic Aptitude Test (SAT) is administered to high school students applying to college. The test, which provides a standardized reading on a student's aptitude for higher education, is believed to grant opportunities to a wider range of students. EDUC

1926   American writer Carl Sandburg publishes the two-volume *Abraham Lincoln— The Prairie Years*. He will publish the four-volume *Abraham Lincoln—The War Years* in 1939. American historian Albert Beveridge will publish the two-volume *Abraham Lincoln, 1809–1850* in 1928. These biographies will be seen as three of the best of the many hundreds of books published about Lincoln over the years. HIST

1926   Chinese political scientist Wang Shijie publishes *Bijiao Xienfa* (*Comparative Constitutions*), one of the best-known works in early Chinese political studies. POL

1926   Russian physiologist Ivan Pavlov publishes *Conditioned Reflexes*, an account of experiments in which he conditioned a dog to salivate at the sound of a bell associated with food (*see* 1877, PSYCH). Pavlov's experiments support the theory that human learning and behavior are based, in part, on conditioned reflex. PSYCH

1926   Indian poet and philosopher Sri Aurobindo Ghose retires into seclusion until his death in 1950. His spiritual community, or ashram, is officially founded under his disciple, the French-born Egyptian Mira Richard. Aurobindo's philosophy of Integral Yoga (*Purna Yoga*) offers a way of achieving higher consciousness that does not require renunciation of the world. REL

1926–1927   English theosophist Annie Besant declares Indian mystic Jiddu Krishnamurti to be the new Messiah. REL

1927   Czech composer Alois Hába describes the use of microtones in musical composition in *New Harmonic Theory.* CRIT

1927   American dancer Isadora Duncan publishes *The Art of the Dance*. CRIT

1927   American historian Charles Homer Haskins publishes *The Renaissance of the Twelfth Century*, a revisionist view of medieval Europe which focuses on the cultural and intellectual achievements of the Middle Ages, seeing the era as a time of great creativity.   HIST

1927   American historians Charles Beard and Mary Ritter Beard publish *The Rise of American Civilization*, a history that emphasizes the role of ideas and of economic and social factors in the development of America. The Beards, who are married to each other, will collaborate on several other books, including *A Basic History of the United States* (1944). Their work is highly influential in its day. *See also* 1913 and 1946, HIST.   HIST

1927   American historian Samuel Eliot Morison publishes *Oxford History of the United States*. Morison will publish other survey histories, as well as influential naval biographies and histories such as *Admiral of the Ocean Sea: A Life of Christopher Columbus* (1942) and *History of U.S. Naval Operations in World War II* (1947–1962). He will be among the most prolific, highly regarded, and widely read of 20th-century American historians.   HIST

1927–1948   American historian George Sarton publishes his three-volume *Introduction to the History of Science*, a landmark work. Many will see Sarton as the greatest historian of science and the person most responsible for establishing the field as a separate discipline.   HIST

1927–1940   American philosopher George Santayana publishes the four-volume *Realms of Being*, in which he develops a philosophy that combines materialism and Platonism. Other works include *Skepticism and Animal Faith* (1923).   PHIL

1927   English painter and writer Wyndham Lewis publishes the treatise *Time and Western Man*, in which he argues for classicism and fixity and denounces the stream-of-consciousness literary technique and French philosopher Henri Bergson's beliefs in intuition and flux.   PHIL

1927–1930   American scholar Vernon Parrington publishes *Main Currents in American Thought*, a major liberal intellectual history.   PHIL

1927   American physicist Percy Williams Bridgman publishes *The Logic of Modern Physics*. Bridgman is known for espousing operationalism, a theory that defines scientific concepts in terms of empirical operations.   PHIL

1927   German physicist Werner Heisenberg states the uncertainty principle or principle of indeterminism, which says that it is impossible to know both the position and momentum of a subatomic particle with complete precision. The principle deals a severe blow to mechanistic or deterministic conceptions of the universe. *See also* 1812, PHIL.   PHIL

1927   German philosopher Martin Heidegger publishes *Being and Time*, in which he examines "being in the world" (*Da Sein*) in terms of people's consciousness of being. His explorations of such themes as care, mood, inauthenticity, and death will influence existentialism. In later works, such as *An Introduction to Metaphysics* (1953), Heidegger will elaborate on such ideas as the dehumanization of modern life. He will also be associated with Nazism (*see* 1933, POL).   PHIL

1927   American parapsychologist Joseph Banks Rhine begins researching extrasensory perception (ESP). He will also seek evidence of psychokinesis, clairvoyance, telepathy, and precognition.   PSYCH

1927   Canadian-born American evangelist Aimee Semple McPherson, known for her rousing Pentecostal prayer services, founds the International Church of Foursquare Gospel.   REL

1928   In *Anthropology and Modern Life*, American anthropologist Franz Boas criticizes long-standing theories of racial superiority.   ANTH

1928   American anthropologist Margaret Mead publishes *Coming of Age in Samoa*, a milestone study of cultural traditions related to becoming an adult in Polynesian society.   ANTH

1928   French poet André Breton writes *Surrealism and Painting*, a work that certifies him as the principal theorist of surrealism. He will publish two more surrealist manifestos in 1930 and 1934.   CRIT

Philosopher of the Third Reich

In 1927, German philosopher Martin Heidegger wrote what would become his most influential work, *Sein und Zeit* (*Being and Time*), in which he explored the nature of being in ways that would inform decades of existentialist thinkers. Over the next few years, he gained stature in his profession, being named in 1928 to the chair of the philosophy department at the University of Freiberg, and in 1933, appointed rector of Freiberg. In his inaugural speech as rector, "The Role of the University in the New Reich," he envisioned a glorious future for Germany, now that it was led by Adolf Hitler.

Heidegger had supported Hitler for years and belonged, albeit reluctantly, to the Nazi Party. In fact, he was named rector only after his Jewish predecessor had been forced to resign. Soon after Hitler took power, however, Heidegger renounced Nazi practices. Even before his death in 1976, he was championed for his relentless questioning of humanity's "sense of being." But he is also remembered for once proclaiming, "The Führer himself, and he alone, is the German reality, present and future, and its law."

1928   German writer Walter Benjamin publishes *The Origin of German Tragic Drama*. Later a member of the Frankfurt School (*see* 1923, PHIL), he will apply Marxist ideas to the analysis of literature, language, history, and culture. CRIT

1928–1943   American historians Arthur Schlesinger and Dixon R. Fox edit *A History of American Life*, the first major anthology of American social history. Schlesinger has published and will continue to publish a number of other influential books on American social and urban history, including *New Viewpoints in American History* (1922), *The Rise of the City, 1878–1898* (1933), and *The American Reformer* (1950).   HIST

1928   German philosopher Rudolf Carnap publishes *The Logical Structure of the World*, a major work of logical positivism.   PHIL

1928   German philosopher Hans Reichenbach publishes *The Philosophy of Space and Time*, in which he introduces the concept of coordinative definitions, or coordination of a theoretical concept in physics with an actual physical process. PHIL

1928   German mathematician Richard von Mises publishes *Probability, Statistics, and Truth*, in which he states the frequency theory of probability: the view that the probability of an event can be stated in terms of frequency of occurrence of events of that kind, in a hypothetical population of occurrences of the same situation.   PHIL

1928   Soviet leader Joseph Stalin enacts the program for economic growth known as the Five-Year Plan.   POL

1928   The Kellogg-Briand Pact, an international agreement banning war as an instrument of national policy, is signed by 15 nations. It is originated by U.S. secretary of state Frank Kellogg and French foreign minister Aristide Briand, in response to the destruction of World War I. The pact eventually will be signed by 62 nations.   POL

1928   Japanese holy man Taniguchi Masaharu founds Seicho no Ie (the House of Growth), which teaches that all religions are expressions of one God.   REL

1928–1929   Indian poet and philosopher Sir Muhammad Iqbal delivers the six lectures known as *The Reconstruction of Religious Thought in Islam*, in which he outlines his Islamic modernist views. In 1930, he will call for the creation of a separate Muslim state; his vision will later take form as Pakistan.   REL

1929   Russian filmmaker Sergey Eisenstein writes an essay describing his conception of montage as a conflict between one shot and its successor. This conflict produces the tense, violent rhythms that are Eisenstein's trademark and that express the Marxist director's dialectical principle. The essay will be published posthumously in the collection *Film Form* (1949).   CRIT

1929   On October 29, prices on the New York Stock Exchange drop sharply; at the end of the day, a record 16.4 million shares have traded, and the Dow Jones Industrial Average has lost 30.57 points. The stock market crash symbolizes, and some will say precipitates, the Great Depression (*see* 1930s, ECON). The causes of the rampant selling, which results in the disappearance of $30 billion from the economy, include the ease with which speculators were allowed to buy stocks on margin. To prevent future crashes from being so devastating, various economic controls will be put into place, the Securities and Exchange Commission will be established (1934), and legislation to protect investors will be passed as part of President Franklin D. Roosevelt's New Deal (*see* 1933–1941, POL).   ECON

1929   English historian Lewis Bernstein Namier publishes *Structure of Politics at the Accession of George III*, which helps create a Namier school of history—an approach involving the close analysis of political institutions and events in an effort to ascertain the motivations of a certain period's principal figures.   HIST

1929   American historian Ulrich Phillips publishes *Life and Labor in the Old South*, a cultural and social history which examines the 19th-century South from a Southern viewpoint. In 1918, he had published *American Negro Slavery*, a popular defense of slavery in which he claimed the institution had benefited blacks as well as whites.   HIST

1929–1936   Italian philosopher Giovanni Gentile edits and oversees publication of the 35-volume *Enciclopedia Italiana*, which presents a fascist view of the world. Gentile will become a leading intellectual apologist for Mussolini's regime.   HIST

1929   German philosopher Otto Neurath publishes the first manifesto of the Vienna Circle. *See also* 1924, PHIL.   PHIL

1929   Nikolay Ivanovich Bukharin loses power in the Communist Party of the Soviet Union for opposing the rapidity of Stalinist collectivization. A former editor of the newspaper *Pravda*, he will be executed for treason in 1938.   POL

1929–1935   Italian communist theorist Antonio Gramsci writes his *Prison Notebooks*, which will be published posthumously. Imprisoned in fascist Italy, he advocates a humanistic Marxism.   POL

1929   Soviet communist Leon Trotsky is exiled from the Soviet Union for his ideological conflicts with Soviet dictator Joseph Stalin. His beliefs, known as Trotskyism, center on the need to sustain a worldwide "permanent revolution." He will be assassinated in 1940, possibly under Stalin's orders.   POL

1929   In Germany, the Nazi secret police originates in Heinrich Himmler's SS, or *Schutzstaffel* (defense echelon), Nazi Party leader Adolf Hitler's bodyguard organization. The SS's intelligence arm, the SD, or *Sicherheitsdienst* (security service), will form in 1931. After Hitler takes power in 1933, the Gestapo, or secret state police, will be organized under Hermann Goering. In 1936 Himmler will take formal control of the Gestapo, thus merging all three secret police organizations into a terrorist juggernaut that will run the Nazi concentration camps throughout the Holocaust (*see* 1933–1945, REL). Although secret police forces have always existed, reaching back in their modern incarnation to Ivan the Terrible's *oprichniki* in 16th-century Russia, secret police will be an inescapable characteristic of 20th-century totalitarian regimes, most notoriously in Germany and in the Soviet Union (*see* 1936, POL).   POL

1929   American humorist James Thurber and essayist Elwyn Brooks White satirize modern sexual psychology in *Is Sex Necessary?*   PSYCH

1929   The Lateran Treaty between the Holy See and Italy is signed. It resolves the Roman Question (*see* 1870, REL) by creating the sovereign state of Vatican City and making Roman Catholicism Italy's state religion in return for papal recognition of Italy.   REL

1929   American linguist Edward Sapir and his pupil Benjamin Lee Whorf advance the Sapir-Whorf linguistic relativity thesis, which holds that social perceptions are determined by the descriptive tools available in a given language.   SOC

1929   American sociologists Robert and Helen Lynd publish *Middletown*, a detailed study of an Indiana town. The authors use the community as an ideal research setting—a relatively self-contained unit with a well-developed social structure. SOC

1929   German sociologist Karl Mannheim publishes *Ideology and Utopia*, detailing his work on the sociology of knowledge. Mannheim studies the social context and determinants of knowledge, and how perceived truth may vary with one's location in the social structure.   SOC

1929   In her book *A Room of One's Own*, English novelist Virginia Woolf asserts that to express oneself artistically, one must have "money and a room of one's own." Her statement refers to women's need to gain not only economic independence but also an artistic identity separate from the pervasive male-dominated aesthetic.   SOC

1930s   Keynesian economic theory, which advocates government intervention to boost a recessionary economy, introduces the concept of econometrics, a technique combining theory with statistical and mathematical analysis in an attempt to improve the accuracy of economic forecasts. *See also* 1936, ECON.   ECON

1930s   The Great Depression in the United States has been caused by, among many other factors, domestic production's having outpaced domestic consumption, the contraction of the foreign market for U.S. goods due to Europe's postwar impoverishment, and easy credit policies that engendered excessive stock market speculation (*see* 1929, ECON). Unlike other cyclical economic recessions, the Great Depression is characterized by severe and prolonged economic and social dislocation. In the United States, a third of the labor force will find itself unemployed in 1932–1933, at the nadir of the depression. In Europe, the crisis will contribute to the rise of fascism, especially in Germany, whose economy has been devastated by World War I and by postwar reparations. The New Deal policies (*see* 1933–1941, POL) of President Franklin D. Roosevelt provide some relief in the United States, whose economy will not fully recover until it is bolstered by the defense spending for the Allied effort during World War II (*see* 1939–1945, POL).   ECON

1930s   In their university positions, American educational reformers Robert Maynard Hutchins and Alexander Meiklejohn blend the new humanist devotion to classical texts and pursuit of metaphysical truths (*see* 1908, CRIT) with the pragmatic cultivation of critical intelligence. Hutchins will be president of the University of Chicago from 1929 to 1945; Meiklejohn will hold positions at Amherst and the University of Wisconsin.   EDUC

1930s   The term *totalitarianism* is used to describe the political philosophy of such modern nations as fascist Italy, Nazi Germany, and the Communist Soviet Union. A totalitarian government is an authoritarian one that attempts to control all aspects of its people's lives—political, economic, cultural, intellectual—and repressively discourages dissent.   POL

1930s   Australian-American psychologist George Elton Mayo performs the Hawthorne experiments in industrial psychology. These studies show that work is a group activity and that a sense of belonging contributes to worker morale. Later research in social organization will rely on Mayo's findings.   PSYCH

1930s   In Jamaica, the religious and political movement called Rastafarianism originates. Taking its name from Ethiopian emperor Haile Selassie, once known as Ras (Prince) Tafari, the movement emphasizes the wickedness of Western civilization and the inevitable return of Africans to Africa.   REL

1930s   Martinican poet Aimé Césaire coins the term "Négritude," or "blackness," for the unique experience of black Africans and their descendants. Césaire and his theory of Négritude will influence African liberation movements.   SOC

1930   In accepting the Nobel Prize for literature, American novelist Sinclair Lewis delivers the speech "The American Fear of Literature," in which he criticizes conservative antagonism toward contemporary writing.   CRIT

1930   German Nazi spokesman on art and culture Alfred Rosenberg publishes *The Myth of the Twentieth Century*, claiming that all modern art is the product of a communist-Jewish conspiracy that undermines the Aryan race. Modern art will therefore be deemed *entartete* or degenerate.   CRIT

1930   English poet and critic Sir William Empson publishes *Seven Types of Ambiguity*. With Ivor Armstrong Richards, Frank Raymond Leavis, and others, he is one of the Cambridge critics, who emphasize close scrutiny of texts. Their work is related to new criticism (*see* 1941, CRIT). Other works by Empson will include *Some Versions of Pastoral* (1935) and *Milton's God* (1961).   CRIT

1930–1932   German-born American scholar Edith Hamilton becomes known as a popularizer of the ancient world with the publication of *The Greek Way* (1930) and *The Roman Way* (1932).   HIST

1930   French philosopher Jean Nicod publishes *Foundations of Geometry and Induction*, in which he proposes what will become known as Nicod's criterion, which regards the circumstances under which pieces of evidence can authentically confirm a general hypothesis.   PHIL

1930   Spanish philosopher José Ortega y Gasset, a dedicated republican, publishes *The Revolt of the Masses*.   POL

1930   American political scientist Harold Lasswell publishes *Psychopathology and Politics*, which draws connections between psychology and politics. Lasswell and Charles E. Merriam (*see* 1925, POL) are leaders of the Chicago School of political science, which stresses psychological factors and statistical analysis. It will influence the development of behavioralism in the late 1940s (*see* c. 1945, POL).   POL

1930   Austrian psychoanalyst Sigmund Freud publishes *Civilization and Its Discontents*. His *Moses and Monotheism* will appear in 1939. In these works, Freud applies the psychoanalytic concepts he developed to the study of history.   PSYCH

1930   At Nag Hammadi, Egypt, Manichean papyri are discovered; finds of Coptic Gnostic papyri will follow c. 1945. The discoveries yield new knowledge about early Christian heresies; among those who will study the Coptic Gnostic papyri is American scholar Elaine Pagels, who will discuss her analysis in *The Gnostic Gospels* (1979).   REL

1931   American writer and critic Edmund Wilson publishes the collection of literary essays *Axel's Castle*. Its subjects include Irish writers James Joyce and William Butler Yeats and American writer Gertrude Stein. Other works by Wilson will include *The American Earthquake* (1958), a social history of the Great

Depression, and *Patriotic Gore* (1962), a survey of American literature of the
Civil War.   CRIT

1931   American critic Kenneth Burke publishes his first book of criticism, *Counter-
        Statement* (1931). In this and other works, including *The Philosophy of Literary
        Form* (1941) and *Language as Symbolic Action* (1966), he develops an approach
        to literature that emphasizes rhetorical effect and language as symbol.   CRIT

1931   Norwegian economist Ragnar Frisch founds the Econometric Society. Econometrics,
        the mathematical analysis and statistical testing of economic theory, will become
        important this decade in the emerging field of macroeconomics.   ECON

1931   American historian and journalist Frederick Lewis Allen publishes the informal
        chronicle of the 1920s *Only Yesterday*. It will be followed by a book on the Great
        Depression, *Since Yesterday*, in 1940.   HIST

c. 1931 Japanese moral philosopher and playwright Watsuji Tetsuro publishes *Ethics as
        Anthropology*, which draws on Buddhism and Confucianism to emphasize com-
        munal ethics.   PHIL

1931   Austrian mathematician Kurt Gödel publishes what will become known as
        Gödel's theorems, which state that in any system based on any set of axioms
        there will always be statements that are true but not provable, and statements
        that cannot be proven or disproven; and that no such system can prove its own
        consistency.   PHIL

1931   German philosopher Edmund Husserl publishes *Cartesian Meditations*.   PHIL

1931   On September 8 American journalist Walter Lippmann begins writing "Today and
        Tomorrow," a political column in the New York *Herald Tribune*. The column will
        win two Pulitzer Prizes (1958 and 1962) and establish Lippmann as the most influ-
        ential political commentator of his time.   POL

1931   English economic historian Richard Henry Tawney publishes his influential
        book, *Equality*, in which he argues against any justification for political or social
        inequality.   POL

1932–1938   Hungarian-born English art historian Frederick Antal writes *Florentine
            Painting and Its Social Background*, in which he rejects the purely formal analy-
            sis of style currently popular in the study of art. He stresses the need to study
            the economic, social, and political conditions of any period in order to
            understand an artist's motives.   CRIT

1932   German painter Hans Hofmann writes "On the Aims of Art," an essay that
               will anticipate Clement Greenberg's writings by stressing the medium, the
               picture plane, and the unity of a piece of art.   CRIT

1932   Mexican painter Diego Rivera writes the essay "The Revolutionary Spirit in
               Modern Art," in which he positions Mexico's mural art program as a counter
               to the tradition of easel art.   CRIT

1932–1953   English critic Frank Raymond Leavis edits the literary review *Scrutiny*, a major
               vehicle for the ideas of Leavis and his fellow Cambridge Critics. Leavis's works
               from this period include *New Bearings in English Poetry* (1932), which helps to
               place the poetry of Gerard Manley Hopkins, T. S. Eliot, and Ezra Pound in high
               esteem.   CRIT

1932   English critic Ivor Armstrong Richards considers the nature of imagination in
               Mencius on the Mind. Later works will include *Coleridge on Imagination* (1934)
               and *Interpretation in Teaching* (1938).   CRIT

1932   American historian Charles Beard writes *A Charter for the Social Sciences in the
               Schools*, which will bring change to the way history is taught in U.S. schools. EDUC

1932   German psychiatrist and philosopher Karl Jaspers publishes the three-volume
               Philosophie.   PHIL

1932   French philosopher Jacques Maritain publishes *The Degrees of Knowledge*. In
               this and other works, such as *True Humanism* (1936), Maritain seeks to revive
               Aristotelian and Thomistic realism.   PHIL

1932   German philosopher Otto Neurath publishes "Protokollsätze," one of several
               papers advocating a physicalist and holistic theory of knowledge.   PHIL

1932   Austrian psychoanalyst Melanie Klein publishes *The Psychoanalysis of Children*.
               A pioneer in the field, she shows how anxieties affect a child's developing psy-
               che and may lead to emotional disturbances. She develops play therapy, in
               which children show and release anxieties through playing with toys.   PSYCH

1932   American child psychologist Beth Wellman is the first to show that children's
               intelligence can diminish in deprived environments and increase in enriched
               environments.   PSYCH

1932   Indian poet and philosopher Sir Muhammad Iqbal publishes *Jāvīd-nāmeh*, or
               The Song of Eternity, a Persian, Muslim version of Italian poet Dante's *Divine
               Comedy* (see 1307–1321, PHIL).   REL

1932   American theologian Reinhold Niebuhr attacks the limits of secular progres-
                sivism in *Moral Man and Immoral Society*.   SOC

1933   American-born English poet and critic T. S. Eliot publishes *The Use of Poetry and
                the Use of Criticism*. He will also write social criticism in such works as *After
                Strange Gods* (1934) and *The Idea of a Christian Society* (1939).   CRIT

1933   English poet and critic Herbert Read helps organize the Unit 1 exhibition of
                contemporary British art and publishes *Art Now*, an argument for anarchism
                and the need for art in education.   CRIT

1933   German psychologist and film aesthetician Rudolf Arnheim publishes *Film*, a
                work that presents antirealist concerns by defining film's opportunity to orig-
                inate, interpret, and mold. It will be revised with four other essays and pub-
                lished as *Film as Art* in 1957.   CRIT

1933   English economist Joan Violet Robinson publishes *The Economics of Imperfect
                Competition*. She will be known as a critic of economic injustice against devel-
                oping nations.   ECON

1933   English philosopher and historian Robin Collingwood publishes *Essay on
                Philosophical Method*. His *The Idea of History* will appear in 1946. He views phi-
                losophy as inevitably historical in nature, as always reflecting the assumptions
                of the age in which it is developed, and he sees the study of history as involv-
                ing the reconstruction of past ways of thinking.   HIST

1933   Spanish leader José Antonio Primo de Rivera founds the fascist Spanish polit-
                ical party known as the Falange. From 1937 it will be dominated by Spanish
                leader Francisco Franco and will merge with his Carlist militia to become the
                national party of Spain. In the Spanish Civil War, its militia will run with the
                Insurgents.   POL

1933–1941   U.S. president Franklin D. Roosevelt enacts the New Deal, his far-reaching
                reform program meant to aid the country during the Great Depression (*see*
                1930s, ECON). Among the programs initiated in the first hundred days of his
                administration alone are the Emergency Banking Relief Act, the Securities Act,
                the Federal Deposit Insurance Corporation (FDIC), and the creation of the
                Civilian Conservation Corps (CCC), Tennessee Valley Authority (TVA), and
                the Public Works Administration. Later reforms include the Social Security Act,
                the Investment Company Act, and the creation of the Federal Housing
                Authority (FHA) and the Works Progress Administration (WPA; renamed the
                Work Projects Administration in 1939).   POL

1933–1945   Through her humanitarian sensibilities and works throughout her husband
                Franklin D. Roosevelt's 12 years as U.S. president, Eleanor Roosevelt extends

the possibilities for the role of first lady. In 1933 she holds the first press conference ever called by a first lady. In 1935 she will begin writing a syndicated
newspaper column called "My Day," and from 1941 to 1942 she will serve as
assistant director of the Office of Civilian Defense. She will travel and lecture
widely to further causes related to civil rights and social welfare.   POL

1933   German philosopher Martin Heidegger delivers the speech "The Role of the
            University in the New Reich," in which he expresses support for the Nazi party in
            terms of his philosophy of "powers of Being."   POL

1933–1945   The systematic persecution and mass murder of European Jews known as the
            Holocaust takes place. The culmination of centuries of anti-Semitism, it origi-
            nates in Germany under Nazi leader Adolf Hitler, who assumes power in 1933.
            Its methods include legal disenfranchisement, ghettoization, and ultimately,
            extermination in concentration camps—a program called by Hitler "the final
            solution to the Jewish question." By the end of World War II, some six million
            Jews and five million others will have perished in the Holocaust, which will
            lead theologians, philosophers, legislators, and artists, among others, to recon-
            sider the nature of organized evil.   REL

1933   German Jewish leaders Leo Baeck and Otto Hirsch found the National Agency
            of Jews in Germany to help protect Jews and aid their emigration in the face
            of growing Nazi attacks. Both men will eventually be sent to concentration
            camps; Hirsch will die in one, but Baeck will survive. Considered the spiritual
            leader of German Jews during the Holocaust, Baeck will later write such works
            as This People Israel: The Meaning of Jewish Existence (1955).   REL

1933   German theologian Paul Tillich is dismissed from his teaching position for his
            criticism of the Nazi government. He immigrates to the United States.   REL

1933   In New York, American journalist and reformer Dorothy Day and French
            philosopher Peter Maurin found the Catholic Worker, an anarchist, pacifist
            movement built on Catholic social teaching and dedicated to performing
            works of mercy. The movement's ideas are put forth in the newspaper the
            Catholic Worker, also founded this year.   REL

1933   American political scientist Paul Lazarsfeld and colleagues Marie Jahoda and
            Hans Zeisel publish Marienthal, a study of the effects of unemployment in an
            Austrian town. The study features ingenious ways of measuring discontent
            among the unemployed.   SOC

1934   American anthropologist Ruth Benedict publishes Patterns of Culture, an
            account of her research among the Zuni and Hopi, two Native American peo-
            ples. The book will help develop the field of cultural psychology.   ANTH

1934   American critic Malcolm Cowley publishes *Exile's Return,* a memoir of the American writers of the "lost generation" (*see* 1920s, CRIT) who departed for Europe in the years after World War I, including Ernest Hemingway, F. Scott Fitzgerald, John Dos Passos, Gertrude Stein, and Hart Crane.   CRIT

1934   French art historian Henri-Joseph Focillon publishes *The Life of Forms in Art,* in which he generalizes about recurrent features in art history. He discusses three phases of styles: the experimental, the classical, and the baroque.   CRIT

1934   German writer Walter Benjamin writes his influential essay "The Author as Producer," which demonstrates his concern for the material basis of art. He will write "The Work of Art in the Age of Mechanical Reproduction" in 1936. His writings will best be exemplified in the translated selections published as *Illuminations* in 1968 and *One-Way Street* in 1979.   CRIT

1934   American philosopher and educator John Dewey publishes *Art as Experience.*   CRIT

1934   American editor and historian Douglas Southall Freeman publishes *R. E. Lee,* a biography of the Confederate military leader. He will later publish *George Washington* (1948–1954). Both books will win Pulitzer prizes, and both will be seen as exemplary biographies of American leaders.   HIST

1934–1954   English historian Arnold Toynbee publishes his ten-volume *History of the World,* a sweeping study of the world's great civilizations.   HIST

1934   German philosopher Rudolf Carnap publishes *The Logical Syntax of Language,* in which he analyzes the structure of mathematical and scientific language.   LING

1934   English linguist Charles Kay Ogden and critic Ivor Armstrong Richards publish *The System of Basic English,* in which they promulgate Ogden's simplified version of English, which is intended for use as an international language.   LING

1934   French philosopher Gaston Bachelard publishes *Le Nouvel esprit scientifique,* in which he considers the nature of scientific thought as a dynamic, changing field.   PHIL

1934–1943   American psychiatrist Harry Stack Sullivan develops his theory of interpersonal relations, arguing that personality development and adjustment are affected by interaction with other people, such as family and friends, and not just by biological and sexual factors.   PSYCH

1934   Japanese holy man Nakano Yonosuke breaks away from the Shinto sect of Omoto to found the Ananaikyo religion.   REL

1934   Swiss theologian Emil Brunner publishes *The Mediator*. This and other works, such as *Divine Imperative* (1937), will influence such thinkers as American theologian Reinhold Niebuhr.
REL

1934   Lithuanian-born American rabbi Mordecai Kaplan publishes *Judaism as a Civilization*. Kaplan is the founder of Reconstructionist Judaism, a movement linked to Conservative Judaism that accepts all forms of Jewish practice, regarding Judaism in cultural rather than theological terms.
REL

1934   *Mind, Self, and Society*, a compilation of lecture notes by students of American philosopher George Herbert Mead, is issued in his memory. The volume details Mead's views on how the self is formed, and was influenced both by behaviorism and pragmatism. A member of the faculty of the University of Chicago, he was in close contact with that school's sociologists, and is considered a founder of symbolic interactionism.
SOC

1935   American anthropologist Margaret Mead publishes *Sex and Temperament in Three Primitive Societies*, a study of gender-based social expectations in three cultures.
ANTH

c. 1935   Czech writer Jan Mukarovsky publishes *Aesthetic Function*, which argues for the importance of aesthetic value in art.
CRIT

1935   American critic Ronald S. Crane of the University of Chicago publishes "History versus Criticism in the Study of Literature." The essay upholds criticism rather than history as the principal component of literary studies. Together with the work of University of Chicago philosopher Richard McKeon, Crane's ideas give birth to the Chicago critics, a school that emphasizes critical pluralism and an expanded interpretation of Greek philosopher Aristotle's *Poetics*.
CRIT

1935   American critic Richard P. Blackmur, an influential theorist of new criticism (*see* 1941, CRIT), publishes *The Double Agent*, in which he argues that the meaning of poetry consists of both form and content. Blackmur's other works will include *Language as Gesture* (1952) and *New Criticism in the United States* (1959).   CRIT

1935–1942   American critic Cleanth Brooks and American writer Robert Penn Warren coedit the *Southern Review*, a distinguished "little magazine" of essays, fiction, and poetry. Its critical essays are representative of new criticism (*see* 1941, CRIT), a movement in which the two editors are leading participants. During this period, Brooks and Warren also collaborate in writing *Understanding Poetry* (1938) and *Understanding Fiction* (1943).
CRIT

1935   British officer Thomas Edward Lawrence, known as Lawrence of Arabia, combines philosophy and military history in *The Seven Pillars of Wisdom*, an

account of his role in the Arab revolt against the Ottoman empire. This
book had been privately printed in 1926.   HIST

1935   Austrian philosopher Karl Popper publishes *The Logic of Scientific Discovery*. He
develops a theory of scientific knowledge, arguing that the scientific method is
hypothetico-deductive, not inductive-deductive, and that validity is established by the falsifiability of claims ("falsificationism").   PHIL

1935   In Akron, Ohio, stockbroker Bill W. and surgeon Bob S. found Alcoholics
Anonymous (AA), the first self-help fellowship. AA will inspire numerous
other programs based on mutual support and recovery from addiction.   PSYCH

1935   American psychologists Henry A. Murray and Conway Lloyd introduce the
Thematic Apperception Test to study personality. The test consists of 30 pic-
tures, plus one blank, to which patients assign stories.   PSYCH

1935   The Omoto group of religions is suppressed by the Japanese government.   REL

1935   American pollster George Gallup founds the American Institute of Public
Opinion at Princeton, New Jersey. Gallup's correct prediction of the outcome
of the 1936 presidential election will confirm the validity of sampling as a
method of determining public opinion. Scientific polling will become an
important instrument of social science and political and market research. SOC

1936   English critic Lord Raglan publishes *The Hero*, an influential study of the hero
figure in literature and legend.   CRIT

1936   American art historian and writer Alfred H. Barr Jr., who, as the first director
of the Museum of Modern Art, mounts the landmark exhibition called *Cubism
and Abstract Art* and publishes the influential book of the same name to
accompany the exhibition. He believes abstract and near-abstract avant-garde
art express a unique freedom that is suppressed in Stalinist Russia and Nazi
Germany.   CRIT

1936   Lithuanian-born American art historian Meyer Schapiro presents the paper
"The Social Bases of Art," in which he applies the resources of Marxist theory to
the problems of analysis of modern art.   CRIT

1936   German-born English art historian Nikolaus Pevsner traces the evolution of
20th-century functional architecture in *Pioneers of Modern Design*, a work based
on a lecture course held at Göttingen University.   CRIT

1936   American writer Van Wyck Brooks publishes *Flowering of New England*, a major
history of American literature that will win the Pulitzer Prize.   CRIT

1936   English economist John Maynard Keynes publishes *The General Theory of Employment, Interest, and Money,* in which he advocates government intervention in the market and deficit spending as remedies for recession. Keynes is a principal architect of modern macroeconomic theory.   **ECON**

1936   American editor Henry Luce founds *Life* magazine, taking advantage of the growing art of photojournalism, which develops in response to the refinement of the handheld camera. According to Luce, *Life* means to "present the moment, as it is experienced." The weekly will be in print until 1972, and will later resume as a monthly.   **JOURN**

1936   English philosopher Alfred Jules Ayer publishes *Language, Truth, and Logic,* which brings greater notice in the English-speaking world to logical positivism. He will later publish *The Problem of Knowledge* (1956).   **PHIL**

1936   American philosopher Arthur Oncken Lovejoy publishes *The Great Chain of Being,* an examination of the Neoplatonic and medieval idea that there is a hierarchy of actual things from lowest to highest, including animals, humans, and angels.   **PHIL**

1936   American political scientist Harold Lasswell, one of the first political scientists to apply psychoanalytical research methods to the empirical study of politics, publishes *Politics: Who Gets What, When, How.*   **POL**

1936–1939   The Spanish Civil War is fought, pitting the forces of conservative nationalists against the moderate and liberal republicans of the country. The bitter struggle will result in worldwide involvement, with fascist Italy and Nazi Germany aiding the nationalists and helping to effect the Spanish government takeover by General Francisco Franco. Communists, socialists, and radicals, among others from the United States and Europe, support the failed Loyalist cause.   **POL**

1936   The Soviet secret police inaugurates the phase of the Stalinist purges of the Communist Party known as the Yezhovshchina (1936–1938), for Nikolai Yezhov, the head of the NKVD, or People's Commissariat for Internal Affairs, as the secret police is known from 1934 to 1943. The Soviet secret police originated in the Cheka in 1917; the organization will go through several incarnations before becoming known as the KGB, or Committee of State Security, in 1953. *See also* 1929, POL.   **POL**

1936   Austrian psychoanalyst Anna Freud, daughter of Sigmund Freud, introduces the theory of ego-defense mechanisms. Well known for her psychoanalysis of children, she will found the Hampstead Child-Therapy Clinic in London in 1947.   **PSYCH**

1936	American lecturer and writer Dale Carnegie publishes *How to Win Friends and Influence People*, a highly popular self-help book on building confidence. PSYCH
1936–1962	Swiss theologian Karl Barth publishes his four-volume *Church Dogmatics*, a systematic exposition of his dialectical theology, which focuses on close attention to the word of God and the revelation of God in Christ. REL
1936	American anthropologist Ralph Linton publishes *The Study of Man*, the work credited with introducing the concept of "role" to social science. SOC
1937	Yale University begins compiling its Human Relations Area Files (HRAF), a collection of ethnographic data for statistical comparison of cultures. ANTH
1937	English anthropologist Edward Evans-Pritchard publishes *Witchcraft, Oracles, and Magic Among the Azande*, which offers an original perspective on the role of magical belief in sustaining social order. ANTH
1937	American critic Sterling Brown publishes *The Negro in American Fiction*. CRIT
1937	American novelist Richard Wright publishes "Blueprint for Negro Writing," in which he tries to define the relation of African-American writers to their community. CRIT
1937	The *Partisan Review*, founded three years earlier as a Communist Party journal, is revived as an independent left-wing review. Its highly influential critics and avant-garde writers, known as the New York intellectuals, will include cofounder and editor Philip Rahv, Dwight Macdonald, Mary McCarthy, Alfred Kazin, Delmore Schwartz, John Ashbery, Lionel and Diana Trilling, Saul Bellow, Irving Howe, Leslie Fiedler, and Hannah Arendt. CRIT
1937	Nigerian journalist and activist Nnamdi Azikiwe founds a chain of nationalist newspapers, including the *West African Pilot*. In 1963, he will become the first president of the republic of Nigeria. JOURN
1937	French philosopher Gaston Bachelard publishes *The Psychoanalysis of Fire*. PHIL
1937	Italian mathematician and philosopher Bruno de Finetti publishes *Foresight: Its Logical Laws, Its Subjective Sources*. De Finetti argues that probability does not exist. PHIL
1937	Swedish political scientist Herbert Tingsten publishes *Political Behavior: Studies in Election Statistics*, a work that anticipates one of the main fields of study in political science in the 1950s. POL

1937–1939   British prime minister Neville Chamberlain practices his appeasement policy toward Germany, offering territorial concessions in the hope of avoiding war. The policy's catastrophic failure will serve as an object lesson for future politicians and diplomats.   POL

1937   German-born American psychoanalyst Karen Horney publishes *The Neurotic Personality of Our Time*, in which she discusses social factors in child development related to the occurrence of basic anxiety. She also outlines the cultural and environmental bases of neurosis. Her challenge to strict Freudianism becomes central to the development of a psychology of women.   PSYCH

1937   American psychologist Gordon Willard Allport publishes *Personality: A Psychological Interpretation*.   PSYCH

1937   American sociologist Talcott Parsons publishes *The Structure of Social Action*, in which he brings together American and European sociological schools. Parsons will become known for his structural-functional theory, a grand theory of nearly all aspects of society.   SOC

1937–1941   Russian-born American sociologist Pitirim Sorokin publishes his massive *Social and Cultural Dynamics*, which theorizes on the social process and typology of cultures. The book describes how civilizations shift between "sensate" and "ideational" forms of culture.   SOC

1937   American sociologist Willard Waller publishes *The Rating and Dating Complex*, a paper that details the ways in which men and women seek to elevate self-esteem through their dating partners.   SOC

1938   American philosopher and educator John Dewey publishes *Logic: The Theory of Inquiry*. Dewey's philosophy, known as instrumentalism, is related to pragmatism; it argues that truth is an instrument used to solve problems and that it is subject to change.   PHIL

1938   The U.S. Congress passes the Wages and Hours Act (also known as the Fair Labor Standards Act). It sets minimum-wage and work-week standards at 25 cents per hour and a 44-hour week. Overtime rates and child labor age limits are also set.   POL

1938   American behaviorist psychologist B. F. Skinner publishes the results of his experiments with the Skinner box, a piece of laboratory equipment used for systematic experiments in operant conditioning on rats and pigeons.   PSYCH

1938   American evangelist Frank Nathan Daniel Buchman, formerly the leader of an evangelical movement known as Buchmanism or the Oxford Group, founds the Moral Re-Armament (MRA) movement.   REL

1938	Japanese religious leaders Niwano Nikkyo and Naganuma Myoko found the Nichiren Buddhist movement Risshokoseikai. REL

| 1938 | American sociologist Robert K. Merton publishes "Social Structure and Anomie," a paper that attempts to explain deviant behavior through the relationship between widely held social goals and varying access to the proper means to achieve them. The article replies to theorists who contend that deviance is a congenital trait. SOC |

| 1939 | German-born American art historian Erwin Panofsky publishes his famous *Studies in Iconology* where he draws the distinction between the study of art's conventional subject matter and the study of its intrinsic meanings. *Meaning in the Visual Arts*, a collection of his essays, will be published in 1955. *Gothic Architecture and Scholasticism* will be published in 1951. CRIT |

| 1939 | American art critic Clement Greenberg publishes the essay "Avant-Garde and Kitsch," finding that the avant-garde ultimately functions to keep culture alive in the face of capitalism. CRIT |

| 1939 | English critic and writer Cyril Connolly founds the literary magazine *Horizon*, which he edits until 1950. His critical works will include *The Condemned Playground* (1945). CRIT |

| 1939–1953 | American scholar Perry Miller publishes the two-volume analysis of Puritan thought and influence, *The New England Mind*. CRIT |

| 1939 | Sir John Richard Hicks publishes *Value and Capital: An Inquiry into Some Fundamental Principles of Economic Theory.* ECON |

| 1939–1945 | World War II occurs, as the Allies (including England, France, the Soviet Union, and, from 1941, the United States) struggle against the aggression of the Axis powers (Germany, Italy, and Japan). Among the many factors driving the war are the fascist ideologies of the Axis nations, which found fertile ground in the economic distress that followed World War I and deepened during the Great Depression (*see* 1930s, ECON). German Nazi leader Adolf Hitler's attempt to eradicate European Jews (*see* 1933–1945, REL) is a product of one of those ideologies. The war ends in 1945, after the United States drops atomic bombs on the Japanese cities of Hiroshima and Nagasaki. By war's end, combat, purges, concentration camps, and famine have taken tens of millions of lives. The United States will soon become the free world's dominant power, England and France will become lesser powers, Germany will be divided into two countries, and the Soviet Union will become the other leading nuclear power and the chief rival of the United States; the seeds of the Cold War (*see* 1948, POL) are sown. POL |

1939   American psychologist David Wechsler introduces the Wechsler-Bellevue Adult
            Intelligence Scale, one of several intelligence assessments that bear his name.
            He will be the first to combine verbal and nonverbal tests into a composite
            scale and to introduce the idea of nonintellective factors of intelligence. PSYCH

1939   Pope Pius XII succeeds Pius XI upon the latter's death; his tenure will last until
            1958. During World War II, he maintains formal relations with all the bel-
            ligerents. He will later be criticized for not objecting forcefully to the Nazi per-
            secution of Jews and for not working harder to protect Jews in Italy. *See also*
            1950, REL.   REL

1939   Anglican theologian D. R. Davies publishes *On to Orthodoxy*, an example of the
            kind of biblical theology that will be popular in England into the 1950s.   REL

1939   In the United States, the Methodist Church is formed from the union of the
            Methodist Episcopal Church; the Methodist Episcopal Church, South; and the
            Methodist Protestant Church. The new church will later unite with the
            Evangelical United Brethren Church to form the United Methodist Church
            (1968).   REL

1939   American sociologist Edwin Sutherland publishes *Principles of Criminology*,
            celebrated for its theory of differential association. The theory accounts for
            deviant behavior by identifying patterns of association and acquaintance
            that might encourage deviant conduct.   SOC

1939   American sociologists Fritz Roethlisberger and William J. Dickson publish
            Management and the Worker, a study of the relationship between changes in
            various working conditions and output at a Western Electric plant. The authors
            discovered that even when working conditions were experimentally worsened,
            output improved, due to the solidarity brought about by the fact of being
            studied.   SOC

1940s   French scholars Leo Spitzer, Jules Marouzeau, and Marcel Cressot write on styl-
            istics, building on the earlier work of Charles Bally (*see* 1905, LING).   CRIT

1940s   Psychologists at the University of Minnesota develop the Minnesota
            Multiphasic Personality Inventory (MMPI), which is able to measure more
            than one personality dimension at a time and will become widely used. PSYCH

1940   English anthropologist Edward Evans-Pritchard publishes *The Nuer*, the first
            work in the important trilogy that also includes *Kinship and Marriage Among
            the Nuer* (1951) and *Nuer Religion* (1956).   ANTH

| 1940 | American critic Harold Rosenberg publishes the essay "The Fall of Paris," anticipating the establishment of New York as the new center of Modernist culture in the 1940s. CRIT |

1940 American critic Harold Rosenberg publishes the essay "The Fall of Paris," anticipating the establishment of New York as the new center of Modernist culture in the 1940s. CRIT

1940 American art critic Clement Greenberg publishes the essay "Towards a Newer Laocoön," hoping to establish the quality of abstract art and to justify abstraction as the fulfillment of an inevitable historical tendency. CRIT

1940–1960 The Geneva school of literary criticism flourishes. Its adherents include Georges Poulet, Marcel Raymond, Albert Béguin, Jean Starobinski, Jean-Pierre Richard, and Jean Rousset. With roots in phenomenology and hermeneutics, the school emphasizes close attention to the themes and imagery of a text in an attempt to understand the particular consciousness or subjectivity behind it. CRIT

1940 English philosopher and historian Robin Collingwood publishes *Essay on Metaphysics*; his other works include *The Principles of Art* (1937) and *The Idea of History* (1946). His work stresses the historical basis for philosophical ideas, and discusses the process of interpreting history. PHIL

1940 English mathematician and philosopher Bertrand Russell publishes *An Inquiry into Meaning and Truth*. PHIL

1941 Russian linguist Roman Jakobson, known for his work in the Russian formalist movement (*see* 1916–1922, CRIT), flees Czechoslovakia and comes to the United States to teach. There his ideas will influence such scholars as structuralist anthropologist Claude Lévi-Strauss. CRIT

1941 American scholar Francis Otto Matthiessen publishes *American Renaissance: Art and Expression in the Age of Emerson and Whitman*. CRIT

1941 English critic George Thomson combines Marxist and ritualist approaches in describing the development of culture in *Aeschylus and Athens*. CRIT

1941 Swiss art historian Sigfried Giedion publishes *Space, Time and Architecture*, a work that places modern architecture both in an historical perspective and in the context of cultural and technological change. He will also publish *Mechanization Takes Command* (1948) and *The Eternal Present: The Beginnings of Art* (1962). CRIT

1941 American poet and critic John Crowe Ransom publishes *The New Criticism*, which gives a name to the movement in literary scholarship that focuses on close reading of texts as harmonious, autonomous wholes without regard to authorial intention or historical context. Prominent members of the school include Ransom, Kenneth Burke, Yvor Winters, Richard P. Blackmur, and

Cleanth Brooks. Enormously influential, new critical methods will long remain accepted practice in the teaching of literature. *See also* 1925, CRIT. CRIT

1941   Italian philospher and historian Benedetto Croce's *History as the Story of Liberty* appears in an English translation. The strong opposition to totalitarianism that Croce expresses in the book leads to his severe censure in Fascist Italy, but, after Mussolini's fall, he will play a leading role in resurrecting Italian liberalism. HIST

1941   In a speech delivered on January 6 to the U.S. Congress, in which he proposes lend-lease legislation, President Franklin D. Roosevelt introduces the Four Freedoms, which he believes should be open to all people: freedom of speech, freedom of worship, freedom from want, and freedom from fear. The ideas become policy objectives, and two of them—freedom from want and from fear—are integrated into the Atlantic Charter, a joint British-American statement of peace aims declared on August 14. The idea of the Four Freedoms also gains popularity in the United States. Thanks to a poster series executed by American illustrator Norman Rockwell, the term becomes common coin during World War II, which the United States enters after the Japanese bomb Pearl Harbor, Hawaii, on December 7. POL

1941   German-born American political philosopher Herbert Marcuse, a member of the Frankfurt School (*see* 1923, POL) of critical Marxism, publishes his first English work, *Reason and Revolution*, an introduction to the works of German philosophers Georg Wilhelm Friedrich Hegel and Karl Marx. POL

1941   German-born American psychoanalyst Erich Fromm publishes *Escape from Freedom*. Fromm's works emphasize social influences, particularly alienation, on individual personalities. PSYCH

1942   American philosopher Susanne Langer publishes *Philosophy in a New Key*, which calls for an exact symbolism of art equal to the symbolism of language and science. Her *Feeling and Form*, which will include the essay "The Symbol of Feeling," will be published in 1953. CRIT

1942   Austrian-born American economist Joseph Alois Schumpeter publishes *Capitalism, Socialism, and Democracy*. He argues that entrepreneurship is the key to fostering business growth. ECON

1942   American historian Thomas C. Cochran and William Miller publish *The Age of Enterprise: A Social History of Industrial America*, a pioneering business history which considers the social and political implications of business's rise. Joseph Dorfman's *The Economic Mind in American Civilization* (1946–1949) will consider the impact various economic concepts and developments have had on the country. HIST

1942   Algerian-born French writer Albert Camus publishes the philosophical essay
              The Myth of Sisyphus and the novel *The Stranger*. Both explore existentialist
              themes, as will such later works as the novel *The Plague* (1947) and the essay
              The Rebel (1951).   PHIL

1942–1946   Internment camps for Japanese-Americans, whose loyalty to the United States
              during World War II is deemed questionable, are operated in the United States.
              Years later, the internment will be officially regretted.   POL

1942   American psychologist William Herbert Sheldon publishes his constitutional
              theory of personality, which claims that body structure alone determines per-
              sonality. Body type is classified in terms of ectomorphy, endomorphy, and
              mesomorphy.   PSYCH

1942   The Institute of Sex Research is founded in affiliation with Indiana University
              by Alfred Kinsey. In the next five years, Kinsey and his colleagues will publish
              their research on male and female sexuality. These findings, which will
              become known as the "Kinsey reports," will address misconceptions about
              female sexual arousal, childhood sexuality, and homosexuality.   PSYCH

1942   *The Gospel of Sri Ramakrishna*, a compendium of the 19th-century Hindu mys-
              tic's sayings, translated into English by Swami Nikhilananda, is published. *See*
              1855, REL.   REL

1942   English scholar and writer C. S. Lewis publishes *The Screwtape Letters*, a satiri-
              cal epistolary work presenting a Christian perspective on evil. Lewis's other
              popular works on Christian faith will include *Mere Christianity* (1952).   REL

1942   German-born American scholar Edith Hamilton publishes *Mythology*, which
              will become a long-standing classic in its field.   REL

1943   Economist and historian Francis Klingender links communist tradition to the
              utopian socialism of the 19th-century English poet and artist William Morris
              in *Marxism and Modern Art*.   CRIT

1943   African-American painter and art historian James Amos Porter publishes
              Modern Negro Art, an influential reference work encompassing African,
              European, Cuban, and Haitian art.   CRIT

1943   French novelist and critic Georges Bataille publishes *L'Expérience intérieure*. In
              this and other philosophical works, such as *Sur Nietzsche* (1945) and *La Part
              maudite* (1947), Bataille promulgates a critical philosophy centered on trans-
              gression, eroticism, and the craving for escape from bourgeois Christian val-
              ues. His writings will be widely admired by the French avant-garde of the early

1960s, and will influence later French theorists such as Michel Foucault and Jacques Derrida.   CRIT

1943   American-born English poet and critic T. S. Eliot meditates on time, eternity, and artistic creativity in the poem *Four Quartets*.   PHIL

1943   French writer and aviator Antoine de Saint-Exupéry publishes the philosophi- cal fable *Le Petit Prince* (*The Little Prince*), about the search for what is impor- tant in life. An earlier collection of stories and meditations is *Wind, Sand, and Stars* (1939).   PHIL

1943   French philosopher and writer Jean-Paul Sartre publishes *Being and Nothingness*, a systematic study of the human condition and human con- sciousness based on existentialist principles. Sartre argues for the freedom and potentialities of human beings in a world without God or meaning. He will elaborate on these ideas in the 1946 lecture *Existentialism Is a Humanism*, and in dramatic and fictional works, such as the play *No Exit* (1944) and the novel trilogy *The Roads to Freedom* (1945–1949).   PHIL

1943   Russian-born American writer Ayn Rand publishes *The Fountainhead*, a novel about the rise of a talented but self-involved architect. In this and other works, notably the novel *Atlas Shrugged* (1957), she expounds her philosophy of objectivism, which supports capitalism, individualism, and limited gov- ernment.   PHIL

1943   Austrian mathematician Kurt Gödel begins to concentrate on philosophy, including the philosophy of mathematics, of cosmology, and of general rela- tivity. His views include Platonic elements.   PHIL

1943   American sociologist William Foote Whyte publishes *Street Corner Society*, an early field work study employing participant observation. Whyte spent time with a group of youths in Boston, gaining their confidence and taking steps to ensure their behavior was not affected by his research.   SOC

1944   American film critic Parker Tyler publishes *The Hollywood Hallucination*, a book that claims American films are myth and not art; the claim is based on the mythological symbolism of Hollywood stars. His concerns will be further elaborated in *Magic and Myth of the Movies* (1947) and the psychoanalytic study *Chaplin: Last of the Clowns* (1948).   CRIT

1944   American painter Robert Motherwell writes "The Modern Painter's World" for *Dyn* magazine, discussing the conditions of the contemporary world which force an artist into isolation.   CRIT

1944   The G.I. Bill, which pays for college costs for World War II veterans, opens high-
            er education to a historically large percentage of the American population.   EDUC

1944   American political scientists Paul Lazarsfeld, Bernard Berelson, and Hazel
            Gaudet publish *The People's Choice: How the Voter Made Up His Mind in a
            Presidential Campaign*, a major advance in the quantitative study of political
            behavior.   POL

1944   German economist Friedrich Hayek publishes *The Road to Serfdom*, in which he
            argues that economic liberty is the only bulwark against government control
            and that planned societies are intrinsically destructive of free political
            societies.   POL

1944   Austrian-born psychoanalyst Helene Deutsch, the first female psychoanalyst to
            be analyzed by Austrian psychoanalyst Sigmund Freud, publishes *The
            Psychology of Women*.   PSYCH

1944   American Southern Baptist clergyman Billy (William Franklin) Graham begins
            his evangelical work. His tours (which he calls "crusades") will extend
            throughout the world and will continue through the 1990s. He will become
            the most respected public conservative Christian evangelist of his day, serving
            presidents and other national leaders.   REL

1944   Swedish economist Gunnar Myrdal publishes *An American Dilemma*, detailing
            the conflict between the American rhetoric of equal opportunity and the real-
            ity of racial discrimination.   SOC

1944   The term *genocide* is first used, to describe the systematic elimination of a racial
            or ethnic group. It is coined to refer to the attempted extermination of Jews
            and other groups deemed inferior by the Nazis. *See also* 1933–1945, REL.   SOC

1945   American anthropologist Ralph Linton publishes *Cultural Background of
            Personality*, which takes an interdisciplinary approach to the study of culture
            and personality.   ANTH

1945   Australian art historian Bernard William Smith publishes *Place, Taste, and
            Tradition*, a Marxist approach to the ways in which Australia's art was
            shaped by local and historical influences. He will publish *European Vision
            and the South Pacific: 1768–1850* in 1960.   CRIT

1945   At Harvard, American classicist John H. Finley Jr. and other academics pub-
            lish *General Education in a Free Society*, which outlines the principles of a lib-
            eral education in the modern age. A synthesis of classical liberal arts influ-
            ences and modern interest in furthering intellectual freedom, it will become

the standard in building Harvard curricula and framing general discussion of
the state of liberal education.   EDUC

1945   American historian Arthur Schlesinger Jr. publishes *The Age of Jackson*, perhaps
                the best of the many histories of Jacksonian America.   HIST

1945–1997   In the decades following World War II, a number of scholars write histories of
                American intellectual life. Examples include Henry Steele Commager's *The
                American Mind: An Interpretation of American Thought and Character Since the
                1800s* (1950), Merle Curti's *Human Nature in American Historical Thought* (1968)
                and *Growth of American Thought* (1982), and Ralph H. Gabriel's *American Values:
                Continuity and Change* (1974).   HIST

1945–1997   An enormous number of books are published about World War II, covering
                virtually all aspects of the conflict. Examples include such general refer-
                ences as J. F. C. Fuller's *The Second World War, 1939–1945: A Strategical and
                Tactical History* (1949) and A. R. Buchanan's two-volume *The United States
                and World War II* (1964). William Shirer's *The Rise and Fall of the Third Reich:
                A History of Nazi Germany* (1959) is very popular. Samuel Eliot Morison
                writes comprehensively about naval operations (*see* 1927, HIST).   HIST

1945–1997   Many well-written histories and biographies aimed at educated general read-
                ers are published; a number of them become best-sellers. Examples include
                the works of Bruce Catton (*see* 1953, HIST); Theodore White's *The Making of the
                President* series (most notably his book on the 1960 campaign); Barbara
                Tuchman's *The Guns of August* (1962) and *A Distant Mirror: The Calamitous
                Fourteenth Century* (1978); Antonia Fraser's biographies, such as *Mary Queen
                of Scots* (1969); and William Manchester's biographies and histories, such as
                American Caesar: Douglas MacArthur, 1880–1964 (1978).   HIST

1945   French philosopher and writer Jean-Paul Sartre founds the literary, philosoph-
                ical, and political journal *Les Temps modernes*.   PHIL

1945   French philosopher Maurice Merleau-Ponty publishes *The Phenomenology
                of Perception*, which draws on both phenomenology and empirical psy-
                chology to consider the world of human experience.   PHIL

1945   English mathematician and philosopher Bertrand Russell publishes *A History
                of Western Philosophy*.   PHIL

c. 1945   Inspired by the Chicago School (*see* 1930, POL), behavioralism becomes a dom-
                inant movement in political science, holding sway until the 1960s.
                Behavioralists try to explain and predict political behavior across cultures and
                historical periods, using empirical methodologies previously employed by
                other social sciences. *See also* 1960s, POL.   POL

1945   In England, Austrian-born philosopher Karl Popper publishes *The Open Society and Its Enemies*, in which he attacks totalitarian political philosophy. His concept of democratic society will later be championed by Hungarian-born American philanthropist and financier George Soros, among others.   POL

1945   The charter for the United Nations is signed, providing a structure for an international organization aimed at addressing problems threatening world peace. The first meeting will be held on January 10, 1946, in London; official headquarters will be built in New York City, on land funded by American financier John D. Rockefeller Jr. Membership will eventually exceed 160 countries.   POL

1945   The United States ushers in the Atomic Age on August 6 by dropping an atomic bomb on Hiroshima, Japan. Three days later a second bomb is dropped on Nagasaki, Japan. The mass destruction and long-term effects of the bombs lead to an ongoing debate about their regulation. The use of atomic power for any purpose (as for public power systems) is also debated, and the possibility of nuclear apocalypse fosters a worldwide sense of uncertainty.   POL

1945   In occupied Japan, state Shinto collapses as Shinto is removed from government auspices. In 1946, Emperor Hirohito will disavow his divinity; in 1947, freedom of religion will become law in Japan.   REL

1945   German theologian Dietrich Bonhoeffer is hanged for his role in a plot to assassinate German Nazi leader Adolf Hitler. His *Letters and Papers from Prison* will be published in English in 1953. Urging Christians to conform themselves to the suffering Christ who lays down his life for others, he will influence a generation of Christian radical theologians.   REL

1945   Following the end of World War II, Arab nations receive full independence from their colonial masters, fostering a revival of Islamic political thought and action.   REL

1945   American sociologists Kingsley Davis and Wilbert Moore publish the paper *Some Principles of Stratification*, an attempt to explain how occupations are differentially rewarded and esteemed. The authors assert that jobs which are difficult and important to society are more highly prized than those that are not, and they suggest that some class structure is inevitable.   SOC

1946   American anthropologist Ruth Benedict publishes *The Chrysanthemum and the Sword*, a study of Japanese culture and society.   ANTH

1946   German scholar Erich Auerbach publishes *Mimesis*, a survey of the representation of reality in Western literature. In this and other works, Auerbach refines methods of close reading through philological and stylistic analysis.   CRIT

1946   Argentine-born Italian artist Lucio Fontano publishes his "White Manifesto" in Buenos Aires, launching the concept of *spazialismo*, which combines dada with concrete art principles.   CRIT

1946   American feminist and historian Mary Ritter Beard publishes *Women as a Force in History*. Beard, who will be the only American scholar to give serious attention to women's history between the 1930s and the 1950s, stresses the positive in her writing, focusing on the power women have held and the contributions they have made over the years and downplaying their historic victimization.   HIST

1946   American journalist John Hersey publishes *Hiroshima*, an account of the effects of the first atomic bomb to be used against a city. The work appeared in the *New Yorker* magazine before being published in book form.   JOURN

1946–1950   Italian existentialist philosopher Nicola Abbagnano publishes his monumental *History of Philosophy*. He will expound his "philosophy of the possible" in *Possibility and Liberty* (1956).   PHIL

1946   French novelist and critic Georges Bataille founds the journal *Critique*.   PHIL

1946   In a speech in Missouri, British statesman and writer Sir Winston Churchill coins the phrase "iron curtain" to describe the Soviet practice of political and

---

Raised on Spock

In the 1940s, when American G.I.s were fighting the Axis powers overseas, a young doctor stationed on naval duty outside New York City was completing the book that would help them raise their postwar children. In 1946, Dr. Benjamin Spock published *The Common Sense Book of Baby and Child Care* to immediate success. A generation of parents were ready to dispel the hardship and rigors of the Great Depression and World War II, at least for their children. Dr. Spock's authoritative medical information and attention to developing a child's personal sensibilities was the humane combination they chose to follow.

For several years after the book's publication, *Baby and Child Care*, as it was retitled, was a best-seller. Millions of children are said to have been raised by it and are now raising their own Spock-influenced families. To critics who, in the wake of the 1960s radicalism, accuse Dr. Spock of encouraging permissiveness, the doctor says, "I've always advised parents to respect their children, but to remember to ask for respect for themselves, to give firm, clear leadership, and to ask for cooperation and politeness."

cultural isolation from the West. The phrase will be commonly used to suggest the division between Soviet-bloc countries and the West.   POL

c. 1946   The field of artificial intelligence (AI) begins as the first computers are developed. AI is a multidisciplinary field encompassing computer science, neuroscience, philosophy, psychology, robotics, and linguistics.   PSYCH

1946   American pediatrician Benjamin Spock publishes *The Common Sense Book of Baby and Child Care*, which encourages a generation of parents to show more affection toward their infants and be less structured in feeding. Retitled *Baby and Child Care*, Spock's book will be a perennial best-seller on the subject of child-rearing.   PSYCH

1946   The idea of short-term therapy begins to evolve. This kind of therapy is goal-specific and can be completed in a limited number of sessions, while traditional psychoanalysis can continue indefinitely.   PSYCH

1946   Japanese religious leader Miki Tokuharu founds the P. L. (Perfect Liberty) Kyodan religious movement, which emphasizes the divine meaning of ordinary human activity.   REL

1947   American critic Yvor Winters publishes *In Defense of Reason*, in which he argues his view that poetry must be both rational and moral.   CRIT

1947   German film historian Siegfried Kracauer publishes *From Caligari to Hitler*, a study of the German cinema from 1919 to 1933 that traces the decline of German political culture as reflected in the history of its filmmaking.   CRIT

1947   American critic Cleanth Brooks publishes the classic work of New Criticism, *The Well Wrought Urn*.   CRIT

1947   The term *postmodernism* is first used in reference to architecture. It will later become associated with various movements in literature, the arts, philosophy, criticism, and other cultural fields.   CRIT

1947   The diary of German Jewish writer Anne Frank is published posthumously by her father. An English translation, *The Diary of a Young Girl*, will appear in 1952. Frank's work will sell millions of copies in many different editions and translations over the years, and it will be widely regarded as among the greatest personal documents to have emerged from the Holocaust.   HIST

1947   American historian John Hope Franklin publishes *From Slavery to Freedom: A History of American Negroes*, a scholarly history of the African-American experience.   HIST

1947–1971   American historian Allan Nevins publishes his eight-volume *Ordeal of the Union*, one of the best comprehensive histories of the American Civil War. HIST

1947   American pilot Kenneth Arnold is the first to report seeing "flying saucers"— wingless, disk-shaped airborne objects moving at very high apparent speeds. Over the coming decades people around the world will report seeing unidentified flying objects (UFOs) of many shapes and sizes. Many people will believe them to be visiting spacecraft from other planets. *See also* 1969, MISC.   MISC

1947   French writer Simone de Beauvoir publishes *The Ethics of Ambiguity*, which explores the ethical implications of existentialist philosophy. Beauvoir, together with her lifelong companion Jean-Paul Sartre, is instrumental in developing existentialist thought.   PHIL

1947   German philosopher Theodor Adorno publishes *Dialectic of Enlightenment*, which offers a philosophy of history focused on Western man's desire to dominate nature. Adorno is a cofounder of the Frankfurt School (*see* 1923, POL) of neo-Marxist critical theory.   PHIL

1947   Great Britain moves to divest itself of its empire as India gains its political independence on August 15.   POL

1947   The U.S. Congress passes the Taft-Hartley Act, which restricts the power of unions by prohibiting closed shops and a variety of strikes, among other provisions. It is passed over the veto of President Harry S. Truman.   POL

1947   The Dead Sea Scrolls are discovered in caves at Qumran on the Dead Sea. Believed to represent the secret library of the Jewish sect the Essenes (*see* 100s B.C.–100s A.D., REL), they were written or copied between the first century B.C. and the first century A.D. They include portions of the Hebrew Bible and Apocrypha and such distinctive documents as *The Manual of Discipline* and *The War of the Sons of Light with the Sons of Darkness*.   REL

1948   American anthropologist Margaret Mead publishes *Male and Female: A Study of the Sexes in a Changing World*, in which she claims that many aspects of gender identity are determined by cultural practices.   ANTH

1948   American film critic Robert Warshow writes "The Gangster as Tragic Hero," an essay reflecting the social, political, moral and cultural implications of the genre. His interest in the sociological significance of the cinema will again appear in his essay "The Westerner" (1954). These and other writings will be published posthumously in *The Immediate Experience* (1962).   CRIT

1948   French philosopher and writer Jean-Paul Sartre writes "The Search for the Absolute" for the catalogue of the exhibition *Alberto Giacometti: Sculptures,*

Paintings, Drawings at the Pierre Matisse Gallery in New York. He stresses the search for "origins" and the need to begin again with naked material.   CRIT

1948   American writer James Agee defines realism as poetry with a combination of surface and depth in his reviews of Georges Rouquier's *Farrebique* and Carl Dreyer's *Day of Wrath*. Agee will later state that a filmmaker's task is to record living authenticity and criticize those who confine their approach to the objective world. His reviews will be collected posthumously in *Agee on Film: Reviews and Comments* (1958).   CRIT

1948   American painter Barnett Newman writes the essay "The Sublime Is Now," in which he distinguishes between American and European forms of abstract art. CRIT

1948   English critic F. R. Leavis publishes *The Great Tradition*, in which he accepts only Jane Austen, George Eliot, Henry James, Joseph Conrad, and D. H. Lawrence into his pantheon of great fiction writers. Leavis's principal criterion for literary greatness is a "reverent openness before life."   CRIT

1948   American Keynesian economist Paul Samuelson publishes *Economics*, which will become a standard textbook. Samuelson will win the 1970 Nobel Memorial Prize in economic sciences (established as one of the Nobel Prize categories in 1969), for his role in developing the mathematical basis of economics.   ECON

1948   American historian Allan Nevins organizes the Oral History Project at Columbia University, the first such archive ever to be established.   HIST

1948–1954   British statesman and writer Sir Winston Churchill publishes his six-volume *The Second World War*. He is awarded the Nobel Prize for literature in 1953 and will publish his four-volume *History of the English-Speaking Peoples* from 1956 to 1958.   HIST

1948   English mathematician and philosopher Bertrand Russell publishes *Human Knowledge: Its Scope and Limits*.   PHIL

1948   American businessman and statesman Bernard Baruch coins the term *Cold War* to describe the burgeoning state of conflict between capitalist nations (most notably the United States) and Communist nations (most notably the Soviet Union).   POL

1948   The policy of apartheid, or legal separation of the races, is legalized in South Africa following the election of Afrikaner Nationalist Party member Daniel F. Malan. Apartheid requires the separation of whites from nonwhites as well as nonwhites from one another. In South Africa, nonwhites are in the vast majority. The decades-long reform movement of South African leader Nelson Mandela helps to bring about the nearly complete repeal of apartheid in 1991–1992. POL

1948   The United Nations General Assembly proclaims a Universal Declaration of Human Rights, outlining a series of rights due to people of all governments.   POL

1948   Democrats from southern states opposed to their party's civil rights stance, as embodied in the programs of President Harry S. Truman, form the political faction known formally as the States' Rights Democrats and informally as the Dixiecrats. Their presidential candidate in 1948 is Governor Strom Thurmond of South Carolina, whose long tenure in the United States Senate will begin in 1955, after a successful write-in candidacy. He will switch parties, becoming a Republican, in 1964.   POL

1948   West Indian activist and writer C. L. R. James, born in Trinidad, publishes *Notes on Dialectics* and *The Revolutionary Answer to the Negro Problem in the United States*. In the U.S. since 1938, he will be expelled from the U.S. in 1953 for his communist views.   POL

1948   The Organization of American States (OAS) is formed to promote peace and economic cooperation between the Americas.   POL

1948   Macedonian-born Roman Catholic nun Mother Teresa (Agnes Goxha Bojaxhiu) begins caring for the poor on the streets of Calcutta, India. As the founder of the international Order of the Missionaries of Charity, she will be revered for her saintliness and will win the Nobel Peace Prize in 1979.   REL

1948   American religious writer Thomas Merton publishes *The Seven Storey Mountain*, an account of his conversion to Catholicism and entry into a Trappist monastery. His spiritual books, including *Mystics and Zen Masters* (1967), will long remain popular.   REL

1948   The World Council of Churches is founded in Amsterdam to encourage ecumenical cooperation. Its members will include all major Protestant, Anglican, and Eastern Orthodox denominations.   REL

1948   English poet, novelist, and critic Robert Graves publishes *The White Goddess*, a study of mythology in relation to poetic inspiration.   REL

1948   Indian poet and philosopher Sri Aurobindo Ghose publishes *The Synthesis of Yoga*. See also 1926, REL.   REL

1948   On January 30, Indian political and spiritual leader Mohandas Gandhi is assassinated by a Maratha Hindu nationalist who considers him too conciliatory toward the region's Muslims.   REL

1948   On May 14, the modern state of Israel is founded in Palestine, marking the success of the Zionist movement in establishing a Jewish homeland. *See also* 1897, REL.   REL

1948   German existentialist theologian Rudolf Karl Bultmann publishes *Theology of the New Testament*, in which he seeks to demythologize New Testament texts.   REL

1948   German-born American theologian Paul Tillich publishes *The Shaking of the Foundations*. His work shows the influence of French existentialism in trying to correlate human concerns and Christian symbolism.   REL

1948   American religious writer Norman Vincent Peale publishes *A Guide to Confident Living*, which outlines his view of practical, scientific Christianity, providing "a simple, workable technique of thinking and acting." The combination of self-help and religion becomes a best-seller.   REL

1948   American sexologist Alfred Kinsey publishes *Sexual Behavior in the Human Male*, the most comprehensive report on the subject to date. It is followed five years later by a similar report on female sexuality.   SOC

1948   American president Harry S. Truman issues an executive order to desegregate the armed forces.   SOC

1949   French anthropologist Claude Lévi-Strauss publishes his first major work, *Elementary Structures of Kinship*. In this and later works, he contributes greatly to the development of structuralism, which will influence not only anthropology but such fields as philosophy and literary studies. Drawing on Saussurian linguistics (*see* 1916, LING), structuralists seek to analyze the interrelations among fundamental signs that underlie the apparent diversity of human cultural phenomena.   ANTH

1949   American drama critic Francis Fergusson publishes *Idea of a Theater*.   CRIT

1949   U.S. senator George Dondero delivers two speeches to Congress targeting left-wing groups and accusing modern artists of harboring communist sentiments.   CRIT

1949   American critics René Wellek and Austin Warren publish *Theory of Literature*, which offers a philosophical foundation for new criticism. The Austrian-born Wellek will be highly influential in shaping the modern discipline of comparative literature.   CRIT

1949   English scholar Walter Wilson Greg delivers the lecture "The Rationale of Copy-Text," an important work in the developing methodology of textual criticism, the scholarly analysis of texts with a view toward arriving at a complete synthesis of various versions, e.g., as in biblical criticism.   CRIT

1949   French philosopher and writer Simone de Beauvoir publishes *Le Deuxième Sexe*. This study of women's second-class status, which will be published in English as *The Second Sex* in 1953, will become a feminist classic. It draws on many fields of learning, including history, literature, sociology, and biology.   MISC

1949   English philosopher Gilbert Ryle publishes *Concept of Mind*, which introduces the derisive term "ghost in the machine" for French mathematician and philosopher René Descartes's theory of mind. Other works will include *Plato's Progress* (1966).   PHIL

1949   American philosopher Wilfrid Sellars edits and publishes *Readings in Philosophical Analysis*; he will follow it with *Readings in Ethical Analysis* (1952). Both prove influential in combining analytic philosophy and logical positivism, a project he also pursues in the journal he cofounds, *Philosophical Studies*.   PHIL

1949   English writer George Orwell (pseudonym of Eric Arthur Blair) publishes his nightmare vision of a totalitarian society, *1984*. The novel, which satirizes contemporary tendencies toward political control of thought in both East and West, introduces such phrases as "brainwashing" and "Big Brother is watching you." Also known for his literary criticism and essays, Orwell comments on the corruption of the language in the essay "Politics and the English Language."   POL

1949   The People's Republic of China is proclaimed in China on October 1, following a civil war. The victory of the Communist forces led by Mao Zedong represents a major advance in the spread of Marxist ideology throughout the world and an intensification of the Cold War (*see* 1948, POL). *See also* 1893–1976, POL.   POL

1949   U.S. president Harry S. Truman presents his domestic platform, called the Fair Deal. Among its positions are civil rights and labor reform and the creation of a national health program.   POL

1949   Following the Nuremberg trials of Nazi war criminals, a convention of the United Nations yields a bill defining genocide and rules for international punishment of its perpetrators. Objecting to its calls for international tribunals, the United States does not ratify the bill until 1986.   POL

1949   American mythologist Joseph Campbell publishes *The Hero with a Thousand Faces*, a study of the hero figure that ties together religion, myth, legend, and literature from numerous cultures.   REL

1949	Although religion in China is discouraged under its new Communist rulers, ordinary Chinese continue to practice a popular religion that includes ancestor worship, a pantheon of deities, and elements of Buddhism, Taoism, and Confucianism. REL
1949	In India, the "untouchable" caste, lowest and most despised of the Hindu hereditary classes, is abolished. SOC
1949	American sociologist Samuel Stouffer and his colleagues publish *The American Soldier: Adjustment During Army Life*, sponsored by the U.S. War Department. The influential questionnaire-based study advances the idea of relative deprivation, the experience of needs relative to one's expectations. SOC
1949	American anthropologist George Peter Murdock publishes *Social Structure*, a comprehensive study that compares a range of social practices cross-culturally, such as marriage rules. SOC
1950s	Critics gaining prominence in the pages of *The Partisan Review* (*see* 1937, CRIT) include Susan Sontag, Norman Podhoretz, Stephen Marcus, and Hilton Kramer. CRIT
1950s	Cliometrics, which combines mathematical modeling and statistical analysis of historical data, becomes an important tool for economic historians. ECON
1950s	Many scholars focus on the history of reform movements in the United States, studying populism, the Progressive Era and the New Deal. Examples of major works include Eric Goldman's *Rendezvous with Destiny* (1952) and Richard Hofstadter's *The Age of Reform* (1955). HIST
1950s	Chinese linguists begin systematic study of the nation's minority languages, including Uighur, Tibetan, and Mongolian. LING
1950s	Responding to fears of Communist influence in American society, a number of investigations are launched, particularly aimed at government officials and artists. The fears are crystallized in several events in 1950: Senator Joseph McCarthy's unfounded accusation that the U.S. State Department is infiltrated by Communists; the book *Red Channels*, which claims that there is widespread Communist infiltration in the entertainment industry (which had, in fact, been investigated in 1947, resulting in the Hollywood Ten's being sentenced to prison); and the perjury conviction of suspected spy and former State Department official Alger Hiss, whose hearings during the late 1940s under the auspices of the House Un-American Activities Committee (HUAC) brought national exposure to one of its members, California representative Richard Nixon. POL

1950s   The quantitative study of voting behavior and public opinion assumes tremendous importance in the study of politics. The Survey Research Center at the University of Michigan becomes a leading institution for the collection and analysis of American voting behavior.   POL

1950s   English mathematician and philosopher Bertrand Russell is a leader in the nuclear disarmament movement in Europe and America. The movement's slogan is "Ban the Bomb."   POL

1950s   American lawmakers use states' rights provisions of the Tenth Amendment to the Constitution to defend segregation in some states.   POL

1950s   Swiss psychoanalyst Ludwig Binswanger develops a form of therapy based on existentialism. His therapy emphasizes personal values and experience and respect for each patient.   PSYCH

1950s   German-born American psychologist Stanley Milgram experiments with human obedience. He finds that people are willing to obey authority figures even to the extent of torturing other people. Milgram suggests this tendency helps explain compliance with Nazi brutality during World War II. *See also* 1963, soc.   PSYCH

1950s   American psychologists Neal Miller and John Dollard hypothesize that frustration always causes a certain amount of aggression, an idea that will be instrumental in the treatment of mental health problems such as depression.   PSYCH

1950s–1960s   In Indonesia, nationalist and communist movements court the support of the *abangan*, or "brown ones." Historically, this Javanese peasant community has been regarded as "unclean" by the Muslim majority. *Abangan* religion and culture, while Muslim in name, incorporates aspects of Hindu and pre-Hindu belief.   REL

1950s   According to a United Nations report, slavery is still practiced in some parts of Africa, Asia, and South America.   SOC

1950   American designer Lee Simonson publishes *The Art of Scenic Design*.   CRIT

1950   Austrian-born English art historian Ernst Gombrich publishes *The Story of Art*.   CRIT

1950   English critic F. W. Bateson publishes *English Poetry: A Critical Introduction*, in which he stresses the relationship between poetry and the historical circumstances of its composition.   CRIT

1950   American critics Caroline Gordon and Allen Tate publish *The House of Fiction*, a widely disseminated anthology with commentary.   CRIT

1950   American critic Lionel Trilling publishes *The Liberal Imagination*. In this and
                other works, including *The Opposing Self* (1955) and *Beyond Culture* (1965), he
                develops an eclectic approach to literary criticism within an Arnoldian human-
                istic tradition. His essentially conservative views bring him into increasing
                conflict with more liberal and radical intellectuals.   CRIT

1950–1958   Chinese historians try to rewrite their nation's history to conform to Marxist
                theory, but are thwarted by the particulars of China's past; periodization
                according to Marxist stages is especially elusive. In 1958, China's leaders urge
                historians to "emphasize the present and de-emphasize the past," for example,
                by writing current histories of factories and communes.   HIST

1950–1997   A number of histories and biographies are published that shed new light on
                colonial and revolutionary America by exploring the intellectual underpin-
                nings of the era's events and the personal conflicts of some of its key figures.
                Examples include Edmund S. Morgan's *The Birth of the Republic, 1763–1789*
                (1956) and *The Puritan Dilemma: The Story of John Winthrop* (1958); Bernard
                Bailyn's *Ideological Origins of the American Revolution* (1967) and *The Ordeal of
                Thomas Hutchinson* (1974); and Joseph J. Ellis's *American Sphinx: The Character
                of Thomas Jefferson* (1997).   HIST

1950   German philosopher Rudolf Carnap publishes *Logical Foundations of
                Probability*, a major work of confirmation theory, which purports to measure
                the degree to which evidence supports a theory.   PHIL

1950–1967   French philosopher and critic Paul Ricoeur publishes the series of books called
                Philosophy of the Will, which draws on existentialism and phenomenology. PHIL

1950   T. S. Ch'ien publishes *The Government and Politics of China*, a standard work of
                Chinese political science.   POL

1950   German-born American political philosopher Leo Strauss publishes one of his
                most influential works, *Natural Right and History*, in which he argues for the
                existence of natural right and timeless, transcendent political virtue. He will be
                credited with reviving the study of classical political philosophy at a time
                when it was being eclipsed by empirical political science.   POL

1950   American psychiatrist Jacob L. Moreno develops psychodrama, therapy involv-
                ing role-playing to bring about emotional catharsis, and sociometry, a tech-
                nique to measure attraction and repulsion among people.   PSYCH

1950   German-born American psychoanalyst Erik H. Erikson publishes *Childhood
                and Society*, in which he introduces his theory of developmental stages. He ana-
                lyzes trust versus mistrust, autonomy versus doubt, industry versus inferiority,

and other states of conflict. In later works, such as *Young Man Luther* (1958), he will apply these ideas to the study of historical figures.   PSYCH

1950   American social psychologist Stanley Schachter begins developing a psychological cognitive theory of emotion.   PSYCH

1950   The bodily assumption of Mary into heaven is defined as dogma by Pope Pius XII. His encyclical *Humani Generis*, also issued this year, condemns such current intellectual tendencies as existentialism.   REL

1950   American science-fiction writer L. Ron Hubbard publishes *Dianetics: The Modern Science of Mental Health*. The best-seller becomes the founding document of the Church of Scientology, which seeks to relieve physical and mental stress by clearing the soul of negative energy through a ceremony called "processing." Regarded by many as a cult, the church will gain many adherents worldwide even as it is subjected to government investigations in several countries.   REL

1950   American sociologist George Homans publishes *The Human Group*, a review of small group research that seeks to identify universal properties of small associations.   SOC

1950   German philosopher Theodor Adorno and his associates publish *The Authoritarian Personality*, a post–World War II questionnaire study of personality types most vulnerable to fascist appeals.   SOC

1950   Sociologist D. F. Aberle and his colleagues publish *The Functional Prerequisites of Society*, a discussion of the basic tasks a society must carry out for it to persist and thrive.   SOC

1950   American sociologist David Riesman and his colleagues publish *The Lonely Crowd*, an examination of the isolating effects of modern, pluralistic society. The authors identify three personality types: inner-directed, outer-directed, and other-directed.   SOC

1951   French writer André Malraux publishes *The Voices of Silence*, a history and philosophy of art. He will publish *The Metamorphosis of the Gods* in 1957.   CRIT

1951   French film critic and theorist André Bazin founds the highly influential film journal *Les Cahiers du Cinéma* with French director and journalist Jacques Doniol-Valcroze. The journal concentrates on developing the realist aesthetic of cinema. The magazine's theories and ideas, particularly the *auteur* theory, will help shape the emerging French New Wave filmmakers.   CRIT

1951   American historian C. Vann Woodward publishes *Origins of the New South, 1877–1913,* which argues that Southern agrarianism was destroyed largely by indigenous Southern capitalism rather than by Northern exploitation. He will publish *The Strange Career of Jim Crow,* a revisionist view of racial segregation, in 1995, and many will come to see him as the dean of historians of the American South.   HIST

1951   French existentialist philosopher Gabriel Marcel publishes *The Mystery of Being.* Other works will include *The Existentialist Background to Human Dignity* (1963).   PHIL

1951   German-born American political scientist Hannah Arendt publishes *The Origins of Totalitarianism,* which ties the rise of fascist regimes to the demise of the traditional nation-state. Her other works include *On Violence* (1970).   POL

1951–1963   German-born American theologian Paul Tillich publishes *Systematic Theology,* which combines elements of existentialism, Jungian psychology, and neoscholasticism.   REL

1951–1956   The notebooks of French mystic Simone Weil are published posthumously. Weil emphasizes the contradictory nature of rational thought and the need to seek union with divine love.   REL

1951   Indian religious leader Vinoba Bhave, widely considered the successor to Mohandas Gandhi, founds the Bhudan, or land-gift, movement, which seeks voluntary redistribution of land.   SOC

1951   American social psychologist Herbert Blumer publishes *Collective Behavior,* an essay identifying types of crowd behavior. A student of George Herbert Mead, Blumer distinguishes between expressive and acting crowds, the former acting to convey emotion, the latter acting to achieve a wider end.   SOC

1951   American sociologist Edwin Lemert publishes *Social Pathology,* a precursor to labeling theory. Lemert establishes the distinction between primary and secondary deviance, the former term referring to acts of deviance, the latter to the ways in which society categorizes persons committing those acts.   SOC

1951   American sociologist Talcott Parsons publishes *The Social System,* presenting his macrosociological view of societies as relatively interdependent wholes.   SOC

1952   English anthropologist Alfred Reginald Radcliffe-Brown publishes *Structure and Function in Primitive Society,* explaining his theory of structural functionalism. His analyses of the interdependent components of social systems help build social anthropology as a science.   ANTH

1952   English sculptor Henry Moore publishes the essay "The Sculptor in Modern Society," which attempts to strike a balance between complete state control of the arts and laissez-faire capitalism.   CRIT

1952   American critic Harold Rosenberg identifies "Action Painting" and emphasizes existential drama within American abstract expressionism in his essay, "The American Action Painters."   CRIT

1952   By now, sociology and political science have been suppressed in China and discredited as "bourgeois." History and economics continue, but are heavily influenced by Marxist doctrine and Soviet research.   MISC

1952   In American writer Ralph Ellison's novel *Invisible Man*, which will be ranked with the works of Jean-Paul Sartre (*see* 1943, PHIL) and Albert Camus (*see* 1942, PHIL), the eponymous African-American narrator's existensialist search for self takes him on a journey from rejection of the role prescribed for him by white Southerners through a stint with a black nationalist group in New York City.   PHIL

1952   English moral philosopher Richard Mervyn Hare publishes *The Language of Morals*, in which he develops the theory of prescriptivism, the view that moral commitment can be modeled on the giving or accepting of commands.   PHIL

1952   German-born American philosopher of science Carl Gustav Hempel publishes *Fundamentals of Concept Formation in Empirical Science*, an influential work on the nature and structure of scientific theory.   PHIL

1952   English philosopher Arthur John Wisdom publishes *Other Minds*, in which he takes a discursive, open-ended approach that examines multiple philosophical viewpoints.   PHIL

1952   In Egypt, Gamal Abdel Nasser leads a military coup to overthrow the monarchy of King Farouk. As president from 1956 until his death in 1970, Nasser will inspire Arabs in many countries with the spirit of Arab nationalism and unity. He will also co-found the nonaligned movement to keep developing nations independent of the Western and Eastern blocs.   POL

1952   Martinique-born, French-educated psychiatrist Frantz Fanon analyzes racism and cultural prejudice in *Black Skin, White Masks*, in which he alleges that racial oppression can contribute to debilitating mental illness among the oppressed. In 1954 Fanon will join the Algerian liberation movement in an attempt to throw off French rule. He will eventually advocate armed revolution to end colonial tyranny (*see* 1961, POL).   PSYCH

1953   American literary critic M. H. Abrams publishes *The Mirror and the Lamp*, which establishes him as the premier American authority on English romanticism. He will later be general editor of the widely used *Norton Anthology of English Literature*.   CRIT

1953   French critic Roland Barthes publishes *Writing Degree Zero*, in which he discusses modern writers' quest for a language of zero degree (free from the associations of the past). In this and other works, he approaches language as a system of signs and contributes to the development of semiotics (or semiology), the study of signs. Drawing on the work of Charles Sanders Peirce (*see* 1878 and 1907, PHIL) and Ferdinand de Saussure (*see* 1916, LING), semiotics will be a powerful force in subsequent criticism.   CRIT

1953   American economist Robert Heilbroner publishes *The Worldly Philosophers*, a popular study of such celebrated persons as Scottish economist Adam Smith and German political philosopher Karl Marx. He will also establish himself as a social critic in such works as *The Future as History* (1960).   ECON

1953–1972   American biographer Leon Edel publishes his five-volume *The Life of Henry James*. In 1959, American scholar Richard Ellmann publishes *James Joyce*. These two works are often considered the greatest literary biographies in English of the mid-20th century.   HIST

1953   American writer Bruce Catton publishes *A Stillness at Appomattox*. He will publish *This Hallowed Ground* in 1956. In these and other books, Catton provides vivid, detailed accounts of the American Civil War that are aimed at the general reader.   HIST

1953   American philosopher Willard Quine publishes *From a Logical Point of View*, in which he denounces the distinction between analytic and synthetic. His prevailing concerns are with meaning and convention.   PHIL

1953   English philosopher George Edward Moore publishes *Some Main Problems of Philosophy*.   PHIL

1953   Irish-born British philosopher and novelist Iris Murdoch publishes *Sartre, Romantic Rationalist*. In this and other philosophical writings, such as *The Sovereignty of Good* (1970), and in her novels, she examines the role of religion and morality in an apparently meaningless universe in which free will is an illusion.   PHIL

1953   *Philosophical Investigations*, by Viennese-born British philosopher Ludwig Wittgenstein, is published posthumously.   PHIL

1953   Latvian-born English political philosopher Isaiah Berlin publishes *The Hedgehog and the Fox: An Essay on Tolstoy's View of History*.   PHIL

1953   American political scientist David Easton publishes *The Political System*, an influential work that borrows the terminology of natural sciences (inputs, feedback, output) to describe governments and political processes.   POL

1953–1960   English economist George Douglas Howard Cole publishes *A History of Socialist Thought*, which becomes one of the standard works on the subject.   POL

1953   African-American psychologist Mamie Phipps Clark assists in preparing a social science brief on self-awareness and self-esteem in black children. The brief will be the basis for the 1954 U.S. Supreme Court decision on public school desegregation.   SOC

1954   American poet Wallace Stevens publishes *Collected Poems*, drawing together work from four decades. Many of his poems present an explicit theory of poetry that is radically skeptical about linguistic reference. Some of these include "Theory" and "The Ultimate Poem Is Abstract."   CRIT

1954   In the United States, "separate but equal" schooling is struck down with the Supreme Court ruling in *Brown* v. *Board of Education*. It initiates nationwide desegregation of schools at all levels.   EDUC

1954   American philosopher Nelson Goodman publishes *Fact, Fiction, and Forecast*. In this and other works, including *The Structure of Appearance* (1951) and *Languages of Art* (1969), he develops views with nominalist and idealist tendencies.   PHIL

1954   American political scientists Angus Campbell, Gerald Gurin, and Warren Miller publish *The Voter Decides*, a landmark study of voting behavior and public opinion.   POL

1954   Wisconsin senator Joseph McCarthy is censured by the U.S. Congress for his unsupported attacks on colleagues and public figures as Communist or Communist-leaning individuals. His inquisitions in the name of anti-Communism become known pejoratively as "McCarthyism."   POL

1954   Following a U.S.-aided military coup in Guatemala this year, "disappearances" become a common way for the government to deal with dissidents. During the Guatemalan civil war, which will last from 1960 through 1996, as many as 50,000 Guatemalans will be categorized by human rights organizations as "disappeared"—abducted, tortured, killed. Other Latin American governments, notably those of Chile, Argentina, and El Salvador, will adopt the practice, inspiring human rights movements in behalf of *los desaparecidos*, or "the disappeared."   POL

1954   After the fall of Dien Bien Phu, Vietnam is divided into Communist North
                Vietnam and non-Communist South Vietnam. The split represents a victory
                for North Vietnam's leader, Ho Chi Minh, who has fought the Japanese and
                French and will later fight the Americans for control of Vietnam. As a Marxist
                thinker, Ho is significant for joining anticolonial nationalism with leftist rev-
                olution.   POL

1955   American anthropologist Julian Steward publishes *Theory of Culture Change:
                The Methodology of Multilinear Evolution*, a study of cultural evolution.   ANTH

1955   French critic and writer Maurice Blanchot publishes *L'Espace littéraire* (*The
                Space of Literature*), one of several critical works in which he considers the roots
                and contradictions of artistic creation. The reclusive author's thought about lit-
                erature is highly metaphysical, pessimistic, and obscure. Other works will
                include *Le Pas au-delà* (1973).   CRIT

1955–1993   Austrian-born American critic René Wellek publishes the eight-volume *History
                of Modern Criticism*.   CRIT

1955   American editor and writer William F. Buckley, Jr. founds the *National Review*,
                which will become a leading vehicle for conservative thought. Buckley also
                expounds his right-wing views in newspaper columns, books such as *God and
                Man at Yale* (1951), and the television show *Firing Line* (from 1966).   POL

1955–1970   The study of how power is distributed in local communities becomes a major
                focus of American political scientists, including Robert Dahl, Nelson Polsby,
                and Edward Banfield.   POL

1955   German-born American political philosopher Herbert Marcuse publishes *Eros
                and Civilization*, which combines Freudian and Marxist thought.   POL

1955   American clinical psychologist Albert Ellis develops rational-emotive therapy,
                which emphasizes the detrimental effects of unrealistic expectations and irra-
                tional thinking.   PSYCH

1955   American clinical psychologist George Kelly publishes *The Psychology of
                Personal Constructs*. Kelly argues that an individual's conception of the world
                is the most important determinant of behavior.   PSYCH

1955   French paleontologist and philosopher Pierre Teilhard de Chardin dies (*b.*
                1881). Long prohibited from teaching by the Roman Catholic church, he
                achieves fame with the posthumous publication this year of his book *The
                Phenomenon of Man*, in which he integrates Darwinian and Christian thought
                in his view of cosmic evolution, with Christ at the apex.   REL

1955–1956   In the United States, both Presbyterian and Methodist denominations decide to permit ordination of women.   REL

1955–1956   Social reforms enacted in India include enforcement of monogamy, easier divorce, and equal inheritance rights for women.   SOC

1955   American social psychologist Solomon Asch publishes an influential paper on group pressure to conform. The paper describes his famed experiment in which subjects were often persuaded that the shorter of two drawn lines was actually the longer.   SOC

1955   American sociologists Talcott Parsons and Robert Bales publish *Family, Socialization and Interaction Process*, stating that families and other small groups tend to produce instrumental and expressive leaders. Instrumental leaders spearhead task development in groups, while expressive leaders maintain their emotional well-being.   SOC

1955–1956   African-American civil rights leader Martin Luther King Jr. leads a successful boycott against the segregated bus lines in Montgomery, Alabama. The boycott marks the beginning of the modern civil rights movement and of King's prominence as one of its leaders. He will continue to lead boycotts and, later, marches (*see* 1963, SOC) until his assassination in 1968. Throughout his career, he adheres faithfully to Gandhian nonviolence (*see* 1919, POL). The civil rights movement will lead to passage of much historic legislation, including the 1964 Civil Rights Act and the 1965 Voting Rights Act.   SOC

1956   Americans William C. Boyd and his wife, Lyle Boyd, identify 13 human "races," based on blood groups.   ANTH

1956   American critic Murray Krieger publishes *The New Apologists for Poetry*. Other works will include *The Tragic Vision* (1960) and *A Window to Criticism* (1964). Krieger emphasizes the primacy and uniqueness of literary works.   CRIT

1956   American economist Robert M. Solow proposes his influential model of economic growth. He will also write on employment policy and on the theory of capital.   ECON

1956–1957   Chinese leader Mao Zedong launches the Hundred Flowers period, in which he encourages intellectuals to flourish and critique his party's regime. Social scientists, notably in sociology and political science, propose a revival of their disciplines. However, the period ends with renewed suppression of independent thought.   MISC

1956   Polish-born American mathematician and philosopher Alfred Tarski publishes *Logic, Semantics, and Metamathematics*.   PHIL

1956   Following a speech at the 20th Party Congress condemning Soviet dictator Joseph Stalin, Soviet premier Nikita Khrushchev pursues a "de-Stalinization" of the Soviet Union. During his lifetime, the process will be only partly successful, but by the 1990s, the Soviet Union and its government will have dissolved and been replaced by a more democratic one.   POL

1956   In an attempt to rebuff Soviet domination, Hungarians revolt in Budapest on October 23. The new government of Imre Nagy withdraws from the Warsaw Pact and declares its neutrality between East and West. A countergovernment is formed by János Kádár, who calls in Soviet military support, and within one month of its inception, the rebellion is brought to a bloody end by Soviet forces.   POL

1956   Guinean revolutionary Amílcar Cabral founds the African Party for the Independence of Guinea and Cape Verde. As a result of his war of independence against the Portuguese, much of Guinea is liberated prior to his assassination in 1973. His writings on the relation of culture to nationalist consciousness will have a wide influence.   POL

1956   American social psychologist Muzafer Sherif publishes *Experiments in Group Conflict*, a report on the ways in which group loyalty is intensified by conflict with other groups, and weakened by devotion to a larger, common cause. Sherif studied the formation of cliques among 11-year-old boys at a summer camp.   SOC

1956   American sociologists Seymour Martin Lipset, Martin Trow, and James Coleman publish *Union Democracy: The Inside Politics of the International Typographical Union*. The study examines a union characterized by democratic governance, in opposition to prevailing models of unions as autocratic and alienating.   SOC

1956   German-born American sociologist Lewis Coser publishes *The Functions of Social Conflict*. Heavily influenced by Georg Simmel, Coser describes the potentially positive effects of conflict. His work attempts to reconcile functionalism and conflict theory.   SOC

1956   American sociologist C. Wright Mills publishes *The Power Elite*, a study of the distribution of political and economic power in the United States among a relatively small class. His work disputes the pluralistic view, which sees power as widely dispersed.   SOC

1956   American editor William Hollingsworth Whyte publishes *The Organization Man*, in which he analyzes corporate culture and the collective ethic.   SOC

1957   Swiss critic and psychiatrist Jean Starobinski publishes *Jean-Jacques Rousseau: La Transparence et l'obstacle*. In this and other critical works, he combines literary interpretation with an interest in psychology (especially melancholy) and the phenomenology of consciousness.   CRIT

1957   American critic Northrop Frye publishes *Anatomy of Criticism*, in which he systematically classifies literature into four categories—comic, tragic, romantic, and ironic—associated with a theory of myths. Frye's later works wil include *The Well-Tempered Critic* (1963) and *The Secular Scripture* (1976).   CRIT

1957   French critic Roland Barthes publishes *Mythologies*. In this and other works, such as *On Racine* (1963) and *The Fashion System* (1967), he analyzes cultural and literary signs.   CRIT

1957   French novelist and critic Georges Bataille publishes *Literature and Evil*, in which he argues that art should be a vehicle for annihilating rationality.   CRIT

The Source of the Power Elite

In 1955, a slender novel by Sloan Wilson entitled *The Man in the Gray Flannel Suit* introduced an unsettling national icon: the man who had sold out to win what he thought was the American dream. In its title character, the best-selling book offered a literary symbol of the cultural conformity of the flourishing post–World War II capitalist economy. Perhaps the foremost observer of the impending gray age of corporate oppression in all its forms was American sociologist C. Wright Mills.

Mills had always been an iconoclast and outsider since his childhood in Waco, Texas (a place whose culture he described as "one man, one rifle"). He became a professor at Columbia University by age 30, after making a name for himself in 1951 with *White Collar*, his critique of the dominance of salesmanship in American life.

But it was his 1956 work, *The Power Elite*, in which the flannel-shirted, motorcycle-riding critic developed his view of the centers of American power. To him, power was centered in the "power elite . . . those political, economic, and military circles which as an intricate set of overlapping cliques share decisions having at least national consequences." According to Mills, this decision-making process, which affected, yet eluded, the average person, created a general sense of alienation that permeated work and everyday life and contributed to the decade's description as the Age of Anxiety.

As notorious as Mills was in his day, he would have even more influence after his early death in 1962. Later that decade, his life and works would become an idealistic touchstone of the campus New Left, the tribe built by the children of the men in gray flannel suits.

1957   German-born English art historian Nikolaus Pevsner investigates his theory
        of "cultural geography" in *The Englishness of English Art*, a work that examines
        the national characteristics of English art in terms of contradictory qualities.
        He will further elaborate this theory in the monumental, 46-volume *Buildings
        of England*, a county-by-county study, completed in 1974, of historical English
        architecture.   CRIT

1957   American scholar George Bluestone publishes *Novels into Film*, which argues
        that film leaves behind those contents of thought that only language can
        approximate. He finds film creates a form that is only sensual and perceptual.   CRIT

1957   English critic Frank Kermode publishes *Romantic Image*, an analysis of the use
        of image by Symbolist and romantic poets. Later works by Kermode will
        include *The Sense of an Ending* (1967) and *The Genesis of Secrecy* (1979), both
        on fiction.   CRIT

1957   Six European nations form an alliance known as the European Economic
        Community (EEC), or Common Market. It is aimed at improving trade and
        commerce among the nations with the ultimate goal of effecting a political
        union. In 1973, the Market is joined by Denmark, Great Britain, and Ireland.
        In 1992, the Maastricht Treaty of European Union proposes a central banking
        system and uniform monetary unit.   ECON

1957   American linguist Noam Chomsky publishes *Syntactic Structures*, in which he
        proposes the revolutionary theory of transformational-generative grammar.
        Claiming that innate mental structures are the basis for human languages, he
        seeks to uncover the deep structure and rules that govern linguistic per-
        formance.   LING

1957   China adopts pinyin as its official spelling system for rendering Chinese words
        and names in the Latin alphabet. It will be decades, however, before pinyin
        (e.g., Mao Zedong) fully supplants the older Wade-Giles system of romaniza-
        tion (e.g., Mao Tse-tung) in Western countries.   LING

1957   English philosopher Gertrude Anscombe publishes *Intention*. She is also the trans-
        lator (in 1953) of Viennese-born British philosopher Ludwig Wittgenstein's
        Philosophical Investigations and author of *An Introduction to Wittgenstein's Tractatus*.
                                                                                PHIL

1957   English political scientist Anthony Downs publishes *The Economic Theory of
        Democracy*, a work that heavily influences contemporary political theory with its
        emphasis on game theory and rational choice models of human behavior. POL

1957   Yugoslav political leader and writer Milovan Djilas publishes *The New Class*, a famous critique of the communist ruling class which portrays it as a privileged elite interested in protecting its status rather than transforming society.   POL

1957   U.S. president Dwight Eisenhower introduces the Eisenhower Doctrine, a foreign policy plan aimed at aiding Mideast countries facing communist infiltration.   POL

1957   American social psychologist Leon Festinger publishes *Theory of Cognitive Dissonance*. Defining cognitive dissonance as the sense that something is amiss in one's belief system, and discussing the drive to eliminate that dissonance, he develops a theory of belief formation and retention.   PSYCH

1957   The United Church of Christ is formed through the union of various American Congregationalist bodies.   REL

1957   On publication, American novelist Jack Kerouac's novel *On the Road* becomes a signature work of the Beat Generation. In the post–World War II 1940s and 1950s, these groups of artists, writers, and Bohemians have sprouted in New York, San Francisco, and other American locales. They advocate rejection of traditional values and authority, living in the present, unconventionality, and distaste for "squares" or conformists.   SOC

1957   American sociologist Edward Franklin Frazier publishes *Black Bourgeoisie*, a classic early statement on the subject.   SOC

1957   American writer C. Northcote Parkinson publishes *Parkinson's Law*, a semi-satirical look at bureaucracy. The book is famed for its assertion that in bureaucracies "work expands to fill the time available for its completion."   SOC

1957   The concept of a "space race" between the United States and the Soviet Union arises when the Soviet Union becomes the first country to launch an artificial satellite, *Sputnik*. The "race," which will extend to all elements of culture, will be partially resolved with the 1969 U.S. landing of men on the moon.   SOC

1958   French anthropologist Claude Lévi-Strauss publishes *Structural Anthropology*.   ANTH

1958   English critic Raymond Williams publishes *Culture and Society, 1780–1950*. In this and *The Long Revolution* (1961), he contributes to the development of cultural studies by analyzing the interrelation of literature, culture, and politics from a left-wing perspective.   CRIT

1958–1962   *What Is Cinema?*, a four-volume collection of essays by French film critic and theorist André Bazin, is published posthumously.   CRIT

1958　English critic Lawrence Alloway coins the term "Pop Art" in his essay "The Arts and the Mass Media." He attempts to create an adequate theory of culture to confront the implications of the new mass media and the subsequent practices of art that are best exemplified by the Independent Group.　CRIT

1958　American philosopher Monroe C. Beardley publishes *Aesthetics: Problems in the Philosophy of Criticism*, which includes his essay, "The Instrumentalist Theory."　CRIT

1958　African-American author and critic Arna Wendell Bontemps publishes *The Book of Negro Folklore* to show the rich heritage of mainstream black music, art, and poetry.　CRIT

1958　At a national convention for artists and art historians, American art historian and editor of *Art Bulletin* James Ackerman comments on the danger of teaching art history surveys rather than focusing on ideas, themes, and philosophies.　CRIT

1958–1964　The Moscow-Tartu school of Soviet linguists, folklorists, and literary scholars takes shape. Drawing on many disciplines, they attempt to develop systematic theories of cultural and literary products. During this period, the focus is on mathematical and linguistic models; later semiotic and global models will be introduced. Prominent members include Valery Ivanov, Eleazar Meletinskij, Aleksandr Piatigorskij, Jurij Levin, and Jurij Lotman.　CRIT

1958　American economist John Kenneth Galbraith publishes *The Affluent Society*. In this and other popular works, he advocates government spending to alleviate unemployment and improve public services.　ECON

1958–1960　China institutes the Great Leap Forward, an economic program aimed at rapidly transforming the country into a major industrial power. The program does not succeed, and crop failures and food shortages force China's leaders to focus again on agricultural production.　ECON

1958　English philosopher Peter Winch publishes *The Idea of a Social Science*, which argues that reality is a social construction.　PHIL

1958　The U.S. Supreme Court reaffirms its 1954 decision to desegregate schools when it rules in *Cooper v. Aaron* that schools in Little Rock, Arkansas, must implement integration procedures.　POL

1958　American psychologist Alfred Lazarus is the first to use the term *behavior therapy* for certain strategies for treating mental illness.　PSYCH

1958　American psychologists Harry F. Harlow and John Bowlby experiment with infant monkeys and maternal deprivation. They show that behavioral disturbances occur when adequate interaction, holding, and bonding does not take place between mother and child.   PSYCH

1958   American social psychologist Fritz Helder publishes his balance theory in *The Psychology of Interpersonal Relations*. He argues that individuals strive for cognitive consistency, attempting to organize beliefs and perceptions in a consistent way.   PSYCH

1958–1963   John XXIII reigns as pope. He convenes Vatican II (*see* 1962–1965, REL.) and works for church reform, social justice, and cooperation with other faiths. *See also* 1961, REL.   REL

1958   The American sociologists August Hollingshead and Fredrick Redlich publish *Social Class and Mental Illness*, an important study of the way in which rates and types of mental illness vary by class.   SOC

1958   The staunchly anticommunist John Birch Society is founded in the United States by manufacturer Robert Welch. Named for an intelligence officer killed in China, it fights domestic communist infiltration, busing as a means of achieving school desegregation, and graduated income tax.   SOC

1959   American anthropologist Edward T. Hall publishes *The Silent Language*, a study of the ways in which nonverbal behavior contributes to and is affected by social relations.   ANTH

1959   American anthropologist Elizabeth Thomas publishes *The Harmless People*, describing the peaceful ways of the African !Kung people.   ANTH

1959   Frank N. Sibley, professor of philosophy at the University of Lancaster, in England, publishes his essay "Aesthetic Concepts."   CRIT

1959   German philosopher Theodor Adorno publishes *Theory of Modern Music*.   CRIT

1959   Economist Gerard Debreu publishes *Theory of Value*, in which he develops the general theory of market value. The book helps drive the trend toward more mathematical modeling in economics.   ECON

1959   American philosopher Saul Aaron Kripke publishes the paper "A Completeness Theorem in Modal Logic." With two semantical papers of his in 1963, this work will make an important seminal contribution to the study of modal logic systems.   PHIL

1959   American philosopher Norman O. Brown publishes *Life Against Death: The Psychoanalytical Meaning of History*.   PHIL

1959   Cuban revolutionary Fidel Castro overthrows the dictatorship of Fulgencio
            Batista. In 1961, Castro will declare himself a Communist and accept support
            from the Soviet Union.   POL

1959   U.S. vice-president Richard Nixon and Soviet premier Nikita Khrushchev
            engage in an informal "kitchen debate" in the kitchen of an American model
            home at a trade show in Moscow. The American press reports that Nixon stood
            up to the Soviet leader, helping to clinch the Republican Party's nomination of
            him for U.S. president during the 1960 campaign. He will lose the general
            election to his Democratic rival, John F. Kennedy.   POL

1959   In Switzerland, voters reaffirm that only men may vote in national elections
            and that only men may run for national office when they reject a proposed
            constitutional amendment that would have opened both activities to female
            participation.   POL

1959   German-born American psychiatrist Viktor Frankl publishes *Man's Search for
            Meaning,* a popular mental health book emphasizing the importance of free
            will.   PSYCH

1959   Swiss psychiatrist Carl Gustav Jung publishes *Flying Saucers—A Modern Myth,*
            in which he argues that belief in the extraterrestrial origin of unidentified fly-
            ing objects (UFOs) is the modern equivalent of ancient beliefs in angels and
            divine portents in the skies. *See also* 1947, MISC.   PSYCH

1959   The Dalai Lama, temporal Buddhist ruler of Tibet, flees to India after a revolt
            in his country is crushed by the Chinese, who have been in power there since
            1950. The Chinese attempt to suppress Buddhism in the region.   REL

1959   Indian guru Maharishi Mahesh Yogi introduces transcendental meditation (TM)
            to the West. His disciples will include the English rock group the Beatles.   REL

1959   American sociologist William Goode publishes his paper "The Theoretical
            Importance of Love," in which he asserts that, rather than being a cultural uni-
            versal, romantic love exists only in certain societies, particularly those in which
            nuclear families predominate.   SOC

1959   Canadian-born American sociologist Erving Goffman publishes *The
            Presentation of Self in Everyday Life,* a study of the ways in which the self is por-
            trayed and fashioned by features of the situations in which persons interact.   SOC

1959   German sociologist Ralf Dahrendorf publishes *Class and Class Conflict in
            Industrial Society.* Dahrendorf shifts the study of conflict from the power rela-
            tionships between classes and their ownership of property to other groups,
            e.g., unions and employers.   SOC

1959   English writer and physicist C. P. Snow delivers the lecture "The Two Cultures,"
                in which he analyzes the gulf between the scientific and literary-humanistic
                cultures in England.   soc

1959   American sociologist C. Wright Mills publishes *Sociological Imagination*.   soc

1960s   The emerging field of cognitive anthropology examines the structure of cul-
                tures as systems of knowledge.   ANTH

1960s–1970s   The field of postcolonial cultural studies begins to develop. It offers analytical
                "counterdiscourses" grounded in the experience of peoples who have under-
                gone European colonialization. Major works include George Lamming's *The
                Pleasures of Exile* (1960), Frantz Fanon's *The Wretched of the Earth* (*see* 1961,
                POL), Roberto Fernández Retamar's "Caliban" essays in the 1970s, and Edward
                W. Said's *Orientalism* (*see* 1978, CRIT). *See also* 1980s, CRIT.   CRIT

1960s   A "new math," which stresses conceptual learning of numerical systems, is
                introduced to school systems across the United States.   EDUC

1960s   Beginning this decade, historians sometimes do computer-aided statistical
                analyses involving huge amounts of data as part of their research. Examples
                include E. A. Wrigley's *Population and History* (1969) and Stephen Innes's *Labor
                in a New Land: Economy and Society in 17th Century Springfield* (1983).   HIST

1960s   The history of ideas becomes the basis for new degree programs at several
                American universities. Development of the discipline will continue in 1973
                with publication of the five-volume *Dictionary of the History of Ideas. See also*
                1922–1923, PHIL.   PHIL

1960s   Poststructuralism develops in France. A reaction against structuralism, its adher-
                ents include Jacques Derrida, Michel Foucault, and Julia Kristeva. The movement
                combines Saussurian linguistics, postmodernist disdain for the possibility of
                objectivity, and exploration of the roots of language in political power and
                unconscious feeling.   PHIL

1960s   Many political scientists react against behavioralism (*see* c. 1945, POL), which
                they believe overemphasized methodology and preservation of the status quo.
                They argue instead for more stress on contemporary problems and human
                values.   POL

1960s   The French word *détente* is used to refer to any movement aimed at lessen-
                ing tensions between the United States and the Soviet Union. The 1969
                Strategic Arms Limitation Talks (SALT) is a prime example of the process
                of détente.   POL

1960s   English mathematician and philosopher Bertrand Russell and French philosopher
               and writer Jean-Paul Sartre are leaders in the European movement to oppose
               American involvement in the Vietnam War.   POL

1960s   Biofeedback becomes popular as a way of helping people learn healthy
               responses to stress. The patient uses a training machine to learn how to con-
               trol such responses as heart rate, breathing, and muscle tension.   PSYCH

1960s   Encounter groups begin gaining popularity as a way of helping already healthy
               people achieve higher levels of mental health.   PSYCH

1960s   Family therapy develops as psychologists call for treatment of entire families in
               cases of abnormal family communication patterns.   PSYCH

1960s   The Irish Republican Army (IRA) mounts terrorist attacks aimed at separating
               Northern Ireland from Britain and uniting it with the Republic of Ireland.
               Protestant terrorists respond in kind against the Catholic IRA, leading to years
               of bloodshed.   REL

What Is Obscene?

In America during the decade that gave birth to *Hair*, Lenny Bruce, and *Penthouse*, challenges to the definition of obscenity were commonplace. Most cases were tried in the
marketplace or in local courts. In a few cases, however, each branch of the U.S. government grappled with the definition of obscenity. Among the decisions:

—A 1966 Supreme Court ruling (*Memoirs v. Attorney General of Massachusetts*) says that
  any material that contains "redeeming social value" cannot be censored. Material is
  to be judged obscene when, "to the average person applying contemporary standards, the dominant theme taken as a whole appeals to a prurient interest."

—A 1969 Supreme Court decision deems a Georgia antipornography law unconstitutional,
  with the majority opinion writing, "If the First Amendment means anything it means that
  a state has no business telling a man, sitting alone in his own house, what books he may
  read or what films he may watch."

—A 1970 report by the Congressional Commission on Obscenity and Pornography
  determines that pornography does not encourage crime or sexual aberration and rec-
  ommends that laws prohibiting its sale be rescinded. President Nixon disagrees with
  the findings of the "morally bankrupt" commission and vows to do what he can
  under his powers to "control and eliminate smut from our national life."

1960s   The successors to the Beat Generation (*see* 1957, soc) are the Love Generation, also known as Flower Children or hippies. Like their predecessors, they believe in living in the present and defying convention. They also advocate free sexual practices and the use of drugs, reject materialism, dabble in Eastern religion, and aim for a gentle, free, egalitarian society.   soc

1960s   In the United States, black nationalism gains strength, particularly among the younger generation. The movement, which calls for blacks to establish a separate identity based on a common African heritage, had its beginnings in the 19th century.   soc

1960   Austrian-born English art historian Ernst Gombrich reflects Aby Warburg's "formula" in *Art and Illusion*, a work that explores the means through which we perceive visual reality. These principles will be further elaborated in *The Sense of Order* (1978) and *The Image and the Eye* (1982).   crit

1960   German film historian Siegfried Kracauer publishes *Theory of Film*, a comprehensive work that promotes film's obligation to record and reveal physical reality. His argument ultimately makes it impossible for film to be an expression of an artist's formal intentions or emotions.   crit

1960   French critic Pierre Restany contributes his essay "The New Realists" for the catalog *Identité Italienne* at the Galerie Apollinaire in Milan. His thoughts deal with the world of modern consumption and the mass media and provoke the formation of the group Nouveau Réalisme in Paris.   crit

1960   American filmmaker Maya Deren publishes "Cinematography: The Creative Use of Reality" for *Daedalus*, a synthesis of realist and formalist theories to describe a program based upon photography's perceptual reality.   crit

1960   German philosopher Hans-Georg Gadamer publishes *Truth and Method*. Gadamer will be known for contributing to "reader-response" theories of literary interpretation. *See also* 1967, crit.   crit

1960   Italian philosopher Galvano della Volpe examines aesthetics in *Critique of Taste*.   crit

1960   The French journal *Tel Quel* is founded, which will become the vehicle for much of what is known as French theory, combining linguistic, semiotic, psychoanalytical, literary-critical, social, and historical strands. French thinkers associated with *Tel Quel* include Jacques Derrida, Michel Foucault, Julia Kristeva, Jacques Lacan, Roland Barthes, Gilles Deleuze, Tzvetan Todorov, Gérard Genette, and the journal's founding editor, Philippe Sollers.   crit

1960   American economist Walt Whitman Rostow publishes *The Stages of Economic Growth*. His theories of economic growth are highly influential, as will be his support for military intervention in Vietnam during his tenure as adviser to President Lyndon Johnson.   ECON

1960   American philosopher Willard Quine publishes *Word and Object*. In this and other works, he examines the implications of treating language as a logical system.   PHIL

1960   The Age of Aquarius dawns, according to astrologers, who believe that the 2,000-year period dominated by the zodiac sign of Pisces (the fishes) is ending and a transition is beginning to a new period dominated by Aquarius (the water-bearer). The Aquarian Age is predicted to be a peaceful one of harmony and understanding.   PHIL

1960   Aid from the Soviet Union to China is terminated as the two communist powers are dvided by an ideological rift, with the Soviets more inclined toward conciliation with the West.   POL

1960   French philosopher and writer Jean-Paul Sartre, for decades a committed left-wing activist, expounds his political philosophy in *Critique de la dialectique*.   POL

1960   American sociologist W. Lloyd Warner and his colleagues publish *Social Class in America*, a study of how social class is perceived in a small New England community. The authors found that residents considered church and club affiliation, residential location, and other variables in addition to economic standing in perceptions of class.   SOC

1960   American sociologist William Goode writes "A Theory of Role Strain," a paper asserting that some conflict within an individual's set of role obligations is virtually unavoidable. The paper represents an implicit reply to functional theorists, who tend to assume roles are typically integrated without tension.   SOC

1960   In England, Enovid 10 becomes the first commercially available oral contraceptive. It and its successors will be important elements in fostering a more open attitude toward sexuality.   SOC

1961   French philosopher Maurice Merleau-Ponty publishes his essay "Eye and Mind," in which he applies neo-Marxist theory to the task of revising phenomenological concepts of perception.   CRIT

1961   American art critic Clement Greenberg publishes "Modernist Painting," an essay that epitomizes the modernist critical agenda with respect to the visual arts.   CRIT

1961   American critic Wayne C. Booth publishes *The Rhetoric of Fiction*, which intro-
           duces the notion of an "implied author" and criticizes the aesthetic tradition
           stemming from American writer Henry James.   CRIT

1961   French critic René Girard publishes *Deceit, Desire, and the Novel*, which con-
           siders the nature of desire in the works of several great European novelists.   CRIT

1961   American historian John Hope Franklin publishes *Reconstruction After the Civil
           War*, in which he challenges the conventional wisdom about the post–Civil
           War period by discussing the positive contributions of Northerners who
           moved to the South and of Southern blacks and whites. Franklin's balanced
           view will greatly influence Reconstruction scholars. He will publish *The
           Emancipation Proclamation* in 1963. *See also* 1947, HIST.   HIST

1961   French philosopher Michel Foucault publishes *Madness and Civilization: A
           History of Insanity in the Age of Reason*. Combining history, philosophy, linguis-
           tics, and psychoanalysis, this and other works by Foucault analyze social insti-
           tutions and fields of learning (particularly science) as instruments of power
           and control.   HIST

1961   Czech-born American philosopher Ernest Nagel publishes *The Structure of
           Science*, which maintains an empiricist view of scientific theory.   PHIL

1961   In his farewell address, U.S. president Dwight Eisenhower coins the term "mil-
           itary-industrial complex" to refer to the growing military establishment and its
           interdependence with American industry and public policy.   POL

1961   Martinique-born psychiatrist Frantz Fanon publishes *The Wretched of the Earth*,
           which advocates the use of violence in overthrowing colonial domination. His
           views will influence black nationalism in the coming years.   POL

1961   American political scientist Robert Dahl publishes *Who Governs? Democracy
           and Power in an American City*, the most influential study of political power in
           an American community to date. Dahl argues that all power is not controlled
           by a single ruling elite but dispersed among various decision-making groups. POL

1961   American political scientist Sidney Verba publishes *Small Groups and Political
           Behavior*, a basic work on how power is distributed in small groups.   POL

1961   English philosopher of law Herbert Lionel Hart publishes *The Concept of Law*, in
           which he argues that law is a system of rules embedded in social practice.   POL

1961   Pope John XXIII issues the encyclicals *Mater et Magistra* and *Pacem in Terris*, in
           which he calls for social reform, workers' rights, aid to poor nations, and world
           peace.   REL

1961	American sociologist Dennis Wrong publishes *The Oversocialized Conception of Man*, an essay decrying the tendency to account for behavior with sociological categories to the exclusion of an individual's free will. **soc**
1961	American sociologist George Homans publishes *Social Behavior: Its Elementary Forms*, a study of the basic structures of human associations. Homans uses behaviorism as his main explanatory tool and rejects the idea that social systems exist as a reality apart from the persons they comprise. **soc**
1961	Canadian-born American sociologist Erving Goffman publishes *Asylums*, a study of mental hospitals that introduces the idea of total institutions, social organizations that dominate and resocialize individuals. **soc**
1961	Hungarian-born American psychiatrist Thomas Szasz publishes *The Myth of Mental Illness*, insisting that mental illness is a term applied by agents of control to describe behavior that violates standard norms. **soc**
1961	American sociologists Richard Cloward and Lloyd Ohlin publish *Delinquency and Opportunity*. Extending Robert Merton's early work in *Social Structure and Anomie*, the authors maintain that deviance is encouraged by varying access even to illegitimate routes to success. **soc**
1962	French anthropologist Claude Lévi-Strauss publishes *The Savage Mind*. Later works will include *The Raw and the Cooked* (1964). **ANTH**
1962	English anthropologist Victor Turner publishes *Forest of Symbols*, an influential work on African ritual and symbolism. **ANTH**
1962	American critic George Kubler publishes *The Shape of Time*, a work that seeks to broaden the conception of art history beyond the Wölfflinian understanding of evolving styles. **CRIT**
1962	American painter Ad Reinhardt publishes "Art as Art," an essay employing a series of negations to resist the need to find meaning in abstract art. **CRIT**
1962	American film critic Andrew Sarris publishes his famous "Notes on the *Auteur* Theory in 1962," an essay outlining the premises that distinguish a director's personality and technical competence over individual films. Sarris's auteur theory will claim American cinema as consistently superior to that of the rest of the world. Sarris will further articulate auteurism in *The American Cinema* (1968) and "Notes on the *Auteur* Theory in 1972." **CRIT**
1962	In a U.S. Supreme Court ruling, the ban on prayer in public schools is upheld. The constitutional separation of church and state is the basis for the decision. **EDUC**

1962   French historian Philippe Aries publishes *Centuries of Childhood: A Social History of Family Life*, a landmark work in the relatively new field of family history. Other significant books in this area will include John Demos's *Little Commonwealth: Family Life in Plymouth Colony* (1970), Edward Shorter's *The Making of the Modern Family* (1975), and Elizabeth Pleck's *Domestic Tyranny: The Making of American Social Policy Against Family Violence from Colonial Times to the Present* (1989).   HIST

1962–1966   In China, the discipline of history is neglected, with only about 50 new historical titles published each year, compared to between 200 and 300 annually in the 1950s.   HIST

1962   *Sense and Sensibilia* and *How to Do Things with Words,* by English linguistic philosopher John Langshaw Austin, are published posthumously. Before his death in 1960, he was a leading figure in the linguistic philosophy movement (also known as Oxford or "ordinary language" philosophy).   LING

1962   *Studies in Empirical Philosophy,* by Scottish-born Australian philosopher John Anderson, is published posthumously.   PHIL

1962   American philosopher of science Thomas Kuhn publishes *The Structure of Scientific Revolutions*, in which he examines the process by which a scientific paradigm, or system of assumptions, is replaced by another.   PHIL

1962   American behaviorist Abraham Maslow publishes *Toward a Psychology of Being.* In this work, as in his earlier *Motivation and Personality* (1954), he distinguishes two types of human motivation: deficiency motivation, the need for shelter, food, and water; and growth motivation, the striving for knowledge and self-actualization.   PSYCH

1962   English philosopher Charles Dunbar Broad publishes *Lectures on Psychical Research,* in which he seriously considers psychic phenomena.   PSYCH

1962–1965   The Second Vatican Council (Vatican II) is convened by Pope John XXIII and completed under Pope Paul VI. Aimed at the renewal of the church in the modern world, it includes observers from Protestant and Eastern Orthodox denominations, encourages ecumenicism, and institutes many reforms. The council's statements encourage greater lay participation in the church, introduce the use of the vernacular rather than Latin in the liturgy, and denounce anti-Semitism.   REL

1962   American political activist Michael Harrington publishes *The Other America,* in which he describes the extent of poverty in the United States. The book is credited with sparking the "War on Poverty."   SOC

| 1962 | American sociologist Alvin Gouldner publishes *Anti-Minotaur: The Myth of a Value-Free Sociology*, a paper urging sociologists to act on political issues. The paper is a reply to Max Weber's view that the social sciences must refrain from such nonscientific judgments. **soc** |

| 1962 | American sociologist Herbert Gans publishes *Urban Villagers*, a study that counters the idea of cities as overwhelming, impersonal places. Gans identifies various types of communities likely to arise in the urban context. **soc** |

| 1962 | American sociologist Neil Smelser publishes *Theory of Collective Behavior*, a study of how various "value-added" conditions combine to produce various large-group outcomes. Smelser is a student of Talcott Parsons (*see* 1937, 1951, and 1955, **soc**). **soc** |

| 1963 | Nigerian critic Obiajunwa Wali publishes the article "The Dead End of African Literature?," in which he decries the cultural domination of African letters by the West. **CRIT** |

| 1963 | American film critic Pauline Kael provides a harsh, point-by-point critique of Andrew Sarris's auteur theory (*see* 1962, **CRIT**) in her essay "Circles and Squares: Joys and Sarris," claiming that a great artist continues to create new standards and rises above technical incompetence. Sarris responds later this year with "The *Auteur* Theory and the Perils of Pauline." **CRIT** |

| 1963 | American filmmaker Stan Brakhage argues that the supposed reality of the photographic image is itself a conventionalized illusion in his essay "Metaphors on Vision." **CRIT** |

| 1963 | Russian critic M. M. Bakhtin publishes a revised version of his *Problems of Dostoevsky's Poetics*, first published in 1929. In it, he introduces the concept of "unfinalizability," the openness of human potential that he finds best represented in novels. **CRIT** |

| 1963 | French writer Alain Robbe-Grillet publishes *Towards a New Novel*, which makes him a leading figure in the French New Wave movement in literature (affiliated with the New Wave movement in film). **CRIT** |

| 1963 | German philosopher Jürgen Habermas, a proponent of the Frankfurt School (*see* 1923, **PHIL**) of critical Marxist theory, publishes *Theory and Practice*. **PHIL** |

| 1963 | American philosopher Ernest Gettier presents exceptions to the long-standing definition of knowledge as true belief justified by a reason; these exceptions will be known as the Gettier examples. **PHIL** |

1963   American philosopher Wilfrid Sellars publishes the paper "Empiricism and
           the Philosophy of Mind," in which he introduces the approach known as func-
           tionalism: defining mental states by their relations to their causes, other men-
           tal states, and behavior. Sellars examines the nature of experience and thought
           in many works, including the collections *Science, Perception, and Reality* (1963)
           and *Essays in Philosophy and Its History* (1974).   PHIL

1963   English-born Australian philosopher J. J. Smart publishes *Philosophy and
           Scientific Realism*.   PHIL

1963   Five years of negotiations pay off when representatives of Great Britain, the
           United States, and the Soviet Union meet in Moscow to sign the limited nuclear
           test-ban treaty, which forbids nuclear weapons testing in the atmosphere,
           under water, and in space.   POL

1963   The word *psychedelic* is coined. Originally meaning "mind-manifesting," it
           will become associated with drug intoxication, visual hallucinations, and the
           subculture that values such experiences.   PSYCH

1963   Following an ancient Chinese Mahayana Buddhist practice, some Vietnamese
           Buddhist monks burn themselves to death in protest against persecution by
           the government of Ngo Dinh Diem, who is assassinated on November 1.   REL

1963–1978   Paul VI reigns as pope. He presides over the close of Vatican II (*see* 1962–1965,
           REL) and implements many of its reforms, while also reasserting papal prima-
           cy and taking a conservative stand on such issues as birth control, divorce,
           priestly celibacy, and the role of women in the church. *See also* 1968, REL.   REL

1963   English theologian John A. T. Robinson publishes *Honest to God*.   REL

1963   British theologian Thomas J. Altizer's *The Gospel of Christian Atheism* is among
           the works urging acceptance of the consequences of 19th-century German
           philosopher Friedrich Nietzsche's ideas concerning the "death of God." Other
           radical theologians attempting to work out a form of progressive religion with-
           out a personal God include Paul Van Buren and William Hamilton.   REL

1963   German-born American psychologist Stanley Milgram publishes "Behavioral
           Study of Obedience", an account of experiments concerning the willingness
           of people to follow extreme orders under duress (*see* 1950s, PSYCH). It is con-
           sidered one of the most controversial studies in social science history because
           of the stress imposed on its subjects, and the results lead to the placing of var-
           ious controls on university experiments.   SOC

1963   American sociologist Howard Becker publishes *Outsiders*, a set of essays pro-
           moting labeling theory. This approach to deviant behavior asserts that

deviance does not inhere in a social act, but rather must be labeled as such by persons capable of enforcing the definition.   soc

1963   American sociologist Philip Slater publishes "On Social Regression," a psy-choanalytically based article on the ways in which society pressures its members not to withdraw from the wider community.   soc

1963   In response to post–World War II stratification of the sexes, American writer Betty Friedan publishes *The Feminine Mystique.* In the book, she calls women's dismissal and subsequent alienation from society "the problem that has no name." Her work is credited with helping to found contemporary feminism.   soc

---

The Problem That Has No Name

Once the confetti hit the ground on V-J Day, millions of women who had built air-planes and fixed phones were dismissed from their jobs to make room for returning GIs. While some women took less prestigious positions at lower pay, many others believed their new civic duty was at home, raising the children of the victors and main-taining their households. The 1950s cult of domesticity held that women's fulfillment required neither intellectual exercise nor remuneration. The home, preferably in an isolated suburban development, was all.

But in 1957 a Smith College alumna writing a magazine article on the dreams of her graduating class 15 years later was astonished at the discontent she found. Despite family pleasures, the women felt trapped, isolated, and unfulfilled. They felt like the author herself, a former labor writer and Greenwich Village resident named Betty Goldstein Friedan.

For the next several years, Friedan shuttled between her suburban home and three children to research and write at the New York Public Library three days a week. The result of her efforts was *The Feminine Mystique* (1963), which posed the nagging ques-tion on the minds of thousands of postwar women: "As she made the bed, shopped for groceries, matched slip cover materials, ate peanut butter sandwiches with her chil-dren, chauffeured Cub Scouts and Brownies, lay beside her husband at night, she was afraid to ask of herself the silent question—'Is this all?'" This, Friedan wrote, was "the problem that has no name." It was sustained, she alleged, in part by the women's mag-azines, which purveyed an image of fulfilling family life, and in part by society as a whole, which bought this image.

Friedan's analysis touched a nerve, eventually resulting in the sale of three million copies of *The Feminine Mystique.* In giving voice to a nameless problem, she became a catalyst for the "second wave" of the feminist movement.

1963   American sociologists Nathan Glazer and Daniel Patrick Moynihan publish *Beyond the Melting Pot*, a study of New York City's ethnic groups. The authors try to dispel the popular idea that ethnicities tend to lose their identity over time.   soc

1963   At a civil rights march on Washington, D.C., American civil rights leader Martin Luther King Jr. delivers what will become known as his "I Have a Dream" speech: "I still have a dream. It is a dream deeply rooted in the American dream that one day this nation will rise up and live out the true meaning of its creed—'We hold these truths to be self-evident, that all men are created equal.'"   soc

1964   American critic Leo Marx writes on American culture in *The Machine in the Garden: Technology and the Pastoral Ideal in America*.   crit

1964   French critic Roland Barthes publishes *Elements of Semiology*.   crit

1964   Canadian social critic Marshall McLuhan publishes *Understanding Media*, a study of the impact of the information explosion and new mass media on society and culture. His other works include *The Mechanical Bride* (1951) and *The Gutenberg Galaxy* (1962).   crit

1964   American critic and art historian Michael Fried amends Clement Greenberg's account of modernism (*see* 1961, crit) with "Modernist Painting and Formal Criticism."   crit

1964   The Centre for Contemporary Cultural Studies is founded at the University of Birmingham in England, marking the rise of this new interdisciplinary field of study, which focuses on social and ideological aspects of cultural products.   crit

1964   American historian Richard Hofstadter publishes *Anti-Intellectualism in American Life*, a study of the persistent antipathy to intellectuals throughout the nation's history.   hist

1964   By now, more than 2,000 characters in Chinese script have been simplified by China's government, in an effort to reform the complex system of writing. ling

1964   German-born American political philosopher Herbert Marcuse publishes *One-Dimensional Man*. In this and other works, Marcuse argues that Western democracies have replaced traditional restraints on freedom with new types of repression based on consumer capitalism and manipulation of tastes by the mass media. Marcuse's claim that revolution must come from such elements as students and minorities proves highly influential among radicals in the 1960s.   pol

1964   The first edition of the *World Handbook of Political and Social Indicators*, the most comprehensive collection of cross-national data to date, is published.   POL

1964   The Palestine Liberation Organization (PLO) is founded by a number of Arab guerrilla groups dedicated to recapturing Palestine from Israel. Led by Yasir Arafat, the group becomes known for terrorist activities, including bombings and hijackings.   POL

1964   The U.S. Congress passes the Civil Rights Act of 1964, the most sweeping civil rights legislation to date. Because previous Civil Rights Acts (1866, 1870, 1871, 1875, 1957, and 1960) had failed to guarantee equal rights for all Americans, the civil rights movement of the 1950s and early 1960s culminated in the 1964 Civil Rights Act, which outlaws discrimination on the basis of race, color, religion, or national origin (but not sex except for Title VII). Title VII of the Civil Rights Act, which establishes the Equal Employment Opportunity Commission (EEOC), forbids discrimination in employment on the basis of race., color, religion, sex, or national origin. The EEOC will have a mandate to enforce, among other laws, Title VII, the Equal Pay Act of 1963, and various statutes protecting the rights of Americans with disabilities. The Voting Rights Act of 1965 will forbid discrimination at the polls, and the Civil Rights Act of 1968 will apply to housing and real estate. *See also* 1972, POL.   POL

1964   Canadian psychologist Eric Berne publishes *Games People Play*. As the founder of transactional analysis, he shows how people can exchange feelings and thoughts more effectively.   PSYCH

1964   The Sacred Hall in Tokyo is opened by members of Risshokoseikai, a Nichiren Buddhist movement.   REL

1964   American sociologist Peter Blau publishes *Exchange and Power in Social Life*, an explanation of social life tied to the exchange model of behavior. The model studies how persons seek to maximize benefits in relationships through a system of mutually rewarding exchanges.   SOC

1964   American sociologists Robert Hodge, Paul Siegel, and Peter Rossi publish "Occupational Prestige in the United States, 1925–1963," a paper showing only small changes in occupational prestige evaluations over time.   SOC

1964   The free speech movement among students at the University of California at Berkeley anticipates the campus unrest and antiwar protests of the late 1960s. SOC

1965   American artist Allan Kaprow, a leading figure among the New York avant-garde, publishes *Assemblages, Environments, and Happenings* to promote a more synthetic art form involving performances.   CRIT

1965   English art critic and novelist John Peter Berger emerges as one of the most
              original writers on art since World War II upon publication of *Success and
              Failure of Picasso*, a work that relates the artist to society. In 1973 he will pub-
              lish *Ways of Seeing*.   CRIT

1965   American film critic Pauline Kael promotes the relevancy of a critic's own life
              experiences and knowlege of other arts in her book *I Lost It at the Movies*.   CRIT

1965   Russian critic M. M. Bakhtin publishes *Rabelais and His World*, the first of his
              works to gain attention in the United States. Bakhtin's critical theory emphasizes
              creativity, ethical responsibility, and a concept of truth as dialogue. In certain
              works, such as the essay "Discourse in the Novel," he develops the approach
              called prosaics, which focuses on small and prosaic events as described in nov-
              els and other prose works.   CRIT

1965   In China, prominent historian Wu Han writes a historical drama, *The Dismissal
              of Hai Rui*, which is covertly critical of Chinese leader Mao Zedong; China's
              government condemns Wu in response. In the Cultural Revolution that fol-
              lows (*see* 1966–1969, POL), history will be one of many academic disci-
              plines to be suppressed.   HIST

1965   In China, a trial edition of a comprehensive dictionary, the *Xiandai hanyu cid-
              ian*, is published, though general publication will be hampered for years as a
              result of the turmoil during and after the Cultural Revolution (*see* 1966–1969,
              POL).   LING

1965   French Marxist philosopher Louis Althusser publishes *For Marx* and *Reading
              Capital*, in which he combines structuralism and dialectical materialism to
              argue that the subject and its apparent actions are simply the locus of warring
              social forces.   PHIL

1965   Argentinian-born leftist revolutionary Ernesto "Ché" Guevara publishes
              Guerrilla Warfare, a manual for rebels. Having helped Cuban revolutionary
              Fidel Castro come to power (*see* 1959, POL), he will fight as a guerrilla in the
              Congo before being executed in Bolivia in 1967. His teachings and example
              will be an inspiration to revolutionaries throughout the world.   POL

1965   English philosopher of law Herbert Lionel Hart publishes *The Morality of the
              Criminal Law*, which emphasizes the limits of law in sexual and other moral
              matters.   POL

1965   American feminist Betty Friedan, author of *The Feminine Mystique* (*see* 1963,
              SOC), founds with several others the National Organization for Women, which
              will work for passage of the Equal Rights Amendment (*see* 1972, POL) and other
              women's rights legislation.   POL

1965   Austrian psychoanalyst Anna Freud publishes *Normality and Pathology in Childhood*, a summation of her theories on child psychotherapy and prevention of mental illness.   PSYCH

1965   American pediatrician and psychoanalyst Donald Winnicott presents infancy as a critical time in human development relevant to later psychopathology. Winnicott stresses the importance of "good enough" mothering.   PSYCH

1965   The Roman Catholic and Eastern Orthodox churches officially remove their anathemas of excommunication from one another.   REL

1965   In Los Angeles, California, Hindu teacher Swami Pradhupada founds the International Society of Krishna Consciousness.   REL

1965   American sociologist Daniel Patrick Moynihan publishes *The Negro Family*, alleging that impaired family structures have brought about many of the difficulties besetting African-Americans. Moynihan, a Democrat from New York, will be elected to the U.S. Senate in 1976.   SOC

1965   In February, Muslim minister and black nationalist Malcolm X (born Malcolm Little) is assassinated in New York City. Originally a supporter of black separatism, he later came to see possibilities for racial coexistence in the United States. In life and death, he was a leading voice for black power, control, and freedom. His book *The Autobiography of Malcolm X* (as told to Alex Haley), published in 1964, will continue to serve as an inspiration.   SOC

1966   American anthropologist Oscar Lewis publishes *La Vida*, a study of Mexican society that advances the concept of "the culture of poverty." Lewis holds that values transmitted from parent to child help instill a mindset of poverty, making it difficult for the poor to overcome their circumstances.   ANTH

1966   American writer Ralph Ellison publishes *Shadow and Art*, in which he relates racial issues to American democracy and the novelist's art.   CRIT

1966   American writer and philosopher Susan Sontag publishes *Against Interpretation*, in which she argues that art should be an emotional and sensuous rather than intellectual experience. The collection of essays includes one in which she examines the concept of "camp." Sontag will become known as an observer and promoter of the avant-garde. Later works will include *Styles of Radical Will* (1969).   CRIT

1966   Austrian-born English art historian Ernst Gombrich publishes *Norm and Form*, a collection of 20 essays on the Italian Renaissance that emphasizes the revival of classicism in art, literature, and ideas. His thoughts will be further elaborated in *Symbolic Images* (1972).   CRIT

1966   American film critic Stanley Kauffmann publishes *A World on Film,* a collection of his reviews from the *New Republic* dating back to 1958. His attitude is skeptical about aesthetic values and the distinction of standards between film and life. Another collection, *Figures of Light,* will be published in 1970.   CRIT

1966   American critic Katharine M. Rogers examines literature from a feminist perspective in *The Troublesome Helpmate: A History of Misogyny in Literature.*   CRIT

1966   American sociologist Daniel Bell publishes *The Reforming of General Education,* which posits that the aim of liberal education is to refine and enlarge a student's ability to engage in inquiry. He says, "All knowledge, thus, is liberal . . . when it is committed to continuing inquiry."   EDUC

1966   The Freedom of Information Act is signed into law by President Lyndon B. Johnson. The act makes a great number of previously classified government documents available to the public. It will be a particular boon for historians studying Cold War policies and practices.   HIST

1966   French philosopher Michel Foucault publishes *The Order of Things.* He will publish *The Archaeology of Knowledge* in 1969.   HIST

1966   American linguist Noam Chomsky publishes *Cartesian Linguistics,* in which he develops the rationalist, antiempiricist implications of his linguistic views (*see* 1957, LING).   LING

1966–1974   French linguist Émile Benveniste publishes *Problems in General Linguistics,* a collection of essays originally published from 1939 to 1972. In these, he develops theories of communication and reference that greatly influence contemporary critical theory.   LING

1966   German philosopher Theodor Adorno publishes *Negative Dialectics.*   PHIL

1966   English philosopher Peter Strawson publishes *The Bounds of Sense,* in which he reexamines Kantian metaphysics. His work tends to defend the common-sense way of perceiving oneself and the world.   PHIL

1966–1969   Chinese leader Mao Zedong leads the Cultural Revolution, a violent movement to restore Communist purity by purging the nation of cultural and intellectual influences deemed bourgeois.   POL

1966   American gynecologist William Howell Masters and American psychologist Virginia Johnson publish *Human Sexual Response,* their first report on human sexual activity. They will become known for their methods of sex therapy.   PSYCH

1966–1971	French psychoanalyst Jacques Lacan publishes *Écrits*, his collected lectures. Lacan's combination of Freudian thought and Saussurian linguistics proves highly influential in literary theory, among other fields. PSYCH
1966	American sociologist Thomas Scheff publishes *Being Mentally Ill: A Sociological Theory*, a study of which persons are identified as being mentally ill, and which are not. The book draws heavily on labeling theory. SOC
1966	American sociologist James Coleman and his colleagues issue *The Coleman Report*, a government-sponsored study of public schools which finds that students' scores on standardized tests are affected more by their values than by their educational environment. The report features complex quantitative methods. SOC
1966	American sociologists Peter Berger and Thomas Luckmann publish *The Social Construction of Reality*, an examination of how the everyday sense of reality is sustained by society's members. SOC
1966	American sociologist Gerhard Lenski publishes *Power and Privilege: A Theory of Social Stratification*. In this study of the evolution of classes, Lenski postulates that modernization brings long-term pressure toward greater equality. SOC
1966	American poet and critic Imamu Amiri Baraka (born LeRoi Jones) reflects on the African-American experience in *Home: Social Essays*. SOC
1966	English feminist scholar Juliet Mitchell examines the relation of women to socialist theory in "Women: The Longest Revolution." She will expand the work as *Woman's Estate* (1971), which includes a history of women's liberation movements. Later works will include *Psychoanalysis and Feminism* (1974). SOC
1967	African American playwright and critic Loften Mitchell publishes *Black Drama*, a personal memoir which becomes the most complete history of African American theater. CRIT
1967	American film and drama critic John Simon publishes *Private Screenings*, a work that finds few films are genuine works of art through his definitions of art, pseudoart, nonart, and entertainment. He will later publish *Movies into Film* (1971) and *Ingmar Bergman Directs* (1972). CRIT
1967	American art historian Michael Fried publishes "Art and Objecthood," an essay that underscores the abstractionist tendency of modernism's characteristics and virtues. CRIT
1967	In his *Of Grammatology*, French philosopher Jacques Derrida introduces the critical approach called deconstructionism, which rests on the impossibility of

finding a single, coherent meaning in a text. Derrida's method depends on uncovering contradictions within a text that subvert its superficial meaning. He also argues against "phonocentrism," the privileging of speech over writing by expecting that the author can say what the text is intended to mean. Other seminal deconstructionist works by Derrida include *Writing and Difference* (1967), *Speech and Phenomena* (1967), *Margins of Philosophy* (1972), and *Dissemination* (1972).　　　　CRIT

1967　American critic Stanley Fish publishes *Surprised by Sin: The Reader in "Paradise Lost,"* which initiates a new movement he calls reader-response criticism.　CRIT

1967　American hermeneuticist E. D. Hirsch Jr. publishes *Validity in Interpretation*, in which he distinguishes between a literary work's meaning, which is fixed and objective, and its significance, which is subjective and changes with the place and time of the reader.　　　　CRIT

1967–1982　American historian Dumas Malone publishes his massive six-volume biography of Thomas Jefferson, running from *Jefferson the Virginian* through *Jefferson and His Time: The Sage of Monticello*. It is perhaps the most thoroughly researched, comprehensive biography of an American political figure ever written.　　　　HIST

1967–1968　The Anglo-American journals *Style* (1967) and *Language and Style* (1968) are founded, marking the introduction of stylistics in Britain and the United States as a distinct field of study related to linguistics.　　LING

1967　American philosopher Richard Rorty edits *The Linguistic Turn*, an important introduction to analytical philosophy. Rorty will be known for his postmodernist skepticism about truth and knowledge and his ironic, detached attitude.　PHIL

1967　English philosopher Philippa Foot proposes the ethical dilemma known as the "trolley problem" in the paper "The Problem of Abortion and the Doctrine of the Double Effect." Envisioning a situation in which a runaway trolley is threatening the lives of several people working on a track, Foot asks whether a bystander should switch the trolley down a track where only one person is threatened.　　　　PHIL

1967　*Quotations from Chairman Mao Zedong* is published. Distributed widely in a "little red book," the Chinese leader's sayings inspire adulation at home and inform radicals and guerrillas in many countries abroad.　　　　POL

1967　American psychologist Aaron T. Beck designs the Beck Depression Inventory (BDI), a test to measure the extent of a person's depression.　　PSYCH

1967   American sociologist Elliot Liebow publishes *Tally's Corner*, a celebrated rebuttal to the culture-of-poverty thesis. Liebow studied street-corner denizens in Washington, D.C., concluding that their economic situation was brought about by discrimination and lack of opportunity, not by defeatist values. **soc**

1967   American sociologist Harold Garfinkel publishes *Studies in Ethnomethodology*, a look at the ways in which persons make their actions intelligible to others, and the role of context in supplying the means for doing so. **soc**

1967   American sociologist Robert N. Bellah publishes *Civil Religion*, advancing the notion that America as a nation possesses a generic, unaffiliated public religion. This faith is promoted through such credos as the Pledge of Allegiance. **soc**

1967   The American sociologists Peter Blau and Otis Dudley Duncan publish *The American Occupational Structure*, a cross-generational study of 20,000 American men and their fathers. The authors argue that class mobility as measured from fathers to sons is largely restricted to the same general occupational brackets, with little movement into different categories. **soc**

The Ruling Class?

Determining what makes a good leader has changed drastically over the course of history. To Greek philosopher Plato, writing in Book 5 of *The Republic* (fourth century B.C.), the only worthy ruler of a just society is the "philosopher king," who seeks the truth and has attained the greatest good. To English romantic poet Percy Bysshe Shelley, writing in *A Defence of Poetry* (1821), "Poets are the unacknowledged legislators of the world."

In modern nations, however, the ruler is neither poet nor philosopher but the professional legislator, trained in the workings of government and willing to devote part of a lifetime in service to a country. Over the short history of the United States, the perception of such leaders has devolved from statesmen, who upheld the Constitution and the Bill of Rights, to mere politicians, categorized in the 1920s by American journalist H. L. Mencken as "plainly and depressingly inferior, both in common sense and in common decency."

In recent decades, public opinion of politicians has grown even worse than that expressed by Mencken, with callers ranting on radio talk shows and voters evicting seasoned politicians from their lifelong posts. Even the politicians themselves have joined in the ridicule: a famous exchange saw one senator chastise another with the epithet, "You're no John Kennedy."

If philosophers, poets, and politicians are incapable, the question still remains: who shall rule?

1967   Former Harvard professor Timothy Leary crystallizes youthful interest in mind-altering substances when he tells a group of 20,000 young adults, "Turn on to the scene, tune in to what is happening, and drop out—of high school, college, junior executive—and follow me, the hard way." A shortened version will become a generation's rallying cry—"Turn on, tune in, and drop out."
SOC

1968   Anthropologist Napoléon Chagnon publishes *The Fierce People*, a classic study of the militaristic Yanomamo people of South America.
ANTH

1968   French philosopher Gaston Bachelard writes on the poetic imagination in *La Psychoanalyse du feu* (*The Psychoanalysis of Fire*), one of several works in which he applies to literature Jungian views regarding archetypes and the collective unconcious.
CRIT

1968   French film semiotician Christian Metz publishes *Film Language: A Semiotics of the Cinema*, a work that sets out the specific terms of how films produce meaning and the nature of cinematic language. In 1971 he will publish *Language and Cinema*, a further elaboration of his concerns.
CRIT

1968   Italian semiotician and critic Umberto Eco publishes *La struttura assente*, in which he critiques existing forms of structuralism and semiotics and sets forth his own position. Eco will translate into English and revise this work as *A Theory of Semiotics* (1976). His many works include critiques of mass culture and novels, most notably *The Name of the Rose* (1980), which incorporates many of his scholarly concerns.
CRIT

1968   American critic Mary Ellmann publishes *Thinking About Women*, in which she analyzes the subordinate place given in the literary canon to books by women.
CRIT

1968   French-born American writer and educator Jacques Barzun publishes *The American University*.
EDUC

1968   Brazilian educator Paolo Freire publishes *Pedagogy of the Oppressed*, an argument and methodology for the teaching of critical awareness in all people. He bases his book on his work with peasants in the developing world.
EDUC

1968   The Nuclear Nonproliferation Treaty, meant to stem the spread of nuclear weapons technology, is approved by the United Nations General Assembly. POL

1968   American antiwar activists, including college students, begin leading large-scale protests against the country's involvement in the Vietnam War. Vocal congressional opponents include Senators Robert Kennedy and Eugene McCarthy. Sizable demonstrations are held in Washington, D.C.; on major college campuses; and at the Democratic National Convention in Chicago, which turns violent as police confront demonstrators. Antiwar forces will be galvanized in May 1970 when four students are killed by U.S. National Guard troops at Kent State University in Ohio.   POL

1968   Although the Tet offensive by North Vietnamese forces against numerous South Vietnamese cities is ultimately unsuccessful, it is nonetheless considered a turning point in the Vietnam War because it demonstrates beyond a doubt the formerly downplayed strength of North Vietnam.   POL

1968   On March 16, American troops under Lieutenant William L. Calley Jr. massacre hundreds of Vietnamese civilians in the village of My Lai in South Vietnam. The American public will not learn of the atrocities for another 20 months. The soldiers' defense, that they were only following orders, will bring to mind issues of conscience brought up during the Nuremberg trials of Nazi war criminals (*see* 1949, POL).   POL

1968   Soviet troops invade Czechoslovakia on August 20, quashing the hopes of all who had welcomed the relaxation of Communist Party control during this year's "Prague Spring."   POL

1968   American behaviorist psychologist B. F. Skinner publishes *The Technique of Teaching*, in which he presents his technique of programmed instruction, built on behaviorist principles. It will be the basis of many teaching machines.   PSYCH

1968   Pope Paul VI issues the encyclical *Humanae Vitae*, in which he reaffirms the church's condemnation of artificial contraceptives. His position brings protests from many in the church.   REL

1968   The American social psychologists Robert Rosenthal and Lenore Jacobson publish *Pygmalion in the Classroom*, a study of the ways in which teacher expectations and perceptions affect student performance.   SOC

1968   The Kerner Commission, headed by Illinois governor Otto Kerner, publishes its findings after the urban riots of 1968. The commission states that racial divisions are producing what are in effect two nations within the United States.   SOC

1968   The assassination of Martin Luther King Jr. on April 4 in Memphis, Tennessee, incites riots in a number of American cities.   SOC

1968   The American Indian Movement (AIM) is founded in Minneapolis, Minnesota, as a militant group demanding civil rights for Native Americans. Protests involving AIM members will include the occupation of Alcatraz Island in 1969–1971 and of Wounded Knee, South Dakota, in 1973.   SOC

1968   Iranian scholar Seyyed Hossein Nasr publishes *Science and Civilization in Islam*. In Muslim countries, the book stimulates a renewed interest in science as a component of Islamic civilization.   SOC

1968   American feminist Ti-Grace Atkinson breaks away from the National Organization for Women to form a more radical feminist group. During the late 1960s and early 1970s, groups such as hers will emphasize analysis of patriarchal structures and militant action.   SOC

1969   English film critic Peter Wollen publishes his highly influential *Signs and Meaning in the Cinema*, a book that examines the relationship of the cinema to the other arts through Eisenstein's theories, the auteur theory, and the study of signs. It will be enlarged and revised in 1972.   CRIT

1969   Bulgarian-born French linguist Julia Kristeva publishes *Semeiotike: Recherches pour une semanalysis*, a critique of Western assumptions about language and the sign. In 1970 she will become a member of the editorial board of the avant-garde review *Tel Quel*.   CRIT

1969   French philosopher Michel Foucault publishes the essay "What Is an Author," which delivers a structuralist attack on the "privilege" of the author in modernism.   CRIT

1969   French writer Philippe Jullian publishes *Dreamers of Decadence*, a study of surrealist painters.   CRIT

1969   Joseph Kosuth publishes "Art after Philosophy" for *Studio International* in London, a revision of art history which places Marcel Duchamp's ready-mades as the initiation of modern art and successfully promotes the avant-garde concern of "art as idea."   CRIT

1969   Algerian-born French feminist scholar Hélène Cixous publishes *Dedans (Inside)*. Her later works will include *Révolutions pour plus d'un Faust* (1975). Associated with the Psych et Po (psychology and politics) movement in Paris in the 1960s and 1970s, she emphasizes psychoanalytic themes in developing a feminist literary theory.   CRIT

1969   American philosopher Stanley Cavell publishes *Must We Mean What We Say?*, a collection of studies linking aesthetics, literary criticism, and the philosophy of language.   CRIT

1969   French critic Tzvetan Todorov introduces the term *narratology* in *Grammaire du Décaméron*. The term refers to the structuralist study of narratives as rule-governed systems.   CRIT

1969	English linguist Geoffrey N. Leech applies linguistic methodologies to literary texts in *A Linguistic Guide to English Poetry*. With English critic Roger Fowler, he will later publish *Linguistic Criticism* (1986). <div align="right">LING</div>
1969	The U.S. Air Force Project Bluebook, which has been investigating reports of unidentified flying objects (UFOs), closes operations after determining that most of the reports were unfounded. The independent Condon Committee reached a similar conclusion in 1968. Even so, belief in the extraterrestrial origin of UFOs will remain strong among many people. *See also* 1947, MISC. <div align="right">MISC</div>
1969	American philosopher Willard Quine publishes *Philosophy of Logic*. <div align="right">PHIL</div>
1969	American philosopher David Lewis publishes *Convention: A Philosophical Study*. <div align="right">PHIL</div>
1969	Strategic Arms Limitation Talks (SALT) begin between the United States and the Soviet Union. <div align="right">POL</div>
1969	Latvian-born English political philosopher Isaiah Berlin publishes *Four Essays on Liberty*. <div align="right">POL</div>
1969	On August 15–19, Woodstock, a rock music festival, is held near Bethel, New York. The event is attended by approximately 300,000 people and becomes a symbol of youthful 1960s counterculture and aesthetic solidarity. <div align="right">SOC</div>
1969	Gays and lesbians fight back against a police raid at the Stonewall Tavern in New York City, marking the birth of the gay liberation movement in the United States. Scholarly works related to that movement in the coming decade will include Dennis Altman's *Homosexual Oppression and Liberation* (1971), Robert Martin's *The Homosexual Tradition in American Poetry* (1979), and John Boswell's *Christianity, Social Tolerance, and Homosexuality* (1980). <div align="right">SOC</div>
1970s	The field of cultural studies begins to challenge the distinction between high and mass culture, treating the products of both as "texts" or "signifying practices." The film studies of Stephen Heath, Colin MacCabe, and others linked with the British journal *Screen* contribute to these changes. Louis Althusser's Marxism, Jacques Lacan's psychoanalytic theory, and semiotics strongly influence the developing field. <div align="right">CRIT</div>
1970s	At Yale University, the Yale school of critics becomes the center for deconstructionist theory and criticism in the United States. Its principal members are Geoffrey Hartman, J. Hillis Miller, and Paul de Man. <div align="right">CRIT</div>
1970s	Discourse analysis and theory develops as a multidisciplinary field of study, combining approaches from linguistics, the social sciences, and literary studies. Prominent practitioners in the 1970s and 1980s include Robert Longacre,

Robert de Beaugrande, Pierre Bourdieu, Wolfgang Dressler, Barry Hindess, Paul Hirst, Malcolm Coulthard, and Diane Macdonnell.   CRIT

1970s   Women's studies develops as an academic field of study. Journals publishing feminist scholarship include *Feminist Studies* and *Women's Studies*, both founded in 1972. Prominent feminist literary critics who emerge during this period include Elaine Showalter, Florence Howe, Catharine Stimpson, Annette Kolodny, Carolyn Heilbrun, Sandra M. Gilbert, Susan Gubar, Carol Ohmann, Fraya Katz-Stoker, Lillian S. Robinson, Lise Vogel, Annis Pratt, Jane Marcus, and Judith Fetterley. *See also* 1979 and 1980s, CRIT. CRIT

1970s   Thought to promote cross-disciplinary study and offer a wider range of teaching styles, team teaching gains popularity in American classrooms.   EDUC

1970s–1990s Some American lawmakers, educators, and parents champion the teaching of "values" as part of the general curriculum. Difficulties arise in reaching consensus on the definition of values.   EDUC

1970s   Following the civil rights movement of the 1960s, a great number of books about black American history are published. Some examples include Norman E. W. Hodges' *Breaking the Chains of Bondage* (1972), Lerone Bennett Jr.'s *The Shaping of Black America* (1975), August Meier and Elliot Rudwick's *Along the Color Line* (1976), William Jeremiah Moses's *The Golden Age of Black Nationalism: 1850–1925* (1978), and Howard Rabinowitz's *Race Relations in the Urban South: 1865–1890* (1978).   HIST

1970s   Under the presidency of Richard Nixon, U.S. policy in the Vietnam War comes to be known as Vietnamization. It is meant to allow for a face-saving withdrawal of American forces and a corresponding strengthening of the South Vietnamese military presence against the North Vietnamese.   POL

1970s   American cardiologists Meyer Friedman and Ray Rosenman identify the behavior pattern known as Type A, which is characterized by impatience, rapid pace, and trying to do many things at once.   PSYCH

1970s   Assertiveness training in group settings is used to enhance individual social skills and self-awareness.   PSYCH

1970s   Psychological self-help groups, characterized by mutual support and sharing of experiences, become widespread.   PSYCH

1970s   European feminist writers such as Suzanne Brogger, Françoise d'Eaubonne, and Carla Lonzi argue that the physical survival of the world depends on the rejection of traditionally male-centered concepts of dominance and the embrace of traditionally female-centered ideas of nurturing and preservation. SOC

1970   French anthropologist Louis Dumont publishes *Homo Hierarchicus*, a study of
            the caste system in India.   ANTH

1970   American film critic Parker Tyler publishes *Underground Film: A Critical History*,
            a negative critique of contemporary avant-garde cinema and declaration for
            the creation of artistic standards to judge experimental film.   CRIT

1970   *Illuminations*, a collection of essays by German writer Walter Benjamin, is pub-
            lished posthumously, marking his continuing influence 30 years after his
            death in 1940.   CRIT

1970   American Marxist literary critic Fredric Jameson helps to introduce neo-Marxist
            literary theory to the English-speaking world in *Marxism and Form*. Subsequent
            works by Jameson will include *The Prison-House of Language* (1972), a critique
            of structuralism, and *The Political Unconscious: Narrative as a Socially Symbolic Act*
            (1981).   CRIT

1970–1997   Many American historians write from a Marxist or neo-Marxist perspective.
            Examples of such work include Herbert Gutman's *Work Culture and Society in
            Industrializing America: Essays in America's Working Class and Social History*
            (1977), David Montgomery's *Worker's Control in America: Studies in the History
            of Work, Technology and Labor Struggles* (1980), and Eugene Genovese's *Roll,
            Jordan, Roll: The World the Slaves Made* (1976).   HIST

1970–1997   The women's movement prompts an outpouring of books about women's his-
            tory. Examples of significant work include Nancy Cott's *The Bonds of
            Womanhood: "Woman's Sphere" in New England, 1780–1835* (1978), Judith
            Walkowitz's *Prostitution and Victorian Society: Women, Class and the State* (1982),
            and Gerda Lerner's *What Women Thought: The Creation of Feminist Consciousness,
            700 A.D.–1870* (1993).   HIST

1970–1997   Social and cultural history is published that shows great imagination and innova-
            tion in its approach. Exemplary works include Peter Gay's *The Bourgeois Experience:
            Victoria to Freud* (three volumes, beginning in 1984) and Ann Douglas's *The
            Feminization of American Culture* (1977) and *Terrible Honesty: Mongrel Manhattan in
            the 1920s* (1994).   HIST

1970   *Aesthetic Theory*, by German philosopher Theodor Adorno, is published posthu-
            mously.   PHIL

1970   German-born American philosopher of science Carl Gustav Hempel publish-
            es *Aspects of Scientific Explanation*.   PHIL

1970   American moral philosopher Thomas Nagel publishes *The Possibility of
            Altruism*. Most of his works are concerned with the nature of moral motivation

and political commitment. He will also be known for his paper "What Is It Like to Be a Bat?," in which he argues that there is a subjective dimension to experience that cannot be comprehended objectively.   PHIL

1970   Salvador Allende is elected president of Chile, becoming the world's first Marxist head of state to win power democratically. He will be overthrown in 1973 by a military coup supported by the U.S. Central Intelligence Agency.   POL

1970   Indian mystic and poet Sri Chinmoy Ghose publishes *Yoga and the Spiritual Life*. Residing in and leading meditation centers in the United States since 1964, he advocates the practice of "love, devotion, and surrender" as the path to union with the Supreme Being.   REL

1970   American social critic Alvin Toffler publishes *Future Shock*. Toffler's vision of technological and social revolution will be further described in such works as *The Third Wave* (1980) and will influence American politician Newt Gingrich (*see* 1995, POL).   SOC

1970   American sociologist Laud Humphreys writes "Tearoom Trade: Impersonal Sex in Public Places," a study of anonymous homosexual encounters. The study is highly controversial for its methodology, in which the author served as a lookout for the encounters and gained follow-up interviews by taking down license plate numbers of participants.   SOC

1970   American sociologist Robin Williams publishes *American Society: A Sociological Interpretation*, an attempt to identify basic values held by the majority of Americans.   SOC

1970   Swiss-born American psychiatrist Elisabeth Kübler-Ross publishes *On Death and Dying*, in which she conceives of facing death as a process consisting of denial, anger, bargaining, depression, and acceptance. She will counter this theory in her 1995 book, *On Life After Death*.   SOC

1970   Feminist works published this year include Kate Millett's *Sexual Politics*; *Sisterhood Is Powerful: An Anthology of Writing from the Women's Liberation Movement*, edited by Robin Morgan; *Women's Liberation: A Blueprint for the Future*, edited by Sookie Stambler; Shulamith Firestone's *The Dialectic of Sex: The Case for Feminist Revolution*; Germaine Greer's *The Female Eunuch*; and Eva Figes's *Patriarchal Attitudes*.   SOC

1971   American philosopher Stanley Cavell publishes *The World Viewed*, a study on how film can render its audience absent and give expression to the modern experience of privacy and anonymity.   CRIT

1971   Philosopher and aesthetician Francis Sparshott publishes the essay "Basic Film Aesthetics," an account of how film is unique in representing space, time, and motion.   CRIT

1971   Belgian-born American deconstructionist critic Paul de Man publishes his first book, *Blindness and Insight*. His writings, which include the posthumously published *The Resistance to Theory* (1986), emphasize the rhetorical character of texts.   CRIT

1971   French philosopher Jean-François Lyotard publishes *Discours, figure*, in which he analyzes the aesthetics of "difference" underlying deconstructionist thought. He will discuss semiotics, Marxism, and Lacanian thought in *Des dispositifs pulsionnels* (1973) and *Économie libidinale* (1974).   PHIL

1971   American philosopher John Rawls publishes *A Theory of Justice*, one of the most influential contributions to political philosophy in the 20th century. In it he argues that all social rewards should be distributed equally, unless unequal distribution benefits everyone.   POL

1971   American behaviorist psychologist B. F. Skinner publishes *Beyond Freedom and Dignity*, in which he argues that free will is an illusion and that behavior is always shaped by past conditioning.   PSYCH

Whatever Happened to est?

In Woody Allen's film *Annie Hall* (1977), a woman at a Los Angeles party asks the character portrayed by Woody Allen if he is into est. When he replies no, she asks, "Then how can you criticize it?" Indeed, in the 1970s, anyone who hoped to avoid criticism was putting out hundreds of dollars for a weekend est seminar, at which they hoped to transform themselves, eliminate fears and flaws, take responsibility, and in the words of the est philosophy, "get it." Founded in 1971 by former car salesman Werner Erhard (a.k.a. Jack Rosenberg and Jack Frost), "erhard seminars training," or "est," was a packaged form of group therapy in which seminar leaders berated and coaxed confessions from participants for hours, not even allowing them to go to the bathroom. At the end, est alumni were supposed to emerge with their selves realigned, able to focus completely on individual fulfillment—an aim widely recognized in the 1970s as the primary goal of life.

Not surprisingly, a phenomenon so rooted in its time could not long survive, at least not without a name change. In 1984, Erhard refashioned and renamed his program "the Forum," in which incarnation it continued to do business.

1971   American sociologist Alvin Gouldner publishes *The Coming Crisis of Sociology*, in which he critiques both the emphasis on functional analysis in the West, and the stress on Marxism in the East.   soc

1971   Neville Thomas Bonner becomes the first Aboriginal Australian to be elected to his country's parliament. He is outspoken in promoting Aboriginal rights and social welfare.   soc

1971   American feminist scholars Vivian Gornick and Barbara K. Moran edit *Woman in Sexist Society: Studies in Power and Powerlessness*. It includes many contributors who will become prominent as academic feminist theorists, including Wendy Martin, Linda Nochlin, and Naomi Weisstein.   soc

1972   American critic Addison Gayle publishes the critical anthology *Black Aesthetic*, a milestone in the Black Arts movement, which, in its advocacy of black nationalism, is connected to the Black Power movement.   CRIT

1972   American art historian Leo Steinberg publishes *Other Criteria*, a book of essays that relates modern art to the Renaissance through a changing continuum of self-reference and representation.   CRIT

1972   Vernon Young publishes *On Film: Unpopular Essays on a Popular Art*, an ethnological approach to film criticism that stresses the complicated relationship between an artist and his or her culture.   CRIT

1972   English film critic and theorist V. F. Perkins includes his essay "Form and Discipline" in his book *Film as Film*, an attempt to incorporate the insights of both realist and antirealist theories. He claims that fictional narratives reveal film's central aim by blending photographic realism with dramatic illusion.   CRIT

1972   Rosalind Krauss publishes "A View of Modernism," an essay that criticizes the inability of Greenbergian modernism (*see* 1961, CRIT) to address contemporary art.   CRIT

1972   American critic Stanley Fish publishes *Self-Consuming Artifacts: The Experience of Seventeenth-Century Literature*.   CRIT

1972   Puerto Rican essayist and fiction writer Rosario Ferré founds one of Latin America's most renowned literary magazines, *Zona de carga y descarga* (*Loading and Unloading Zone*).   CRIT

1972–1976   Turkish scholar Fuat Sezgin publishes *Geschichte des arabischen Schrifttums*, a survey of the early history of Islamic science and technology.   HIST

1972   To provide a feminist voice for women, American journalist Gloria Steinem and others found *Ms.* magazine. Although it first appeared as a sample insert in the December 1971 issue of *New York* magazine, its first complete issue is published in January this year. It begins monthly publication this summer.   JOURN

1972   French philosopher and writer Simone de Beauvoir writes on the social and psychological dimensions of aging in *The Coming of Age*.   PHIL

1972   Philosopher P. T. Geach introduces the term *Cambridge change* in his book *Logic Matters*. The term refers to changes that are not substantial but merely the result of a changing relationship to an external object.   PHIL

1972   American political scientist James David Barber publishes *The Presidential Character: Predicting Performance in the White House*, in which he develops a typology of presidential personalities.   POL

1972   American political scientists Sidney Verba and Norman Nie publish *Participation in America: Political Democracy and Social Equality*, a comprehensive study of political participation in the United States.   POL

1972   A break-in on June 17 by men affiliated with Republican U.S. president Richard Nixon's reelection committee at Democratic Party headquarters at the Watergate office-and-apartment complex in Washington, D.C., escalates into a political scandal that will result in a congressional investigation, and ultimately, on August 9, 1974, in the resignation of President Nixon. The Watergate affair, and eventually the suffix -gate, will come to be used as shorthand for political corruption and the decline of trust in government.   POL

1972   Chinese leader Mao Zedong receives U.S. president Richard Nixon in Beijing, signalling a warming of relations between the two countries. The improving relations promote scholarly exchanges in many disciplines.   POL

1972   Drafted by suffragist Alice Paul in 1921 and repeatedly introduced in Congress since 1923, the Equal Rights Amendment (ERA) is finally passed by both houses. It states in full: "Equality of Rights under the law shall not be denied or abridged by the United States or any state on account of sex. The Congress shall have the power to enforce, by appropriate legislation, the provisions of this article. This amendment shall take effect two years after the date of ratification." After the ERA fails to meet its seven-year deadline for ratification, it will be given a three-year extension, which will expire (*see* 1982, POL) before the ERA has been ratified by the necessary two-thirds of the states.   POL

1972   French critic René Girard turns from literary to religious studies with *Violence and the Sacred*, which proposes an original theory of sacrifice and scapegoating. REL

1972   The American sociologist Christopher Jencks and his colleagues publish *Inequality*, a controversial study of the effects of family, genetic inheritance, and schooling on life chances.   SOC

1973   American anthropologist Clifford Geertz publishes *The Interpretation of Cultures*, which offers a new approach to the study of cultural symbols.   ANTH

1973   American anthropologist Steven Goldberg publishes *The Inevitability of Patriarchy*, in which he argues that patriarchy is biologically determined. A revised edition will follow in 1974.   ANTH

1973   American critic Hayden White publishes *Metahistory: The Historical Imagination in Nineteenth-Century Europe*, in which he unites historiography and literary criticism in describing the "poetics of history."   CRIT

1973   French critic Roland Barthes publishes *The Pleasure of the Text*, a collection of aphorisms that focus on the enjoyment of texts. Other important Barthes works of this period include *S/Z* (1970) and *Camera Lucida* (1980), his last work published at the time of his death.   CRIT

1973   Feminist film critic Joan Mellen publishes *Women and Their Sexuality in the New Film*, a study of how sexism and racism affect the study of film art.   CRIT

1973   American feminists Anne Koedt, Ellen Levine, and Anita Rapone edit and publish *Radical Feminism*, which includes essays by Koedt, Carol Hanisch, Pat Mainardi, Radicalesbian, and others.   CRIT

1973   American feminist critic Carolyn Heilbrun publishes *Toward a Recognition of Androgyny*.   CRIT

1973   American critic Harold Bloom publishes *The Anxiety of Influence*, in which he expresses his theory of the poet's Oedipal need to displace poetic predecessors by "misreading" previous poets' work. Other works include *Blake's Apocalypse: A Study in Poetic Argument* (1963) and *A Map of Misreading* (1975).   CRIT

1973   American philosopher David Lewis publishes *Counterfactuals*, in which he develops the "possible worlds" approach to counterfactuals (conditional propositions in which the "if" clause is contrary to known fact).   PHIL

1973   In *Roe v. Wade*, the U.S. Supreme Court decides to legalize abortion. The 7–2 decision invalidates antiabortion statutes in many states and leads to decades of controversy over whether abortion should remain legal.   POL

1973   American social psychologist Phillip Zimbardo reports on his experimental study of authority, in which subjects are recruited to act like prison guards assigned to oversee another group of subjects. Zimbardo has to abandon the experiment when the "guards" begin acting with unexpected cruelty. *See also* 1950s, PSYCH, and 1963, SOC.   PSYCH

1973   Peruvian priest and theologian Gustavo Gutierrez coins the term *liberation theology* for the Latin American school of thought that believes the Gospel requires the church to work for liberation of the poor of the world from oppression. Other prominent liberation theologians of the 1970s and 1980s will include Brazilian Leonardo Boff and Uruguayan Juan Luis Segundo. The movement, which makes use of Marxist ideas and supports revolution, will draw conservative fire inside and outside the church. *See also* 1985, REL.   REL

1973   Lithuanian-born American rabbi Mordecai Kaplan publishes *And If Not Now When? Toward a Reconstitution of the Jewish People. See also* 1934, REL.   REL

1973   The American sociologist Daniel Bell publishes *The Coming of Post-Industrial Society*, proclaiming a gradual shift in the American workforce from producers of tangible goods to producers of information.   SOC

1974   French-born American writer and educator Jacques Barzun analyzes contemporary arts in *The Use and Abuse of Art* and discusses the influence of psychoanalysis on historical interpretation in *Clio and the Doctors*.   CRIT

1974   Bulgarian-born French linguist Julia Kristeva publishes *Revolution in Poetic Language*. In this and other works, she combines psychoanalytic, linguistic, and Marxist influences.   LING

1974   Philosopher Richard Montague introduces the formal language that will become known as a Montague grammar in the paper "The Proper Treatment of Quantification in English."   PHIL

1974   U.S. president Richard Nixon resigns on August 9. *See* 1972, POL.   POL

1974   American political theorist Robert Nozick publishes *Anarchy, State, and Utopia*, which argues that any government action beyond protecting individuals from violation of their rights is illegitimate.   POL

1974   Belgian feminist theorist Luce Irigaray publishes *Speculum of the Other Woman*. Her works analyze the nature of sexual difference, positing a connection between the distinctiveness of the female mind and that of the female body.   PSYCH

1974   American psychologists Eleanor Maccoby and Carol Jacklin publish *The Psychology of Sex Differences*, an exhaustive review of a decade of studies on the subject.   PSYCH

1975   Poet and art critic David Antin formulates his views about video art and its relation to television in his essay, "Video: The Distinctive Features of the Medium."
CRIT

1975   Australian art critic Ian Burn, cofounder of the Society for Theoretical Art and Analysis, publishes the essay "The Art Market: Affluence and Degradation," in which he criticizes the conditions of the New York art world.
CRIT

1975   American critic Norman Holland publishes *Five Readers Reading*, in which he analyzes the responses of readers within a psychoanalytic framework.
CRIT

1975   English art critic Laura Mulvey links the pleasures of film and of much modern art to a repressive social structure in "Visual Pleasure and Narrative Cinema," an essay that relates types of looking to gender differences.
CRIT

1975   French philosopher Michel Foucault publishes *Discipline and Punish: The Birth of the Prison*.
HIST

"New" Movements

In the flux of intellectual movements, the one thing that remains the same is that something is always being called "new." Here is a guide to some "new" movements of the 20th century:

new criticism—Literary-critical movement focusing on close reading of texts as autonomous wholes without reference to authorial intention. *See also* 1941, CRIT.

new economics—Term for the economic theories of English economist John Maynard Keynes, which emphasized government economic planning and deficit spending. *See also* 1936, ECON.

new historicism—Literary-critical movement that studies texts in relation to the network of cultural institutions, practices, and beliefs at the time they were written. *See also* 1982, CRIT.

new humanism—Movement in education, literary criticism, and philosophy aimed at the restoration of classical principles and humanistic values. *See also* 1908, CRIT.

New Wave—French aesthetic movement advocating radically new directions for films and novels. Its views were embodied both in critical writings and artistic works. *See also* 1951 and 1963, CRIT.

1975   Philosopher Ernest Adams publishes *The Logic of Conditionals*, in which he proposes the hypothesis that will become known as Adams's thesis, regarding conditional probability.   PHIL

1975   American philosopher of language David Kaplan publishes the article "How to Russell a Frege-Church," in which he reintroduces the concept of haecceity— "thisness" or individuating essence—originally used by scholastic philosopher Duns Scotus.   PHIL

1975   American entomologist Edward O. Wilson publishes *Sociobiology: The New Synthesis*. Coined by Wilson, the term *sociobiology* refers to the study of human and animal social behavior based on the premise of its evolutionary utility and genetic basis. Though highly controversial, the approach influences much future work in psychology, ethics, and the social sciences.   SOC

1975   In *Against Our Will: Men, Women, and Rape*, American writer Susan Brownmiller develops the idea that the sexual assault of women is an act of male violence and the assertion of power, not an act of desire.   SOC

1976   English critic Raymond Williams publishes *Keywords*, in which he presents a vocabulary of culture and society consistent with his theoretical orientation.   CRIT

1976   French philosopher Jean Baudrillard publishes "The Hyper-realism of Simulation," a view of the media-dominated contemporary world in which reality has been replaced by "simulacra" or manifestations drawn from surrealism, pop art, and photography.   CRIT

1976   Victor Burgin publishes "Socialist Formalism," an essay that invokes the practical tradition of Russian constructivism and the theoretical concerns of linguistic semiology.   CRIT

1976   American literary scholar Robert Scholes publishes the essay "Narration and Narrativity in Film."   CRIT

1976   German philosopher Hans-Georg Gadamer publishes *Philosophical Hermeneutics*, a collection of critical essays.   CRIT

1976   American critic Jonathan Culler publishes *Structuralist Poetics*. Other works will include *The Pursuit of Signs* (1981) and *On Deconstruction* (1982). Culler's work emphasizes analysis of the conventions and operations of literary discourse.   CRIT

1976   American critic J. Hillis Miller, a member of the Yale school of deconstruction, publishes two essays on deconstructionist principles: "Ariadne's Thread" and "Stevens' Rock and Criticism as Cure, II."   CRIT

1976   French philosopher and critic Paul Ricoeur publishes *Interpretation Theory: Discourse and the Surplus of Meaning*. Drawing on phenomenology and hermeneutics, he develops a theory of text and interpretation founded on a dialectic of explanation and understanding. His later works on literary theory will include *Hermeneutics and Human Sciences* (1981) and the three-volume *Time and Narrative* (1984–1985).   CRIT

1976   Nigerian poet, playwright, and critic Wole Soyinka publishes *Myth, Literature, and the African World*, which examines Yoruba myth, ritual, and tragedy. Soyinka's work is influential in postcolonial discussion of language, literature, and politics. Other works will include *Art, Dialogue, and Outrage* (1988).   CRIT

1976   American critic Roberto Mangabeira Unger publishes *Knowledge and Politics*. Unger is a prominent voice in the field known as critical legal studies, which critiques the legitimacy of such dualisms as law-politics, fact-value, and private-public.   CRIT

1976–1984   French philosopher Michel Foucault publishes the three-volume *History of Sexuality*.   HIST

1976   English zoologist Richard Dawkins publishes *The Selfish Gene*, in which he coins the term *meme* for a cultural object (e.g., an idea, a fashion, a dogma) that can be replicated and transmitted. Dawkins argues that memes are subject to evolutionary processes analogous to those involved in biological evolution. More generally, Dawkins claims that living things, including humans, are "survival machines" designed to serve the interests of "selfish" genes.   PHIL

1976   One month after the death of Chinese leader Mao Zedong in September, four radical leaders of the Cultural Revolution (*see* 1966–1969, POL)—the "Gang of Four"—are arrested for plotting to overthrow the government. Jian Qing (Mao's widow), Zhang Chunqiao, Wang Hongwen, and Yao Wenyuan will be tried in 1980 and convicted in 1981.   POL

1976   The General Secretariat of the Organization of African Unity publishes *Cultural Charter for Africa*, which advocates resistance to and overthrow of cultural domination by the West.   POL

1976   Austrian psychologist Bruno Bettelheim publishes *The Uses of Enchantment*, in which he claims that the "evil" presented in fairy tales is of value to children learning about their own psychological makeup.   PSYCH

1976   American psychologist Herbert Benson publishes *The Relaxation Response*, in which he discusses therapeutic techniques to control panic and anxiety.   PSYCH

1976   American faith healer Harry Edwards dies. Followers from around the world
        have sought healing from his spirit guides.   REL

1976   German theologian Karl Rahner publishes *Foundations of Christian Faith*, a
        summation of the systematic theology he has developed over several decades. REL

1976   The American social psychologists Bibb Latane and John Darley publish *Help
        in a Crisis: Bystander Response to an Emergency*, a report on the ways in which
        bystanders respond to incidents requiring their help. Inspired by the Kitty
        Genovese murder in 1964, the authors found that bystanders were more like-
        ly to respond to a person in trouble when they witnessed the event alone. soc

1976   In her essay "It is the Lesbian in Us . . . ," American poet Adrienne Rich sug-
        gests that a "lesbian" leaning encompasses not only sexuality but a broader
        intimacy among women that can generate creative expression. Her essay col-
        lection that year, *Of Woman Born: Motherhood as Experience and Institution*,
        reflects on the ambiguities of motherhood. Other essay collections will include
        On Lies, Secrets, and Silence (1979) and *Blood, Bread, and Poetry* (1986).   soc

1977   American anthropologist Marvin Harris publishes *Cannibals and Kings*. He is
        known for his influential work in developing the theory of cultural material-
        ism, and for his field studies in Latin America and Africa.   ANTH

1977   A seminar on Afro-American Literature and Course Design is held at Yale
        University. It results in publication next year of *Afro-American Literature: The
        Reconstruction of Instruction*, edited by Robert Stepto and Dexter Fisher.   CRIT

1977   French film semiotician Christian Metz develops a metapsychology of cinema
        in *Le Signifant imaginaire*, a work that examines the structure of viewing rela-
        tions between film and spectator.   CRIT

1977   Leading American Marxist literary critic Fredric Jameson publishes "Reflections
        on the Brecht-Luckacs Debate," an essay that concludes that both socialist real-
        ism and modernism are inadequate to the experiences of modern society.   CRIT

1977   Italian semiotician and critic Umberto Eco publishes the essay "On the
        Contribution of Film to Semiotics," which draws on the Peircian theory of signs
        (*see* 1878 and 1907, PHIL). Eco encourages the analysis of the codes and conven-
        tions of iconic signs as a means of understanding how film communicates. CRIT

1977   German critic Hans Robert Jauss publishes the first part of his *Aesthetic
        Experience and Literary Hermeneutics*, in which he develops the school of criti-
        cal thought known as reception theory. It emphasizes the historical "horizon
        of expectations" through which the reader makes sense of a text.   CRIT

1977   American critic Elaine Showalter publishes *A Literature of Their Own*, which offers a new history and analysis of novels written by English women from 1840 to the present.   CRIT

1977   American political theorist Michael Walzer publishes *Just and Unjust Wars*. POL

1977   American sociologist and feminist Alice Rossi publishes the article "A Biosocial Perspective on Parenting," in which she argues that there is a biological influence on behavioral differences between the sexes.   SOC

1977   The first court ruling in which sexual harassment is found to be a form of discrimination is that of the U.S. Court of Appeals for the District of Columbia in *Barnes v. Costle*. *See also* 1986, SOC.   SOC

1978   Conservative American sociologist Daniel Bell publishes "Modernism and Capitalism," a critique of Marxist theory that promotes "theoretical knowledge" as the central dynamic of change for the late 20th century.   CRIT

1978   German critic Wolfgang Iser publishes *The Act of Reading: A Theory of Aesthetic Response*. Emphasizing the reader's role in determining literary meaning, his work is associated with the Constance school of reception theory.   CRIT

1978   Palestinian-born American critic Edward W. Said publishes *Orientalism*, in which he relates the development of the Orientalist field of scholarship to Europe's patterns of imperialism and colonialism. The work is a landmark in postcolonial cultural studies (*see* 1960s, CRIT). Related works by Said will include *The Question of Palestine* (1979).   CRIT

1978   American writer and philosopher Susan Sontag publishes *Illness as Metaphor*, in which she examines the representation of illness in literature and modern culture.   CRIT

1978   American critic and biographer W. J. Bate publishes *Samuel Johnson*, in which he closely analyzes his subject's moral and intellectual concerns as related to his writing.   HIST

1978   American philosopher Nelson Goodman publishes *Ways of Worldmaking*. PHIL

1978   English philosopher Michael Dummett publishes the essay collection *Truth and Other Enigmas*. Dummett's views on logic, language, and mathematics will be highly influential. His other works include *Frege: Philosophy of Language* (1973) and *The Game of Tarot* (1980).   PHIL

1978   American psychiatrist M. Scott Peck publishes *The Road Less Traveled*, a guide to psychological and spiritual growth that will remain a perennial best-seller into the 1980s and 1990s.   PSYCH

1978   American feminist scholar Nancy Chodorow publishes *The Reproduction of Mothering: Psychoanalysis and the Sociology of Gender*.   PSYCH

1978   Pope John Paul I briefly succeeds Paul VI before dying a month after his accession. He is succeeded by the Polish-born John Paul II, the first non-Italian pope since the Dutch Adrian VI (1522–1523). John Paul II's reign will be marked by many international trips, increased international representation in the College of Cardinals and Roman Curia, and conservative positions on a range of moral and ecclesiastical issues.   REL

1979   The field of black feminist criticism begins to gain ground with such works as *Sturdy Black Bridges: Vision of Black Women in Literature*, edited by Roseann P. Bell, Bettye J. Parker, and Beverly Guy-Sheftall, and *Talking Back: Thinking Feminist, Thinking Black*, by bell hooks (Gloria Watkins). Critics in this field in the 1980s will include Barbara Smith, Marjorie Pryse, Hortense Spiller, Joanne M. Braxton, Deborah McDowell, and Andrée McLaughlin. *See also* 1970s and 1980s, CRIT.   CRIT

1979   French philosopher Jean-François Lyotard publishes *The Postmodern Condition*, a work that seeks new explanations for the conditions of contemporary capitalism.   CRIT

1979   American scholar of popular culture John Cawelti examines film genre as a manifestation of underlying social attitudes in his essay "*Chinatown* and Generic Transformation in Recent American Films."   CRIT

1979   English cultural critic Dick Hebdige publishes *Subculture: The Meaning of Style*, which offers a poststructural analysis of postwar English working-class subcultures.   CRIT

1979   French critic Pierre Bourdieu publishes *Distinction: A Social Critique of the Judgment of Taste*.   CRIT

1979   American feminist critics Sandra M. Gilbert and Susan Gubar publish *The Madwoman in the Attic: The Woman Writer and the Nineteenth-Century Literary Imagination*. The team's later works will include *No Man's Land* (1987–1989) and an edition of *The Norton Anthology of Literature by Women* (1985).   CRIT

1979   American philosopher Richard Rorty publishes *Philosophy and the Mirror of Nature*, which opposes the traditional view of philosophy as a form of higher knowledge.   PHIL

1979   American critic and writer Norman Podhoretz publishes *Breaking Ranks*, an
            account of his conversion from left-wing to right-wing politics. As editor of
            Commentary, he leads the journal in the same direction, as he becomes one of
            the nation's chief conservative commentators. His other works will include
            Why We Were in Vietnam (1982).   POL

1979   Swiss theologian Hans Küng is prohibited from officially teaching Roman
            Catholic doctrine as a result of his criticism of papal authority in works such
            as *Infallible? An Inquiry* (1971).   REL

1979   A revolution in Iran topples the Shah's regime, leaving in its place a Shiite
            Muslim fundamentalist government, headed by Ayatollah Ruhollah Khomeini.
            In the coming decades, Islamic fundamentalism will become a destabilizing
            force throughout the Middle East.   REL

1979   American sociologist William Julius Wilson publishes *The Declining
            Significance of Race*, which asserts that class has come to play an increasingly
            influential role over race in the experience of African-Americans.   SOC

1979   The use of affirmative action programs, designed to lessen discrimination in
            hiring practices, is upheld by the U.S. Supreme Court in *United Steelworkers of
            America* v. *Weber*.   SOC

1980s   American anthropologist Robert Carneiro publishes studies of the rate of con-
            solidation of autonomous political units from prehistory to the present. His
            studies indicate a gradual process of centralization from over 500,000 units
            worldwide in 1000 B.C. to fewer than 200 at present.   ANTH

1980s   A number of new academic fields of study associated with "postcolonial cul-
            tural studies" (*see* 1960s, CRIT) emerge or gain new prominence in this decade.
            These include various ethnic or minority studies, African studies, Latin
            American studies, Caribbean studies, and third world studies. *See also* 1970s
            and 1979, CRIT.   CRIT

1980s   Materialist feminist literary criticism flourishes in this decade, influenced by
            Lacanian psychoanalytic theory and Althusserian Marxism. Prominent works
            include Rosalind Coward's *Patriarchal Precedents* (1983), Catherine Belsey's
            Critical Practice (1980), Toril Moi's *Sexual/Textual Politics* (1985), and Cora
            Kaplan's *Sea Changes* (1986).   CRIT

1980s   Because the equal pay legislation of the 1960s failed to even out the earnings dis-
            crepancy between men and women, the idea of comparable worth is introduced
            in American courtrooms and legislative chambers. Arguing that equal pay for
            equal work does not address the gender stratification of the American economy,
            comparable worth advocates note that female-dominated professions, which they

describe as belonging to a "pink collar" ghetto, generally pay less on average than male-dominated professions requiring similar levels of education, training, and experience. To rectify this situation, proponents of comparable worth propose that jobs performed primarily by women that are deemed to be of comparable worth to those performed primarily by men carry equal remuneration. Opponents, who will generally prevail, argue that legislators should not and cannot interfere with the fair market value of such jobs.   ECON

1980s–1990s   Biographers write with unprecedented candor about their subjects' sexuality, mental illness, and alcohol and drug addiction. Examples include Sharon O'Brien's *Willa Cather: The Emerging Voice* (1987), Diane Middlebrook's *Anne Sexton: A Biography* (1991), and Nicola Beauman's *Morgan: A Biography of the Novelist E. M. Forster* (1994).   HIST

1980s   In the United States, antigovernment right-wing survivalists establish wilderness residences, largely in the Midwest and Northwest. Many are racist and anti-Semitic and protect themselves from government invasion with large quantities of firearms. The movement reflects a growing distrust of American government. *See also* 1990s, SOC.   POL

1980s   Televangelism gains strength, due in part to the growth of cable television, which provides more video outlets. Among the best-known televangelists are Jerry Falwell, Jim Bakker, and Pat Robertson. Some of the video evangelists will use their religious position to effect political change by lobbying and running for office.   REL

1980s   New Age beliefs proliferate in the United States. The term *New Age* encompasses a variety of movements rooted in the 1960s counterculture that embraced the Age of Aquarius (*see* 1960, PHIL). These movements share a faith in a dawning transformation of human consciousness; they incorporate such ideas and practices as pyramidology, healing crystals, astrology, and reincarnation.   REL

1980s   Conceiving of pornography as a violation of women's civil rights, American feminists Catharine A. MacKinnon, a lawyer, and Andrea Dworkin, a writer, draft legislation, including a widely copied local ordinance, that would enable women to sue for civil damages if they could prove that they have been harmed by a specific piece of pornography. Although the ordinance will be adopted in some communities, it will be rejected on appeal in each case; other such legislation will meet a similar fate. *See also* 1992, SOC.   SOC

1980   *Toward the Decolonization of African Literature* is published by African critics Chinweizu, Onwuchekwa Jemie, and Ihechukwu Madubuike, who discuss what is involved in defining the "Africanness" of a text.   CRIT

1980   In an address given in Frankfurt, German philosopher Jürgen Habermas maintains a commitment to the critical potential of modernist high art. He inter-
prets recent theorization of the postmodern as a reactionary tendency to
counter economic systems. His address will be published as *Modernity: An
Incomplete Project* in 1981.   CRIT

1980   American critic Stanley Fish publishes *Is There a Text in This Class? The Authority
of Interpretive Communities*, a collection of essays in which he shifts away from
reader-response theory to a theory of interpretive communities.   CRIT

1980   American critic Geoffrey Hartman calls for an eclectic, dialectical, creative
form of criticism in *Criticism in the Wilderness: The Study of Literature Today*.
Other works will include *Easy Pieces* (1985) and *The Unremarkable Wordsworth*
(1987).   CRIT

1980   American critic Stephen Greenblatt publishes *Renaissance Self-Fashioning*, in
which he examines the shaping of identity in 16th-century England. The work
is one of the earliest in the critical movement known as new historicism (*see*
1982, CRIT). Other Greenblatt works will include *Shakespearean Negotiations*
(1988).   CRIT

1980   American writer George W. S. Trow publishes *Within the Context of No Context*,
an indictment of lack of history and content in American culture, especially
television.   CRIT

1980   With the publication of American historian John Boswell's *Christianity, Social
Tolerance, and Homosexuality: Gay People in Western Europe from the Beginning of
the Christian Era to the Fourteenth Century*, gay and lesbian history begins to be
viewed as a field meriting serious, unbiased inquiry by scholars. Other signif-
icant works will include John D'Emilio's *Sexual Politics, Sexual Communities:
The Making of a Homosexual Minority in the United States, 1940–1970* (1983),
Lillian Faderman's *Odd Girls and Twilight Lovers: A History of Lesbian Life in
Twentieth-Century America* (1991), and George Chauncey's *Gay New York:
Gender, Urban Culture, and the Making of the Gay Male World, 1890–1940*
(1994).   HIST

1980   American philosopher J. R. Searle publishes the article "Minds, Brains, and
Programs," in which he introduces the thought experiment of the Chinese box.
By speculating about a non-Chinese-speaking person who is mechanically
manipulating batches of Chinese characters according to prespecified rules, he
reaches the conclusion that artificial intelligence (AI) is not capable of achieving
true understanding or cognition.   PHIL

1980   Canadian philosopher of science Bas van Fraassen publishes *The Scientific Image*, in which he develops the theory of scientific knowledge known as constructive empiricism.   PHIL

1980   American philosopher Donald Herbert Davidson publishes *Essays on Actions and Events*; he will also publish *Inquiries into Truth and Interpretation* (1983). He develops the philosophy of mind known as anomalous monism and the linguistic concept of the radical interpreter.   PHIL

1980   American philosopher Saul Aaron Kripke publishes *Naming and Necessity*, which influentially examines the topic of reference.   PHIL

1980   The Chinese rulers of Tibet reopen the Potala Palace in Lhasa to pilgrimage by exiled Tibetan Buddhists.   REL

1980   The Church of England introduces its Alternative Service Book, an alternative to the Book of Common Prayer.   REL

1980   Signaling greater toleration of religion, the Chinese government sponsors the renovation of certain historic Buddhist temples and monasteries and the largest Taoist temple in Beijing.   REL

1980   English feminist scholar Michèle Barrett publishes *Women's Oppression Today*, which argues for a feminist reexamination of Marxist class analysis.   SOC

1981   English critic Raymond Williams publishes *Contact: Communication and Culture* and *Culture*, in both of which he analyzes culture as a signifying system.   CRIT

1981   American critic Murray Krieger publishes *Arts on the Level: The Fall of the Elite Object*, in which he argues for fundamental differences between literary language and ordinary language. Later works will include *Words about Words about Words* (1988).   CRIT

1981   American economist Milton Friedman publishes *Free to Choose*. A leader of the monetarist school, a branch of neoclassical economics that opposes Keynesian government intervention, Friedman supports laissez-faire policies and argues that monetary policy (control of the money supply) is the most significant factor in stabilizing the economy.   ECON

1981   American economist James Tobin wins a Nobel Prize for his studies of the impact of financial markets on spending and investment.   ECON

1981   American economists Robert Heilbroner and Lester Thurow publish *Five Economic Challenges*.   ECON

1981   American linguist Donald Freeman publishes *Essays in Modern Stylistics*, in which he argues for a joining of stylistics to the theory of transformational-generative grammar.   LING

1981   German Marxist philosopher Jürgen Habermas publishes *The Theory of Communicative Action*, in which he discusses the nature of communication as related to social action. Subsequent works will include *Philosophical Discourse on Modernity* (1985).   PHIL

1981   American philosopher Hilary Putnam publishes *Reason, Truth, and History*, in which he takes a position known as internal realism. Other works include *Philosophy of Logic* (1971).   PHIL

1981   English moral philosopher Richard Mervyn Hare publishes *Moral Thinking: Its Levels, Method, and Point*, one of several works in which he takes a utilitarian position.   PHIL

1981–1989   Throughout his two terms as U.S. president, Republican Ronald Reagan effects laws and provisions to reduce the scope of federal powers, increase deregulation, and devolve more power to the states. The trend will continue into the administration of Republican president George Bush (1989–1993) and under the Republican majority elected to Congress in 1994. The Reagan administration also cuts taxes in the hope of spurring economic growth, a tactic advocated by the supply-side (or "trickle-down") economics of such thinkers as Arthur Laffer.   POL

1981   American psychologist Eleanor Rosch expands her theory of prototypes and basic level categories, thereby challenging Greek philosopher Aristotle's classical theory of categorization and making categorization a subfield of cognitive psychology.   PSYCH

1981   Pope John Paul II survives an assassination attempt by a Turkish terrorist.   REL

1981   Islamic fundamentalists assassinate Egyptian president Anwar al-Sadat in reaction to his reconciliation with Israel and his domestic reforms.   REL

1981   American critic Robert Alter publishes *The Art of Biblical Narrative*, in which he calls for the application of "new critical" analysis to Bible texts. He and Frank Kermode will advance this project further by editing *The Literary Guide to the Bible* (1987).   REL

1982   English anthropologist Victor Turner publishes *From Ritual to Theater*, in which he explores the concept of culture as dramatic performance.   ANTH

1982 | The critical anthology *Writing Culture* is published. Edited by James Clifford and George E. Marcus, the volume emphasizes the poetics and politics of anthropological writing. **ANTH**

1982 | American anthropologist Melvin Konner publishes *The Tangled Wing*, in which he considers the influence of evolution on human behavior. **ANTH**

1982 | American Marxist literary critic Frederic Jameson gives a talk entitled "Postmodernism and Consumer Society," in which he discusses the post-modern in relation to architecture, art, literature, and economics. The address will develop into a paper to be published as "Post-Modernism: Or the Cultural Logic of Late Capitalism" (1984). **CRIT**

1982 | In his essay "What Is Postmodernism?," French philosopher Jean-François Lyotard argues that the postmodern and the modern are continually bound in a dialectical relationship. He proposes a new distinction claiming that the modern strives for an unattainable wholeness whereas such attempts at whole-ness are impossible for the postmodern. **CRIT**

1982 | American art critic Hal Foster publishes the essay "Subversive Signs," in which he identifies two types of postmodernism: one complicit in contemporary cap-italism and another in resistance. It will be republished in his collection of essays entitled *Recordings: Art, Spectacle, Cultural Politics* (1985). **CRIT**

1982 | American critic Stephen Greenblatt coins the term *new historicism* for a grow-ing movement in criticism that examines the relationship of texts to the net-work of institutions, practices, and beliefs in which they were written. New his-toricist methods and ideas are originally associated with English Renaissance texts, but will spread to those of other times and places. Prominent critics asso-ciated with this school include Greenblatt, Louis Montrose, Jonathan Goldberg, and Walter Benn Michaels. **CRIT**

1982 | The first national news daily, *USA Today*, begins publication. Its creation reflects the growing mobility of Americans. **JOURN**

1982 | The deadline for ratification of the Equal Rights Amendment (ERA) expires on June 30, by which time the ERA has been ratified by 35 states, just three short of the two-thirds required for its adoption into the U.S. Constitution. The amendment was given ten years for ratification since its passage by both hous-es of Congress (*see* 1972, **POL**). It will be reintroduced in Congress two weeks later only to be narrowly defeated by the House of Representatives in November 1983. **POL**

1982 | American psychologist Carol Gilligan publishes *In a Different Voice: Psychological Theory and Women's Development*. Taking issue with previous theories of ethical development, she argues that women develop practical reasoning in a way different from men, with more of an emphasis on the web of actual relationships and less on abstract principles.   PSYCH

1982   In a historic step toward reconciliation, Pope John Paul II meets with Anglican church leaders and worships with Archbishop of Canterbury Robert Runcie.   REL

1983   American anthropologist Clifford Geertz publishes *Local Knowledge*.   ANTH

1983   American novelist and critic Alice Walker publishes *In Search of Our Mothers' Gardens: Womanist Prose*, which examines the writing of African-American women.   CRIT

1983   Italian semiotician and critic Umberto Eco writes on mass culture, semiotics, and philosophy in the eclectic essay collection *Travels in Hyperreality*.   CRIT

1983   English critic Terry Eagleton publishes *Literary Theory: An Introduction*, a widely read guide to the subject.   CRIT

1983   Palestinian-born American critic Edward W. Said publishes *The World, the Text, and the Critic*, in which he calls for an oppositional form of cultural criticism, one that consciously and skeptically intervenes in the formation of culture.   CRIT

1983   A U.S. government report on education, *A Nation at Risk*, argues that the educational system fails to prepare American students as well as do schools in other industrialized countries. The report becomes a call to arms for educational reformers, conservative and progressive alike.   EDUC

1983   The Center for the Study of Language and Information is established at Stanford University, combining resources from such language-related fields as linguistics, psychology, philosophy, and computer science.   LING

1983   Bulgarian-born French linguist Julia Kristeva publishes *Love Stories*.   LING

1983   American philosopher Saul Aaron Kripke publishes *Wittgenstein on Rules and Private Language*.   PHIL

1983   English philosopher of law Herbert Lionel Hart publishes *Essays in Jurisprudence and Philosophy*.   POL

1983   The United Presbyterian Church of North America and the Presbyterian Church in the United States merge to form the Presbyterian Church (U.S.A.). *See also* 1858, REL.   REL

1983   American sociologists Richard Gelles and Claire Pedrick Cornell publish *International Perspectives on Family Violence*, the first of a series of influential books by Gelles and various colleagues on domestic violence.   soc

1983   Guatemalan activist and Quiché Indian Rigoberta Menchú publishes her auto-biography, *I, Rigoberta Menchú*. Her account of the deaths of several family members at the hands of Guatemala's military spurs worldwide indignation against human rights abuses in that country (*see* 1954, POL). She will win the Nobel Peace Prize in 1992.   soc

1984   American critic Henry Louis Gates Jr. publishes "Criticism in the Jungle," in which he tries to establish a theoretical basis for the formation and analysis of an African-American literary canon. Gates will also publish *"Race," Writing, and Difference* (1986) and *The Signifying Monkey* (1988).   CRIT

1984   American critic Houston Baker Jr. publishes *Blues, Ideology, and Afro-American Literature*.   CRIT

1984   American film critic J. Hoberman writes the essay "After Avant-Garde Film," in which he discusses the commercialization of the avant-garde in the 1970s and how present filmmakers and music video directors are able to return to a sense of the avant-garde through the development of an authentically nonnarrative, nonlinear film mode.   CRIT

1984   English philosopher Derek Parfit publishes *Reasons and Persons*, an examination of the self from a moral and metaphysical perspective.   PHIL

1984   French philosopher Jean-François Lyotard publishes *The Postmodern Condition*. The book describes the postmodern viewpoint, which includes skepticism about the possibility of objective knowledge, mistrust of institutional power and its control over social and intellectual life, and an attitude that is playful, detached, ironic, and parodic. It includes such movements as poststructuralism (*see* 1960s, PHIL).   PHIL

1984   Robert Axelrod publishes *The Evolution of Cooperation*, in which he addresses the philosophical problem of the prisoners' dilemma with a strategy from game theory known as "tit for tat."   PHIL

1984   German psychoanalyst Adolf Grünbaum's *Foundations of Psychoanalysis* is one of a number of works in this period questioning the scientific basis of psychoanalysis.   PSYCH

1984   Hundreds of militant Sikhs occupying the Golden Temple in Amritsar, India, are killed when Prime Minister Indira Gandhi sends in troops to remove them. The Sikhs demand independence for the Punjab state in which they live.

Gandhi is assassinated later this year by Sikh extremists, and anti-Sikh riots follow. REL

1984   Belgian feminist theorist Luce Irigaray publishes *Éthiques de la différence sexuelle*. SOC

1985   American critic Elaine Showalter publishes *The New Feminist Criticism: Essays on Women, Literature, and Theory*. The collection includes such seminal pieces as Barbara Smith's "Toward a Black Feminist Criticism" and Deborah McDowell's "New Directions for Black Feminist Criticism." Showalter coins the term "gynocritics" for critics who attempt to construct an exclusively female framework for analysis of women's literature. CRIT

1985   American critic Robert Scholes publishes *Textual Power*, which advocates a transition from literary to cultural studies: studies of texts of many sources, visual and verbal, rather than of an exclusively literary canon. CRIT

1985   English critic Janet Batsleer publishes *Rewriting English: Cultural Politics of Gender and Class*. CRIT

1985   American critic J. Hillis Miller publishes *The Linguistic Moment*. Subsequent works will include *The Ethics of Reading* (1987) and *Theory Then and Now* (1991). CRIT

1985   English philosopher Bernard Williams publishes *Ethics and the Limits of Philosophy*. In this and other works, he adopts a subtle form of moral relativism. PHIL

1985   American computer scientist Marvin Minsky, one of the founders of the field of artificial intelligence (AI), publishes *The Society of Mind*. Minsky argues that human intelligence arises from a network of simpler processes, or agencies, that are not themselves intelligent. PSYCH

1985   The Roman Catholic church censures Brazilian theologian Leonardo Boff for his promulgation of liberation theology. REL

1985   Conservative Judaism approves ordination of women as rabbis. REL

1986   *Flash Art* publishes "The Cultural-Historical Tragedy of the European Continent," a transcript of a discussion between artists Joseph Beuys, Jannis Kounellis, Anselm Kiefer, and Enzo Cucchi, who relate radical art to radical politics. CRIT

1986   American critics Tony Bennett, Colin Mercer, and Janet Woollacott publish *Popular Culture and Social Relations*, in which they try to reconcile culturalist and structuralist approaches to cultural studies. CRIT

1986   American philosopher David Lewis publishes *The Plurality of Worlds*.   PHIL

1986   The essay "Toward a Philosophy of the Act," by Russian critic M. M. Bakhtin, is published posthumously.   PHIL

1986   American philosopher of law Ronald Dworkin publishes *Law's Empire*. His other works include *Taking Rights Seriously* (1977) and *A Matter of Principle* (1985). A political liberal, Dworkin advocates legal realism, which emphasizes pragmatic and moral considerations in creating and applying law.   POL

1986   The U.S. Supreme Court hears its first sexual harassment case, *Meritor Savings Bank v. Vinson*, ruling unanimously that the prohibition on sex discrimination in employment covered by Title VII of the Civil Rights Act of 1964 applies not just to quid pro quo cases, in which continued employment or promotion is dependent upon sexual favors, but also to the form of sexual harassment defined as "hostile environment," in which an employee's job performance is impaired by the harassment.   SOC

1987   Anthropologist Gilbert Herdt publishes *The Sambia: Ritual and Custom in New Guinea*, an account of the Sambia people of highland Papua New Guinea, who are notable for being among the most belligerent and misogynistic people in the world.   ANTH

1987   American critic Hayden White publishes *The Content of the Form: Narrative Discourse and Historical Representation*, in which he analyzes historical texts as narratives influenced by ideology.   CRIT

1987   American critic Flint Schier delivers the speech "Painting After Art," in which he argues that art can only exist within a context of concerns shared between artist and spectator. The speech will be published as an essay in *Visual Theory: Painting and Interpretation* (1991).   CRIT

1987   The international journal *Cultural Studies* is founded.   CRIT

1987   The late Belgian-born American deconstructionist critic Paul de Man (d. 1983) becomes the focus of controversy upon the discovery that he had written for a collaborationist newspaper during the Nazi occupation of Belgium, and that one article included anti-Semitic language.   CRIT

1987   American critic Hazel Carby publishes *Reconstructing Womanhood*, which criticizes black feminist criticism as an example of bourgeois humanism.   CRIT

1987   Austrian philosopher of science Paul Feyerabend publishes *Farewell to Reason*. In this and other works, such as *Against Method* (1975), he takes a skeptical approach to the rationality of science, arguing that rhetoric and politics have much to do with the success of a scientific proposition.   PHIL

1987   American philosopher Jerry Fodor publishes *Psychosemantics*. A realist about mental functioning, he develops many of his ideas from the analogy between thought and computation. Other works include *The Language of Thought* (1975).   PHIL

1987   The Vatican expresses its opposition to *in vitro* fertilization, artificial insemination, surrogate motherhood, and other medical practices concerned with manipulating conception.   REL

1987   University of Chicago professor Allan Bloom publishes *The Closing of the American Mind*, an analysis of the decline of American intellect and moral thinking. The book becomes a best-seller and is championed by some conservative groups.   SOC

1988   American anthropologist Clifford Geertz publishes *Works and Lives*, in which he argues that anthropology is basically a rhetorical attempt at persuasion.   ANTH

1988   American feminist critic Catharine R. Stimpson publishes *Where the Meanings Are*.   CRIT

1988   Ghanaian critic Kwame Anthony Appiah publishes "Out of Africa: Typologies of Nativism," in which he explores the continuing effect of the language of empire on African criticism of African literature.   CRIT

1988   James Clifford publishes *The Predicament of Culture: Twentieth-Century Ethnography, Literature, and Art*, a work that defines both modernism and tribal art as abstract and simplifying.   CRIT

1988   American philosopher Richard Rorty publishes *Contingency, Irony, and Solidarity*.   PHIL

1988   French philosopher Jean-François Lyotard publishes *Peregrinations, The Differend*, and *Heidegger and "the Jews."*   PHIL

1988   American law professor Robert Unger publishes *Politics, a Work in Constructive Social Theory*, which emphasizes the difficulty of organizing planned economies and calls for a reorganization of government to develop a noncentralized socialism.   POL

1988   American psychologist Richard Haier reports that high intelligence may be the result of an efficiently organized brain.   PSYCH

1989   American anthropologist Marvin Harris publishes *Our Kind*, an exploration of
            the origins of human culture.   ANTH

1989   Australian critics Bill Ashcroft, Gareth Griffiths, and Helen Tiffin publish *The
            Empire Writes Back: Theory and Practice in Post-Colonial Literatures.*   CRIT

1989   Roy Harris and Talbot J. Taylor write on the history of linguistics in *Landmarks
            in Linguistic Thought: The Western Tradition from Socrates to Saussure.*   LING

1989   American social scientist Francis Fukuyama publishes the essay "The End of
            History." On the basis of recent world events, he argues that the ancient debate
            over the ideal form of government has been resolved in favor of democratic
            capitalism.   POL

1989   American political scientist Roger Masters publishes *The Nature of Politics*,
            which interprets the rise of the centralized state in terms of animal behavior
            and an evolutionary perspective.   POL

1989   In April, Chinese students begin a protest in Tiananmen Square in Beijing to
            promote national democratic reform. The group, which comes to include
            workers and intellectuals, soon numbers over a million. On June 3 and 4, the
            Chinese military invade the square, killing thousands and ending the
            movement.   POL

1989   In November, the Berlin Wall, a symbol of the Cold War since its erection in 1961
            along the border between East and West Berlin, begins to be dismantled. The
            event is a milestone in the decline of Soviet-bloc communism. The collapse of
            East Germany and unification with West Germany will follow in 1990.   POL

1990s   The concept of tracking, or segregating students by levels of ability and
            achievement, is challenged in primary and secondary schools across the
            United States. Opponents to tracking believe it deprives average students of
            opportunities throughout their school careers.   EDUC

1990s   Communication via the Internet, the international network of computers
            linked by telephone lines, becomes a major force in the dissemination of
            ideas. With film, radio, and television—mass media that came into their own
            earlier this century—the world of computer communication, or cyberspace,
            begins to revolutionize commerce, various industries, and lifestyles in indus-
            trialized nations. *See also* 1454, MISC.   MISC

1990s   In the United States and elsewhere, computer hackers such as New Yorker
            Mark Abene (a.k.a. Phiber Optik) are prosecuted for illegally entering protect-
            ed computer systems and obtaining private information. Such intrusion grows
            with the complexity and availability of computer equipment.   MISC

1990s   The Christian Coalition, a conservative American advocacy group, attempts to effect political change that reflects its religion-based views. The coalition is successful in helping to unseat incumbent moderates and liberals in the 1994 U.S. congressional elections.   REL

1990s   The United States experiences a surge of interest in angels, both as objects of spiritual belief and as decorative or artistic motifs.   REL

1990s   Informed by the writings of French philosopher Michel Foucault and others, as well as a more libertine attitude toward sexual practices, a pain-as-pleasure attitude becomes favored among some, prompting such ritualistic practices as tattooing, branding, and body piercing.   SOC

1990s   In pockets of the United States, right-wing antigovernment conspiracists form private militias to defend themselves against a government that they believe to be out to destroy them. Among states with private militias are Michigan and Montana. *See also* 1980s, POL.   SOC

1990s   In the United States, conservative political ideology is promulgated widely through public avenues such as talk radio and television. Commentators include Rush Limbaugh, Pat Buchanan, and George Will, among others.   SOC

1990s   In Western nations, increased life expectancy and a growing number of people over 65 are among the factors prompting a more positive view of aging and the perception of a "new," late stage of life. The aging of the work force also means that older workers may be disproportionately affected by downsizing policies that mandate their replacement by younger, cheaper workers.   SOC

1990   American critic Henry Louis Gates Jr. publishes *Reading Black, Reading Feminist*. CRIT

1990   Art historian Lucy Lippard promotes multicultural art in *Mixed Blessings: New Art in a Multicultural America*, a work that encourages criteria for looking at art based on class, culture, and gender.   CRIT

1990   Art critic Michael Brenson writes the essay "Is Quality an Idea Whose Time Has Gone?," a reevaluation of the definition of quality in discussions about art, aesthetic standards, multiculturalism, and American culture.   CRIT

1990   Critic Eve Kosofsky Sedgwick writes on literature and homosexuality in *Epistemology of the Closet*. Her other works include *Between Men* (1985).   CRIT

1990   American critic Gayatri Chakravorty Spivak publishes *The Post-Colonial Critic*. Her works, which combine Marxism, feminism, deconstructionism, and post-colonial cultural critique, also include *In Other Worlds* (1987).   CRIT

1990   American critic Camille Paglia publishes *Sexual Personae,* an analysis of gender roles and identity in which she debunks notions of the depth of female influence on civilization. The controversial book becomes a favorite of some conservative thinkers, some of whom misunderstand the author's radicalism, and sparks a lively debate within the feminist movement.   CRIT

1990   American economist David M. Kreps publishes *Game Theory and Economic Modeling.*   ECON

1990   Controversy about the origins of homosexuality is stirred by studies suggesting that genes may have an important effect on sexual orientation.   PSYCH

1990   American critic Regina Schwartz edits and publishes *The Book and the Text: The Bible and Literary Theory.*   REL

1991   Feminist anthropological theory is developed in Trinh T. Minh-Ha's *When the Moon Waxes Red* and Micaela di Leonardo's *Gender at the Crossroads of Knowledge.*   ANTH

1991   American critic Houston Baker Jr. publishes *Workings of the Spirit: The Poetics of Afro-American Women's Writing.*   CRIT

1991   English critic Antony Easthope publishes *Literary into Cultural Studies.*   CRIT

1991   American Marxist literary critic Fredric Jameson publishes *Postmodernism, or, The Cultural Logic of Late Capitalism* and the essay collection *Signatures of the Visible.*   CRIT

1991   English philosopher of language Paul Grice publishes *The Conception of Value.* Other works include *Studies in the Way of Words* (1989).   PHIL

1991   American philosopher Allen Gibbard publishes *Wise Choices, Apt Feelings,* in which he develops an ethical theory that emphasizes the feeling of guilt.   PHIL

1991   American philosopher David Lewis publishes *Parts of Classes,* in which he examines set theory in the light of the relationship of parts to whole.   PHIL

1991   American moral philosopher Thomas Nagel publishes *Equality and Partiality.*   PHIL

1991   Following years of economic and internal decline, and the inability of Soviet president Mikhail Gorbachev to effect *perestroika* ("restructuring") and *glasnost* ("openness"), the Union of Soviet Socialist Republics is dissolved on December 31. The collapse of the world's first and most powerful Communist nation symbolizes the defeat of Marxist-Leninist ideology in its struggle with democratic capitalism (*see* 1948, POL). The union is replaced by

a number of independent states attempting to govern themselves democratically and form free markets.   POL

1991   American psychologist Jan Belsky argues that girls brought up in dangerous
            environments are encouraged by evolution to have children early and often, to
            increase the chances that some offspring will survive.   PSYCH

1991   American philosopher Daniel C. Dennett publishes *Consciousness Explained*,
            in which he claims that there is no central, conscious "audience" in the
            brain. Instead, he argues that consciousness consists of multiple drafts com-
            posed by neural processes of "content fixation" that generate the illusion of
            a single, conscious self. His other works include *Brainstorms* (1978) and *The
            Intentional Stance* (1987).   PSYCH

1991   American critic Harold Bloom presents new arguments about biblical author-
            ship in *The Book of J*.   REL

1992   Mexican writer Carlos Fuentes, known for his fictional explorations of Latin
            American history in such novels as *The Death of Artemio Cruz* (1962), publish-
            es a book of essays in English, *The Burried Mirror: Reflections on Spain and the
            New World*.   CRIT

1992   In her book *The Beauty Myth*, American writer Naomi Wolf charts the history
            of women's obsession with limited ideas of the cultural phenomenon of
            beauty.   CRIT

1992   American philosopher Hilary Putnam publishes *Renewing Philosophy*.   PHIL

1992   English philosopher and novelist Iris Murdoch publishes *Metaphysics and
            Morals*.   PHIL

1992   The carnage of the Bosnian civil war exposes the West's inability to deal with
            genocide even within its own domain of Europe. It raises questions about how
            the international community should respond to genocide and about the pur-
            pose of the Western alliance after the collapse of the Soviet Union.   POL

1992   Rioting erupts in Los Angeles following the acquittal of white police officers
            accused of beating black motorist Rodney King. The acquittal and the riot
            spark renewed debate about race relations in the United States.   SOC

1992   Canada becomes the first country whose Supreme Court includes in its defin-
            ition of obscenity materials deemed to subordinate, degrade, or dehumanize
            women. In *R. v. Butler*, the Canadian Supreme Court upholds the obscenity
            provision of its criminal code and rules that the potential harm to women that
            may result from obscene materials may justify the materials' suppression.

American lawyer Catharine A. MacKinnon, whose antipornography crusade has been less successful in the United States (*see* 1980s, **soc**), helped write the brief in this case.   **soc**

1993   Former secretary of education William Bennett publishes *The Book of Virtues*, a collection of historical writings on the subject of virtue. The book, which becomes a best-seller, ties in with popular debate on the teaching of values in schools.   **EDUC**

1993   In her book *You Just Don't Understand*, American linguist Deborah Tannen posits that the root of much discord and miscommunication between the sexes lies in differing uses and expectations for language.   **LING**

1993   The movement toward digital libraries, accessible via the Internet, attains two notable landmarks when the Library of Congress begins to put its holdings online and the British Library begins digitizing the 11th-century manuscript of *Beowulf*.   **MISC**

1993   The administration of U.S. president Bill Clinton calls for the development of a National Information Infrastructure, a meganetwork of telecommunications technologies allowing for maximum access to information and media.   **MISC**

1993   American philosopher of law Ronald Dworkin publishes *Life's Dominion: An Argument about Abortion, Euthanasia, and Individual Freedom*.   **PHIL**

1993   English philosopher Bernard Williams publishes *Shame and Necessity*.   **PHIL**

1993   On April 19, U.S. government forces storm the Waco, Texas, compound of self-proclaimed religious leader David Koresh and his followers. The encounter results in an exchange of gunfire, the destruction of the compound, and the deaths of dozens of its residents. The event enrages antigovernment groups, allegedly influencing the bombing of a government building in Oklahoma City, Oklahoma (*see* 1995, **POL**).   **REL**

1993   Reflecting the increasingly shared family responsibilities of modern families, the U.S. Congress passes the Family Leave Act, which permits workers to take up to 12 weeks off work without pay in order to care for a family member.   **soc**

1994   American literary critic Harold Bloom defends the value of reading Western literature in *The Western Canon*.   **CRIT**

1994   American sociologists Charles Murray and Richard J. Herrnstein publish *The Bell Curve*, a study of the possible influence of fixed characteristics, such as race, on intelligence. The book sparks controversy, with critics questioning its findings and methodology.   **EDUC**

1994   Controversy erupts in the U.S. over the National History Standards, a set of education standards that critics say are far too multicultural and left-wing. **HIST**

1994   After several months of existence, *Wired* magazine becomes an influential periodical of the digital age. **JOURN**

1994   English philosopher Michael Dummett publishes the essay collection *The Seas of Language*. **PHIL**

1994   American philosopher Jerry Fodor continues his explorations into the nature of the mind in *The Elm and the Expert*. **PHIL**

1994–1995   The U.S. Supreme Court makes a series of decisions that point to its growing interest in reconsidering, and in some cases, limiting, the scope of power of the federal government. **POL**

1994   Brazilian sociologist and political scientist Fernando Cardoso wins his country's presidency. In the 1960s, his democratic left-leaning views won him recognition abroad and resulted in his persecution at home at the hands of Brazil's military rulers. Since then, many Brazilians came to support him and his inflation-fighting, free-market policies. **POL**

1994   American psychologists Amos Tversky and D. J. Koehler propose support theory, a theory of belief tying subjective probability to descriptions of events rather than events themselves. **PSYCH**

1994   American sociologist John Gagnon and his colleagues publish the most comprehensive study of sexuality since the Kinsey reports (*see* 1942, **soc**). **soc**

1994–1995   In the United States, the highly publicized criminal trial and acquittal of former football player O. J. Simpson for the murders of Nicole Brown Simpson and Ronald Goldman generate heated debates about race, the legal system, and domestic violence. **soc**

1995   Works of literary criticism include Joseph Tabbi's *Postmodern Sublime: Technology and American Writing from Mailer to Cyberpunk*; Rita Felski's examination of European fin de siècle texts in *The Gender of Modernity*; and literary theorist Michael Joyce's *Of Two Minds: Hypertext, Pedagogy, and Poetics*. **CRIT**

1995   American scholar of Latin American culture Neil Larsen publishes *Reading North by South: On Latin American Literature, Culture, and Politics*. **CRIT**

1995   American economist Paul Krugman publishes *Development, Geography, and Economic Theory*. **ECON**

1995   Economist Nasrul Islam discusses changes in growth in relation to different levels of productivity across countries in "Growth Empirics: A Panel Data Approach."   ECON

1995   American historian Gertrude Himmelfarb publishes *The De-Moralization of Society: From Victorian Virtues to Modern Values.*   HIST

1995   American historian Robert Darnton publishes *The Forbidden Best-Sellers of Pre-Revolutionary France,* a study of illegal books and their impact in the years preceding the French Revolution. Darnton argues that these books, which often mixed pornography with political radicalism, played a role—though probably not a great one—in bringing about the Revolution by convincing some already sympathetic readers that it was indeed time for change.   HIST

1995   American political scientist Robert Putnam publishes *Making Democracy Work: Civic Traditions in Modern Italy,* which explores the relationships between stable democracies and civic culture.   POL

1995   On April 19, two years after the U.S. government storming of the Koresh compound in Waco, Texas (*see* 1993, REL), the Alfred P. Murrah federal building in Oklahoma City, Oklahoma, is destroyed by a bomb, killing 167 people. It is believed to be an unprecedented act of domestic terrorism perpetrated on Americans by Americans and raises questions about the power of antigovernment forces in the country.   POL

1995   U.S. Speaker of the House of Representatives Newt Gingrich leads the new congressional Republican majority to attempt large-scale restructuring of the federal government through a plan known as the Contract with America. Among its goals are the balancing of the federal budget; the reduction of federal regulations on business and industry; the diminution of entitlements, social programs, and federal mandates; a greater emphasis on states' rights; and a decrease in taxes for individuals and businesses.   POL

1995   At Oxford University, scraps of a manuscript are unearthed that may reveal the oldest reference to Jesus as a divine being. The scraps are believed to date from the middle of the first century A.D.   REL

1995   American professor of theology Elaine Pagels publishes *The Origin of Satan,* about the transformation of the demon in religious thought. *See also* 1930, REL.   REL

1995   For the first time, the Church of England ordains women as priests.   REL

1995   On October 16, Nation of Islam leader Louis Farrakhan leads the Million Man March, a rally of African-American men in Washington, D.C., stressing personal responsibility.   SOC

1995   In several decisions on minority businesses, school desegregation, and redistricting for minorities, the U.S. Supreme Court curtails a number of orders and practices meant to encourage minority participation.   soc

1996   The American critical journal *Social Text* publishes an article by physicist Alan Sokal arguing that modern physics proves reality is subjective. Written in academic babble, the article is soon revealed to be a hoax intended to satirize postmodernist views. The journal's editors take offense at the deception, while opponents of postmodernism take comfort.   crit

1996   The diversity of contemporary approaches to art history is displayed in *12 Views of Manet's 'Bar'*, edited by Bradford R. Collins.   crit

1996   American scholar Julie A. Reuben publishes *The Making of the Modern American University*.   educ

1996   The Nobel Prize in economics is awarded to Canadian-American William S. Vickrey, who dies this year, and Briton James A. Mirrlees, for their separate contributions to the economic theory of incentives in situations where parties possess asymmetric (differing and incomplete) information.   econ

1996   American economists Lester Thurow and Paul Krugman publish books in which they take contrary positions on such issues as how to achieve economic growth and the effects of global competition on American wages. Thurow's book is *The Future of Capitalism*, Krugman's *Pop Internationalism*.   econ

1996   American economists David Johnson and Stephanie Shipp publish "Changing Inequality in the U.S. from 1980–1994: A Consumption Viewpoint."   econ

1996   American historian Daniel Jonah Goldhagen publishes *Hitler's Willing Executioners*, which argues for the responsibility of ordinary Germans in carrying out the Holocaust.   hist

1996   American historian Alan Taylor wins the Pulitzer Prize for history for *William Cooper's Town*.   hist

1996   The school board of Oakland, California, decides that the "black English" spoken by many of their students is really a separate language called ebonics. The idea generates controversy about linguistic differences among American ethnic groups and about the best way to educate minority students.   ling

1996   American scholar James L. Kloppenberg reflects on the renewal of the American pragmatic tradition in such disciplines as literary criticism and history in "Pragmatism: An Old Name for Some New Ways of Thinking."   phil

| 1996 | In Montana, an antitax, antigovernment group called the Freemen surrenders to federal agents after an armed standoff of 81 days. **POL** |

| 1996 | Michael Dillon publishes *Politics of Security: Towards a Political Philosophy of Continental Thought.* **POL** |

| 1996 | Social scientist Sherry Turkle publishes *Life on the Screen: Identity in the Age of the Internet.* **SOC** |

| 1996 | The MacArthur Foundation establishes a research network on the link between socioeconomic status and health, to be directed by psychologist Nancy Adler. **SOC** |

| 1996 | American biotechnology critic Jeremy Rifkin challenges patenting of a gene implicated in early-onset breast cancer. Supported by women's health advocacy groups, Rifkin argues that genes should be regarded as an unpatentable natural resource and warns against genetic tests that could pose a threat to privacy. **SOC** |

| 1996 | In an example of new law being generated by advances in gene research, U.S. president Bill Clinton signs a bill prohibiting insurance companies from treating a genetic susceptibility as a preexisting condition for which coverage can be denied. **SOC** |

| 1996 | The U.S. Congress makes it a crime to display indecent material on an interactive computer network in a way accessible to minors. The law will be challenged before the Supreme Court. **SOC** |

| 1996 | Montana recluse Theodore J. Kaczynski is charged with being the Unabomber, who had been linked to a series of bombings over 17 years. In 1995, the Unabomber had published a manifesto entitled *Industrial Society and Its Future,* attacking the modern world and its technologies. **SOC** |

| 1996 | Falling crime rates in the United States spark debate as to the causes of the decline, including changing demographics and improved police work. **SOC** |

| 1997 | For his studies of wage inequalities, American economist Kevin M. Murphy wins the prestigious John Bates Clark Medal from the American Economic Association. **ECON** |

| 1997 | Hungarian-American financier and philanthropist George Soros publishes "The Capitalist Threat," an essay warning against the hazards posed to democracy by the spread of free-market values into all areas of life. **ECON** |

1997   American economist Daphne A. Kenyon analyzes theories of state and local economic development policies in "Theories of Interjurisdictional Competition." ECON

1997   Irish historian R. F. Foster publishes the first of two volumes of *W. B. Yeats: A Life*. HIST

1997   American journalists Richard Bernstein and Ross H. Munro, in their book *The Coming Conflict with China*, are among the international analysts debating the significance of China's growth as a world power. POL

1997   In Britain, Labor Party leader Tony Blair is elected prime minister, ending 18 years of Conservative control that began with Margaret Thatcher's 1979 election. Blair has been credited with, and criticized for, helping the Labor Party become less socialist and more moderate than it was in the past. POL

1997   American political theorist Michael J. Sandel publishes *Democracy's Discontent*, in which he distinguishes between "procedural liberalism" and "formative republicanism" as two ways of understanding freedom and democracy. POL

1997   Thirty-nine members of a California cult called Heaven's Gate kill themselves in the worst mass suicide on American soil. (In November 1978, 912 members of the People's Temple, a cult that had recently relocated from California to Guyana, died in a mass suicide orchestrated by cult leader Jim Jones.) The Heaven's Gate cultists, led by Marshall Herff Applewhite, believed their deaths would free them to join a spaceship accompanying the Hale-Bopp comet. REL

1997   A University of Georgia poll finds that about 40 percent of scientists believe in God, the same proportion as in a 1916 poll. The data undermine the assumption that religious belief among educated people has been declining in the 20th century. REL

1997   *The Gift of Peace*, a memoir by Joseph Cardinal Bernardin, Archbishop of Chicago, is published posthumously. The account of his last years inspires others facing terminal illness. REL

1997   The Presbyterian Church (U.S.A.) votes to ban practicing homosexuals from the clergy. The issue of whether to ordain openly gay people has divided many Protestant churches in recent years. REL

1997   In Terekhovo, Russia, a woman is murdered and several others are assaulted for allegedly practicing witchcraft. Belief in the occult has been on the rise in Russia since the fall of Communism. REL

1997   American sociologists Kathryn Edin and Laura Lein document the economic situation and survival strategies of women on welfare in *Making Ends Meet*. SOC

1997   Anti-smoking activists gain a victory when the Liggett Group Inc. becomes the
            first leading American cigarette manufacturer to acknowledge that tobacco is
            addictive and causes cancer. The admission is part of a settlement of lawsuits
            filed by 22 states.   **soc**

1997   The heads of three United Nations agencies join in the growing international
            appeal to end female genital mutilation, a cultural practice common in Africa
            and parts of the Middle East.   **soc**

Appendix:
Birth and Death Dates

Abbagnano, Nicola	1901–	Anthony, Susan B.	1820–1906
ʿAbd al-Qādir al-Jīlanī	c. 1077–1166	Antiochus of Ascalon	130–68 B.C.
Abd al-Rahman al-Jabarti	1753–1825	Antiphon	480–411 B.C.
Abduh, Muhammad	1849–1905	Antisthenes	445–360 B.C.
Abelard, Peter	1079–1144	Apollinaire, Guillaume	1880–1918
Abrabanel, Judah	c. 1460–c. 1523	Arcesilaus	316–242 B.C.
Abrams, M. H.	1912–	Arendt, Hannah	1906–1975
Abū Bakr	573–624	Aristotle	384–322 B.C.
Abufazl	1551–1602	Aristoxenus	4th century B.C.
Adams, Hannah	1755–1831	Arius	250–336
Adams, Henry	1838–1918	Arius Didymus	fl. 20 B.C.
Adams, Herbert Baxter	1850–1901	Arjun	1563–1606
Addams, Jane	1860–1935	Arminius, Jacobus	1560–1609
Addison, Joseph	1672–1719	Arnauld, Antoine	1612–1694
Adler, Alfred	1870–1937	Arnheim, Rudolf	1904–
Adler, Felix	1851–1933	Arnold, Matthew	1822–1888
Adorno, Theodor	1903–1969	Ashʿari, Abū al-Hasan al-	873–936
Agee, James	1909–1955	Aśoka	273–232 B.C.
Ahmad Khan, Sir Sayyid	1817–1898	Athanasius	293–373
Akiba ben Joseph	50–135	Atīśa	982–1054
Alberti, Leon Battista	1404–1472	at-Tabarī	839–923
Albertus Magnus	c. 1200–1280	Auerbach, Erich	1892–1957
Alcott, Bronson	1799–1888	Augustine of Hippo	354–430
Alcuin (Albinus)	753–804	Aulard, François	1849–1928
ʿAlī ibn Abī Tālib	600–661	Aurobindo Ghose, Sri	1872–1950
ʿAlī Mohammad of Shiraz, Mīrza	1819–1850	Austin, John Langshaw	1790–1859
Alloway, Lawrence	1926–1990	Avenarius, Richard	1843–1896
Allport, Gordon Willard	1897–1967	Averroës (Ibn Rushd)	1126–1198
Althusser, Louis	1918–1990	Avicenna (Ibn Sina)	980–1037
Ambrose	340–397	Babbitt, Irving	1865–1933
Ammonius Saccas	175–242	Babeuf, François	1760–1797
Anaxagoras of Clazomenae	500–428 B.C.	Bach, Carl Philipp Emanuel	1714–1788
Anaxarchus	4th century B.C.	Bachelard, Gaston	1884–1962
Anaximander of Miletus	610–547 B.C.	Bacon, Francis	1561–1626
Anaximenes of Miletus	fl. 546 B.C.	Bacon, Roger	1220–1292
Anselm	1033–1109	Bahā Allāh (Bahaullah)	1817–1892
Antal, Frederick	1887–1954	Bahr, Hermann	1863–1934
Anthony of Egypt	250–355	Bain, Alexander	1818–1903

Bakhtin, M. M.	1895–1975		Biddle, John	1615–1662
Bakunin, Mikhail	1814–1876		Binet, Alfred	1857–1911
Bancroft, George	1800–1891		Binswanger, Ludwig	1881–1966
Barr, Alfred H., Jr.	1902–1981		Blackmur, Richard P.	1904–1965
Barth, Karl	1886–1968		Blackstone, Sir William	1723–1780
Barthes, Roland	1915–1980		Blake, William	1757–1827
Barzun, Jacques	1907–		Blanc, Louis	1811–1882
Basilides	fl. 120–145		Blavatsky, Helena Petrovna	1831–1891
Bataille, Georges	1897–1962		Bleuler, Eugen	1857–1939
Bate, W. J.	1918–		Bloom, Harold	1930–
Baudelaire, Charles	1821–1867		Bloomer, Amelia Jenks	1818–1894
Baudrillard, Jean	1929–		Blumenbach, Johann	1752–1840
Baumgarten, Alexander Gottlieb	1714–1762		Blumer, Herbert	1900–1987
Bayes, Thomas	1702–1761		Boas, Franz	1858–1942
Bayle, Pierre	1647–1706		Boccaccio, Giovanni	1313–1375
Bazin, André	1918–1958		Bodin, Jean	1530–1596
Beard, Charles	1874–1948		Boethius	480–524
Beard, Mary Ritter	1876–1958		Böhme, Jakob	1575–1624
Beauvoir, Simone de	1908–1986		Boileau-Despréaux, Nicolas	1636–1711
Beck, Aaron T.	1921–		Bolton, Herbert	1870–1953
Beecher, Lyman	1775–1863		Boltzmann, Ludwig	1844–1906
Belinsky, Vissarion	1811–1848		Bonaventure	1217–1274
Bell, Clive	1881–1964		Bonhoeffer, Dietrich	1906–1945
Bell, Daniel	1919–		Boniface	675–754
Bellah, Robert N.	1927–		Bontemps, Arna Wendell	1902–1973
Bellori, Giovanni Pietro	1615–1696		Boole, George	1815–1864
Benedict, Ruth	1887–1948		Booth, William	1829–1912
Benedict	480–547		Bosanquet, Bernard	1848–1923
Benjamin, Walter	1892–1940		Boscovich, Ruggiero	1711–1787
Bennett, William	1943–		Bossuet, Jacques	1627–1704
Bentham, Jeremy	1748–1832		Boswell, James	1740–1795
Bentley, Arthur	1870–1957		Bradford, Gamaliel	1863–1932
Berenson, Bernard	1865–1959		Bradford, William	1590–1657
Berger, John Peter	1926–		Brakhage, Stan	1933–
Bergson, Henri	1859–1941		Breasted, James Henry	1865–1935
Berkeley, George	1685–1753		Brentano, Franz	1838–1917
Berkman, Alexander	1870–1936		Breton, André	1896–1966
Berlin, Isaiah	1909–		Breuer, Josef	1842–1925
Bernard of Clairvaux	c. 1090–1153		Bridgman, Percy Williams	1882–1961
Berne, Eric	1910–1970		Brik, Osip	1888–1945
Besant, Annie	1847–1933		Brill, Abraham Arden	1874–1948
Bettelheim, Bruno	1903–1990		Broca, Pierre-Paul	1824–1880
Beuys, Joseph	1921–1986		Brooks, Cleanth	1906–1994
Beveridge, Albert	1862–1927		Brooks, Van Wyck	1886–1963
Bhave, Vinoba	1895–1982		Brouwer, Luitzen	1881–1966

Browne, Robert	c. 1550–1633
Browne, Sir Thomas	1605–1682
Brownson, Orestes	1803–1876
Bruno, Giordano	1548–1600
Brunschvicg, Léon	1869–1944
Bryan, William Jennings	1860–1925
Bryce, James	1838–1922
Buber, Martin	1878–1965
Bucer, Martin	1491–1551
Buchman, Frank Nathan Daniel	1878–1961
Buckley, William F., Jr.	1925–
Buddhaghosa	5th century
Bukharin, Nikolay Ivanovich	1888–1938
Bultmann, Rudolf Karl	1884–1976
Bunyan, John	1628–1688
Burckhardt, Jakob	1818–1897
Burgess, John	1844–1931
Burgin, Victor	1941–
Buridan, Jean	c. 1300–1358
Burke, Edmund	1729–1797
Burke, Kenneth	1897–1993
Burn, Ian	1939–
Burnet, Gilbert	1643–1715
Burney, Charles	1726–1814
Butler, Joseph	1692–1752
Calvin, John	1509–1564
Camden, William	1551–1623
Campion, Edmund	1540–1581
Campion, Thomas	1567–1620
Camus, Albert	1913–1960
Caritat, Marie-Jean de	
(Marquis de Condorcet)	1743–1794
Carlyle, Thomas	1795–1881
Carnap, Rudolf	1891–1970
Carneades	214–129 B.C.
Carnegie, Dale	1888–1955
Carrà, Carlo	1881–1966
Cassel, Gustav	1866–1945
Cassiodorus	490–585
Cassirer, Ernst	1874–1945
Castiglione, Baldassare	1478–1529
Cato the Elder	234–149 B.C.
Cavell, Stanley	1926–
Cavendish, George	1500–1561
Cellini, Benvenuto	1500–1571

Celsus	2nd century
Cennini, Cennino	c. 1370–1440
Chaitanya	fl. c. 1500
Chambers, Ephraim	c. 1680–1740
Chang Ling	1st century
Cheng Hsüan	2nd century
Child, Francis James	1825–1896
Chodorow, Nancy	1944–
Chomsky, Noam	1928–
Chrysippus of Soli	280–207 B.C.
Chu Hsi, Sushigaku	1130–1200
Chu Tao-sheng	fl. 397–434
Chuang-tzu	369–286 B.C.
Churchill, Sir Winston	1874–1965
Cibber, Colley	1671–1757
Cicero, Marcus Tullius	106–43 B.C.
Cixous, Hélène	1937–
Clark, John Bates	1847–1938
Clarke, Samuel	1675–1729
Clay, Henry	1777–1852
Cleanthes of Assos	331–232 B.C.
Cleisthenes	fl. 6th century B.C.
Clement I (early pope)	d. 101
Clement of Alexandria	150–215
Cobden, Richard	1804–1865
Coleman, James	1926–1995
Coleridge, Samuel Taylor	1772–1834
Collingwood, Robin George	1889–1943
Collins, Anthony	1676–1729
Columban (Irish abbot)	c. 543–615
Comenius Johann Amos	1592–1670
Comte, Auguste	1798–1857
Condillac, Étienne Bonnot de	1715–1780
Confucius	551–479 B.C.
Cooley, Charles Horton	1864–1929
Coomaraswamy, Ananda Kentish	1877–1947
Cotton, Robert Bruce	1571–1631
Cousin, Victor	1792–1867
Coverdale, Miles	1488–1569
Crane, Ronald S.	1888–1967
Cranmer, Thomas	1488–1556
Crates of Thebes	365–285 B.C.
Cratylus	5th century B.C.
Crescas, Hasdai ben Abraham	1340–1410
Crèvecoeur, J. Hector St. John de	1735–1813

Croce, Benedetto	1866–1952	Durkheim, Émile	1858–1917
Crowley, Aleister	1875–1947	Dwight, Timothy	1752–1817
Cucchi, Enzo	1950–	Dworkin, Ronald	1931–
Cudworth, Ralph	1617–1688	Eastman, Max	1883–1969
Culverwel, Nathanael	c. 1618–1651	Ebbinghaus, Hermann	1850–1909
Cumberland, Richard	1631–1718	Eco, Umberto	1932–
Dante Alighieri	1265–1321	Eddy, Mary Baker	1821–1910
Darwin, Charles	1809–1882	Edel, Leon	1907–1997
Davis, Andrew Jackson	1826–1910	Edwards, Jonathan	1703–1758
Day, Dorothy	1897–1980	Einstein, Albert	1879–1955
Dayananda Sarasvati	1824–1883	Eisenstein, Sergey	1898–1948
De Man, Paul	1919–1983	Elijah ben Solomon	1720–1797
De Morgan, Augustus	1806–1871	Eliot, Charles William	1834–1926
Democritus	460–370 B.C.	Eliot, T. S.	1888–1965
Denis, Maurice	1870–1943	Ellis, Havelock	1859–1939
Dennett, Daniel C.	1942–	Ellmann, Richard	1918–1987
Derrida, Jacques	1930–	Elphinstone, Mountstuart	1779–1859
Descartes, René	1596–1650	Emerson, Ralph Waldo	1803–1882
Dewey, John	1859–1952	Empedocles of Acragas	493–433 B.C.
Dhammaceti	15th century	Empson, Sir William	1906–1984
Diaghilev, Sergey Pavlovich	1872–1929	Endell, August	1871–1925
Diderot, Denis	1713–1784	Engels, Friedrich	1820–1895
Dilthey, Wilhelm	1833–1911	Epictetus	55–135
Dio Chrysostom	40–112	Epicurus	341–270 B.C.
Diogenes Laertius	3d century	Erasmus, Desiderius	c. 1466–1536
Diogenes of Sinope	400–325 B.C.	Erastus, Thomas	1524–1583
Dionysius Exiguus	500–560	Erigena, John Scotus	810–877
Dionysius of Halicarnassus	fl. 25 B.C.	Erikson, Erik H.	1902–1994
Dionysius Thrax	170–90 B.C.	Euclid	fl. 300 B.C.
Dix, Dorothea	1802–1887	Eutyches	378–450
Dōgen	1200–1253	Evans-Pritchard, Edward	1902–1973
Doesburg, Theo van	1883–1931	Fa-hsien	fl. 399–414
Dominic (cleric)	c. 1170–1221	Fanon, Frantz	1925–1961
Douglass, Frederick	c. 1817–1895	Félibien, André	1619–1695
Draco	fl. 621 B.C.	Festinger, Leon	1919–1989
Dryden, John	1631–1700	Feuerbach, Ludwig	1804–1872
Du Bois, W. E. B.	1868–1963	Feyerabend, Paul	1924–1994
Dubnow, Simon	1860–1941	Fichte, Johann Gottlieb	1762–1814
Dugdale, Sir William	1605–1686	Ficino, Marsilio	1433–1499
Duguit, Léon	1859–1928	Filarete	c. 1400–c. 1470
Dummett, Michael	1925–	Finney, Charles Grandison	1792–1875
Duncan, Isadora	1878–1927	Fiorillo, Johann Dominicus	1748–1821
Dunlap, William	1766–1839	Fischer, Kuno	1824–1907
Dunning, William	1857–1922	Fish, Stanley	1938–
Duns Scotus, John	c. 1266–1308	Flaubert, Gustave	1821–1880

Fletcher, Alice Cunningham	1838–1923	Garvey, Marcus	1887–1940
Focillon, Henri-Joseph	1881–1943	Gassendi, Pierre	1592–1655
Fokine, Michel	1880–1942	Gates, Henry Louis, Jr.	1950–
Fontano, Lucio	1899–1968	Geertz, Clifford	1923–
Forrest, Nathan Bedford	1821–1877	Geiger, Abraham	1810–1874
Foster, Hal	1955–	Geminiani, Francesco	c. 1687–1762
Foucault, Michel	1926–1984	Gentile, Giovanni	1875–1944
Foucher, Simon	1644–1696	Gersonides (Levi ben Gershom)	1288–1344
Fourier, Charles	1772–1837	Geulincx, Arnold	1624–1669
Fox, George	1624–1691	Ghazālī, Abu Hāmid al-	1058–1111
Foxe, John	1516–1587	Ghiberti, Lorenzo	c. 1378–1455
Francis de Sales	1567–1622	Gibbon, Edward	1737–1794
Francis of Assisi	c. 1181–1226	Giedion, Sigfried	1888–1968
Francis Xavier	1506–1552	Gilligan, Carol	1936–
Frank, Anne	1929–1945	Gilman, Charlotte Perkins	1860–1935
Frankel, Zacharias	1801–1875	Girard, René	1923–
Frankl, Viktor	1905–1997	Gladden, Washington	1836–1918
Franklin, Benjamin	1706–1790	Glanvill, Joseph	1636–1680
Franklin, John Hope	1915–	Gobineau, Joseph-Arthur de	1816–1882
Frazer, James George	1854–1941	Gödel, Kurt	1906–1978
Frazier, Edward Franklin	1894–1962	Godwin, William	1756–1836
Freeman, Douglas Southall	1886–1953	Goethe, Johann Wolfgang von	1749–1832
Frege, Ludwig Gottlob	1848–1925	Goffman, Erving	1922–1982
Freire, Paolo	1921–	Gokhale, Gopāl Krishna	1866–1915
Frelinghuysen, Theodore	1787–1862	Goldman, Emma	1869–1940
Freud, Sigmund	1856–1939	Goldsmith, Oliver	1730–1774
Fried, Michael	1939–	Gombrich, Ernst	1909–
Friedan, Betty	1921–	Goodnow, Frank	1859–1939
Friedman, Milton	1912–	Gorbachev, Mikhail	1931–
Frisch, Ragnar	1895–1973	Graetz, Heinrich	1817–1891
Froebel, Friedrich	1782–1852	Graham, Billy	1918–
Fry, Roger Eliot	1866–1934	Gramsci, Antonio	1891–1937
Frye, Northrop	1912–1991	Green, John Richard	1837–1883
Fuller, Margaret	1810–1850	Green, Thomas Hill	1836–1882
Fuller, Thomas	1608–1661	Greenberg, Clement	1909–1993
Gadamer, Hans-Georg	1900–	Greenblatt, Stephen	1943–
Galbraith, John Kenneth	1908–	Greer, Germaine	1939–
Galen of Pergamum	129–199	Gregory I (Gregory the Great) (pope)	540–604
Gall, Franz Joseph	1758–1828	Gregory VII (pope)	c. 1020–1085
Gallup, George	1901–1984	Gregory of Nazianzus	330–389
Galton, Sir Francis	1822–1911	Grimm, Jacob	1785–1863
Gan, Alexey	1889–1942	Gropius, Walter	1883–1969
Gandhi, Mohandas	1869–1948	Grosseteste, Robert	c. 1175–1253
Gardiner, Samuel	1829–1902	Grotius, Hugo	1583–1645
Garrison, William Lloyd	1805–1879		

Guicciardini, Francesco	1483–1540	Hobbes, Thomas	1588–1679
Guizot, François	1787–1874	Hofmann, Hans	1880–1966
Gumplowicz, Ludwig	1838–1909	Hofstadter, Richard	1916–1970
Gurdjieff, George Ivanovich	1872–1945	Holbach, Paul-Henri d'	1723–1789
Gyogi	670–749	Hölderlin, Friedrich	1770–1843
Habermas, Jürgen	1929–	Holdheim, Samuel	1806–1860
Hahnemann, Samuel	1755–1843	Hōnen	1133–1212
Hakluyt, Richard	c.1552–1616	Hooker, Richard	c. 1553–1600
Hall, Granville Stanley	1844–1924	Horace	65–8 B.C.
Hallāj, al-	858–922	Horney, Karen	1885–1952
Hallam, Henry	1777–1859	Howells, William Dean	1837–1920
Hamann, Johann Georg	1730–1788	Hsüan-tsang	602–664
Hamilton, Alexander	1755–1804	Hsün-tzu	298–230 B.C.
Hamilton, William	1788–1856	Hubbard, L. Ron	1911–1986
Hanotaux, Gabriel	1853–1944	Hui-neng	637–713
Hanslick, Eduard	1825–1904	Hui-yüan	334–416
Harley, Robert	1661–1724	Hulme, Thomas Ernest	1883–1917
Harlow, Harry F.	1905–1981	Hume, David	1711–1776
Harris, Marvin	1927–	Hunt, Leigh	1784–1859
Hartley, David	1705–1757	Husserl, Edmund	1859–1938
Hartman, Geoffrey	1929–	Hutcheson, Francis	1694–1746
Haskins, Charles Homer	1870–1937	Hutchins, Robert Maynard	1899–1977
Hawkins, John	1719–1789	Hutchinson, Anne	c. 1591–1643
Hayek, Friedrich	1899–1992	Hutter, Jacob	d. 1536
Hazlitt, William	1778–1830	Huxley, Thomas Henry	1825–1895
Hearne, Thomas	1678–1735	Hypatia	370–415
Hegel, Georg Wilhelm Friedrich	1770–1831	Ibn Ezra, Abraham ben Meir	1089–1164
Heidegger, Martin	1889–1976	Ibn Daud, Abraham	1110–1180
Heilbroner, Robert	1919–	Ibn Tūmart	1078–1130
Heilbrun, Carolyn	1926–	Ignatius of Loyola	1491–1556
Heisenberg, Werner	1901–1976	Innocent III	c. 1160–1216
Helvétius, Claude-Adrien	1715–1771	Irenaeus (pope)	120–200
Hempel, Carl Gustav	1905–	Irigaray, Luce	1939–
Heracleitus of Ephesus	c. 540–480 B.C.	Isaiah	8th century B.C.
Herbart, Johann	1776–1841	Isocrates	436–338 B.C.
Herbert, Edward,		Israel ben Eliezer	c. 1698–1760
first baron of Cherbury	1583–1648	Isserles, Moses	1525–1572
Herder, Johann Gottfried von	1744–1803	Jacob ben Asher	1270–1340
Herodotus	480–425 B.C.	Jakobson, Roman	1896–1982
Herzen, Aleksandr	1812–1870	James, Henry	1843–1916
Herzl, Theodor	1860–1904	James, William	1842–1910
Hilbert, David	1862–1943	Jameson, Fredric	1934–
Hippocrates	fl. 460 B.C.	Jansen, Cornelis	1585–1638
Hirsch, E. D., Jr.	1928–	Jaspers, Karl	1883–1969
Hitler, Adolf	1889–1945	Jay, John	1745–1829

Jayadeva	12th century	Kristeva, Julia	1941–
Jazuli, al-	d. c. 1465	Kroeber, Alfred Louis	1876–1960
Jefferson, Thomas	1743–1826	Kropotkin, Pyotr	1842–1921
Jerome	347–419	Kubler, George	1912–
Jesus Christ	6 B.C.–30	Kübler-Ross, Elisabeth	1926–
Jevons, William Stanley	1835–1882	Kugler, Franz	1808–1858
Jñāneśvara	1275–1296	Kuhn, Thomas	1922–
John Chrysostom	c. 347–407	Kūkai (Kōbō Daishi)	774–835
John of Salisbury	1115–1180	Küng, Hans	1928–
Johnson, Samuel	1709–1784	K'ung Ying-ta	7th century
Johnson, Virginia	1925–	Kurozumi Munetado	1780–1850
Judah ha-Levi	1075–1141	La Mettrie, Julien de	1709–1751
Julian the Apostate	331–363	Lacan, Jacques	1901–1981
Julian of Norwich	1342–c. 1416	Lamartine, Alphonse de	1790–1869
Jung, Carl Gustav	1875–1961	Lange, Carl	1834–1900
Kabir	1440–1518	Langer, Susanne	1895–1985
Kael, Pauline	1919–	Lanier, Sidney	1842–1881
Kahnweiler, Daniel-Henri	1884–1976	Lanzi, Luigi	1732–1810
Kandinsky, Wassily	1866–1944	Lao-tzu	6th century B.C.
Kant, Immanuel	1724–1804	Laski, Harold	1893–1950
Kaplan, Mordecai	1881–1983	Lasswell, Harold	1902–1978
Kaprow, Allan	1927–	Lawrence, D. H.	1885–1930
Karo, Joseph	1488–1575	Lazarsfeld, Paul	1901–1976
Kautsky, Karl	1854–1938	Le Bon, Gustave	1841–1931
Keble, John	1792–1866	Le Corbusier	1887–1965
Keller, Helen	1880–1968	Leavis, F. R.	1895–1978
Kempe, Margery	c. 1373–c. 1440	Leibniz, Gottfried Wilhelm	1646–1716
Kenko, Yoshida	1283–1350	Leland, John	c.1506–1552
Keshub Chunder Sen	1838–1884	Lenin	1870–1924
Keynes, John Maynard	1883–1946	Leo IX	1002–1054
Kiefer, Anselm	1945–	Lessing, Gotthold	1729–1781
Kierkegaard, Søren	1813–1855	Leucippus of Miletus	450–420 B.C.
King, Martin Luther, Jr.	1929–1968	Lévi-Strauss, Claude	1908–
Kinsey, Alfred	1894–1956	Lévy-Bruhl, Lucien	1857–1939
Klein, Melanie	1882–1960	Lewis, C. S.	1898–1963
Klingender, Francis	1907–1955	Lewis, Clarence Irving	1883–1964
Klyuchevsky, Vasily	1841–1911	Lichtenberg, Georg Cristoph	1742–1799
Knox, John	c.1513–1572	Linton, Ralph	1893–1953
Koffka, Kurt	1886–1941	Livy	59 B.C.–17
Köhler, Wolfgang	1887–1867	Locke, John	1632–1704
Kosuth, Joseph	1945–	Lockhart, John	1794–1854
Kounellis, Jannis	1936–	Lombard, Peter	c. 1095–1160
Kracauer, Siegfried	1889–1966	Lombroso, Cesare	1836–1909
Krauss, Rosalind	1941–	Longinus	1st century
Kripke, Saul Aaron	1940–	Lotze, Rudolf Hermann	1817–1881

Lovejoy, Arthur Oncken	1873–1963
Lucretius	98–55 B.C.
Lukács, György	1885–1971
Luria, Isaac	1534–1572
Luther, Martin	1483–1546
Lynd, Helen	1896–1982
Lynd, Robert	1892–1970
Lyotard, Jean-François	1924–
Ma Jung	2nd century
Mabillon, Jean	1632–1707
Macaulay, Thomas Babington	1800–1859
Maccabaeus, Judas	d. 160 B.C.
Mach, Ernst	1838–1916
Machiavelli, Niccolò	1469–1527
Madison, James	1751–1836
Madox, Thomas	1666–1727
Mahan, Alfred Thayer	1840–1914
Maimonides, Moses	1135–1204
Maitland, Frederic	1850–1906
Makemie, Francis	c. 1658–c. 1707
Male, Émile	1862–1954
Malebranche, Nicolas de	1638–1715
Malevich, Kazimir	1878–1935
Malinowski, Bronislaw	1884–1942
Malraux, André	1901–1976
Malthus, Thomas Robert	1766–1834
Mandeville, Bernard	1670–1733
Mann, Horace	1796–1859
Mannheim, Karl	1893–1947
Mao Zedong	1893–1976
Marcel, Gabriel	1889–1973
Marcion	d. 160
Marcus Aurelius	121–180
Marcuse, Herbert	1898–1979
Maritain, Jacques	1882–1973
Marshall, Alfred	1842–1924
Marsilius of Padua	c. 1280–c. 1343
Martin V (pope)	316–397
Martineau, Harriet	1802–1876
Marx, Karl	1818–1883
Maslow, Abraham	1908–1970
Masters, William Howell	1915–
Mather, Cotton	1663–1728
Mather, Increase	1639–1723
Matthiessen, Otto	1902–1950
Maurin, Peter	1877–1949
Maurois, André	1885–1967
Mauss, Marcel	1872–1950
McDougall, William	1871–1938
McLuhan, Marshall	1911–1980
McMaster, John	1852–1932
McPherson, Aimee Semple	1890–1944
Mead, George Herbert	1863–1931
Mead, Margaret	1901–1978
Meier-Graefe, Julius	1867–1935
Meinecke, Friedrich	1862–1954
Melanchthon, Philipp	1497–1560
Mencken, H. L.	1880–1956
Mendelssohn, Moses	1729–1786
Meng-tzu (Mencius)	372–289 B.C.
Menno Simons	c. 1496–1561
Merleau-Ponty, Maurice	1908–1961
Merriam, Charles	1874–1953
Mersenne, Marin	1588–1648
Merton, Robert K.	1910–
Mesmer, Franz Anton	1734–1815
Metz, Christian	1931–
Metzinger, Jean	1883–1956
Michel, Louise	1830–1905
Michelet, Jules	1798–1874
Michels, Robert	1876–1936
Milgram, Stanley	1933–1984
Mill, James	1773–1836
Mill, John Stuart	1806–1873
Miller, J. Hillis	1928–
Miller, William	1782–1849
Millett, Kate	1934–
Mills, C. Wright	1916–1962
Milton, John	1608–1674
Milyukov, Pavel	1859–1943
Minsky, Marvin	1927–
Mitchell, Loften	1920–
Mitchell, Wesley Clair	1874–1948
Mo-tzu	479–391 B.C.
Mokichi, Okada	1882–1955
Molina, Luis de	1535–1600
Mommsen, Theodor	1817–1903
Montaigne, Michel de	1533–1592
Montalembert, Charles-Forbes-René	1810–1870

Montessori, Maria	1870–1952	Paine, Thomas	1737–1809
Moore, George Edward	1873–1958	Paley, William	1743–1805
Moore, Henry	1898–1986	Palomino, Antonio	1653–1726
Moréas, Jean	1856–1910	Panofsky, Erwin	1892–1968
Morgan, Lewis Henry	1818–1881	Parākramabāhu	14th century
Morison, Samuel Eliot	1887–1976	Pareto, Vilfredo	1848–1923
Morris, William	1834–1896	Park, Robert	1864–1944
Mosca, Gaetano	1858–1941	Parker, Theodore	1810–1860
Moses	fl. 1200 B.C.	Parkman, Francis	1823–1893
Moses de León	1250–1305	Parmenides of Elea	b. 515 B.C.
Motherwell, Robert	1915–1991	Parrington, Vernon	1871–1929
Motley, John Lothrop	1814–1877	Parsons, Talcott	1902–1979
Mott, Lucretia	1793–1880	Pascal, Blaise	1623–1662
M'Taggart, John	1866–1925	Pater, Walter	1839–1894
Muhammad	570–632	Patrick, St.	5th century
Mukarovsky, Jan	1891–1975	Paul (apostle)	d. 67
Mulvey, Laura	1941–	Pavlov, Ivan	1849–1936
Münzer, Thomas	c. 1468–1525	Peale, Norman Vincent	1898–1993
Myrdal, Gunnar	1898–1987	Peirce, Charles Sanders	1839–1914
Namier, Lewis Bernstein	1888–1960	Pelagius	354–418
Nanak Guru	1469–1539	Perry, Ralph Barton	1876–1957
Nestorius	d. 451	Pestalozzi, Johann	1746–1827
Neurath, Otto	1882–1945	Peter (apostle)	d. 64
Nevins, Allan	1890–1971	Petrarch	1304–1374
Newman, Barnett	1905–1970	Pevsner, Nikolaus	1902–1983
Newman, John Henry	1801–1890	Phillips, Ulrich	1877–1934
Nichiren	1222–1282	Philodemus of Gadara	110–35 B.C.
Nicholas, Bishop of Myra	4th century	Piaget, Jean	1896–1980
Nicholas of Cusa	1401–1464	Pickering, John	1777–1846
Niebuhr, Barthold	1776–1831	Pico della Mirandola, Giovanni	1463–1494
Niebuhr, Reinhold	1892–1971	Pigou, Arthur Cecil	1877–1959
Nietzsche, Friedrich	1844–1900	Pirenne, Henri	1862–1935
Norris, Frank	1870–1902	Plato	428–347
North, Roger	1653–1734	Pliny the Elder	23–79
Noverre, Jean-Georges	1727–1810	Plotinus	205–270
Nozick, Robert	1938–	Plutarch	46–119
Ogden, Charles Kay	1889–1957	Podhoretz, Norman	1930–
Origen	185–254	Poe, Edgar Allan	1809–1849
Ortega y Gasset, José	1883–1955	Poincaré, Jules-Henri	1854–1912
Orwell, George	1903–1950	Pokrovsky, Mikhail	1868–1932
Ostrogorsky, Moisey	1854–1919	Popper, Karl	1902–1994
Owen, Robert	1771–1858	Porphyry	233–305
Ozenfant, Amédée	1886–1966	Porter, James Amos	1905–1971
Pacheco, Francisco	1564–1654	Posidonius of Apamea	135–51 B.C.
Pachomius	290–346	Praetorius, Michael	1571–1621

Prescott, William	1796–1859		Ripley, George	1802–1880
Price, Richard	1723–1791		Rivera, Diego	1886–1957
Priestley, Joseph	1733–1804		Rivers, W. H. R.	1864–1922
Priscillian (bishop of Avila)	340–385		Robertson, Dennis	1890–1963
Proclus	410–485		Robertson, William	1721–1793
Protagoras	485–410 B.C.		Robinson, James	1863–1936
Proudhon, Pierre Joseph	1809–1865		Robinson, Joan Violet	1903–1983
Pudovkin, Vsevolod	1893–1953		Roget, Peter Mark	1779–1869
Pyrrho of Elis	360–272 B.C.		Roper, William	1496–1578
Pythagoras	580–500 B.C.		Rorschach, Hermann	1884–1922
Quine, Willard	1908–		Rorty, Richard	1931–
Quintilian (Marcus Fabian			Rosenberg, Alfred	1893–1946
Quintilianus)	35–97		Rosenberg, Harold	1906–1978
Radcliffe-Brown, Alfred Reginald	1881–1955		Rostow, Walt Whitman	1916–
Rahner, Karl	1904–1984		Rousseau, Jean-Jacques	1712–1778
Raleigh, Sir Walter	1554–1618		Rouvroy, Claude-Henri de,	
Ramakrishna	1836–1886		Comte de Saint-Simon	1760–1825
Ramana Maharishi	1879–1950		Royce, Josiah	1855–1916
Ramanand	c. 1400–c. 1470		Ruskin, John	1819–1900
Ramanuja	c. 1017–1137		Russell, Bertrand	1872–1970
Rameau, Jean-Philippe	1683–1764		Russell, Charles Taze	1852–1916
Rand, Ayn	1905–1982		Ryle, Gilbert	1900–1976
Ranjit Singh	1780–1839		Sa'adia ben Joseph	882–942
Rank, Otto	1884–1939		Sade, Marquis de	1740–1814
Ranke, Leopold von	1795–1886		Sadeddin, Hoca	1536–1599
Ransom, John Crowe	1888–1974		Sahagún, Bernardino de	1499–1590
Rashi (Rabbi Solomon bar Isaac)	1040–1105		Saichō (Dengyō Daishi)	767–822
Rask, Rasmus Kristian	1787–1832		Said, Edward W.	1935–
Rasmussen, Knud Johan Victor	1879–1933		Sainte-Beuve, Charles-Augustin	1804–1869
Ratzel, Friedrich	1844–1904		Samuelson, Paul	1915–
Rauschenbusch, Walter	1861–1918		Sandburg, Carl	1878–1967
Rawls, John	1921–		Sanger, Margaret	1879–1966
Read, Herbert	1893–1968		Santayana, George	1863–1952
Reichenbach, Hans	1891–1953		Sapir, Edward	1884–1939
Reid, Thomas	1710–1796		Sarris, Andrew	1928–
Reinhardt, Ad	1913–1967		Sarton, George	1884–1956
Restany, Pierre	1930–		Sartre, Jean-Paul	1905–1980
Reuchlin, Johannes	1455–1522		Saussure, Ferdinand de	1857–1913
Reynolds, Sir Joshua	1723–1792		Savigny, Friedrich Karl von	1779–1861
Rhodes, James	1848–1927		Schapiro, Meyer	1904–1996
Ricardo, David	1772–1823		Schelling, Friedrich von	1775–1854
Ricci, Matteo	1552–1610		Schier, Flint	1953–1988
Richards, Ivor Armstrong	1893–1979		Schiller, Johann von	1759–1805
Ricoeur, Paul	1913–		Schlegel, Friedrich von	1772–1829
Riegl, Alois	1858–1905		Schleiermacher, Friedrich	1768–1834
Riesman, David	1909–		Schlesinger, Arthur, Jr.	1917–

Schlick, Moritz	1882–1936
Schnaase, Carl	1798–1875
Schopenhauer, Arthur	1788–1860
Schumpeter, Joseph Alois	1883–1950
Schweitzer, Albert	1875–1965
Seeley, Sir John	1834–1895
Sellars, Roy Wood	1880–1973
Sellars, Wilfrid	1912–1989
Semper, Gottfried	1803–1879
Seneca	4 B.C.–65
Sextus Empiricus	fl. 200
Shabbetai Tzevi	1626–1676
Shāfi'ī, ash-	767–820
Shaw, George Bernard	1856–1950
Shelley, Percy Bysshe	1792–1822
Shinran	1173–1262
Siddhartha Gautama	563–483 B.C.
Sidgwick, Henry	1838–1900
Sidney, Sir Philip	1554–1586
Siger de Brabant	fl. 1270
Signac, Paul	1863–1935
Simmel, Georg	1858–1918
Simonson, Lee	1888–1967
Skinner, B. F.	1904–1990
Small, Albion	1854–1926
Smith, Adam	1723–1790
Smith, Bernard William	1916–
Smith, John	d. 1612
Smith, Joseph	1805–1844
Snow, C. P.	1905–1980
Socrates	470–399 B.C.
Söderblom, Nathan	1866–1931
Solon	639–559 B.C.
Sontag, Susan	1933–
Sorel, Georges	1847–1922
Sorokin, Pitirim	1889–1968
Soyinka, Wole	1934–
Sparks, Jared	1789–1866
Spencer, Herbert	1820–1903
Spener, Philipp Jacob	1635–1705
Spengler, Oswald	1880–1936
Spinoza, Baruch	1632–1677
Spock, Benjamin	1903–
Sprat, Thomas	1635–1713
Ssu-ma Ch'ien	145–85 B.C.
Ssu-ma Kuang	1019–1086

Staël, Anne-Louise-Germaine de	1766–1817
Stanton, Elizabeth Cady	1815–1902
Starobinski, Jean	1920–
Steele, Sir Richard	1672–1729
Steffens, Lincoln	1866–1936
Steinberg, Leo	1920–
Steinem, Gloria	1934–
Steiner, Rudolph	1861–1925
Stieglitz, Alfred	1864–1946
Stow, John	1525–1605
Stowe, Harriet Beecher	1811–1896
Strachey, Lytton	1880–1932
Stubbs, William	1825–1901
Suárez, Francisco	1548–1617
Suetonius	69–140
Sumner, William Graham	1840–1910
Sun-tzu	4th century B.C.
Sunday, Billy	1862–1935
Swedenborg, Emanuel	1688–1772
Swift, Jonathan	1667–1745
Symonds, John Addington	1840–1893
Tacitus	55–117
Tagore, Rabindranath	1861–1941
Taine, Hippolyte	1828–1893
Tarde, Jean-Gabriel de	1843–1904
Tate, Allen	1899–1979
Tawney, Richard Henry	1880–1962
Teilhard de Chardin, Pierre	1881–1955
Tennent, Gilbert	1703–1764
Teresa of Avila	1515–1582
Terman, Lewis Madison	1877–1956
Tertullian	c. 155–220
Thayer, Alexander Wheelock	1817–1897
Theophrastus	372–287 B.C.
Thérèse de Lisieux	1873–1897
Thomas, John	1805–1871
Thomas à Becket	c. 1118–1170
Thomas à Kempis	c. 1379–1471
Thomas Aquinas	1225–1274
Thoreau, Henry David	1817–1862
Thucydides	460–400 B.C.
Thurow, Lester	1938–
Tilak, Bal Gangadhar	1856–1920
Tillich, Paul	1886–1965
Titchener, Edward	1867–1927
Tocqueville, Alexis de	1805–1859

Toland, John	1670–1722		Watson, John Broadus	1878–1958
Tolstoy, Leo	1828–1910		Webb, Beatrice Potter	1858–1943
Toynbee, Arnold	1889–1975		Webb, Sidney	1859–1947
Treitschke, Heinrich von	1834–1896		Weber, Max	1864–1920
Trevelyan, Sir George	1838–1928		Webster, Noah	1758–1843
Trotsky, Leon	1879–1940		Wechsler, David	1896–1981
Tsou Yen	340–260 B.C.		Weil, Simone	1909–1943
Tsunesaburo, Makiguchi	1871–1944		Weishaupt, Adam	1748–1830
Tubières-Grimoard,			Weld, Theodore Dwight	1803–1895
Anne-Claude-Philippe de,			Wellek, René	1903–
Count of Caylus	1692–1765		Wertheimer, Max	1880–1943
Tubman, Harriet	c. 1820–1913		Wesley, John	1703–1791
Tulsidas	c. 1543–1623		Whewell, William	1794–1866
Tung Chung-shu	179–104 B.C.		Whitefield, George	1714–1770
Turgenev, Ivan	1818–1883		Whitehead, Alfred North	1861–1947
Turner, Frederick Jackson	1861–1932		Whitman, Walt	1819–1892
Turner, Victor	1920–		Whorf, Benjamin Lee	1897–1941
Tyler, Parker	1904–1974		Whyte, William Hollingsworth	1917–
Tylor, Edward Burnett	1832–1917		Wilde, Oscar	1854–1900
Tyndale, William	c. 1494–1536		Williams, Raymond	1921–1988
Tzara, Tristan	1896–1963		Williams, Roger	c. 1603–1683
Unamuno y Jugo, Miguel de	1864–1936		Wilson, Edmund	1895–1972
Vaihinger, Hans	1852–1933		Wilson, Edward O.	1929–
Valla, Lorenzo	1407–1457		Winckelmann, Johann	1717–1768
Vallabha	1479–1531		Winters, Yvor	1900–1968
Vasari, Giorgio	1511–1574		Wittgenstein, Ludwig	1889–1951
Veblen, Thorstein	1857–1929		Wolff, Christian von	1679–1754
Venn, John	1834–1923		Wölfflin, Heinrich	1864–1945
Vergerio, Pier Paolo	1370–1445		Wollstonecraft, Mary	1759–1797
Vico, Giambattista	1668–1744		Wood, Anthony à	1632–1695
Villani, Giovanni	c. 1275–1348		Woodward, C. Vann	1908–
Vio, Tommaso de	1468–1534		Woodworth, Robert Sessions	1869–1962
Vitruvius	1st century B.C.		Woolf, Virginia	1882–1941
Vivekenanda	1863–1902		Worringer, Wilhelm	1881–1965
Voltaire	1694–1778		Wundt, Wilhelm	1832–1920
Wali Allah, Shah	1703–1762		Wycliffe, John	c. 1330–1384
Wallas, Graham	1858–1932		Wyzewa, Teodor de	1862–1914
Waller, Willard	1899–1945		Xenocrates of Sicyon	396–314 B.C.
Walther, Johann Gottfried	1684–1748		Xenophon	431–352 B.C.
Walton, Izaak	1593–1683		Yang Chu	440–c. 360 B.C.
Warburg, Aby	1866–1929		Young, Arthur	1741–1820
Warren, Robert Penn	1905–1989		Young, Edward	1683–1765
Warshow, Robert	1918–1955		Zarlino, Gioseffo	1517–1590
Warton, Thomas	1728–1790		Zeno of Citium	c. 335–c. 263 B.C.
Washington, Booker	1856–1915		Zeno of Elea	c. 495–430 B.C.

Zermelo, Ernst	1871–1953	Zoroaster	628–551 B.C.
Zetkin, Clara	1857–1933	Zunz, Leopold	1794–1886
Zola, Émile	1840–1902	Zwingli, Huldrych	1484–1531

Bibliography

Abramson, Glenda, ed. *The Blackwell Companion to Jewish Culture*. Oxford: Basil Blackwell Inc., 1989.

Anderson, Bonnie S., and Judith P. Zinsser. *A History of Their Own: Women in Europe from Prehistory to the Present*. New York: Harper & Row, 1988.

Appiah, Kwame Anthony, and Henry Louis Gates, Jr., eds. *The Dictionary of Global Culture*. New York: Alfred A. Knopf, 1997.

Barnes, Harry Elmer. *An Introduction to the History of Sociology*. Chicago: University of Chicago Press, 1948.

Barry, Norman. *An Introduction to Political Theory*. New York: St. Martin's Press, 1989.

Blackburn, Simon. *The Oxford Dictionary of Philosophy*. Oxford: Oxford University Press, 1994.

Blunt, Anthony. *Artistic Theory in Italy: 1450–1660*. Oxford: Oxford University Press, 1987.

Britannica Online.

Bullock, Alan, and R. B. Woodings, eds. *Twentieth-Century Culture*. New York: Harper & Row, 1983.

Carlyon, Richard. *A Guide to the Gods: An Essential Guide to World Mythology*. New York: Quill, 1981.

Chernow, Barbara A., and George A. Vallasi. *The Columbia Encyclopedia*, 5th ed. New York: Columbia University Press/Houghton Mifflin, 1993.

Collini, Stefan, Donald Winch, and John Burrow. *That Noble Science of Politics: A Study in Nineteenth-Century Intellectual History*. Cambridge: Cambridge University Press, 1983.

Corsini, Raymond J., ed. *Concise Encyclopedia of Psychology*. New York: John Wiley & Sons, 1987.

Current Biography 1940–Present (electronic). New York: H. W. Wilson.

Dahl, Robert. *Modern Political Analysis*, 4th ed. Englewood Cliffs, NJ: Prentice Hall, 1984.

Dunaway, David K., and Willa K. Baum, eds. *Oral History: An Interdisciplinary Anthology*. Nashville: American Association for State and Local History, 1984.

Eagleton, Terry. *Literary Theory: An Introduction*. Minneapolis: University of Minnesota Press, 1983.

Easton, David, John Gunnell, and Luigi Graziano, eds. *The Development of Political Science*. London: Routledge, 1991.

Ebenstein, William. *Great Political Thinkers: Plato to the Present*, 4th ed. New York: Holt, Rinehart and Winston, 1969.

Fancher, Raymond. *Pioneers of Psychology*. New York: W. W. Norton & Co., 1979.

Gilbert, Katharine Everett, and Helmut Kuhn. *A History of Esthetics*. Bloomington: Indiana University Press, 1953.

Goodman, Norman, and Gary Marx. *Society Today*. New York: Random House, 1978.

Groden, Michael, and Martin Kreiswirth, eds. *The Johns Hopkins Guide to Literary Theory and Criticism*. Baltimore: Johns Hopkins University Press, 1994.

Grolier's Academic American Encyclopedia (online edition).

Grun, Bernard. *The Timetables of History*. New York: Touchstone, 1982.

Harrison, Charles, and Paul Wood, eds. *Art in Theory*. Cambridge MA: Blackwell Publishers, 1993.

Havens, Thomas R. H. *Nishi Amane and Modern Japanese Thought*. Princeton: Princeton University Press, 1970.

Hunt, Elgin F., and David C. Colander. *Social Science: An Introduction to the Study of Society*, 6th ed. New York: Macmillan, 1987.

Hutchinson Dictionary (online edition).

Katz, Ephraim. *The Film Encyclopedia*. New York: Perigee Books, 1979.

Levy, Judith S., and Agnes Greenhall. *The Concise Columbia Encyclopedia*. New York: Avon, 1983.

Low, W. Augustus, and Virgil A. Clift, eds. *Encyclopedia of Black America*. New York: Da Capo Press, 1981.

Magnusson, Magnus, ed. *Cambridge Biographical Dictionary*. Cambridge: Cambridge University Press, 1990.

Mast, Gerald, and Marshall Cohen, eds. *Film Theory and Criticism*. Oxford: Oxford University Press, 1985.

Minor, Vernon Hyde. *Art History's History*. New York: Harry N. Abrams, 1994.

Murphy, Bruce, ed. *Benét's Reader's Encyclopedia*, 4th ed. New York: HarperCollins, 1996.

Murray, Edward. *Nine American Film Critics*. New York: Frederick Ungar, 1975.

Nobel Prize Winners. New York: H. W. Wilson, 1987.

Nobel Prize Winners: 1989–1991 Supplement. New York: H. W. Wilson, 1992.

Nobel Prize Winners: 1992–1996 Supplement. New York: H. W. Wilson, 1997.

Parrinder, Geoffrey, ed. *World Religions from Ancient History to the Present*. New York: Facts on File, 1985.

Perkins, George, Barbara Perkins, and Phillip Leininger. *Benét's Reader's Encyclopedia of American Literature*. New York: HarperCollins, 1991.

Podro, Michael. *The Critical Historians of Art*. New Haven, CT: Yale University Press, 1982.

Popenoe, David. *Sociology*. Englewood Cliffs, NJ: Prentice Hall, 1986.

Scarre, Chris. *Smithsonian Timelines of the Ancient World*. London: Dorling Kindersley, 1993.

Scruton, Roger. *A Short History of Modern Philosophy: From Descartes to Wittgenstein*. London: Routledge, 1984.

Tillman, Frank A., and Steven M. Cahn. *Philosophy of Art and Aesthetics*. New York: Harper & Row, 1969.

Trager, James. *The People's Chronology*. New York: Henry Holt, 1992.

Urdang, Laurence, ed. *The Timetables of American History*. New York: Simon & Schuster, 1981.

Van Der Grinten, Evert. *Enquiries into the History of Artistorical Writing*. Amsterdam: Amsterdam Municipal University, 1952.

Wallis, Brian, ed. *Art After Modernism*. New York/Boston: New Museum of Contemporary Art/David R. Godine, Publishers, 1984.

Webster's New Biographical Dictionary. Springfield, MA: Merriam-Webster, 1988.

Wetterau, Bruce. *Macmillan Concise Dictionary of World History*. New York: Macmillan, 1983.

——. *The New York Public Library Book of Chronologies*. New York: Prentice-Hall, 1990.

Wilson Biographies (electronic). New York: H. W. Wilson.

Zusne, Leonard. *Names in the History of Psychology: A Biographical Sourcebook*. Washington, DC: Hemisphere Publishing, 1975.

Index

P